# From PADEREWSKI to PENDERECKI

## The Polish Musician in Philadelphia…

*From one brass player to another !*

*Paul Krzywicki*

*2017*

Paul Krzywicki

ISBN: 978-1-4834-4267-9 (sc)
ISBN: 978-1-4834-4266-2 (e)

Because of the dynamic nature of the Internet, any web addresses or links contained in this book may have changed since publication and may no longer be valid. The views expressed in this work are solely those of the author and do not necessarily reflect the views of the publisher, and the publisher hereby disclaims any responsibility for them.

Lulu Publishing Services rev. date: 03/11/2016

# CONTENTS

In 1872, when the great violin virtuoso Henryk Wieniawski first performed in Philadelphia, he created a sensation. His success encouraged an influx of Polish musicians to America--significantly contributing to the growth of music in this country. Nowhere was the influence of these artists felt greater than in Philadelphia where the formation of the city's most important cultural and educational institutions was largely molded by Poles such as Leopold Stokowski, Józef Hofmann, Marcella Sembrich-Kochańska, and Artur Rodziński. As teachers, performers and administrators these immigrants had a formidable musical impact, and those successes subsequently encouraged generations of musical celebrities like Mieczysław Horszowski, Edward Steuermann, Szymon Goldberg, Stanisław Skrowaczewski, and Krzysztof Penderecki to flourish in Philadelphia and throughout America. Today, the presence of Polish musicians, whether first or third generation, remains vibrant; more than a century after their musical ancestors first introduced themselves to the American public. Philadelphia continues to embrace today's most brilliant young Polish musicians. The pianists Jan Lisiecki, Piotr Anderszewski and Rafał Blechacz are just a few of the frequent visitors to America. This book brings to life the great array of Polish pianists, violinists, singers, composers, conductors and other instrumentalists who brought their artistry to this city and America from 1870 to the present. One hundred and seventy biographies and images are intermingled with historical information, photos and background so that their accomplishments can be more fully appreciated. A pronunciation guide is also included.

# ACKNOWLEDGMENTS

I could not have documented the opera history of Philadelphia without the painstaking work of John Curtis, continued by Frank Hamilton and housed today at the main branch of the Free Library of Philadelphia. It has been installed online and can be found at http://hamilton.francocorelli.nl/ph/ph1.pdf.

The Philadelphia Orchestra Archives have been closed since 1993 and are still mired in the recovery from bankruptcy. Most of the programs dating from the Orchestra's first concert in 1900 were kept outside that room, however, and they were an invaluable source thanks to the assistance of Darrin Briting, Associate Director of Communications.

The archives of the Israel Philharmonic, Boston Symphony, Cleveland Orchestra, Philadelphia Orchestra, New York Philharmonic and Metropolitan Opera Orchestra were also most helpful.

When it comes to learning about the musicians of America's orchestras there is no better starting, or even ending place than the website, Stokowski.org, a truly incredible website assembled over many years by Larry Huffman. I have garnered information from this site throughout the book.

Leon Blaszczyk's book *Polish Contribution to the Musical Life of America* was a special kind of pathfinder to names that helped me to include as many artists as possible.

Tom DiNardo, friend and longtime Arts Writer for the *Philadelphia Daily News*, was a great help in editing my grammar and nudged me along in a literary area in which I was without experience.

Helene von Rossum, archivist with the Curtis Institute of Music, was most generous with her time and materials, as was Michelle Oswell, Director of the Music Library.

Frank Garber of the Chestnut Hill Camera Shop was invaluable in helping with images for the book.

Many thanks are owed to my dear friend Dariusz Gajos in Warsaw for his material and financial support.

Additional thanks to Allan Evans, Norman Carol, David Arben, Marjan Kiepura, Gary Fitelberg, Ann Schein, Linda Schein Greenebaum, Mary Doane, David Lesniaski, Matt Good, Nigel Nettheim, Peter Obst, Pete Checchia, Barbara Zakrzewska, Jean Wald, Tonya Crawford, Joe Herter, Tyrone Greive, Michelle Drobik, Robert Pettit, Therese Dickman, John Corenswet, Scott Kessler of Marston Records, Takeushi Takahashi, Jennifer Kallend and Cecylia Arzewski.

My brother Philip helped with readings, and my daughter, Jill, helped me through many computer technology issues. My son, John, lent a hand in maneuvering me through the most frustrating task of searching for photos. It is to my wife, Joan, and especially my brother Jan to whom I owe the most thanks for their patience and unflagging interest.

## NOTES

Some of the information presented here was collected from personal interviews or correspondence with the musicians themselves, and have not been footnoted in each instance.

The Polish names in this book are included with all their diacritics (the marks over, under or through a letter, specific to the Polish language), even though they are very seldom used in English journalism. In the case of musicians born in America, I then use the English adaptations of their names throughout the text. For musicians who chose stage names, I refer to those names in their biographies.

A pronunciation guide is also included at the very end of the text for the non-Polish-speaking reader who wishes to confront the challenge of accurately pronouncing the names.

# PREFACE

# WHY THIS BOOK?

In 1972, I had the privilege and good fortune to be invited by Eugene Ormandy to join the Philadelphia Orchestra as principal tubist. In this capacity I spent the next 33 years performing more than 4,000 concerts with the most acclaimed instrumentalists and conductors in all the musical capitals of the world. At the same time, I was invited by Rudolf Serkin, the Director of the Curtis Institute of Music, to join their faculty and continued there after my retirement from the Philadelphia Orchestra in 2005. Meanwhile, I also taught at two other Philadelphia musical institutions, Temple University and the Philadelphia Musical Academy (now part of the University of the Arts).

During my career, I developed some awareness of the role that Polish musicians played in the history of music in Philadelphia, but my knowledge was limited. I knew of Josef Hofmann and Leopold Stokowski, but few others. At the Curtis Institute, I often taught in a large studio called the Horszowski Room that contained pictures and memorabilia of the great pianist and pedagogue Mieczyslaw Horszowski. There was also a bas-relief portrait of Marcella Sembrich hanging in that studio. At the time, I had no idea who Sembrich was, and I wondered why such a portrait would be hanging in a studio named in Horszowski's honor. Several years later, I learned that both musicians were born in Poland, that they came from similar backgrounds and that Horszowski was, in fact, pleased to have Sembrich's presence in the studio named in his honor.

Subsequently, for the 75th anniversary of the Curtis Institute, Diana Burgwyn wrote a wonderful book documenting the school's history that mentioned several prominent Polish musicians, including details of Curtis's first official commencement in 1934. The Polish presence at that ceremony was formidable. It was presided over by the Polish director of the school, included a speech by the Polish attaché to the United States and a performance of the Polish national anthem, and took place in the school's hall, which had been named for a Pole and which prominently displayed the Polish flag. It was then that my interest in that connection both to the Curtis Institute and the Philadelphia Orchestra rose to a level that compelled the research for this book and directed me on a quest to learn more about the early musicians and teachers who established Philadelphia as a cultural landmark in the world of music. I also wanted to follow the careers of all those others not connected to Curtis or the Orchestra who have brought their art to this city and the world. In Part II (Other Remarkable Musicians), I have included some composers because their concert music or film music have been heard in Philadelphia, and celebrated the accomplishments of a few performers who may never have come to Philadelphia, but deemed that more important than their physical presence in the city. On a few occasions I have also included musicians whose Polish-ness may be questionable, but I found their inclusion to be relevant nevertheless. It became important to me that all these amazing artists of Polish descent be remembered, commemorated and recognized for the ethnic sensitivities which formed their unique characters and made them extraordinary. These men and women have given the world much to admire. To students, they have given an artistic standard to which to aspire.

# AN INTRODUCTION

This is a book about the Polish musicians who have played a role in the musical life of America, most specifically in Philadelphia from 1872 onward. It is a book about the Polish artist-performers and conductors who have inspired and thrilled audiences here and throughout the world, the distinguished Poles whose teaching has been important in developing other performers to carry on their legacies, and the great Polish composers whose music has been in our concert halls and in our films. About two hundred Polish musicians are profiled in these pages. Of these, forty were born in the United States while almost all of the rest came from Poland; of that number, about one third became citizens of the United States. All of these Polish musicians contributed, to a greater or lesser extent, to the musical vitality of Philadelphia. In many cases, the history of music in the city is unthinkable without them.

Despite their eventual importance to the development of classical music in Philadelphia, Poles were slow to introduce themselves to this new land. There were probably no Polish musicians in the early years of America. In 1834, according to the Philadelphia newspaper the *United States Gazette*, there were officially only thirty-three Poles in the city.[1] Tracking Poles during much of the nineteenth century, however, is a challenge. After Poland was partitioned by three aggressors in 1795, the nationalities of Polish-speaking immigrants were often changed and designated as Russian, Austrian, or German. The United States census of 1820 made no attempt to clarify the situation; Poland was not even listed

---

[1] In that same year the first book of English for Poles was published in Philadelphia. Sister M. Theodosetta, C.S.F.N., "The Poles in Philadelphia to 1914," *PAS* vol. 8, no. 1/2 (1951): 15.

on a census form until 1918. Nevertheless, music of a popular nature was being composed by Poles and published in Philadelphia: marches, waltzes, quick-steps, and polkas such as "Kaliszanka Polka," "March of the Polish Rifle Corps," "Quick Steps to the Memory of Poland," "Polish Maiden's Farewell," and the "Third of May" song. After the failed Polish Uprising against Russia in 1830–31, Americans developed an empathy for the Polish struggle for independence that may have led to Polish music becoming accepted and fashionable in America.[2] After 1831, most Polish musicians were political refugees, but by the 1850s, economic refugees were entering the United States. Simultaneously, Philadelphia was building the base for a musical culture emulating Europe. Grand performance halls were constructed, music schools were instituted, and artists from allover Europe became interested in touring America.[3]

The first really important, world-renowned Polish musicians began to come to America as part of the "new immigration" from Europe that occurred roughly between 1870 and 1920. During that time, 100,000 Poles were entering the United States each year, seeking jobs in the country's new industries, and Pennsylvania was home to the largest population of Poles in the country. Some chose to return to a free, regenerating Polish Republic, which was recreated in the aftermath of World War I. For the immigrant Poles who chose the long process of assimilation in America, the prospect of bringing up their children with a musical instrument was a welcome change from Europe, where education was suppressed and only the "gentry" could learn to play a musical instrument.[4] Polish-American music-making began to thrive. In 1890, for example, the Halka Choral Society was formed here (later known as the Paderewski Choral Society).

While Germans were by far the largest group to contribute to Philadelphia's early musical scene, Polish musicians were becoming

---

[2] Alexander Janta, "Early Eighteenth Century American-Polish Music," *PR* vol.VI, no. 1–2 (1961): 73–105. Continued in vol. X, no. 2 (1965): 60–87.
[3] The Academy of Music was built in 1857, and the Chestnut Street Theater was rebuilt in 1862. The oldest chartered music school in Pennsylvania, The Philadelphia Musical Academy (now incorporated into the University of the Arts), opened in 1870. The Philadelphia Conservatory (1877), Combs Broad Street Conservatory (1885), Sternberg School (1896), and Leefson-Hille Conservatory (1899) no longer exist.
[4] Michal Kasprzak, "Buying a New Identity: Polish American and Mass Consumerism in the Interwar Years," *PR* vol. LVI, no. 4 (2011): 362.

important in feeding America's craving for European culture.[5] In the first quarter of the twentieth century, renowned Poles such as Josef Hofmann, Marcella Sembrich, and Leopold Stokowski were to have a significant influence on the history of music in Philadelphia. They became, in fact, the principal designers in fashioning the city into a place of importance on the world musical stage due in large part to their pivotal role in the growth of the city's two most important musical institutions, the Curtis Institute of Music and the Philadelphia Orchestra. The history of these two organizations is closely intertwined. An astonishing number of Polish musicians from the Curtis Institute, both alumni and faculty, are profiled in this book. Their presence in the Philadelphia Orchestra, a privileged destination for the world's best musicians, also plays throughout this story. The teaching institutions, creative ensembles, and performance venues in the city that were populated by Polish musicians are also considered in an attempt to trace all the remarkable resident or visiting musicians and teachers of Polish descent who have graced this city with their talents. The biographies of these musicians tell of their extraordinary artistry and relate the incredible lives they led. You will marvel at many of their stories.

---

[5] By 1755, Germans accounted for about one half of Philadelphia's population. Inspired to come here by Penn's religious tolerance, they went on to become the most important group to contribute to Philadelphia's early musical scene. They formed the Mendelssohn Club and the Germania Orchestra; the first conductor of the Philadelphia Orchestra was from Frankenberg, and German was spoken for rehearsals.

# I

# PHILADELPHIA'S MUSICAL INSTITUTIONS

By the end of the nineteenth century, Poland's most famous musicians had come to America and performed in Philadelphia. America welcomed and was willing to pay for Europe's best artists, so it is not surprising that Henryk Wieniawski, Ignacy Paderewski, Marcella Sembrich, Jean de Reszke, his brother Edouard, and Josef Hofmann were appearing here. But if America wanted to attract them as teachers it was going to have to expand its teaching opportunities since at the time the city's most enduring musical institutions had yet to be established. There was still no exceptional music school (nor performing ensembles, for that matter) that Europe could admire. The education of musicians would be addressed by the confluence of a few brilliant musicians, the generosity of a benefactor, and two piano teachers. Without them, the city could easily have missed the opportunity for the remarkable creativity and accomplishments that were to follow.

In 1908, Blanche Wolf and Jeanette Selig offered piano lessons for five cents a lesson to forty immigrant children in a settlement house in one of the poorest sections of Philadelphia. Nine years later, their enrollment had increased several times, and their efforts drew the attention of Cyrus and Louisa Curtis, who decided to provide the funds to erect a new building for music education—the beginning of the Settlement Music Schools that today dot the city and suburbs—with the original goal of musical

1

education for any student and their "Americanization among the foreign population of Philadelphia."

Cyrus and Louisa Curtis had founded the Curtis Publishing Company and launched the most popular magazines in America, including the *Saturday Evening Post* and the *Ladies Home Journal*, the first publication in America to reach a million subscribers. They became one of the wealthiest couples in the United States and important philanthropists to Philadelphia. Their daughter, Mary Louise, was an accomplished pianist and a writer for the *Ladies Home Journal*, helping to make the publication an impressive source of musical interest. Sheet music, information on piano technique, and music education could all be found regularly in its pages, and she enlisted Jozef Hofmann, Moritz Moszkowski, and Antoinette Szumowska, as contributors. Mary Louise inherited a large estate and married Edward Bok, who took over the publishing business and was drawn into his wife's world of music. Mary Bok greatly admired the Polish pianist Josef Hofmann, often described as the greatest pianist of his time, and while on tours in Philadelphia, he entered into a long-lasting friendship with the Curtis family.[6] Hofmann became music editor of the *Ladies Home Journal*, wrote many articles, and for eleven years answered letters in an advice column.[7] On January 28, 1917, Hofmann played the inaugural recital for the opening of the Queen Street Settlement School. Two years earlier, in 1915, Hofmann's only appearance in Philadelphia had been as a fundraiser for the Settlement School.[8] He performed at another fundraising concert in 1921.[9]

The Settlement School prospered. After a few years, however, the talent that was emerging from the school made clear the need for an institution for more advanced students. The Boks, together with Hofmann and the young, soon-to-be-superstar conductor Leopold Stokowski, spent many an evening envisioning a place of musical training in Philadelphia that would attract worldwide attention. The Boks purchased three adjoining buildings on Locust Street, just on Rittenhouse Square, and the Curtis

---

[6] Burgwyn (1999) 2–5.

[7] Dorothy Vogel, "Musical Masterclasses," *American Music Teacher*, August/September 2012.

[8] Viles (1983) 5–8.

[9] Benko and McNeill, "Josef Hofmann and the 7 April 1938 Casimir Hall: Recital," Marston Records.

Institute of Music, named for Mary's parents, was founded. The school opened for classes on October 13, 1924, and was officially chartered by the Commonwealth of Pennsylvania on April 18, 1925, not coincidentally, the birthday of Stokowski, whom Mary Bok called the "prince." To Stokowski, Mrs. Bok was "Marussia."[10] Josef Hofmann became the head of the Piano Department and three years later became Director of the school for eleven years. Prominent musicians from around the world were recruited, and indeed in a very short time, a world-class school of music was established. The Board of Advisers included Stokowski and Hofmann, of course, and they were joined by Marcella Sembrich, another Pole and the diva who was also establishing the vocal department at Juilliard.

The first official commencement at The Curtis Institute of Music was held in 1934.[11] Thirty-four students graduated in the main concert hall, Casimir[12] Hall, named after Jozef Hofmann's father (later renamed Curtis Hall and recently Field Concert Hall). Red and white carnations (the colors of the Polish flag) filled the stage. The American and Polish national anthems were played to honor Hofmann, the director, and Mary Bok, who had previously been decorated by the Polish government for her efforts to promote close ties with Poland.[13] The commencement speaker was Władysław Sokółowski, the Polish attaché to the United States. Marcella Sembrich and Leopold Godowsky, Hofmann's colleagues and close friends, received honorary doctorates.

In ten years' time, an amazing school of music had been established, the likes of which the world had not seen before. It was, and remains, distinctive and revered in the universe of music education. What were the policies established and privileges afforded the students, and who were these especially uncommon musicians and personalities who brought fame to the school and cultivated generations of extraordinary musicians—many known throughout the world?

---

[10] Stokowski's version of *Marysia,* the familiar name of Mary in Polish.

[11] Burgwyn (1999) 34–35.

[12] The Anglicized version of *Kazimierz.*

[13] In a letter to Stokowski dated 24 May 1932 regarding help for a struggling Polish composer, she wrote that she would assist, "as I have adopted the Polish nation." CIMA.

"Arguably the greatest pianist of the twentieth century."
Ward Marston[14]

Curtis Institute of Music Archives

**Józef Kazimierz Hofmann** was born in Podgórze, near Kraków, Poland, in 1877. His mother, Matylda Pindelska, was a singer, and his father, Kazimierz, was a graduate of the Vienna Conservatory and a well-known teacher and conductor at both the Warsaw Conservatory and Warsaw Opera. He was also Józef's teacher in his early years. Józef was extraordinarily gifted, could play at four, and at the age of five made his debut at the Teatr Wielki (Warsaw Opera House).

Józef also had a great aptitude for science and mechanics, patenting dozens of inventions throughout his life. When he could not reach the pedals of the piano, he invented extensions that allowed him to reach them.

---

[14] Liner notes of the Ward Marston CD collection of Hofmann recorded performances. Ward Marston is an internationally recognized recording engineer who specializes in remastering historical recordings. He has won Gramophone and Grammy awards for "best historical recordings" and in 2010 created a four-CD set entitled *A Century of Romantic Chopin*—a collection of recordings dating back to 1895 cylinders featuring the 65 most celebrated interpreters of Chopin.

Anton Rubinstein, the Russian pianist and composer, heard him and encouraged a tour of Europe. Józef's father agreed, and at the age nine, he visited most of Central Europe, Scandinavia, and London. He played the Beethoven Piano Concerto No. 1 with the Berlin Philharmonic under Hans Von Bülow and also with London's Royal Philharmonic Orchestra. The next tour took him to America where he debuted on November 29, 1887. The reviewer for the *New York Herald* of November 30 wrote, "The occasion proved something to be remembered and talked over for the rest of one's life." The program again included the Beethoven Piano Concerto No. 1 in addition to the Weber-Liszt *Polacca* for Piano and Orchestra.

Library of Congress, R.J.Falk

He was booked for a staggering eighty concerts, performing four times a week and causing a sensation not just with his playing but also his improvisation. In New York, however, after his fifty-second concert, the Society for the Prevention of Cruelty to Children stepped in to stop further performances. A benefactor, Alfred Corning Clark, came forward and offered Hofmann $50,000—five times the sum he was to receive for the entire tour—if he would retire from the stage until the age of eighteen, and he did just that.

Back in Europe, this hiatus allowed him to study with the composer Moritz Moszkowski and Eugen d'Albert and to resume his relationship with Anton Rubinstein, whom he considered the greatest influence in his musical life. [15]

Josef Hofmann's official adult debut occurred in Hamburg, where he played the Rubinstein Piano Concerto No. 4 with the composer conducting; he then took up again the life of a touring musician. Especially popular in Russia, he made history in St. Petersburg by playing twenty-one consecutive concerts consisting of 255 pieces from memory, never repeating the same piece twice. . . an unimaginable feat. Once he heard something, it was committed to memory forever, sometimes without even seeing the score, but just hearing it. He made his "second" debut in America in 1887.

On one of his tours of America, he played in Aiken, South Carolina, and was entertained after the concert by the James Biddle Eustis family. He continued to play in Aiken with some frequency, and in 1905 married Marie Eustis, who was eleven years his elder. A daughter, Josefa, was born the following year. Because Marie toured extensively with Josef and kept a detailed diary, we now have a published book that details their life on the road. They spent each Christmas and part of the winter in Aiken, toured in the spring and fall, and spent summers in Switzerland—where they had a house where Josef's close friend Ignacy Jan Paderewski was a neighbor. There he invented the Hofmann air spring shock absorber, which made him a fortune. When he wasn't playing the piano, he tinkered. In 1914, as World War I broke out, he was trapped in Switzerland as an "alien." (He would not become a U.S. citizen until 1926). With the aid of diplomatic friends, they traveled to Genoa, where the Hofmanns obtained Swedish passports with the help of a Belgian diplomat, and then made the

---

[15] While he was Director of the Curtis Institute, Hofmann scheduled, as the school's first opera performance, Eugen d'Albert's seldom heard opera, *Tiefland*. Conducted by Artur Rodziński, it was performed on May 12, 1929.

precarious trip to America, all the while trying to not be discovered by Customs.[16]

The Hofmanns bought a house in Maine and began to spend the summers there, not sure if they would ever get back to Switzerland. Josef owned several boats, but more often than not they were not working because he loved to take apart the motors and put them back together again. He would spend long periods of time without practicing and still return to world class form without difficulty. After the shelling of a tugboat off the coast of Massachusetts by a German submarine in 1918, the Hofmanns stayed in Aiken for the summers.[17]

As their daughter, Josefa, grew older, Marie stayed in South Carolina to care for her and did not tour with her husband. Josef and Marie eventually grew apart and divorced in 1927.

In his first three years at the Curtis Institute, Hofmann's only responsibility was as head of the piano department, although previously he had done little teaching. In 1927, he took over as Director of the Curtis Institute. The mission of the school was stated thus: "To hand down through contemporary masters the great traditions of the past; to teach students to build on this heritage for the future."

Under Hofmann's leadership, many of the policies still in place today were formulated, including no tuition and a stipend for living expenses if needed. Free Steinways were provided to piano students in their apartments. A very active student concert series free and open to the public began, and Philadelphia Orchestra members were included in Student Orchestra concerts. Students could continue their studies in the summer in Warsaw, Kraków, London, Paris, Budapest, Bolton Landing on Lake George, Rockport and Camden Maine, and even Hollywood— with Artur Rodziński when he became Music Director of the Los Angeles Philharmonic.

Curtis also gave students the opportunity to further their careers by sponsoring concert tours. The idea was to create every advantage for students to succeed. An extensive set of concert series were established throughout the area at universities, churches, hotels, festivals, cultural

---

[16] Graydon and Sizemore (1965) 131, 170.
[17] Graydon and Sizemore 187.

centers, and clubs, and in the homes of supporters. The curriculum also included weekly lectures named The Comparative Arts Series, which featured well-known guests from around the country. Olin Downes of the *New York Times*, America's most influential music critic, gave a series of lectures on various subjects, including music criticism.

On December 3, 1927, Hofmann performed the inaugural recital in the newly opened Casimir Hall, named after his father (since changed to Field Concert Hall). Wrought-iron grilles designed by **Samuel Yellin** embellished the balconies and complimented the iron doors that led to the Hall.[18] Other notable landmarks were Wanda Landowska's series of lecture recitals, and the Curtis Orchestra's first concert in the Academy of Music under Artur Rodziński.[19] In 1929, Louis Bailly, acting as curator of intruments for Curtis, purchased a large collection of valuable string instruments – from a 1697 Stradivarius violin to an 1850 Vuilliame cello. It is also interesting to note that 41 percent of the students in that year were women.

The Depression in America was a very difficult time for the Curtis Institute, but Hofmann proved to be a more than able administrator in balancing financial issues. Many activities were curtailed and the budget greatly reduced, but the school survived and continued to graduate the same high level of musical artist.

In 1933, the University of Pennsylvania awarded Hofmann an honorary Doctor of Music degree. In 1934, he became an honorary professor at the Warsaw Conservatory. In 1935, he was decorated by the Polish Government with the Order of Polonia Restituta and the rank of Commander of the

---

[18] Samuel Yellin (Jelen) (1885–1940) was born in Poland on the border with Austria. He became a master blacksmith and left home at the age of 17 to travel Europe. In 1906, he arrived in Philadelphia where his mother and two sisters had moved a few years earlier. He opened a wrought-iron works, and became a well-known craftsman who by 1928 was able to employ as many as 268 workers. Beginning in 1909, the Curtis family together with Edward Bok engaged him for his entire life in designing for both their homes and the Curtis Institute. In 1925, he received the Philadelphia Award. Burgwyn (1999) 17.

[19] Viles (1983) 65.

Rebirth of Poland.[20] Hofmann stepped down as Director of the Curtis Institute in 1937.

Hofmann made a number of recordings even though he did not trust them, saying that he never performed the same piece in the same way twice. Some discography, of varying quality, exists to give the listener a sense of his staggering technique, originality, and clarity. At the age of ten he had been recorded by Thomas Edison, and kept in touch with Edison on matters both scientific and technical as he continued his avid interest in anything mechanical.

After a long career of concertizing that took him to Carnegie Hall an amazing 115 times, he retired from playing in 1945 due largely to the effect his heavy drinking was having on his abilities. (Rachmaninoff, who always admired him, called Hofmann the "greatest pianist alive if he is sober.") Marie Eustis, from whom he was divorced, continued to be devoted to him and appeared at many of his concerts in disguise; she was truly distraught when his great talent diminished later in his life.

In 1937, Hofmann celebrated his Golden Jubilee at the Metropolitan Opera House in New York City, introduced by **Walter Damrosch,** who had been at his debut in 1887.[21] He continued his jubilee celebration

---

[20] The presentation took place at the Ministry of Education, Warsaw, before a distinguished group of people, Konstanty Chyliński, the Minister of Education, conferring the decoration upon Dr. Hofmann. This was an unusual distinction since the rank of Commander in the Order generally is reserved for persons in the diplomatic, military, or official service of the Polish Government. Dr. Hofmann is the only musician to have received this honor in recognition of his art. CIM, *Overtones* (1935).

[21] Walter Damrosch, the man who introduced Hofmann at his Golden Jubilee concert in New York City and accompanied Paderewski's first appearances in America is included here because of all the support he offered to the long line of immigrant Polish musicians arriving in New York City. He was born in 1862 in Breslau, Prussia, which is now Wrocław, Poland. Walter Damrosch was the most important conductor and influential musician in New York City at the time of the arrival of these Polish musicians. He conducted the U.S. premieres of Tchaikovsky's Symphonies Nos. 4 and 6, and arranged for Tchaikovsky to come to New York and conduct his orchestra. Damrosch formed the New York City Symphony, which became the New York Philharmonic and was a major force in getting a new Hall built in New York named after his friend, Andrew Carnegie. He conducted Paderewski's first five concerts in

performing in Philadelphia with the Curtis Institute Orchestra. Ten principal players from the Philadelphia Orchestra and twenty-nine Curtis alumnae excused from their various positions around the country joined the Curtis Orchestra,[22] followed by a performance with Eugene Ormandy and the Philadelphia Orchestra in Beethoven Piano Concerto No. 4. Both concerts were recorded. The Curtis Institute Orchestra concert was conducted by **Ignacy Hilsberg**.[23]

As written in the 50th anniversary issue of the Curtis Institute's *Overtones* publication in 1974, Hofmann's "final concert remains as one of the most moving occasions in the annals of American musical history."

Hofmann did return to Curtis on one occasion, on May 13, 1940, eight months after the start of World War II. The Curtis Orchestra with Hofmann as soloist performed a benefit for Polish Relief at the Academy of Music.[24]

---

America in 1891. He also conducted Paderewski's Opera, *Manru*, at the Metropolitan Opera in 1902 with Marcella Sembrich as Ulana. That remains the only Polish opera by a Polish composer ever performed there. Though clearly a German, he had close associations with many Poles, perhaps because that part of Germany, which was once Polish land, had a fond connection for him. In his biography Damrosch wrote, "It is difficult to define the charm with which the artists of Poland seem to be imbued almost beyond any other race. It is more than a social gift. It is not the result of calculation but seems to be a combination of kindliness of heart and good breeding." He went on to say that if the state of Poland were composed of only an elect like Sembrich, de Reszke, the Adamowskis, Kochański and Lambert "it would soon become the ideal republic of the world." He was also a good friend to Halina and Artur Rodziński. At the Christening of their son, Riki, "Papa" Damrosch presented the infant with a fancy sculpted baton with the blessing "from the oldest conductor to the future one." Rodziński (1976) 276. In 1940, he was the commencement speaker for graduation ceremonies of the Curtis Institute of Music. Burgwyn (1999) 137.

[22] Viles (1983) 114.

[23] Ignacy Hilsberg, brother of Alexander Hilsberg, was born in Warsaw in 1907 and made his first appearance with a symphony orchestra in Warsaw at the age of nine. He was well known as a pianist and was on the faculty of Juilliard, but appeared at Curtis as a conductor. He first performed in America in 1923, and in 1935 he was soloist with the Philadelphia Orchestra under the baton of his brother. Ignacy moved to California, played piano for films, and taught at UCLA. He died there in 1973, twelve years after his brother.

[24] Viles (1983) 129.

Hofmann died of pneumonia in 1957 in Los Angeles. His many patents included automobile windshield wipers,[25] various medical devices, a furnace for burning crude oil, pneumatic shock absorbers for cars and planes, a house that revolved with the sun, improvements in the development of the piano roll, adjustable piano stools, and piano action improvements adopted by the Steinway Company. He also composed many pieces under the pseudonym Michel Dvorsky, supposedly a Frenchman. Some of his most famous students were Shura Cherkassky, Ruth Slenczyńska, Abram Chasins, and Abbey Simon.

"Whatever flaws he possessed, no artistic director did more for the Curtis Institute of Music than Jozef Hofmann in establishing a world class institution of musical learning, putting Philadelphia on the world cultural map. Aside from establishing as great a faculty and student body as had been seen in America, he convinced Mary Bok to endow the school and she donated the astounding sum of $12.5 million."

"Under his guiding hand the Curtis Institute of Music had entered an unparalleled golden age. The caliber of the small group of students he engaged and the progressiveness of the artistic environment he fostered remain unmatched by any conservatory."[26]

What would the Curtis Institute have looked like without Jozef Hofmann? Surely it could not have attracted such a faculty without "arguably the twentieth century's greatest pianist."

A *New York Times* editorial on Hofmann's death said, "Something has gone out of the world of music with the death of Josef Hofmann. He was the symbol, a landmark-almost an institution. It is hard to imagine the piano in our time without him" (February 19, 1957).

In his book, *The Great Pianists* (1976), Harold Schoenberg called Hofmann "The greatest pianist of his time."

---

[25] Hofmann is acknowledged as an inventor of the windshield wiper, but the American Mary Anderson is credited with the first patent for the first operational windshield wiper in 1903.

[26] Liner notes from Marston Records of Josef Hofmann 1938 Casimir Hall recital.

"An artist of the most discriminating taste. . . one of the finest musicians among all the singers of history" Henry Pleasants.[27]

The Metropolitan Opera Archives, Mora
**Sembrich as Lucia in Gaetano Donizetti's *Lucia di Lammemoor* (Metropolitan Opera premiere, 1893)**

---

[27] Pleasants (1966) 278.

Henry Pleasants (1910–2000) grew up on Philadelphia's Main Line, studied voice at the Curtis Institute, and attended the University of Pennsylvania. He became music critic for the Philadelphia *Evening Bulletin* until he entered the Foreign Service in Europe during WWII. He studied voice and composition in Europe, but became the foreign music correspondent for the *New York Times*. He also wrote regularly for *Opera Quarterly*, *Stereo Review*, and for thirty years was the London music critic for the *International Herald Tribune*. He is the author of several books including the translations of Eduard Hanslich's and Robert Schumann's music criticisms and the autobiography of Louis Spohr. The Curtis Institute of Music awarded him an honorary doctorate in 1977. He died in London.

**Marcella Sembrich,** together with Artur Rodziński, formed the opera department of the Curtis Institute of Music in 1924. Sembrich was born Prakseda Marcelina Kochańska in Wiśniewczyk, Galicia, in 1858. She grew up in extreme poverty but was infused with a great love of music by her parents. Her father supported the family of thirteen children by teaching and performing on several instruments. Marcella began piano lessons at the age of four and the violin at six. Marcella, a brother, and her parents formed an ensemble.

Unfortunately, all of their sheet music was borrowed, and Marcella spent hours by candlelight copying parts, to the point where she suffered permanent impairment of her vision. Throughout her career, she could scarcely see the conductor's baton. (She was very self-conscious about a cast in her right eye, and most photographs of her show only her left profile.)[28]

When Marcella was eleven, her parents brought her to study at the University of Lemberg (Lwów) where her teacher on the piano was Karol Mikuli, the Director of the Conservatory who had been a student of Chopin's. She also studied violin and piano with Wilhelm Stengel, eleven years her elder, whom she would marry years later. She met her expenses by playing for dancing classes.

In 1873, she was taken to Vienna to further her study of piano and violin as well as voice.[29] She was introduced to Franz Liszt. She played for him one of his Hungarian Rhapsodies on the piano, and on the violin some Wieniawski. But it was when she sang that Liszt exclaimed, "God has given you three pairs of wings with which to fly through the country of music; they are all equal: give up none of them, but sing, sing for the world, for you have the voice of an angel."[30]

After studying in Italy, Sembrich made her operatic debut at the age of nineteen in Greece in *I Puritani*. She then sang in Dresden, Milan, Vienna, Warsaw, Madrid, and London as her career skyrocketed. In St. Petersburg, she sang for Czar Alexander II a Chopin song in a language that had not been permitted by the Czar: Polish.[31] Fortunately, he was moved by her

---

[28] James and Boyer (1971) 259.

[29] Owen (1950) 11–18.

[30] Sembrich never denied this story but was emphatic in stating that her piano teacher in Vienna, Julius Epstein, discovered her voice. See Larue (1993) 1226.

[31] Owen (1950) 37.

artistry. Her career in Europe rose rapidly. She performed in Warsaw with Paderewski as her accompanist and she acquired considerable prosperity, living on her estate, Villa Marcella, on Canalettostrasse in Dresden. [32]

She came to America in her twenties, already having achieved considerable notoriety using her mother's name, Sembrich—having made the decision that Kochański was too difficult to pronounce.[33] She debuted at the Metropolitan Opera on the second night of its existence in 1883, singing Lucia at the age of twenty-five. During that season, she sang 55 performances in 12 different roles, all premieres. In the span of only 29 days, she sang the Metropolitan Opera's first performances of seven different operas. Later in the season, she added four more, and the Met chose one of those, Charles Gounod's *Romeo e Juliet*, to be performed first in Philadelphia. The Metropolitan Opera had a regular Tuesday night series in Philadelphia which continued for the next 80 years with 900 performances.

All of the Met's productions in that first season came to Philadelphia. Sembrich's initial appearance in Philadelphia was during that first season singing *Lucia di Lammermoor* at the Chestnut Street Theater; two months later, she sang for the first time at the Academy of Music in *Les Huguenots*. At the last performance of that 1883–84 season, in a gala fund raiser, she astonished the audience displaying her amazing talents performing Chopin *Mazurkas* on the piano, de Beriot's Concerto No.7 on the violin, and then providing a violin obbligato for *Ave Maria* which accompanied her colleague, Christine Nilsson. Finally, she sang from *Barber of Seville* and *La Sonnambula*.

---

[32] A location that surely did not go unnoticed to Sembrich-Kochańska. Bernardo Bellotto, known as "Canaletto" in Poland, had painted in Dresden, but at the invitation of King August III of Poland became the court painter in Warsaw and spent the last sixteen years of his life there, passing away in 1780. Canaletto painted the Royal Castle and many buildings in the capitol and the surrounding environs. After the destruction of Warsaw in WWII, his paintings of incredible accuracy were used to restore many landmarks and parts of the city to their original prewar facades.

[33] A part of her possessions were already in America. An elaborate music chest in the music salon of her Villa was taken to Philadelphia and exhibited at the Centennial Exhibition of 1876 and won first prize. Gustav Kobbe, "Mme. Sembrich at Villa Marcella," *The Delineator*, May 1904: 841–846.

The ambitiousness of that first season took a financial toll on the Met, and Sembrich decided to return to Europe; and she did not sing again in America for another 14 years, in 1898. Beginning in 1900, she again sang the first performances of six more operas. In 1902, she sang the role of Ulana in the only Polish opera ever presented at New York's Metropolitan Opera, Paderewski's *Manru*, conducted by Walter Damrosch. In that year, she finally made her first appearance with the Philadelphia Orchestra under its first Music Director, Fritz Scheel, singing works by Mozart, Schubert, and Weber. In 1903, for Enrico Caruso's debut in America, she sang with him in a new Metropolitan Opera production of *Rigoletto,* performed both in New York and in Philadelphia at the Academy of Music. In 1906, she opened another new Metropolitan Opera production singing *Lakmé* by Léo Delibes with its very first performance in Philadelphia. In her final year at the Met, Philadelphia saw one of its most glittering nights as Sembrich teamed with Caruso and the great Polish basso Adam Didur to sing *La bohème.* In eleven seasons, she sang 450 performances with the Metropolitan Opera, and more key roles in more important premiere productions than any other singer in their history. Her farewell opera in 1909 was *The Marriage of Figaro* sung with Didur as Figaro and conducted by Gustav Mahler both in Philadelphia and New York.[34] It is said that her New York farewell performance on February 6th was the most spectacular in Met history.

Sembrich was the preeminent diva of her time, giving many recitals in New York in addition to her frequent operatic appearances; and it was not unusual for her to remove her gloves and accompany herself on the piano in encores of Chopin songs. She would also incorporate lesser-known Polish composers such as Aleksander Zarzycki and Zygmunt Stojowski into her recitals.[35] A full-length portrait of her hangs prominently at the Met in a display of their most famous artists. She still holds the record for Rosina's

[34] Marion (1984) 141–162.

[35] "Modern civilization insists on associating us (Poland) more with political trouble than with culture . . . we are proud of what we have done with music. . . I am hoping that the world will awaken to the realization of our Polish composers, Sowinski, Wielkowski, Zarzycki, Moniuszko and the rest. I need not tell about Chopin." An excerpt from a special edition of the *Etude* magazine, February 1915, featuring Paderewski on the cover page and entitled, "The Music of Proud and Chivalrous Poland."

in *The Barber of Seville,* having sung it 65 of the 67 performances while she was there.[36] In the lesson scene of that opera, Sembrich sometimes substituted the teaching of Chopin's song *Życzenia* (The Maiden's Wish) or a Chopin waltz.[37] She broke the tradition of the diva when she performed recitals of lieder in six different languages in the order of their composition. She participated in the first recordings of opera in America in 1903.

Curtis Institute of Music Archives, Kubey-Rembrandt Studios

Upon her retirement Sembrich became head of the Opera Departments of both the Curtis Institute and New York's Institute of Musical Art (which became the Juilliard School of Music). There is a wonderful property in Bolton Landing, N.Y., on Lake George where she had a home and invited her Curtis students to study in the summer. She held "musicales" featuring the students, which were open to the public or to specially invited musicians and critics. Much of the property was sold after her death, but

[36] Stephen Herx, "Marcella Sembrich's Contribution to the American Vocal Scene," *Marcella Sembrich Memorial Association,* Spring 2008.
[37] MOA.

there remains a small museum with a performance space dedicated to her on a beautiful alcove. From June to September, the Marcella Sembrich Memorial Association holds concerts, lectures and other cultural events there. It is listed in the National Register of Historic Places.

One commentator called her "the best-loved singer known to New York."[38] Throughout her life, she served Polish causes and was President of the American-Polish Relief Committee of New York during World War I, which was wholly devoted to raising money, food, and clothes for her suffering countrymen. Her generosity also aided many other causes for the poor and underprivileged. In a letter, President Theodore Roosevelt honored her, saying, "your singing has meant very much indeed to the American people. And I especially thank you for the generous way in which you have used your great gift for every philanthropic and charitable undertaking."[39]

The Kosciuszko Foundation in New York City holds an annual Marcella Sembrich Voice Competition. Her funeral in St. Patrick's Cathedral in Manhattan in 1935 was to be a simple service as per the family's request. However, seven carloads of flowers were delivered, and 3,500 mourners spilled onto the icy sidewalks.[40]

Sembrich had been a preeminent voice teacher in America, but taught only women. On the roster for the Metropolitan Opera's 1935–1936 season, at least eleven of the fifty-three female singers were her students.[41] Dusolina Giannini,[42] Hulda Lashanska, Alma Gluck, Maria Jeritza, and Queena Mario, who taught for Sembrich when she was ill, were some of her most successful. In 1926, one of Sembrich's first students at the Curtis Institute, Louise Lerch, had accepted a four-year contract with the Metropolitan

---

[38] James and Boyer (1971) 259.

[39] Galazka (1992) 85.

[40] Villamil (2004) 1.

[41] Stephen Herx, "Marcella Sembrich's Contribution to the American Vocal Scene," *Marcella Sembrich Memorial Association*, Spring 2008.

[42] Dusolina Giannini (1902–1986), born in Philadelphia into a remarkably musical family, made her debut at the Met in 1936 singing the role of Amneris in *Aida*, just three months after the death of Sembrich. Her sister, Euphemia Giannini Gregory (d. 1979), taught voice at Curtis from 1927 to 1973. Their brother, Vittorio (1930–1966), taught composition there from 1956 to 1964.

Opera [43] and sang in 129 performances. Natalie Bodanskaya, another Curtis student of hers sang major roles in 157 performances at the Met.[44] Bodanskaya, Josephine Jirak, Genia Mirska and Genia Wiłkomirska also studied with Sembrich on her property on Lake George.

Some of her students went on to become teachers at Curtis and Juilliard. Those vocal successors who have passed on her artistry include Anna Moffo, Judith Blegen, Frank Guarrera, Judith Raskin, Leontyne Price, and David Lloyd.[45]

### The Seventeen First-Performances Sung by Marcella Sembrich with The Metropolitan Opera

In the Met's first season, 1883–84, in the span of 29 days she sang:

*Lucia di Lammermoor* by Gaetano Donizetti
*I Puritani and La Sonnambula* by Vincenzo Bellini
*La Traviata* and *Rigoletto* by Giuseppe Verdi
*Il Barbiere di Siviglia* by Giaochino Rossini
*Don Giovanni* by Wolfgang Amadeus Mozart

Later in the same season she sang:

*Hamlet* by Ambroise Thomas
*Les Huguenots by* Giacomo Meyerbeer
*Don Pasquale by* Gaetano Donizetti
*Romeo e Juliette* by Charles Gounod (premiered first in Philadelphia)

---

[43] Viles (1983) 50.

[44] Bodanskaya and Queena Mario teamed up together in 1927 with the Philadelphia Grand Opera Company in Engelbert Humperdincks's *Hänsel und Gretel*. As with Dusolina Giannini, Sembrich died just months before Bodanskaya's Metropolitan Opera debut as Micaela in Bizet's *Carmen*. Born in New York City, Bodanskaya changed her name to Bodanya after attending Curtis.

[45] George Parrous and Charles B. Mintzer, www.cantabile-subito.de/Sopranos/ Sembrich Marcella/hauptteil sembrich marcella.htm, accessed September 12, 2014.

After a 14 year absence, she then sang the Metropolitan Opera premieres of:

*Die Zauberflöte* by Wolfgang Amadeus Mozart (1900)
*Die Lustigen Weiber von Windsor* by Otto Nicholai (1900)
*Fille de Regiment* by Gaetano Donizetti (1902)
*Ernani* by Giuseppe Verdi (1903)
*Die Fledermaus* by Johann Strauss, Jr. (1905)

*Manru* by Ignacy Jan Paderewski (1902) in its U.S. premiere—the only Polish opera ever presented by the Met.[46]

Sembrich also sang two songs by Richard Strauss, "Allerseelen" and "Ständchen," on the first half of a concert that included the U.S. premiere of Richard Strauss's *Elektra*.

---

[46] Paderewski's opera, *Manru*, has an interesting history in itself. It continues to be the only opera by a Polish composer ever performed by the Metropolitan Opera. The libretto, generally considered the weakest part of the opera, was written by Alfred Nossig (1864–1943), a friend of Paderewski's. Nossig was a Polish Jew born in Lwów. In Poland he studied law; in Zurich he studied philosophy; and in Vienna, medicine. He was a brilliant man and an impassioned Pole who became an impassioned Zionist. His ideas for establishing a Zionist state in what is now Turkey, however, were rejected. He became a peace activist in the late 1920s, but when the Nazis emerged victorious in Poland in WWII, quite unbelievably, he became an intelligence gatherer for the Germans in the Warsaw Ghetto. The Polish Underground discovered his charts for the underground passages to the Ghetto that were to be passed to the Nazis and the Jewish Underground executed him. Years after the *Manru* premiere, Paderewski's association with Nossig was to cause him some distress with the Jewish community in New York who were already inflamed by a rumor that some 30 years earlier Paderewski had supported an anti-Jewish publication in Warsaw.

Curtis Institute of Music Archives, Kubey-Rembrandt Studios

**Leopold Stokowski** predicted that the Curtis Institute of Music would become "the most important musical institution of the country, perhaps of the world," and those exalted expectations have been met for nearly a hundred years. Stokowski was the first conductor of the student orchestra, and he believed that the exceptional instrumentalists that he and the school nurtured would become the future of the Philadelphia Orchestra. Curtis was a kind of training ground for his Orchestra; its alumni and faculty often constituted a third of the membership of the Orchestra. Throughout Stokowski's tenure with the Philadelphia Orchestra, he utilized Curtis students, especially in his lavish productions. They participated in the first American performance of Alban Berg's *Wozzeck*. But he could also be the most complicated man to anticipate. He loved to shroud much about his life and career in mystery, fantasy, and misinformation, so that one never knew what he would do or say next. His interest in the school remained strong but his regular attendance at Curtis waned after two years.

"Leopold Stokowski could only have been invented—by Leopold Stokowski."[47]

Stokowski was born Leopold Antoni Stokowski in 1882 in North London, England. His father, Josef Kopernik Bolesław Stokowski,[48] was a cabinetmaker who married Annie Moore, an illiterate Irish woman who had to sign Leopold's birth certificate with an X.[49] His grandfather, also Leopold Stokowski, had been forced to leave Lublin and Kraków, Poland, in 1848 because of his part in the fight to gain freedom for Poland.[50] He married an English woman. At one point later in his life, however, Stokowski (the younger) somehow managed to convince the writers of the Grove Dictionary of Music, the world's most respected history of music in English, that he had been born in 1887 as Leopold Bolesławowicz Stanisław Antoni Stokowski.[51]

In 1911, he married the famous pianist, Olga Samaroff, who had changed her name from Lucie Hickenlooper. His second marriage, to the Johnson & Johnson heiress Evangeline Johnson, brought them a daughter in 1927. Always the showman, Leopold proposed naming her Gloria Amoris Nadya Luba Marzenka Stanisława Stokowski. Luba was finally settled on, but Stokowski always called her Lyuba because it sounded more exotic.[52]

At the age of thirteen, Stokowski began his musical training in London at the Royal College of Music, at the time the youngest person ever admitted to that school. He studied piano and violin but preferred the organ. Upon graduation, he secured a position at St. James's Church, Picadilly, as organist/choir director and continued studies at Queens College, Oxford.

At the age of 23, he went to New York City as the organist and choir director at St. Bartholemew's. In 1909, a successful conducting debut in

---

[47] David Patrick Stearns, "A Century on, Stokowski Still Burns Bright," *Philadelphia Inquirer*, 18 June 2012.

[48] Opperby (1982) 9.

[49] Lebrecht (1991) 140.

[50] Leopold Stokowski, "Chopin-Poland's National Poet," *Etude*, February 1915.

[51] *Grove's Dictionary of Music and Musicians*, 1954 edition.

[52] Daniel (1982) 204.

Paris helped earn him the position of Music Director of the Cincinnati Symphony Orchestra. At the same time while in Cincinnati, he changed the spelling of his last name to Stokovski- an attempt to steer the English audience away from the "cow" in Sto<u>kow</u>ski. In his London debut in 1912, he led the London Symphony in Queens Hall. In the audience were Sir Edward and Lady Elgar, Joseph Szigeti, Mischa Elman, and numerous other musical and managerial celebrities.[53] Efrem Zimbalist, future director of the Curtis Institute, was the soloist, and the reviews for Stokowski were nothing less than spectacular.

Stokowski was invited to become the third conductor of the Philadelphia Orchestra beginning in 1912. He built a career here that made him the first "superstar" conductor in America, and was for many years the most famous Philadelphian in the world. He became a U.S. citizen in 1915, and it was around this time that he also acquired some peculiarities, one of which was a strange kind of European accent, sort of Slavic, certainly not English. His tenure established both himself and the Philadelphia Orchestra as among the best in the world.

Courtesy of Philadelphia Orchestra Association

---

[53] Daniel 113.

"In 1912 when Stokowski took over the Philadelphia Orchestra, it was far from being one of the better orchestras in America, let alone one of the best in the world. It is one of his greatest achievements that when he left it 25 years later, the Philadelphia Orchestra had no equal anywhere."[54] "His career was the most glamorous of any conductor in this century."[55]

Stokowski died in 1977 at the age of 95. During his time with the Philadelphians, he introduced many masterworks not just for the first time in America, but even the world. In his biography on Stokowski, William Ander Smith estimates that he premiered 2,000 new or unplayed works in his long career.[56] He broke with European tradition and formed the country's first truly American orchestra. He mingled with his players, many of whom were immigrants gathered from around the world, and for the first time, English was the language spoken in rehearsals (previously it had been German). The sound of the orchestra was like no other and was described as sonorous, blended, and burnished. Quite simply, he, more than anyone, placed Philadelphia on the world cultural map. He was very proud to be an American, but he did not forget his Slavic roots and in 1939, formed the Hollywood Committee for Polish Relief, after Germany's attack on Poland. Mary Louise Curtis Bok headed the Philadelphia Committee for Polish Relief.[57]

The Philadelphia Orchestra had a few excellent musicians in its ranks in 1912, but Stokowski went on a quest to find the very best that America had to offer; many came from other orchestras.[58] Players from France, Spain, Russia, the Netherlands, and Italy filled the rosters. Among his principal players were Kincaid, Tabuteau, Torello, Horner, Caston, Kindler, and Bonade. . . names that remain legends among musicians to this day. Poles came also; among them as the **Berw** family.

---

[54] Robinson (1977) 15.

[55] Dubal (1984) 365.

[56] Smith (1990) 29.

[57] *Philadelphia Evening* Bulletin, 6 December 1939.

[58] As examples, Kincaid was second flute and Tabuteau was first oboe in the New York City Symphony. Torello was principal bass in the Boston Opera.

**Arthur Berw (Berv)** was born in Warsaw in 1906.[59] His parents came to the United States during the great influx of Polish immigrants just before World War I and settled in Chisholm, Minnesota. His father, Samuel, ran a general store. Samuel had an intense interest in classical music and chose the trumpet for his son, Arthur. Arthur's three brothers were all born after him and Samuel also made choices for Arthur's three younger brothers: the cello for **Jack** and the piano for **Harry**, while **Henry** chose the violin. Luckily for us, three of them successfully settled on the French horn. Samuel eventually moved the family to Philadelphia where the children could study at the Curtis Institute. Arthur was so talented that when they arrived in Philadelphia Stokowski hired him for the orchestra as a sixteen-year-old, while Jack and Harry entered the Curtis Institute.[60] Arthur left Philadelphia in 1926 to become first horn in Walter Damrosch's Orchestra in New York, but he returned to Philadelphia in 1930 to become assistant first horn under Stokowski. After performing the Richard Strauss Horn Concerto No. 1 with the Orchestra, he became principal horn in 1935. That same year, Harry and Jack now officially graduated from Curtis, and had gained considerable notoriety of their own. Stokowski asked them also to join the Orchestra. The trio was not to stay long in Philadelphia, however. Arturo Toscanini, who was unhappy with his first horn at the NBC Symphony heard them and decided to hire all three brothers for his orchestra. They became first, second, and third horns. (I don't think that has ever been accomplished again on any instrument.) They also played together in the Army Air Corps Band during World War II.[61] Arthur wrote many articles for horn publications, and Harry's book, *A Creative Approach to the French Horn*, was published by Chappell Music in 1977. Henry, the violinist, never become a professional musician.

Other Poles who played with the Philadelphia Orchestra during the Stokowski years included the violinists **Stanisław Dąbrowski**, **Henri**

[59] Larry Huffman, Philadelphia Orchestra Musicians, at www.Stokowski.org, accessed September 12, 2014.
[60] "Join New York Symphony," *New York Times*, 8 August 1926.
[61] "Three Men On a Horn," *New York Times*, 3 March 1945.

**Czaplinski, David Nowiński, Max Seliński, Paul Pitkowski,** and **Israel Siekierka.**[62]

Siekierka played in the Warsaw Philharmonic before joining the Philadelphia Orchestra from 1924–1943, then became an osteopath and shall always be remembered as the man who shot a patient and himself to death in 1960.

There were the **Argiewicz** brothers: **Bernard**, a cellist, played in Philadelphia for eight years (and in Detroit for 25 years), and **Arthur**, a prominent violinist in San Francisco.[63]

Violist **Ludwik Starzyński** was a member of the Philadelphia Orchestra from 1900–1910 and also played in the orchestras of New York, Cincinnati, and St. Louis.

**Emil Latisch** played double bass in the Orchestra until 1917. The five Rozanel brothers came from Warsaw. All played brass instruments and were successful in New York, Cleveland, and Philadelphia. **Elizir Rozanel** was Stokowski's first trumpet before accepting the same position in Cleveland where Rodziński was also attracting Polish musicians. **Waldemar Dąbrowski** (no relation to the violinist, Stanisław) studied conducting at Curtis as a classmate of Leonard Bernstein.[64] **Bronisław Szulc** played French horn from 1922–1933 before returning to Poland.[65]

---

[62] Larry Huffman, Philadelphia Orchestra Musicians, at www.Stokowski.org, accessed September 12, 2014.

[63] Arthur, at the age of nine, just arriving in America in 1893, played a recital in New York that was reviewed by the *New York Times*, which called him a "juvenile prodigy." "A Week's Musical Topics," *New York Times*, 22 October 1893. He taught at the Institute of Musical Art in New York from 1911 to 1913. During this time, he and Zygmunt Stojowski performed a series of recitals at the Mac Dowell Club, premiering a new Stojowski Violin Sonata. "Stojowski's New Sonata," *New York Times*, 19 March 1912. He went on to the San Francisco Symphony, attaining the status of assistant concertmaster. He was arrested in 1922 for non-support of his mother, who he said had abandoned him in Poland. "Son Refuses to Assist Mother," *Oakland Tribune*, 9 December 1922.

[64] During WWII, however, he was in the U.S. Army Air Force, learned electronics, and became a radar officer. After the war he went to work at the Princeton Plasma Physics Lab and retired from that business, but never abandoned his skills as a pianist.

[65] In 1936, Bronisław Szulc and his brother Brotisław, also a horn player, became the first members of Bronisław Huberman's Palestine Symphony.

**Sigmund Hering**, trumpeter from 1925–1964 who also studied double bass at Curtis, was also born in Poland and became a well-known pedagogue on his instrument.

Stokowski was constantly innovating, testing the limits of his audiences and his performers. He radically rearranged orchestra seating to best balance the sound of his players, and he is credited with adopting the seating plan that most orchestras use today. The number of American and world premieres he presented has never been equaled by any conductor in history. But Stokowski had trouble keeping a principal violinist. For example, Mischa Mischakoff, born in the Ukraine, who came to the Orchestra from the Warsaw Philharmonic lasted only two years; as a result, Stokowski experimented with rotating the violins so that more players got the chance to act as concertmaster.[66] This terrorized many of the violinists—not knowing when the rotation would call for them to play the most difficult solos. So for six years the orchestra had no permanent concertmaster, until Alexander Hilsberg was appointed in 1935.

Curtis Institute of Music Archives

---

[66] Daniel (1982) 297–301.

**Aleksander Hillersberg (Alexander Hilsberg)**[67] was born in Warsaw in 1900. He toured Poland and Russia as a child prodigy at the age of nine. His formal training took him to St. Petersburg with Leopold Auer, who had studied with Wieniawski. He toured the Far East for four years, living for a time in Harbin, China. Arriving in the United States in 1923, he joined the Philadelphia Orchestra in 1926 and became a U.S. citizen in 1929. He became a faculty member at the Curtis Institute on Stokowski's recommendation and was appointed conductor of the student orchestra. He was the teacher of Leon Zawisza and of Jacob Krachmalnik, who went on to become concertmaster of the Philadelphia Orchestra. Hilsberg was a highly regarded soloist and conductor, and continued as concertmaster and assistant conductor under Eugene Ormandy when Stokowski left the Philadelphia Orchestra. He led the Orchestra more than one hundred times in concert, including with piano soloists William Kapell and Alexander Brailowsky, and recorded with violinist Isaac Stern. Hilsberg left Philadelphia to become Music Director of the New Orleans Philharmonic and hired Norman Carol as his concertmaster. A few years later, Carol was to take that position with the Philadelphia Orchestra. Hilsberg then hired William de Pasquale as his concertmaster—and a few years later he, too, came to Philadelphia as associate concertmaster.

In a rather radical gesture, Stokowski eventually abandoned his use of a baton, traditionally used by all conductors. Quite often he spoke to, harangued, and tried to educate his audiences, introducing new music, not always to their delight, but nearly always eliciting a significant reaction. He hired harpist Edna Phillips, the first woman to be engaged by a major orchestra. Stokowski tinkered with recording techniques at the Bell Laboratories in Camden, New Jersey, and conducted many of the first recordings ever made in America. No musician had a greater influence on the development of recording techniques. Mistrustful of recording engineers' manipulation, at one stage he demanded the control panel be installed in front of the podium. In 1929, the Philadelphia Orchestra made historic studio broadcasts over American radio and European and Asian shortwave stations. In 1925, they had made the first electrical recording.[68] At one time, when new pieces were being prepared, Stokowski had his

---

[67] *Baker's Biographical Dictionary of Musicians*, 2001.
[68] Daniel (1982) 304–314.

assistant conductor rehearse the orchestra as he sat in the hall, controlling a battery of colored lights onstage that signaled if the orchestra was to play softer, louder, faster, slower, etc.[69]

He was a true autocrat—a conductor's tradition shared by others of prominence[70] that has, thankfully, passed. On tour, the Orchestra created a sensation everywhere it went.

Rachmaninoff called the Philadelphia Orchestra "the finest orchestra the world has ever heard,"[71] and dedicated some of his works to Stokowski. With "Stoky" and the Philadelphians, Rachmaninoff made historic recordings of his concertos with himself as piano soloist. In 1940, he also conducted a recording of his Symphony No. 3 for RCA.

Only Serge Koussevitzky in Boston commissioned more new music than Stokowski, but Stokowski's American premieres of pieces such as Alban Berg's opera *Wozzeck*, several Shostakovich symphonies and the world premiere of Carlos Chavez' Mexican ballet, *H.P.,* produced more notoriety. Stokowski's insatiable drive to experiment often made his concerts in Philadelphia front page news in the daily papers. Those experiments were sometimes "hissed" by the audience and the Board of Directors of the Orchestra was not always supportive, but Stokowski was always unfazed. In an event that garnered much publicity, he conducted the Eastern State Penitentiary Band in Philadelphia.[72] It was his first

---

[69] Rodziński (1976) 155, 255.

[70] Arturo Toscanini craved power and went into frequent, blinding rages with his NBC Symphony. Fritz Reiner was so hated by the Chicago Symphony in his nine years there that it took Georg Solti, a successor, many years to convince the orchestra members that he was not the enemy. Arturo Rodziński also engaged in warfare with the Chicagoans for a year. He arrived there after having fired fourteen musicians as one of his first duties when he was music director of the New York Philharmonic. Conductors in America believed that domination by fear was the way a great conductor should behave. Lebrecht (1991) 78, 96.

[71] Daniel (1982) 300.

[72] Hedda van den Beemt (1880–1925) was a violinist/pianist in the Philadelphia Orchestra for nearly twenty years but also taught and conducted at the Eastern State Penitentiary. He invited Stokowski to guest conduct the penitentiary band. Van den Beemt was born in the Netherlands and was also the Music Director for several productions of the Philadelphia Operatic Society in 1924 and 1925. He is forever immortalized, however, in the well-known 1904 painting by Thomas Eakins entitled *Music*. Daniel (1982) 344.

experience with motion pictures, as it was filmed for newsreels and shown in theaters around the country, preceding another film *Big Broadcast of 1937* by sixteen years.[73] He appeared, acted, and conducted in several Hollywood films.

When Walt Disney decided to make a film about the *Sorcerer's Apprentice,* it was first produced as a "short" with studio musicians. He showed it to Stokowski, who convinced Disney to make a full-length movie, which became *Fantasia.*[74] The film was the first stereophonic production for a theater. It was a tremendous hit, the first in the history of motion pictures in which music was the primary focus.

Stokowski's fascination with children led him to invite youngsters to perform the Haydn *Toy Symphony* with the Orchestra, and beginning in 1921, he created series of concerts for children, the high point of which undoubtedly was his version of Saint-Saens' *Carnival of the Animals.*[75] To the delight and amazement of the children present at that concert, on to the stage trooped three baby elephants, three ponies, two lion cubs, a llama, a kangaroo, a heron, a Galapagos turtle, an ostrich, a kingfisher, a duck hawk, three penguins, a swan, a donkey, and a camel.[76]

During World War II, Stokowski offered his services to the U.S. Army to develop improvements in military bands.[77] In 1922, he was the recipient of the first $10,000 "Philadelphia Award." In 1940, he led a special benefit concert for hospitals in war-torn China, which undoubtedly helped build a long-term cultural relationship with the Chinese.[78] When When Leopold Stokowski finally severed all ties to Philadelphia and the Orchestra in

---

[73] Robinson (1977) 39.

[74] Opperby (1982) 65–72.

[75] Daniel (1982) 191.

[76] Ardoin (1999) 110.

[77] Daniel 424–426.

[78] This gala benefit concert on March 21, 1940, boasted one of the largest orchestras ever assembled and included members of the Curtis Institute as well as the soloists Alexander Kipnis, Rose Brampton, Joseph Szigeti, and Emanuel Feuermann. Stokowski shared the podium with Eugene Ormandy. "Noted Soloists Appear After Some Difficulty," *Galveston Daily News,* March 22, 1940.

During the Richard Nixon administration in 1973, the Orchestra under Eugene Ormandy was the first large group from America sent to China to reignite relations between the two countries, performing in Peking and Shanghai. In 2010, they were

1941, one biographer deemed it "one of the greatest tragedies in the recent history of music." [79]

In California, just before leaving the Philadelphia Orchestra, he was planning the formation of an Electric Orchestra and was in correspondence with the well-known thereminist Elena Moneak. In 1930, Maurice Martenot, inventor of the electronic instrument the *ondes martenot* gave the instrument its first concert performance in America under Stokowski and the Philadelphians.

In 1999, David Mellor in *Gramophone* magazine wrote: "Stokowski is now recognized as the father of modern orchestral standards."

The city saw nothing of Stokowski during the next twenty years. In 1960, however, he again began a stint of engagements with the Orchestra that eventually numbered fifty over the next nine years. In 1961, he debuted with the New York Metropolitan Opera in a legendary performance of *Turandot*, a production he brought to Philadelphia.[80] A 1963 Philadelphia Orchestra Christmas concert featured "traditional Slavic Christmas music." Again in 1969, he departed and did not return again before his death on September 13, 1977.

Philadelphia keeps a historical record of Stokowski in a large collection at the University of Pennsylvania. The Leopold Stokowski Papers, an extensive collection originally given to the Curtis Institute of Music and now held by the library of the University of Pennsylvania, contain his correspondence, notebooks, memorabilia, photographs, penciled manuscripts, and personal papers.[81] There would be much more, but after his death in England, a large container of his possessions was lost overboard from the ship transporting them to the United States.[82]

---

again highlighted at the Shanghai World Expo; at that time a long-term annual residency in China was planned to begin in the 2012 Season.

[79] Opperby (1982) 53.

[80] "One of the highlights of the Met's long performance series is the legendary 1961 production of *Turandot* designed by Cecil Beaton featuring conductor Leopold Stokowski in his company debut and starring Birgit Nilsson, Franco Corelli and Anna Moffo." *Metropolitan Opera News*, October 2012: 41.

[81] University of Pennsylvania Rare Book and Manuscript Library: Stokowski Papers, Ms. Coll. 381.

[82] Daniel (1982) 922–923.

"Stokowski was neither servant nor a priest in the House of music. He was a Dionysian experimenter in music; He was sorcerer rather than priest, sensualist rather than servant. He was a playful pagan in a musical world dominated by serious-minded priests, scribes, and disciples. He was playful in the sense that unregimented youth is playful, that is, curious, delighting in the new and the experimental, and seeing old things with new eyes and hearing with new ears—always his own. His goal was always the innovation of tomorrow rather than the tradition of yesterday."[83]

A memorial service was held at the Curtis Institute on September 23, 1977, led by John DeLancie, then Director of Curtis, and a Conducting Fellowship was established in Stokowski's honor.

Two other conductors who assisted Stokowski are discussed later in this book: **Józef Pasternak (Josef Pasternack)** (see Conductors) and **Tadeusz Jarecki** (see Composers).

Curtis Institute of Music Archives, Kubey-Rembrandt Studios

**Artur Rodziński**, born in Croatia in 1892, became Stokowski's assistant with the Philadelphia Orchestra in 1925 and the following year he took over Stokowski's position as Director of the Orchestral and Opera Departments

---

[83] Smith (1990) 97.

of Curtis. His father, Hermana, was a Polish surgeon conscripted into the Austrian army; his mother, Jadwiga, was a musician.[84] The family was transferred to Lvov (Lwów) in 1897 where Artur began piano studies at age five. Eventually Rodziński went to Vienna, received a law degree from the University of Vienna, and studied music at the Vienna Musical Academy. Back in Lwów, he became choral director of the Lwów Opera and made his principal conducting debut with *Ernani* in 1920. He then became a regular conductor of the Warsaw Opera (Teatr Wielki w Warszawie) for six years at the invitation of Emil Młynarski.

While Stokowski was visiting Poland, he saw Rodziński conduct Richard Wagner's *Die Meistersinger* in Warsaw and invited him to Philadelphia to be his assistant. Rodziński accepted, and the following year he also became Director of the Orchestral and Opera Departments at the Curtis Institute. On January 15, 1929, he conducted the Curtis Orchestra in the first radio broadcast from Casimir Hall. In all there were fourteen radio broadcasts of the Curtis Orchestra in that season, and the radio network expanded to fifty stations. On May 12 of the same year, he led the Curtis Institute in their first opera appearance— *Tiefland* by Eugen d'Albert at the Academy of Music, and also led a twelve performance Thursday evening opera series with the Philadelphia Grand Opera Company. He spent four years in Philadelphia as Mary Curtis Bok's "prodigal son"[85] and made his New York debut conducting the Philadelphia Orchestra in the premiere of a Miaskowsky symphony. He also conducted *The Step* by Zygmunt Noskowski.[86] Rodziński's last performance with the Philadelphia Orchestra was in 1932. After working as Stokowski's assistant in Philadelphia, Rodziński had begun a busy career elsewhere: he was conductor of the Los Angeles Philharmonic (1929–1933), became

---

[84] From the late eighteenth century to the end of WWI, a period of 128 years, Poland was partitioned between Prussia, Austria, and Russia and removed from the world's map. Each of those occupying countries had conscription into their armies which would have forced Poles to fight fellow Poles.

[85] Rodziński (1976) 155, 255.

[86] Noskowski (1846–1909) was a popular Polish Romantic composer and famed composition teacher of Szymanowski at the Warsaw Musical Institute. His symphonic music was quite popular. Stokowski and Rodziński both championed his music. *Step* is generally regarded as the first Polish tone poem.

a U.S. citizen (1933), and was appointed Music Director of the Cleveland Orchestra (1933–1943).

During that time, Rodziński was also engaged to establish the NBC Symphony in New York City for Toscanini. He toured the country, auditioning and hiring the best players available in America and conducted the first concerts in preparation for Toscanini's tenure. He then secured a five-year position as the first Music Director of the newly named New York Philharmonic,[87] followed by one year as Music Director of the Chicago Symphony. He was responsible for helping to launch Leonard Bernstein's career by hiring him in New York as his assistant when Bernstein was only 26 years old.[88] Bernstein had also studied at the Curtis Institute. While living in New York, Rodziński actively maintained a farm, The White Goat, in Stockbridge, Massachusetts, where he raised goats, cows, and bees. It was also a "haven for Polish refugees"[89] and where Rodziński first interviewed Bernstein to be his assistant. Rodziński's resignation from the New York Philharmonic landed him on the cover of *Time* magazine issue of February 17, 1947.

The depth of musical heritage of many of these families is fascinating. Rodziński's second wife, **Halina Lilpop-Rodziński**, was related to the great Wieniawski brothers, Henryk and Józef. Halina's great-great-uncle sang the role of Skolnik in the first performance of Moniuszko's *Halka,* Poland's first national opera. Halina, like her grandmother and mother before her, was named after that *Halka,* which is the affectionate diminutive of Halina.[90] Artur and Halina Rodziński only had one child, a

---

[87] Previously the New York Philharmonic had engaged several of the world's most renowned conductors—Toscanini, Walter, Barbirolli, Mitropoulos, and Reiner—but none assumed the responsibilities of a full-time position, which required controlling repertoire, soloists, auditions, and long-term program planning. Peyser (1987) 105.

[88] Bernstein's appointment was strongly opposed by Arthur Judson, the powerful artists' manager who simultaneously ran the Philadelphia Orchestra and New York Philharmonic. Rodziński prevailed. Bernstein was also recommended by Serge Koussevitzky, the conductor of the Boston Symphony whom Rodziński greatly admired. Peyser (1987) 106.

[89] Rodziński (1976) 205.

[90] Halina's three sisters also had remarkable backgrounds: **Felicja,** an author and painter, was wed to the pianist Kazimierz Kranze. **Aniela** was married to Count Raczyński who became the President of the Polish Government in exile in London.

son born in 1945; his name was Riki (Richard) and his godfather was **Jan Karski**, hero of the Polish Resistance during World War II and honored by President Barack Obama in 2012.[91] Richard Rodziński became General Director of the International Tchaikovsky Competition in Moscow. He was in attendance at the 2010 Chopin International Piano Competition in Warsaw. In 2007, he donated a very large Artur Rodziński collection to the Library of Congress.

When Rodziński became Music Director of the Los Angeles Philharmonic, his successor in the Opera and Conductiong departments at Curtis was **Emil Młynarski**, who also came from Poland.

---

**Maria**, the youngest, married the poet, Zbigniew Unilowska. The family was an icon for the Polish people. Lipton (2011) 91.

[91] Jan Karski (1914–2000), born Jan Kozielewski in Łódź, was a lawyer and a member of the Polish diplomatic corps, serving throughout Europe. During WWII he was twice smuggled into the Warsaw Ghetto so he could see and report on the torture and extermination of the Jews to the rest of the world. He eventually came to America, received a doctorate, lectured extensively and was appointed Professor of History at Georgetown University. He was posthumously awarded the 2012 Presidential Medal of Freedom by President Obama for risking "his life to provide early eyewitness accounts of the Holocaust and press world leaders for action." U.S. Congressman Dan Lipinski, 24 April 2012.

Curtis Institute of Music Archives

Młynarski, one of the most important Polish musicians in the early twentieth century and one of the foremost conductors of opera and symphony orchestras in Europe, was born in 1870 in the Suwałki region. His studies took him to St. Petersburg as a violin student under Leopold Auer and an orchestration student under Rimsky-Korsakoff. He played second violin in the Leopold Auer String Quartet. As an eighteen-year-old, he performed in Petrograd with Marcella Sembrich Kochańska at a ceremony for the Empress of Russia.

He abandoned a successful solo career in Europe and Russia to concentrate on teaching and moved to Warsaw in 1897. He had many successful students to his credit, including Pawel Kochański. He was conductor of the Warsaw Imperial Orchestra and became the first Music Director of the newly formed Warsaw Philharmonic, conducting its inaugural concert in 1901. The soloists for that concert were Ignacy Jan Paderewski and bass-baritone Wiktor Grąbczewski, who had sung the Metropolitan and Philadelphia Opera premieres of *I Pagliacci* in 1893. The program included the works of Chopin, Moniuszko, Żeleński, Paderewski, Noskowski, and Stojowski.

In 1907, Młynarski became the Director of the Institute of Music in Warsaw and conductor of the London Symphony. The following year, he won the Paderewski Composers' Competition in Leipzig for his Violin Concerto No. 1, opus 11. Młynarski spent eleven years working in England and Scotland, and for six of those years was the Music Director of the Scottish Orchestra (now the Royal Scottish National Orchestra). In 1915, he asked Sir Edward Elgar to compose a piece for a wartime Polish Victims' Relief Fund concert. Elgar obliged with *Polonia*, dedicated it to Paderewski, and conducted its first performance in Queen's Hall, London, on a concert shared with Sir John Barbirolli. In 1918, he resumed his involvement with the Warsaw Philharmonic and became Director of the newly formed Warsaw Conservatory.[92]

In 1919, he began a ten-year association with the Warsaw Opera as manager and conductor. In 1926, he premiered Karol Szymanowski's *Król Roger* with Stanisława, the composer's sister, in the principal role of Roxana. As Director of the Warsaw Philharmonic, Młynarski brought in Mischa Mischakoff (born Mischa Fischberg) as concertmaster and Gregor Piatigorsky as assistant first cellist. Fifteen years later, Piatigorsky would be teaching at Curtis, and he appeared more than forty times with the Philadelphia Orchestra as soloist, while Mischakoff would hold the position of Concertmaster under Toscanini in New York's NBC Symphony. It was also during this time that Młynarski engaged Rodziński for Warsaw's Teatr Wielki (Grand Theater), and Leopold Stokowski attended Rodziński's performances of Richard Wagner's *Die Meistersinger*.

When Rodziński left Philadelphia for the Los Angeles Philharmonic, he repaid the kindness by engaging Młynarski as Dean of the Department of Orchestra and Opera at the Curtis Institute. Mary Louise Curtis Bok was also interested in supporting the struggling Philadelphia Opera

---

[92] Formerly the Warsaw Institute of Music associated with the University of Warsaw, it was taken over by the State in 1918 and re-formed as the Warsaw Conservatory. It was destroyed in the Warsaw Uprising of WWII, rebuilt and recreated in 1946 as the Higher State School of Music. In 1979, it was renamed the Fryderyk Chopin Music Academy, and in 2008, it once again changed its name to the Fryderyk Chopin University of Music in Warsaw.

Company but only if it could be restructured. She welcomed Młynarski to help reorganize it so that Curtis students could be incorporated in singing and playing roles in an increased number of productions. During the 1930–31 season, in the span of six months, twenty-one different operas were performed by the newly formed Philadelphia Grand Opera in affiliation with the Curtis Institute (see the following page). To supplement the solo roles of his casts, Młynarski brought in two Polish singers, **Genia Wiłkomirska**, lyric soprano,[93] and **Josef Woliński**, a tenor best suited for Wagnerian roles.[94] In October of 1929 they sang together in *Cavalleria rusticana* as Turiddu and Lola. Natalie Bodanskaya, Josephine Jirak, Genia Mirska, Alexandre Michajłowski and Maurice Janowski also sang roles at that time. Młynarski created the first position of Orchestra Manager for the opera company and Alexander Hilsberg was chosen to solidify the relationship that was to be achieved between the Philadelphia Orchestra and the Curtis Institute.

Młynarski took the Curtis Orchestra to Boston to perform in 1929 and continued the radio broadcast series begun by Rodziński. He conducted the Philadelphia Orchestra on March 14–15, 1930, and continued a policy started by Stokowski of also utilizing members of the Philadelphia Orchestra with the Curtis students in opera productions of the Philadelphia Grand Opera. In the summer of 1930, Młynarski held conducting classes in Warsaw; Louis Vyner from Curtis was one of his pupils who later conducted the Warsaw Philharmonic. In 1931, the Depression ended the support required to continue the Grand Opera in Philadelphia, and Młynarski returned to Poland, once again joining the Warsaw Opera. He had developed crippling arthritis, however, and soon had to retire from conducting. He died in Warsaw in 1935.

Młynarski was also an accomplished composer of roughly twenty compositions. His Violin Concerto No. 2, opus 16 was recorded by Nigel

---

[93] Wiłkomirska came from Poland to study with Marcella Sembrich at the Curtis Institute even though she already had enjoyed some success in Europe. She sang under Młynarski, Rodziński, Reiner, and Goosens in the Philadelphia Grand Opera seasons of 1929–1931, singing Amneris in Philadelphia's first *Aida*.

[94] In 1929 and 1930, Woliński sang *Lohengrin* as well as four non-Wagnerian roles under both Rodziński and Młynarski, including Edgardo in Gaetano Donizetti'e *Lucia di Lammermoor*.

Kennedy and the Polish Chamber Orchestra under Jacek Kaspszyk, and in 2011 *Gramophone* designated it an "Editors Choice." His *Mazur,* opus 7 for violin and piano is still often performed.

### 1930–31 Opera Season of the Philadelphia Grand Opera Company in Affiliation with the Curtis Institute

In a remarkable achievement, during the 1930–31 season, in the span of six months, twenty-one different operas were performed:

*Aida* (October 16, 1930), *La traviata,* and *Rigoletto* by
    Giuseppe Verdi
*Gianni Schicchi, Tosca, Madama Butterfly* and *Pagliacci* by
    Giacomo Puccini
*Lucia di Lammermoor* by Gaetano Donizetti
*Boris Godunov* by Modest Mussorgsky
*Thais* by Jules Massenet
*Hänsel und Gretel* by Engelbert Humperdinck
*Die Puppenfee* by Josef Bayer
*Faust* by Charles Gounod
*L'Heure Espaognole* by Maurice Ravel
*Cavalleria rusticana* by Pietro Mascagni
*Wozzeck* by Alban Berg
*Le jongleur de Notre-Dame* by Jules Massenet
*Les pêcheurs de perles* and *Carmen* by Georges Bizet
*Lohengrin* and *Tannhäuser* (April 16, 1931) by Richard
    Wagner

Also, added to the Curtis Institute of Music faculty were a number of international stars:

Curtis Institute of Music Archives

**Wanda Landowska,** the world's leading authority on the harpsichord, taught at Curtis beginning in 1925 and remained on the faculty for several years. She taught a special unprecedented series of courses in seventeenth- and eighteenth-century music. Landowska was born in Warsaw in 1879, where her father was a lawyer and her mother a linguist who translated Mark Twain into Polish. She studied piano first at the Warsaw Conservatory under **Jan Kleczyński** and **Aleksander Michałowski**, continued study in Berlin, married the Polish folklorist Henry Lew, and moved to Paris in 1900. In 1913, she moved again to Berlin with her newly built, larger harpsichord; however, at the outbreak of World War I, she and Lew were held as civilian prisoners. Finally, they were able to resettle in France. Landowska taught there, became a French citizen, and founded a music school in 1925. Since she was of Jewish heritage, in 1940 she had to leave Paris and sailed to the United States. Her house in France had been looted and all her harpsichords and a library of 10,000 books and manuscripts stolen or destroyed. She arrived in the America without assets and had to reestablish herself as a performer and teacher. She became the world's best-known harpsichordist, bringing great notoriety to a relatively obscure instrument. She worked to improve the instrument in collaboration with the Pleyel Company, the company that provided Chopin with his pianos.

The instrument she developed could project its sound in the concert hall because of its larger body and cast iron frame.

Curtis Institute of Music Archives

Between 1923 and 1927, Landowska appeared with the Philadelphia Orchestra in performances of Bach, Mozart, Handel, and de Falla. She, like Paderewski, knew in her solo appearances how to hold an audience breathless: darkened stage, just enough lighting to illuminate the instrument and her figure. Stylistically she could be a romantic, taking many liberties in her interpretations of Bach, even though she liked to say she was playing it "Bach's way". "Her rubato, incidentally, was a perfectly calibrated means of expression. It was not for nothing that she had Polish blood."[95] After a Town Hall concert, Virgil Thompson wrote in the *New York Herald Tribune*:

> "Wanda Landowska's playing of the harpsichord at Town Hall last night reminded one all over again that there is nothing in the world like it. There does not exist in the world today, nor has there existed in my lifetime,

---

[95] Schonberg (1963) 397–99.

another soloist of this or of any instrument whose work is so dependable, so authoritative and so thoroughly satisfactory. Criticism is unavailing, has been so, indeed, for thirty years."

She transformed all who listened to Bach and Scarlatti, performing on the instrument for which they were originally intended, and she was decorated by both the Polish and French governments. She died in her Connecticut home in 1959, leaving a large collection of recorded works by which to admire her artistry, including an acclaimed Bach *Well Tempered Clavier* that she recorded when she was 70 years old. Landowska was also an accomplished pianist, though not well known on that instrument, who recorded many classical piano works and the early nineteenth century *Polonaises* of Michał Keofas Ogoński.

Curtis Institute of Music Archives

**Maurycy (Moriz) Rosenthal** (1862–1946), "the Napoleon of the Pianoforte," was born in Lemberg (Lwów). He was a pupil of **Karol Mikuli**, his first teacher at the Lwów Conservatory; and it was with Mikuli that he made his first public career appearance at the age of ten as duo-pianist with his teacher.[96] At the age of thirteen, Rosenthal received a three-year stipend for artistic development from the local government and went to study in Vienna where he became a student of Rafael Joseffy. In 1880, he interrupted his career for three years to study philosophy at the University of Vienna. After an introduction from Joseffy, he auditioned for Franz Liszt. "In this boy there hides an artist who will not remain hidden for long," was Liszt's reaction, and Rosenthal became his student intermittently for four years. During his early days in Vienna, he also played for and was a colleague of Johannes Brahms until that great composer died in 1897. At the age of 26, Rosenthal performed in America on a concert with the teenage violinist Fritz Kreisler. Both were making their American debuts. Back in Europe in 1912, he became court pianist for Emperor Franz Josef I of Austria. In 1926, he returned to the United States from Warsaw for a six-month tour of this country and became a member of the faculty of the Curtis Institute for two years. He had a full schedule of twelve students and on occasion shared a pupil with Hofmann. Rosenthal performed much anticipated Curtis recitals in 1927 and 1928 and instead of the standard practice of using the Steinway piano in performance, he supported the Baldwin Piano Company.

In 1888, he performed the Xaver Scharwenka Piano Concerto No. 1 at the Academy of Music in Philadelphia with the Boston Symphony. Twenty years later, he performed the Chopin Piano Concerto in E Minor with the Philadelphia Orchestra at the Academy of Music, as well as in Washington and Baltimore. Though he is not as well known as Hofmann, Rachmaninoff, or Rubinstein, at the time he was indeed included in that exalted company.

"The deep musicality of the Jewish race, the Slavonic temperament, the melancholy of his Polish birthplace and upbringing. . . formed in him a musical outlook of the highest order." [97]

Rosenthal had a "longtime preoccupation" with Paderewski. He believed he was his superior. Paderewski's success drove Rosenthal to

---

[96] **Karol Mikuli** (1821–1897) was born in Czernowice (Czernowitz) and died in Lwów. He was a student of Chopin and his teaching assistant in Paris. Mikuli's detailed notes and observations of Chopin's teaching methods are often quoted by historians, and he was the first to publish an edition of Chopin's works.

[97] *Grove's Dictionary of Music and Musicians*, 1955 ed., 237-238.

play the same programs as Paderewski in cities where he followed him, even down to the encores. He expected the same honorarium and even advertised the fact that he would play the pieces "faster than Paderewski."[98]

When the Nazis occupied Austria in 1938, Rosenthal made the United States his home. He performed his last recital in New York's Town Hall in 1941, became a United States citizen in 1944 and died in New York City in 1946.

Curtis Institute of Music Archives, Albert Peterson

**Mieczysław Munz,** another of the great pianists of the day (Paderewski and Hofmann were admirers of his playing), twice served on the faculty of the Curtis Institute, 1930–32 and 1941–42. In 1931, he performed the Liszt Piano Concerto No. 2 with Leopold Stokowski and the Philadelphia Orchestra. Munz was born in Kraków in 1900 and at the age of twelve made his debut in that city playing the Tchaikovsky Piano Concerto No. 1. He went on to Vienna and Berlin to further his studies, and in 1920 he made his Berlin debut performing three concertos: the Liszt A major, the Brahms D minor, and the Franck Symphonic Variations. Two years later, he made his New York debut in Aeolian Hall and for the next

---

[98] Mitchell and Evans (2006) 159 #19.

twenty years performed with all of America's major orchestras as well as in Europe's capitals. A severe nervous disorder of his right hand cut his career short, and he spent his last 30 years only teaching. [99] He taught at the Peabody Conservatory in Baltimore where Ann Schein was his most famous student, but his longest tenure was at the Juilliard School of Music, where the Lwów-born Emanuel Ax was his most famous student. He also taught Jahja Ling, a piano student who became a conductor and has led both the Curtis Symphony Orchestra and the Philadelphia Orchestra in concerts. At Curtis, Munz also taught the Leschin sisters, the duo-piano team of Joana and Louise who were well known and popular at the time. A Munz recital always contained Chopin, and he did not hesitate to schedule the rarely performed complete *24 Preludes*, for which he was acclaimed by critics. He also enjoyed presenting the transcriptions of Leopold Godowsky and Wiktor Łabuński. Munz died of a heart attack in New York City in 1976.

Curtis Institute of Music Archives, Maurice Goldberg

**Alekander Lambert** "was either student, teacher or close friend of almost every important pianist in the last fifty years" (*New York Times* obituary, January 1, 1930). Lambert was born in Warsaw in 1863 and studied

---

[99] He was a tragic figure who suffered misfortune throughout his life. In addition to a shortened performing career he lost 23 family members to the Nazis and his wife, Aniela, left him for Artur Rubinstein.

piano with his father before entering the Vienna Conservatory at the age of twelve. Two years after graduating, at the age of eighteen, he came to America for three years, concertizing and teaching and performed with Walter Damrosch and his New York Symphony. He then returned to Europe and was encouraged by Moritz Moszkowski to study with Franz Liszt. He went on to appear in concert with Josef Joachim, Pablo Sarasate, and Europe's leading orchestras. He also taught at the Kullaks Akademie der Tonkunst in Berlin.

At the age of 21, Lambert made America his home permanently, but for the next ten years he continued to concertize in both Europe and the United States. In 1888, he was appointed Director of the New York College of Music. He gave up his concert career in 1892, and dedicated the remainder of his life to teaching. His celebrated piano performances can now only be heard on a few piano rolls. He was the piano teacher to Jerome Kern, one of America's best-known and loved theater composers and was also a good friend of Leopold Godowsky, who dedicated many of his compositions to Lambert. Lambert's piano teaching book, *Piano Method for Beginners*, published by G. Schirmer, was much used by piano pedagogues.[100] Before Lambert stopped performing, in his first years at the New York College of Music, he played a benefit for the school with Victor Herbert conducting.

Lambert spent his last years also teaching at the Curtis Institute, but on December 31, 1929, he was fatally struck by an automobile in New York City. Two weeks later, Josef Hofmann, in his Carnegie Hall concert in New York City, memorialized Lambert by opening the concert with the Chopin *Funeral March*, which was dedicated to him. Lambert bequeathed the relics from his extensive music collection to the New York Public Library. Those treasures included hand-colored Gregorian chants, a framed letter from Chopin, and an original score of Richard Wagner.

---

[100] Błaszczyk (1978) 574.

# The First Official Commencement of the Curtis Institute of Music

Curtis Institute of Music Archives

**Seated (L-R) Sokółowski, Gates, Bok, Hofmann, Sembrich, Godowsky**

On the stage of Casimir Hall (named after Hofmann's father) stood the flags of the United States and Poland, and carnations of red and white (the colors of both Poland and the Institute) were placed in front of the American flag. Thomas Sovereign Gates, President of the University of Pennsylvania, was introduced by Mrs. Bok [101] and he addressed the audience commemorating the special event. The Polish national anthem was then sung and the commencement address was delivered by Władysław Sokółowski, the Counselor to the Polish Embassy in Washington, D.C., substituting for the Ambassador, who was ill. Józef Hofmann presented the first honorary doctorates to Marcella Sembrich Kochańska and Leopold

---

[101] It should be noted that previously Mrs. Bok had been awarded the Order of Polonia Restituta (*Order Odrodzenia Polski*) by the Polish government for her meritorious work in promoting Polish-American friendship.

Godowsky. After Hofmann awarded all the diplomas to the graduating class, the American national anthem concluded the ceremonies.

## After Józef Hofmann

Stokowski remained involved in the development of Curtis, seeing to it that the Philadelphia Orchestra's best players and teachers were on the faculty, but after the first several years Stokowski made few appearances at school, and he left Philadelphia in 1940. Josef Hofmann was spending more time away on tours, and when he was replaced in 1938, the new administration avoided any connection with his name.[102]

With the passing of Sembrich and Lambert, and the departure of Hofmann, Rosenthal, Landowska, Munz, Młynarski, and Rodziński, the Curtis Institute had lost a very strong Polish presence on its faculty. The policies and mission of the school had been established, however, and today Curtis continues to adhere to those original principles. A number of great instrumentalists and singers of Polish ancestry attended Curtis. Some of them went on to teach there and carried on a tradition of both teaching and performance of which Hofmann would have been proud. Some of the world's leading musicians who never attended Curtis also were drawn to the school as faculty and performers. Horszowski, Goldberg, Rosand, Steinhardt, Feuermann, Rostropovich, Ax, and Penderecki have all had important roles in the education of the student body and are included in the following pages. Following World War II, under the pall of Communism, America saw little of what the Poles had to offer. In the 1960s, however, with the encouragement of Eugene Ormandy—Stokowski's successor as Music Director of the Philadelphia Orchestra—musicians such as Krzysztof Penderecki and Stanisław Skrowaczewski appeared in America for the first time, marking a new period of artistic freedom, or rather, its tolerance in Poland.

---

[102] His time was not wasted, however. In an interview on January 21, 1952, he stated that he was grateful for the time to continue his inventions and innovations, working on piano action and amplification. www.youtube.com/watch?v=miAbuXDA2aI, accessed September 12, 2014.

Curtis Institute of Music Archives, Joyce Creamer

In 1942, **Mieczysław Horszowski** joined the Curtis faculty. A wonderfully respected pianist (who lived to the age of 100), Miecio, as he was called, was born in Lwów in 1892 to Stanisław Horszowski and Janina Róża Wagner. He began piano studies with his mother who had been a pupil of Karol Mikuli, himself a student of Chopin and an assistant to Chopin in Paris. She took Miecio to Vienna to study with Leschetizky at the age of six, dressed in Polish national costume. His official concert debut was in Warsaw with Emil Młynarski conducting the Beethoven Piano Concerto No. 1. He performed at the Vatican for St. Pius X at the age of fourteen, [103] and in the same year he made his Carnegie Hall debut. While still a teenager, he interrupted his young career to study Literature,

---

[103] He returned again in 1940, performing for Pope Pius XII and recording from the Vatican.

Philosophy, and History of Art in Paris. He resumed his performing career in 1913 in Italy, where he chose to live. Throughout his very busy life, he played in Poland many times, was a good friend of Karol Szymanowski, and championed Chopin's music. As a teenager performing in Spain, he met Pablo Casals, and they embarked on a lifelong friendship with concert tours until Casals's death in 1973. He joined the faculty of the Curtis Institute in 1942 at the age of 50. He played at the White House for the Kennedys in 1961 and again for the Carters in 1979, presenting an all-Chopin concert. In 1967, Switzerland held its first Horszowski Festival in Zermatt, where Horszowski had performed and taught since 1961.

In 1971, Horszowski moved to Philadelphia from New York City where he had been living and commuting. In 1981, at the age of 89, he married Bice Costa, an Italian. Interestingly, he was both Jewish and a devout Catholic. Bice later supervised the publication of his diary and letters. In 1984 he took his Italian bride to Poland, showing her the Kosciół Swiętego Krzyża (Church of the Holy Cross) where Chopin's heart is interred, and to Częstochowa, Poland's most sacred shrine. During that visit, he played in Warsaw for the last time. The final concert of his amazing life took place in 1991 at the Port of History Museum in Philadelphia, just before his 100th birthday . . . thus ended one of the most amazing performing and teaching careers of the twentieth century. His following had always been very devoted and revered him as a celebrity. At one birthday celebration held for him at Curtis, a number of his students performed, including Eugene Istomin, Seymour Lipkin, Peter Serkin, and Richard Goode. He also counted as students Anton Kuerti, Murray Perahia, Steven De Groote, and Marion Zarzeczna.

## FACULTY TODAY AT CURTIS

At the Curtis Institute of Music, every student is required to perform on the piano. Not all can study with the faculty's most famous teachers, however, and some are directed to Marion Zarzeczna. She has been instructing non-majors since 1962.

Courtesy of Marion Zarzeczna

**Marion Zarzeczna** was born in Trenton, New Jersey, in 1930. Both of her parents were born in Poland and came to the United States as teenagers from the region of Rzeszów. Her father, Paweł, had served in the Polish Army during World War I. In Trenton, he and his wife, Anna Wiączek, opened a candy store. Marion, attended a Polish grammar school, and when she was twelve years old came to Philadelphia to study at the New School of Music with Martha Massena and Vladimir Sokoloff. At the age of eighteen, the Polish Arts Club of Trenton sponsored her first recital, and under their auspices, she performed the Chopin F Minor Piano Concerto with the Polish National Radio Orchestra while it was on tour. Zarzeczna was fortunate to study with the legendary Pole Mieczysław Horszowski at Curtis, from which she graduated in 1954. In her senior year, she won first prize in a contest held by the Leschetizky Association of America, which awarded her a recital at New York's Town Hall. Upon her graduation from Curtis, she won a two-year Fulbright Fellowship to study at the Conservatorio Luigi Cherubini in Florence, investigating manuscripts of the earliest music written for piano. She gave concerts throughout Europe, won the Darmstadt Musipreis for modern music, and performed frequently with the 7th Army Symphony in Germany, which was then rebuilding in the aftermath of World War II. She was a finalist in the

Vercelli (1957) and Busoni (1968) International Piano Competitions, both won by Martha Argerich.

Back in America, in 1965, Zarzeczna performed another recital at Town Hall. It included the music of Chopin and Tadeusz Kassern, and in the *New York Times* of June 2, 1965, the reviewer commented that "her technique is exceptional." In 1969, she accompanied Nadia Koutzen in that violinist's 30th anniversary concert of her professional debut at Town Hall. Zarzeczna maintained a private studio but also taught at the Westminster Conservatory of Rider University. She was also a vocal coach for Temple University's Ambler Music Festival and performed for a special Chopin concert for Philadelphia's Polish Heritage Society.

This writer, **Paul Krzywicki**, teacher of tuba and brass orchestral performance, joined the Curtis Institute in 1972 at the invitation of Rudolf Serkin. Between 1880 and 1915, Krzywicki's great-grandparents and grandparents came to America from Nowy Wieś (Gmina Tomaszów), Nowy Sącz, Suwałki, and Białystok, and settled in the coal mining region of upstate Pennsylvania. Paul's father was a physician and his mother a nurse, but the house was filled with music, and all four children, Paul, Jan, Philip, and Teofila, became musicians by profession. Their father was an accomplished pianist who had studied with Bernard Cortese, a student of Józef Hofmann; all the children followed suit, also studying piano.

In 1959 at the age of fifteen, Paul began to play the tuba and attended the Aspen Music Festival in 1963. There he studied with William Bell, America's most renowned teacher, and eventually followed him to Indiana University where Paul received both Bachelor's and Master's degrees, as well as the Performers' Certificate. He also became teaching assistant to Mr. Bell. Krzywicki joined the Army in 1967 and spent three years as a member of the United States Military Academy Band at West Point. His career after the Army brought him many opportunities in many places: the New York Brass Sextet, the Cambridge Brass Quintet of Boston, the Boston Ballet, the Portland (Maine) Symphony, summers as a faculty member of the Aspen Music Festival, assistant professor at Youngstown State University, and a position with the Buffalo Philharmonic. In 1972, Eugene Ormandy invited him to join the Philadelphia Orchestra, and he remained there for 33 years playing more than 4,000 concerts around the world under Maestros Muti, Sawallisch, and Eschenbach, in addition to his first eight years with Ormandy. In 1985, the orchestra presented him with the C. Hartman Kuhn Award for showing "ability and enterprise of such character as to enhance the standards and reputation of the Philadelphia Orchestra."

That same year, the Philadelphia Orchestra commissioned a new work, *Music for Three Trombones and Tuba* by Raymond Premru, which Krzywicki performed that May. He had already appeared as soloist with the Orchestra: in 1965, he performed the premiere of *Fantasy* for Tuba and Strings, a composition by his brother, Jan. He also appeared as soloist on four Youth programs over his first fifteen years. He played the first performance of Jan's Concerto for Tuba and Orchestra with the Temple University Orchestra in 1997 and soloed under John Williams at the Saratoga Performing Arts Center. He was the recipient of a Fromm Foundation Fellowship to Tanglewood and for three years was a member of the Fulbright Fellowship Screening Committee in New York. He has taught master classes around the United States, including in Warsaw and Żywiec, Poland. In 1983, he participated in an International Music Festival at the University of Maryland, performing before musicians from around the world. At that festival, he shared a recital with Zdzisław Piernik from Warsaw.

His graduating students from Curtis have held positions in the Dallas, Pittsburgh, San Francisco, San Jose, New World, Jacksonville, and Syracuse Symphonies, the Aspen Festival Orchestra, the Australian National Opera and Ballet Company in Sydney, the Scottish National Symphony in Glasgow, the Flensburg Symphony in Germany, the United States Military Academy Band at West Point, and the United States Army Band at Fort Meyer, Virginia.

Paul's wife, **Joan Grahek Krzywicki**, is a pianist and teacher-trainer of the Suzuki Method. She has been a lecturer and teacher on three continents and is a board member of the Suzuki Association of the Americas.

Courtesy of Susan Nowicki

**Susan Nowicki,** piano accompanist and opera coach, has been on the faculty of the Curtis Institute since 1987. A native of Trenton, New Jersey, she attended the Philadelphia College of Performing Arts where she graduated *summa cum laude*. Her first piano teacher was her uncle, a very talented pianist who had toured Poland with an ensemble in 1936. (In America, he and Susan's father owned and operated a bar. Susan's lessons took place every Saturday morning, and like his good friend, Ernie Kovacs, Uncle Feliks was never without a cigar in his mouth, dropping ashes on the keyboard.) In high school, she studied with Marion Zarzeczna, alumna and faculty member of Curtis. She then attended the Philadelphia Musical Academy, studying with Donn-Alexander Feder[104] and later Edna Golandsky.

---

[104] A native of Philadelphia, Feder performed with Eugene Ormandy and the Philadelphia Orchestra when he was thirteen, and became the first American pianist to have been awarded a two-year U.S.-Polish government grant for intensive study in Poland for the music of Szymanowski and Chopin, mentoring with Zbigniew Drzewiecki. He recived a "diploma of distinction" at the seventh International Chopin Competition, and in 1965, he was the first American invited by the Chopin Society of Poland to perform at Żelazowa Wola, Chopin's birthplace.

The Curtis Institute has nurtured an astounding number of singers to become among the world's best, and Nowicki has been an integral part of their education.[105] Her talent in coaching contemporary operatic repertoire has made her indispensable at Curtis.

She has also been a member of the piano faculty of the Taubman Institute. In 2004, she became a founding member of the piano wellness program, "The Well Balanced Pianist."[106] She has toured under the auspices of Columbia Artists Management and has performed throughout the United States on piano, fortepiano, and harpsichord, as a soloist and in collaboration with singers and instrumentalists such as Pamela Frank, Peter Lloyd, and Emily Golden. She has recorded for the Albany, North-South, de Haske, and Capstone labels.[107] She has been a pianist for the Philadelphia Orchestra and, as a member of Philadelphia's well-known Network for New Music, has collaborated with some of the world's best players and singers in bringing many premieres to the city and world.

In 2012, the Curtis Institute of Music celebrated the teaching anniversaries of several faculty members, including Marion Zarzeczna concluding her 50th year of teaching, Paul Krzywicki his 40th year, and Susan Nowicki her 25th.

Two highly esteemed violinists of Polish background also are members of the Curtis faculty.

---

[105] "Meet the Faculty: Susan Nowicki," CIM *Overtones*, October 1995.
[106] www.wellbalancedpianist.com/, accessed September 12, 2014.
[107] Liner notes from Carol Jantsch CD *Cascades*.

Curtis Institute of Music Archives, George Bilyk

**Arnold Steinhardt** joined the violin faculty of Curtis in 1968. He was born in Los Angeles in 1937. His parents both came from Poland. They met in New York City after their arrival in America and moved to California before Arnold was born. His mother was from a Polish shtetl, Długosiodło, not far from Warsaw. At the age of fourteen, she came alone to the United States. His father came from the vibrant Jewish community of Będzin in Silesia at the end of World War I. Steinhardt's early training in California earned him a solo debut with the Los Angeles Philharmonic at the age of fourteen. He came to the Curtis Institute in 1954 to study with Ivan Galamian and was an audition winner of the Philadelphia Orchestra Youth Competition three years later, for which he was awarded a performance of the Wieniawski Violin Concerto No.2 with the Orchestra. Before he graduated, he went on to win the Leventritt Award in New York. After Steinhardt received a bronze medal in the Queen Elizabeth International Violin Competition in 1963, George Szell appointed him Assistant Concertmaster to Josef Gingold in the Cleveland Orchestra. It was not to last long, however, for in 1964 he formed the Guarneri Quartet, which endured for 45 years as one of the world's finest chamber ensembles. In 1968, he began teaching chamber music at Curtis and, a few years later, also took on private students. On one of the Guarneri Quartet tours, his mother accompanied him to Warsaw where the quartet performed at the National Philharmonic Hall (Filharmonia). They took an emotional tour together to the town where she had been born.

Although the quartet has now retired, Steinhardt keeps a very busy schedule teaching from coast to coast and has authored two books, *Violin Dreams* and *A String Quartet in Pursuit of Harmony*. In addition to the many recordings that the Quartet made, Steinhardt also made solo recordings that occasionally featured him on the viola. He has been the recipient of honorary doctorates and received the award of distinguished cultural service from the City of New York.[108] Steinhardt plays a late-eighteenth-century Lorenzo Storioni violin from Cremona, Italy. He contributes regularly to a number of periodicals, including *Strad* and *Listen*.[109]

Curtis Institute of Music Archives, Neil Benson

**Aaron Rosand,** a longtime violin faculty member of the Curtis Institute, was born in 1927. His father came to America from outside Warsaw in the

---

[108] Mayor Edward Irving Koch (1924–2013) was born in the Bronx, New York, the second son of Polish immigrants.

[109] Arnold Steinhardt website, www.arnoldsteinhardt.com/, accessed September 12, 2014.

1920s; his mother came from Minsk. They settled first in Calumet City, just outside Chicago, where Rosand studied with Leon Sametini at the Chicago Musical College. He performed with the Chicago Symphony at the age of ten. His studies later took him to Curtis where his teacher was Efrem Zimbalist, famed soloist and also the Director of the School. In the year of his graduation, 1948, he made his New York debut playing at Town Hall with Arthur Balsam as his accompanist. The opening line of the review, "A tone of unusual quality and a technique of near-perfection marked the debut recital of Aaron Rosand at Town Hall last night,"[110] should have signaled the start of a brilliant career, but for Rosand success was slow going in America. He was to spend more time in Europe than in the United States for more than twenty years.

He recorded in Europe and performed throughout the continent, including in Warsaw, Kraków, and Gdańsk. With his first wife, Eileen Flissler, he made a number of highly acclaimed, well-received recordings, including all the works for violin and piano by Beethoven. When he returned to Town Hall in recital in 1968, he was again heralded for his extraordinary technique in a difficult program that included the Paganini-Szymanowski *Caprices*.[111] He was known as "one of the romantic violinists supreme"[112] and performed not just Sibelius, Mendelssohn, Brahms, Tchaikovsky, and Wieniawski, but also the lesser-heard romantic works of Jeno Hubay, H. W. Ernst, Joseph Joachim, Benjamin Godard, and Eugene Ysaye.

Rosand is a much sought-after teacher and has been on the Curtis Institute faculty since 1981. In 2002 to mark his 75th birthday, Rosand performed the Sibelius Violin Concerto in concert with the Curtis Symphony Orchestra.[113]

In 1957 Rosand purchased Paweł Kochański's famed violin, the 1741 Guarnieri *del Gesu* named the "Kochański." He sold it in October of 2009

---

[110] C. H. "Rosand, Violinist, Scores at Debut," *New York Times*, 28 December 1948.

[111] Allen Hughes, "Aaron Rosand Meets Demands of Challenging Violin Program," *New York Times*, 7 December 1968.

[112] Harold Schonberg, "Music Violin Virtuoso," *New York Times*, 30 April 1970.

[113] Aaron Rosand biography page, www.allmusic.com/artist/aaron-rosand-mn0001230894#discography, accessed September 12, 2014.

to a Russian businessman for the highest price ever paid for an instrument, $10 million. He donated $1.5 million to the Curtis Institute of Music.

## There Were Other Schools
## Temple University

Temple University's music school was founded in 1913. Thaddeus Rich, the first concertmaster of the Philadelphia Orchestra, was an early influence and became Dean in the 1930s after his departure from the Orchestra. Today the school is named the Esther Boyer College of Music and Dance and, as has been a long tradition, some faculty members of the Curtis Institute of Music also teach at Temple. Three Poles have had long tenures at the school: two acclaimed artist-teachers and an esteemed Professor of Musical Studies.

The pianist, **Marian Filar,** brought an international presence to Philadelphia's Settlement School of Music and Temple University.

> . . . . incomparable technical facility is at the service of this utterly elegant musicianship. The performances are fleet, supple, and beautifully nuanced. He plays with flair and rhapsodic freedom, but never at the expense of musical structure and textual lucidity. . . truly impressive performances, and just another indicator that exceptional talent does not guarantee wide public recognition in the often unjust world of classical music. Anthony Tommasini, *New York Times*[114]

Filar was born in Warsaw in 1917 and performed with the Warsaw Philharmonic at the age of twelve. His first teacher and an influence throughout his life was Zbigniew Drzewiecki at the Warsaw State Conservatory. At that time, Poland's greatest musical luminaries had gathered to study in Warsaw: Lutosławski, Małcużyński, Panufnik,

---

[114] Quote from inside cover of Filar's book, *From Buchenwald to Carnegie Hall.*

and Koprowski as well as Filar. He survived several Nazi death camps, including Buchenwald and Majdanek, but lost his parents.

After his liberation by the Polish Army, he studied with the great German pianist, Walter Gieseking, and then performed all over Europe before arriving in the United States in 1950, accompanied by two brothers and 114 other Jewish passengers. In 1951, he appeared with the Philadelphia Orchestra under Eugene Ormandy for the first of several times, playing in all, Chopin, Beethoven, and Tchaikovsky. In 1952, Filar made his debut in Carnegie Hall performing the Chopin Concerto in F minor with the Philadelphia Orchestra and, that very same year, made his first recording. In 1953, he joined the faculty of the Settlement School, where his students often won the Philadelphia Orchestra Concerto Competition which rewarded them with a performance with the Philadelphians. He toured the United States, South America, and Europe, and in 1957, he performed the Schumann Piano Concerto in A minor in a benefit for the Israel Philharmonic. In 1958, he was appointed Chairman of the Piano Department of Temple University, and the next year returned to Poland for the first time since the war, meeting Drzewiecki again and performing with the Warsaw Philharmonic. In 1988, he became an Emeritus Professor in the new Boyer School of Music and Dance at Temple. He made his home in Jenkintown, Pennsylvania, just outside Philadelphia. In 1992, he once again returned to Warsaw and played with the Warsaw Philharmonic under the leadership of Kazimierz Kord. He continued to live in the suburbs of Philadelphia suburb until his death in 2012.[115]

---

[115] Len Lear, "Legendary pianist, teacher of local students," *Chestnut Hill* (PA) *Local*, 19 July 2012.

Courtesy of Lambert Orkis

**Lambert Orkwiszewski (Orkis)**, one of America's most respected pianists, was born in Philadelphia in 1946. His father, Stanley Orkwiszewski, one of six siblings, came from a family rooted in Warsaw all of whom eventually settled in Philadelphia. He was a baker for the commercial firm Freihofer, and he played the guitar. Lambert first took piano lessons at the age of four and at age ten began studies with Eleanor Sokoloff, who continued as his teacher at the Curtis Institute. In 1957, at age eleven, he won the Philadelphia Orchestra competition and played the Mendelssohn *Capriccio Brillante* with the Orchestra. After graduating from Curtis in 1965, Orkis went to Temple University to receive a Masters degree under Marian Filar; he joined Temple's faculty in 1968. It is his career as accompanist to the world's best musicians that has secured him an international reputation. He was Rostropovich's accompanist for eleven years playing for Presidents Reagan, Bush, and Clinton, King Hussein, Emperor Akahito, and Gandhi. He also developed a long artistic partnership with Anne-Sophie Mutter that led to concerts for the presidents of France and Germany, the Queen of Spain, and the monarchs of Sweden. In 1988, they gave 85 performances of the complete Beethoven Violin Sonatas and won awards for their recording. In 2013, they performed in Carnegie Hall to celebrate the 25<sup>th</sup> anniversary of their debut in the hall. Their tours also took them to Warsaw's Filharmonia in 1993 and 1997. New CDs by the pair are regularly released on Deutsche Gramophone, and are frequently nominated for Grammy Awards. Orkis has an interest in all forms of chamber music, performs Classical and Romantic composers on early instruments, and has commissioned many contemporary composers to write for him. The Richard Wernick Concerto for Piano and Orchestra was commissioned and premiered by Orkis at Carnegie Hall and the Kennedy Center in 1991. He is the pianist for the National Symphony in Washington, D.C., and still finds time to teach regularly at Temple University, where he has received the Faculty Award for Creative Achievement.

Courtesy of Jan Krzywicki

**Jan Krzywicki** (brother of Paul; see above) was born in Philadelphia in 1948, second of the four children of Paul Krzywicki and Teofila Tokarczyk, all four of whom became professional musicians. Between 1880 and 1915, both families came to America from Nowy Wieś (Gmina Tomaszów),

Nowy Sącz, Suwałki and Białystok. They settled in an area of Pennsylvania largely populated by the peoples of Eastern Europe. Even though Paul and Teofila became a physician and a nurse, respectively, everyone in the family had their turn at the piano, and music was a vital part of each day. Dr. Paul Krzywicki, who had studied piano with Bernard Cortese, himself a student of Józef Hofmann, always impressed family and guests with his Mendelssohn, but particularly with his ability to improvise, a la George Shearing.

While in high school, Jan began his composition studies at the Philadelphia Musical Academy with Joseph Castaldo. He studied in New York at the Juilliard School with Vincent Persichetti and Elliott Carter, and in France at the Ecole des Beaux Arts Americaines with Nadia Boulanger. He spent the summer of 1968 at the Aspen Music Festival under Darius Milhaud before receiving his Bachelor's degree from the University of Kansas.

In 1965, at the age of only seventeen, Jan received his first major performances when his *Fantasy* for Tuba and Strings was premiered by the Philadelphia Orchestra with his brother Paul as soloist. The following year, the work was performed at the Juilliard School. In 1976, *Continuum* was commissioned by the Pennsylvania Ballet and was subsequently played on U.S. tours. In 1988, The Grammy Award–winning Chestnut Brass Company commissioned and recorded his *Deploration* for brass quintet, written as a tribute to Persichetti. Jan is primarily a composer of chamber music and his works have been recorded by many of America's best artists, including a long list of Philadelphia Orchestra members. In 2012, *Fanfare* magazine had the highest recommendation for his album of five original Krzywicki compositions entitled *Alchemy*, recorded for Albany Records (Troy1317), and called Jan a "supremely talented Philadelphia based composer." Seventeen of his compositions are included in the catalogue of the Theodore Presser Publishing Company. His String Quartet recorded by the Colorado Quartet, his Trumpet Sonata recorded by Terry Everson, and the *Ballade* for Tuba recorded by Craig Knox are some of his most successful works.[116] Alphonse Leduc & Cie, Tenuto Publications, Lyra

---

[116] The 2009 International Trumpet Competition listed the Trumpet Sonata as one of its required compositions for that event; the *Ballade* was a requirement for the 2012 Falcone Competition. The *Ballade* had its first performance in 1983 at an

Music Corporation, Penn Oak Press, and Heilman Music also publish his compositions; and Albany Records, Capstone Records, North-South Recordings, De Haske Recordings, and Centaur Records have recorded his works.

Krzywicki has received many ASCAP Awards and a Rockefeller Grant and has been a Pew Fellow in the Arts. Since 1987, he has been a Professor of Music at Temple University in the music theory department and has developed extensive and detailed teaching materials for the instruction of music history, harmony, and theory. Before his appointment at Temple, he was on the faculty of the Philadelphia Musical Academy (now the University of the Arts). He has been Director of the Paderewski Choral Society in Philadelphia and the Chorale Polonaise in Hackensack, New Jersey, and a judge for the Polish Singers Alliance of America (PSAA) competition. Since 1988, Krzywicki has been its conductor of the Network for New Music, the well-known performance group dedicated to the introduction of new compositions to the public, which was founded in 1984. He has led no less than seventy-five works in their world premieres in Philadelphia with this ensemble, and they have made three recordings for Albany records. His scholarly interest in the music of Vivaldi has guided him in the publishing of bass realizations of Vivaldi works for Les Productions D'oz, Quebec, Canada (1998), and Theodore Presser (1991), as well as a book review on Vivaldi for *Opera Quarterly*.[117]

He is married to pianist Susan Nowicki (see above), who has been a faculty member of the Curtis Institute in the opera and vocal studies department since 1987.

### Philadelphia Musical Academy

The Philadelphia Musical Academy was established in 1870, when it received the first charter granted to a music school in Pennsylvania. After three separate mergers between 1877 and 1987, the school is now part of the University of the Arts. Two native Poles who taught there are

---

International Tuba Conference where Paul Krzywicki (the author) presented the work on a program shared with the Polish tubist Zdzisław Piernik.
[117] Summer 1985, vol. 3, no. 2, 171–173.

mentioned many times in this book as they interact with many of the most outstanding artists—of all nationalities—who came to America.

Courtesy of Clara Steuermann

**Eduard Steuermann** taught at the Philadelphia Musical Academy for sixteen years. He was a very important early to mid-twentieth-century musician, though little-known outside of his musical specialty, the Second Viennese School. He was born in Sambor, near Lvov (Lwów) in 1892. His father was the mayor there for eighteen years, and his family prospered in this Austrian-controlled region. Edward first studied piano in Lwów with Vilem Kurz, a Czech. After playing for Ferruccio Busoni in Basel, he moved to Berlin where he studied composition with Arnold Schoenberg. He also taught in Poland at the Paderewski School in Lwów, in Vienna and Prague, and in 1936, came to America to continue his teaching and performing career in Philadelphia and New York. He became a U.S. citizen in 1944.

A pianist specializing in Schonberg, Berg, and Webern, Steuermann was deeply involved in the development of music in this period and premiered many of the most important pieces written then. He was the vocal coach and pianist for the premiere of Schoenberg's *Pierrot Lunaire*, Op.21 in

1912, and was the pianist for whom Webern composed his Variations for piano, Op.27 in 1936. On February 16, 1944, Steuermann premiered Schoenberg's Piano Concerto, Op.42 with Stokowski conducting the NBC Symphony. He also appeared as soloist with Otto Klemperer, as well as with Artur Rodziński and the New York Philharmonic. Steuermann was the "titular pianist" for the music of the Second Viennese School.[118] Though less known outside of his "specialty," he was highly regarded for his Beethoven recitals in New York,[119] and he edited the complete piano works of Johannes Brahms for Universal Edition, the well-respected publishing company in Vienna.

Although a composer of some note, his arrangements and transcriptions of both modern and classical compositions brought him more attention. In 1949, he married Clara Silvers, a pianist of considerable accomplishment, who left Los Angeles to study with Steuermann in New York. (Clara's father had been born in Poland.) Although she was studying with Jakob Gimpel, a piano faculty member at California State University who was also from Lwów, Arnold Schoenberg encouraged her to travel East and study with her future husband. The Philadelphia Musical Academy (then renamed the Philadelphia College for the Performing Arts) awarded Steuermann an honorary doctorate in 1962. His most famous students were Alfred Brendel, Natalie Hinderas, Joseph Kalichstein, Lorin Hollander, Moura Lympany, and Russell Sherman.

---

[118] The Second Viennese School was named after a group of composers; it endured for roughly 40 years, beginning in 1903. They began as late-Romantic period composers, living, teaching, and performing in Vienna. Their music evolved into chromatic expressionism, and eventually they were led by Arnold Schonberg into the twelve-tone technique of music composition.

[119] *Grove Dictionary of Music and Musicians*, 1980 ed.

Manhattan School of Music Archives, Diane Gorodnitski

Also added to the Philadelphia Musical Academy faculty in 1960 was **Artur Balsam,** born in Warsaw in 1906. He studied in Łódź with **Krzysztof Lewandowski** and in 1930 won first prize in the Berlin International Piano Competition. The following year, in Munich, he won the Mendelssohn Prize for chamber music playing with Roman Totenberg.

Balsam was most celebrated as an ensemble pianist. In 1932, he toured the United States with a fourteen-year-old Yehudi Menuhin. He played in Europe and North America, but with the rise of the Nazis, settled in the United States. He married Rita Miller, a pianist who also had studied in Łódź with Lewandowski. He performed with the best in the world: Milstein, Fuchs, Oistrakh, Szigeti, Rostropovich, Morini, Francescatti, the Budapest and Kroll quartets, and the Polish-born violinists Goldberg, Haendel, Gimpel, and Szeryng, as well as two Carnegie Hall recitals with Henri Temianka. He accompanied Aaron Rosand for his 1948 debut and amassed a recorded discography of some 250 works, which included all the piano sonatas of Haydn and Mozart, the complete violin sonatas of

Mozart and Beethoven, and the cello sonatas of Beethoven.[120] He gave his last Carnegie Hall recital at the age of 87, a year before his death. The Artur Balsam Competition for Duos is held at the Manhattan School of Music where he taught for almost 40 years. A memorial concert in his honor was performed at the Manhattan School of Music on April 25, 1995. Written tributes were sent from around the world, and in a program of music from Bach to Rachmaninoff, more than twenty of America's finest instrumentalists paid tribute to this great artist-collaborator. They included Roman Totenberg, his Polish colleague from their studies together in Berlin in 1927, and Roman Markowicz, Polish-born pianist and student of Balsam's at MSM who was also the music critic for the Polish Daily News (*Nowy Dziennik*).

---

[120] www.naxos.com/person/Artur_Balsam/10886.htm, accessed September 12, 2014.

# ▮▮

# MORE REMARKABLE MUSICIANS

## A. PIANISTS

Every one of Fryderyk Franciszek Chopin's more than two hundred compositions included the piano, and since Chopin's death in 1849, pianists around the world have continued to perform a larger percentage of this composer's total output than any other.[121] The drama and soul of Chopin's music has always been captivating to audiences, and an artistic challenge that is essential to every pianist's training and repertoire. For Poles and non-Poles alike, Chopin plays a prominent part in their musical lives. One does not have to be Polish to feel and interpret the depth of Chopin's *żal*,[122] even in his mazurkas—a dance which must seem exotic to many.

The 2010 International Chopin Piano Competition in Warsaw featured eighty-one previously screened contestants. They numbered thirty-five of Asian background, six Poles, eleven from France, Italy, Austria, Spain, and Switzerland combined, seven from former Soviet territories, ten Russians, three Israelis, two Australians, five Americans, and one Canadian. Clearly,

---

[121] Frank Cooper, Liner notes for the four-CD set *A Century of Romantic Chopin* (Marston 54001–2) 39.

[122] "A beautiful word, impossible to translate. It means sadness, nostalgia, regret, being hurt, and yet it is something else. It feels like a howling inside you, so unbearable that it breaks your heart." Artur Rubinstein.

the level of interest and proficiency of the artists has spread far beyond the land of the *polonez* and *krakowiak*. Chopin's literature has indeed dominated the landscape of Polish piano music, and there was little else coming out of Poland to capture the interest of the concert pianist until late in the century.

After the death of Chopin in 1849, the Chopin family entrusted the publication of the composer's unpublished music to **Julian Fontana.** Fontana was a pianist, composer, and dear friend to Chopin. They were born in the same year, 1810—Chopin in Żelazowa Wola and Fontana in Kraków. They were students together at the Warsaw Lyceum and performed as a duo numerous times. When Chopin went to Paris in 1830, Fontana remained in Warsaw and fought in the November Uprising against the Russians.

Fontana's family had come to Poland from Italy two centuries earlier and were architects in the building of the Church of the Holy Cross (Kosciół Swiętego Krzyża[123]) in Warsaw. After the failed Uprising, Fontana lived in Paris, England, Germany, and Cuba (he translated Cervantes' *Don Quijote de la Mancha* from Spanish to Polish.) He arrived in America in Philadelphia in 1845 but spent most of the following three years in New York as recitalist, accompanist, and publisher. In 1850, his *Third of May Song* was published in Philadelphia in a collection of Polish National Melodies. He was the chief copyist of Chopin's works for publication in Paris and the only authorized publisher of Chopin's unpublished works. He became a naturalized U.S. citizen in 1855. After years of illness and deafness he took his own life in Paris in 1869.[124]

---

[123] The church where Chopin's heart is interred.

[124] There is a well-maintained website dedicated to Fontana, www.julianfontana.com, accessed September 12, 2014.

University of Adelaide Archives' Series 312, Maude Puddy Collection

At the time that Chopin was living in Paris, one of the most famous teachers of any instrument in the history of music was born in Poland. **Teodor Leszetycki (Theodor Leschetizky)** had enormous influence on the piano throughout the period of the late nineteenth century and beginning of the twentieth. As Carl Flesch, a Hungarian, was the most famous teacher of the violin (he was also a disciple of Henryk Wieniawski), so his counterpart on the piano was Theodor Leschetizky.

Leschetizky, a Polish Catholic from Eastern Galicia, was born in 1830 and lived on the estate of the Potocki family in Łancut.[125] His father was the music master for the estate. Twelve hundred students were listed in Leschetizky's lesson books from the time he taught at the St. Petersburg Conservatory until his last days in Vienna;[126] among his students were Paderewski, Horszowski, Friedman, and Małcużyński. Only Franz Liszt

---

[125] Potocka (1903) vii.
[126] Edwin Hughes, "The Leschetitzky Heritage," *Leschetizky Association News Bulletin,* January 1963.

could have competed with him.[127] Leschetizky composed only a few pieces, including *Reminiscences de Halka de Moniuszko*. He taught only advanced students and maintained that there were three indispensables for pianistic greatness and would ask prospective students three questions: Were you a child prodigy? Are you of Slavic descent? Are you a Jew?[128] All three would have made the perfect combination. Unfortunately, Leschetizky never came to America, but the enormous popularity of Paderewski in this country convinced some Americans, especially in the summers, to make the trip to Vienna to study with the man who had an influence in his training. Even Samuel L. Clemens (Mark Twain) went to Vienna in 1897 with his family so that his elder daughter, Clara, could study with Leschetizky. She would eventually marry the well-known pianist Ossip Gabrilowitsch.[129]

The direct descendant of an amazing lineage, Leschetizky studied with Czerny in Vienna and performed a Czerny *Concertino* conducted by Wolfgang Amadeus Mozart's son, Franz Xaver. After settling in Vienna, he taught there until 1915, the year of his death.

---

[127] Generally regarded as Liszt's most famous student, Carl Tausig was a Pole born in Warsaw who died at the age of 29, a victim of typhoid. He was described as "Chopin at the piano." Carl first studied with his father, Aloys, before traveling to Weimar to be with Liszt. Schonberg (1963) 244.

[128] Schonberg (1963) 280.

[129] Martin Nowak, "Mark Twain's Polish Acquaintances," www.google.com/search?q=Mark+Twain+by+Martin+Nowak&ie=utf-8&oe=utf-8&aq=t&rls=org.mozilla:en-US:official&client=firefox-a&channel=np&source=hp, accessed September 12, 2014.

Library of Congress, Arnold Genthe

**Ignacy Jan Paderewski,** who became one of the greatest musicians of any time and perhaps the greatest musician-statesman that the world has known, was Leschetizky's student. As a result of that relationship, he brought an already acclaimed Leschetizky to special prominence in the piano world.

Paderewski was born in 1860 in Kuriłówka, Russian occupied Poland. His mother died several months after his birth, and his father was imprisoned by the Russians for his involvement in the 1863 January Uprising. Adopted by an aunt, Ignacy had little training until he entered the Warsaw Conservatory at the age of twelve; he studied cello and oboe and also became first trombone in the student orchestra.[130] He played for the great Polish actress Helena Modrzejewska (Modjeska in America), and deciding that the piano was his destiny, she helped to finance his studies in Vienna with Leschetizky.[131]

Paderewski generally had great success in Europe, performing in all of the musical capitals of Europe; but he never returned to Berlin after the German press, in 1890, expressed indignation that a Pole should be

---

[130] Kellogg (1956) 19.
[131] Sachs (1995) 54.

playing for them.[132] The following year, he came to America under the auspices of the Steinway Piano Company. Throughout his life he did very little teaching, and often followed a grueling concert schedule around the world, performing hundreds of solo recitals just in the United States alone. Strained and torn tendons in his hand were to make his calendar of programs in America a punishing experience. He performed at the Academy of Music in Philadelphia on his first American tour in 1891, and also performed with the Philadelphia Orchestra in 1914, when he played the Beethoven Piano Concerto No. 5. When the concerto ended, the Orchestra left the stage and Paderewski remained to play a solo recital which lasted for another hour. Except for one Liszt piece, the music was entirely Chopin. In 1915, Stokowski conducted Paderewski's only symphony, the *"Polonia"* Symphony in B Minor (1909).[133] His Concerto for Piano and *Crakovienne Fantastique* also received performances under Stokowski in Philadelphia. Late in life, he took on one student, Witold Małcużyński, whom he coached to win third prize in the 1937 Chopin Piano Competition. In 1932, he faced an audience of 16,000 in Madison Square Garden, the largest crowd in the history of music at that time, and raised $50,000 for the benefit of unemployed American musicians. In that same year, he again performed at the Academy of Music.

Paderewski was the greatest drawing card in American musical history.[134] He traveled like no other, with an entourage and his own pianos in a private railway car. He was a wealthy man, commanding fees unheard of at the time, but he was also a very generous man who supported many causes. If we looked for a classical artist on today's performance circuit to compare in popularity to Paderewski, we would find none. All pale in comparison to the effect he drew from his audiences, especially his female listeners. Olin Downes, the educator and well-known music critic of the *New York Times*, covered a Paderewski recital in New York City and wrote:

> "A Paderewski recital—*séance* might be a better word—is
> an occasion that requires no signboard to identify. The
> crowded stage, the roped-in piano, the scurrying ushers,

---

[132] Brook (1946) 132.
[133] "Intended as a glorification of Poland," according to *Etude* magazine, March 1915.
[134] Schonberg (1963) 290.

the excited twittering of the ladies, the matinee miss and her confidential friend, the whole rows of female colleges— for is not the mighty one meat and drink and bon-bons to them?—and finally, on the pianist's appearance, that species of hushed applause that voices the general spirit of reverential suspense and expectation—all these things combine to impart an atmosphere of rare novelty peculiar to the occasion." [135]

He was described by Camille Saint-Saëns as a "genius who happens to play the piano."[136] The well-known English composer Sir Edward Elgar dedicated his work *Polonia* to Paderewski for the Polish Relief Fund concert in London in 1916. His charisma allowed his patriotic appeals for the Polish cause to succeed, especially during and after World War I when his friendship with President Woodrow Wilson had an enormous influence on the future of his country. Paderewski became Prime Minister of Poland in 1919 and signed the Treaty of Versailles, which restored the territories of Greater Poland, Pomerania and Gdańsk back to Poland. At the peace conference, English Prime Minister Lloyd George reacted with amusement at the presumption of a musician as a political representative, but Lloyd George was no match for Paderewski's mental agility and eloquence as he won over his listeners. "His high standards of honesty, integrity and his impeccable character added to his great triumph of being the father of modern Poland."[137] He then became the Polish Ambassador to the League of Nations. In the 170 or so years between Kosciuszko and Pope John Paul II, no one did more for the Polish cause than Paderewski. He lived much of his later life in Switzerland and at the Buckingham Hotel in New York City, in self-exile at the outbreak of World War II.

A few things worth noting: Paderewski appeared in the 1937 American film *Moonlight Sonata*. He owned a 2,600-acre vineyard near Paso

---

[135] *New York Times*, 7 November 1907.

[136] Kellogg (1956) 45.

[137] Retired General Edward Rowny, former adviser to President Ronald Reagan, facilitated the transfer of Paderewski's remains back to Poland; he maintains a website dedicated to Paderewski, www.paderewskirowny.com/, accessed September 12, 2014. He is also the author of the paper, "Paderewski—Father of Modern Poland."

Robles, California, which still produces well-respected wines with the label Epoch Estates Wines. Paso Robles continues to hold an annual Paderewski Festival[138], and in Los Angeles he has a star on the Hollywood Walk of Fame. He was awarded many honorary doctorates and awards from governments around the world, and donated many of his personal possessions to the Polish Museum of America in Chicago,

Paderewski died in New York in 1941, succumbing to pneumonia. He was honored at a funeral in St. Patrick's Cathedral where the organist performed Paderewski's *Nocturne* and the *Funeral March* from the Chopin B-flat Minor Sonata. The choir sang (Monsignor) Don Lorenzo Perosi's *Mass*, a work admired by Paderewski. Since he was also a world leader, his funeral was carried out with full military honors. An overflow crowd of 40,000 watched as the casket was loaded onto a horse-drawn caisson and brought to Pennsylvania Station. From there, it was taken to Washington and, by order of President Roosevelt, was entombed at Arlington National Cemetery, an honor granted to few foreigners. As per his dying wish, 51 years later when Poland was again free, his body was moved to Warsaw and placed in a crypt in St. John's Cathedral; his heart is forever encased in a bronze sculpture at the National Shrine of Częstochowa in Doylestown, Pennsylvania.

**Jarosław Zieliński (Jarosław de Zielinski)** fought and was wounded in Poland in the failed 1863 Uprising against the Russians. The following year he made his way to America. Arriving in Boston, he joined the Fourth Massachusetts Cavalry Unit of the Union Army and fought in the Civil War. He departed from the service as a bugler in 1865. . . a startling beginning to the biography of such a multi-faceted musician. He was a concert pianist, teacher, composer, critic, and prolific writer yet, unfortunately, to most he is an unknown figure in American musical history. But, through his writings, he was one of the few in America who would educate readers on Slavic music, publishing in the leading music journals of the day, *Etude* magazine, *The Musical Courier,* and *Pianist.* In 1902, he wrote the *Poles in Music* for the Century Library of Music in

---

[138] Daniel Laurie, "The Grapevine: Paderewski land stll producing," *The Tribune,* San Luis Obispo, 17 January 2010.

New York.[139] He was recognized throughout the world as an authority on Polish and Russian music and musicians. In 1905, James Huneker used Zielinski's expertise in assembling information for his book. [140]

Zieliński was born in 1847 on his father's estate in Lubycza Królewska, near Zamość. He studied in Lemberg (Lwów) including piano with Karol Mikuli, Chopin's pupil and friend. He continued studies in Berlin and Vienna and spent a short time studying voice in Milan. After the Civil War, he moved to New York State. Although he taught voice, he was primarily a pianist, concertizing and teaching in many cities throughout America. In 1878, he became the Director of the Music Department at Fairmount College in Monteagle, Tennessee. Two years later he moved to Michigan, living in Detroit and Grand Rapids. Travels continued to Colorado but he finally decided to settle in Buffalo, New York. While residing there, he also helped establish the Music Department at Bailey Springs University in Alabama. In 1910, he left Buffalo and moved to Los Angeles where he was to stay the rest of his life. There he directed another music school and formed the Zielinski Trio Club, performing primarily the works of American composers. He died in Santa Barbara in 1922. The Los Angeles Public Library houses his vast music collection. He composed many pieces for piano and voice, including mazurkas. Much of this biography was drawn from an article written for the *The Musician* in Philadelphia in 1898.[141] A large collection of his papers and memorabilia are located at the Immigration History Research Center at the University of Minnesota. His stay in Buffalo provided a wealth of material for a short biography compiled in 2008 by Keith Kaszubik for the *Pol-Am Eagle* in that city.[142]

---

[139] Jaroslaw Zielinski, "Poles in Music," *Polish Music Journal*, vol. 5, no. 2, Winter 2002.

[140] Huneker (1966).

[141] W. H. Kozlowski, "Jarosław Zielinski," translated from *"Echo Muzyczne I Teatralne"* 1998, no. 744, Warsaw, Poland.

[142] Keith Kaszubik, "Zielinski, Jarosław," *Am-Pol Journal*, 10 April 2008.

Library of Congress

**Leopold Godowski (Godowsky)**, who together with Marcella Sembrich received the first honorary doctorates bestowed by the Curtis Institute of Music in 1934, was born in 1870 in Żośle, near Wilno, in present day Lithuania and was virtually self-taught. He was known to many as the "Buddha of the Keyboard."[143] He was never a member of the faculty of Curtis, but he taught in Philadelphia at the Combs Broad Street Conservatory. He made his first appearance in the United States in 1884 and became an American citizen in 1891. Godowsky toured almost constantly, traveling to nearly every country in the world. He had homes in Paris and London, taught in Berlin and Vienna, but spent most of his time in New York City, where he gave one of the first recitals in the newly opened Carnegie Hall. He performed a Beethoven piano concerto with the Philadelphia Orchestra in 1912, Leopold Stokowski's first year as Music Director, and then in 1916 he performed the Tchaikovsky Piano Concerto No. 1. He is universally recognized as having had one of the most astonishing techniques in the history of piano performance, but

---

[143] Godowsky was short (5'3") and stocky with a round face. The title was given to him by James Huneker, the highly respected music critic. Huneker also wrote many books, including *Chopin: The Man and His Music*. He was born in Philadelphia in 1860, studied in Europe, and worked primarily in New York. Schonberg (1963) 317–319.

unfortunately his career ended too soon, when just after recording the Chopin *Scherzos* he suffered a stroke and spent his last few years primarily as a pedagogue.

He was a composer throughout his life, but perhaps is best known for his transcriptions, editions of various composers and arrangements of other musical masterpieces, such as his *54 Studies on Chopin Etudes*, and the Albeniz *Tango*. Godowsky's compositions and transcriptions were played with some frequency by both faculty and students at Curtis.

He died in 1938. His son, Leopold Godowsky, Jr., a very talented violinist—in the Los Angeles and San Francisco Symphonies—was a co-inventor of the color photography process known as Kodachrome.[144] Leopold, Jr. married George Gershwin's younger sister, Frances, and their son, Leopold Godowsky, III, became a concert pianist. Godowsky's daughter, Vanita, married David Saperton, who was on the piano faculty of the Curtis Institute from its inception in 1924 to 1941.

Courtesy of the University of Missouri-Kansas City Archives

---

[144] Roger Kaza, "No. 2456, Ode to Kodachrome." http://search.aol.com/aol/search?enabled_terms=&s_it=comsearch-txtlnkusaolp00000051&q=Kaza%2C+Roger.+%E2%80%9CNo.+2456%2C+Ode+to+Kodachrome, accessed September 12, 2014.

At the Curtis commencement the following year, in 1935, an honorary doctorate was awarded to **Wiktor Łabuński** (1895–1974). Łabuński grew up in a cultured household speaking four languages and had been the head of the Piano Department of Kraków Conservatory from 1919 to 1928. He was the son-in-law of the conductor Emil Młynarski, having married his eldest daughter, Wanda, and was the brother-in-law of Artur Rubinstein, who wed Młynarski's youngest daughter, Nela (Aniela). Encouraged to come to America by Mieczysław Munz, he made his Carnegie Hall debut in 1928 and toured America both as a solo pianist and with orchestra as a "Steinway artist." Łabuński taught at the Nashville Conservatory (1928-1930), and directed the Memphis College of Music (1931-1937). When Emil Młynarski had to leave Curtis and return to Poland because of ill health, Łabuński took a year's sabbatical from his position in Memphis and went to Warsaw in 1934 to take up some of the conducting duties of Młynarski with the Warsaw Philharmonic, and also became a music critic for the *Warsaw Times*. When he returned to the states he spent the rest of his career teaching at the Kansas City Conservatory where he was its Director for 17 years.[145] Now known as the University of Missouri-Kansas City Conservatory (UMKC), a Wiktor Łabuński Scholarship Endowment was established in his honor. He was also a composer who wrote almost exclusively for the piano. Of his several dozen compositions, many were published in America by Carl Fischer, Summy-Birchard and G. Schirmer, and in Poland by Gebethner & Wolff. Some of his unpublished works are housed at the Fleischer Collection in Philadelphia. Kansas City was privileged to have heard him perform there more than 200 times, and joined by his wife Wanda he played his Concerto for Two Pianos and Orchestra with the Kansas City Symphony. Łabuński was a longtime and admired friend of Hofmann and Rachmaninoff, and as a young music student in St. Petersburg, two of his classmates were Sergei Prokofiev and Jascha Heifetz.

---

[145] Belanger, Richard J. *Wiktor Labunski: Polish-American In Kansas City, 1937-1974: A Case Study*. Diss. Teachers College, Columbia U, 1982. N.p.: U Microfilms International, n.d. Print.

Courtesy of the Archives and Rare Books Library, University of Cincinnati

Wiktor's brother, **Felix Roderyk Łabuński** (1892–1979), also made a successful career for himself in America. He arrived here in 1936, and the following year he presented an important lecture-recital at Curtis entitled "An Outline of Four Centuries of Polish Chamber Music." The performers in that recital represented a who's who of future stars. [146]

Felix, like his brother Wiktor was born in Ksawerynów in Eastern Poland in 1892 and studied at the École Normale de Musique in Paris with Nadia Boulanger and Paul Dukas, thanks to a stipend from Ignacy Jan Paderewski. There, in 1927 he formed the "Association of Young

---

[146] The program began with music of the sixteenth-century composer Sylwester Szarzyński and continued with Adam Jarzębski, Stanisław Moniuszko, Juliusz Zarębski, Karol Szymanowski, Aleksander Tansman, Kazimierz Sikorski, and ended with Felix Łabuński's own String Quartet. The players were violinists Marian Head, who was to wed Jascha Brodsky; and Julius Schulman, who became concertmaster of the San Antonio Symphony; violist David Schwartz, who was to become an executive in the Los Angeles Musicians' Recording Industry; and cellist Leonard Rose, principal cellist of the New York Philharmonic and well-known soloist who had appeared with the Philadelphia Orchestra and taught at Curtis for 26 years. CIMA

Polish Composers in Paris" and became its President for four years. His first orchestral composition, *Tryptique Champetre*, won the 1931 Warsaw Competition for composers. He then took a position as the Director of Classical Music for Polish Radio in Warsaw, and studied conducting with Emil Młynarski. But as so many other Poles before him, Felix decided to make America his home, becoming a naturalized citizen of the United States in 1941.[147] He joined the faculty of the Cincinnati Conservatory in 1945, and although he was a piano soloist, he found more success as a composer. His compositions were played by major orchestras throughout the United States including a performance of his *Canto di Aspirazione* with Leopold Stokowski, and later recorded by the Louisville Orchestra as part of its First Edition series in 1972. A collection of his papers are housed in the New York Public Library.[148]

Pianists seem to have poured out of every Polish city in the early part of the twentieth century. Already mentioned for their great inspiration to Philadelphia's music schools are Hofmann, Rosenthal, Lambert, Godowsky, Landowska, Munz, Balsam, Filar, Steuermann, and Horszowski. Others did not teach here, but as Paderewski did, they had Philadelphia marked on their performance circuit as one of the most important centers of music in the country.

---

[147] Sokol (1992) 221.
[148] Felix Łabuński, Music Division Papers, New York Public Library, 1930–1977, call no: JPB 02-4.

University of Adelaide Archives' Series 312, Maude Puddy Collection

Unarguably, one of the greatest pianists of the twentieth century was a frequent visitor to Philadelphia during his long career. **Artur Rubinstein** was the seventh child born to a well-to-do family in Łódź in 1887. Early piano instruction did not progress easily. His mother, Felicja, took the nine-year-old Artur to Warsaw to play for Alexander Michałowski, Warsaw's most celebrated pianist and teacher, but Michałowski declined to teach a student so young and recommended that the family take him to Aleksander Różycki for a year. His lessons with Różycki did not last long and he was taken to Berlin, where he somewhat successfully studied with Heinrich Barth. He was not the most hard-working student, but was fortunate to have a close relationship with the great violinist Joseph Joachim, who used Artur as an accompanist for his violin classes.[149] There Rubinstein learned literature seldom acquired by a concert pianist that was to serve him well in the future. Disgusted by the Germans, he never returned to Germany again after 1914. In the Second World War, his entire family from Łódź and Warsaw was put to death.

---

[149] Sachs (1995) 17–30.

Rubinstein made his Western Hemisphere debut at New York's Carnegie Hall in 1906 with Fritz Scheel and the Philadelphia Orchestra in the Saint-Saëns Concerto No. 2 in g Minor. Shortly thereafter, his first appearance at the Academy of Music was in the Chopin Piano Concerto No. 2, again with the Philadelphia Orchestra. A career in America was slow to take hold, however, and he returned to Europe destitute and desperate. "Reborn" in the next several years, he revived his career in London and lived there during the First World War. He came to America again in 1921 with the composer Karol Szymanowski and the great violinist Paul Kochański and his wife, Zosia. He did two tours of the United States that year and eventually he became a U.S. citizen (1946), as did Kochański. But before that, Rubinstein withdrew from public appearances and spent his time with intensive practice in Europe. His return-to-America debut with an American orchestra was with Artur Rodziński and the Cleveland Orchestra in 1937.

Rubinstien was very popular in Philadelphia and appeared here many times, playing the Chopin Concertos fourteen times and giving the first performances in Philadelphia of the Szymanowski *Symphony Concertante* for Piano and Orchestra, dedicated to him (he was a strong supporter of Symanowski's music and performed his works whenever possible). No matter which concerto he played here, he always followed it with a Chopin encore. He was fluent in eight languages and had a formidable memory not unlike Hofmann. He did little teaching until late in life.

Throughout his life, Rubenstein had a strong attachment to Poland. He was in London at the outbreak of World War I. He went to Paris to join the newly forming Polish Legion, only to find that the Russian Tsar, who was ruling Warsaw at the time, would not permit it unless they fought under the Russian flag. In 1917, after the war, when Poland was again placed on the map of the world, he obtained one of the first passports from the new Republic of Poland, and saw a country that for the first time in his life was free and rid of the "Russian scourge." In San Francisco, at an inauguration concert for the United Nations in 1945, Rubinstein expressed his deep disappointment that there was no Polish delegation or Polish flag there.

"A blind fury took hold of me, I played the Polish anthem. . . with tremendous impact and very slowly and repeated the last phrase with a big resounding forte. "[150]

The audience gave him a great ovation, and "Poles all over the globe were moved." He donated to the Juilliard School of Music manuscripts and editions that had been stolen from his Paris apartment by the Nazis; this was the first time that Jewish property kept in the Berlin State Library was returned to the legal heirs. When he was twelve years old, this author attended a recital by Rubinstein at the Academy of Music in Philadelphia. . . on the stage in overflow seating, not twenty feet from the pianist. And as a member of the Philadelphia Orchestra, I was also present for Rubinstein's last appearance in Philadelphia in 1976. There was a morning rehearsal ending at 1:00 pm, and a performance that evening. That afternoon, I spotted Rubinstein having lunch in Bookbinder's restaurant, one of Philadelphia's landmark eating establishments at the time. He had just finished a steak accompanied by a bottle of red wine and was about to light a cigar. Yes, the stories of Rubinstein's "bon vivant" lifestyle were true.

In Israel, Rubinstein is much celebrated and memorialized. In Poland, an outdoor sculpture of Rubinstein at the piano stands on Piotrkowska Street in his hometown of Łódź, and the city's orchestra is now named the Artur Rubinstein Philharmonic of Lodz (Filharmonia Łódzka im. Artura Rubinsteina).

---

[150] Sachs (1995) 269.

University of Adelaide Archives' Series 312, Maude Puddy Collection

In 1882, just a few years after Josef Hofmann's birth, **Isaac Solomon Freudmann (Ignaz Friedman)**, another of Leschetizky's most renowned students, was born in Podgórze, Poland, near Kraków. Both Sergei Rachmaninoff and Harold Schonberg, the author of *The Great Pianists,* considered him one of the greatest in this period of extraordinary performers. His father, Wolf Freudmann, played several instruments in local and traveling orchestras, including an orchestra conducted by Kazimierz Hofmann, Józef's father. Since they were frequently on the road, Ignaz had many music teachers until he encountered **Flora Grzywińska**, with whom he credits his extraordinary technique. His public performances began slowly in Poland and the surrounding countries as the family did not want to repeat the exploitation that Hofmann was experiencing. His final training and the beginning of his professional life took place in Vienna with Leschetizky for whom he became a teaching assistant. His debut took place in that city in 1904. In Lwów, to commemorate the 100th anniversary of Chopin's birth, Friedman and Artur Rubinstein held a joint recital which also featured a performance by them as a duo.

His debut in America took place in New York in 1920, and he became a featured artist for the Steinway Corporation. James Huneker, the famed writer (*Chopin, The Man and His Music*, written in 1900), historian, and music critic, wrote a lengthy, enthusiastic review in the *New York World* about a Friedman concert, at which Rachmaninoff and Godowsky were in the audience. He toured the United States, Canada, and Mexico for six years in the 1920s, performing with Stokowski, Monteux, and Koussevitsky. In 1926, he returned to Europe, concertized with the Polish violinist Bronisław Huberman and, in a trio, adding the cellist Pablo Casals. His solo career took him all over the world, visiting every continent except Antarctica. At the outbreak of World War II, he escaped Hitler's Nazis, sailed for Australia, and made his home there, passing away in 1948. For the publisher Breitkopf and Haertel, he edited the complete works of Chopin in 1912. His interpretation of the Chopin nocturnes and mazurkas, which he danced as a child, are especially treasured.[151] "The place of Ignaz Friedman in the history of Chopin playing is unique and unassailable",[152] and we are fortunate that he left a large recorded legacy on piano rolls and discs.

[151] "Ignaz Friedman—What is the Most Difficult Thing in Piano Playing?" *Etude*, May 1921.
[152] Methuen-Campbell (1981), 64.

**Michał (Michael) von Zadora** was born in New York City in 1882, the son of Baron and Baroness Louis von Zadora of Warsaw. Though first raised in America, he went to Europe at age twelve to study with Theodor Leschetizky and Ferruccio Busoni.[153] He taught at the Institute of Musical Art, later to become Juilliard, at the Lwów (Lemberg) Conservatory, and at the Klindworth-Scharwenka Institute in Berlin. Between the wars, he returned to appear more frequently in America. Michael was a busy recitalist, especially in New York City, where in 1935 he teamed with the great pianist Egon Petri in a duo-recital at Town Hall.[154] He was to appear there many more times—with particular success in 1943: "Veteran of the Concert Stage Delights Audience in an Exacting Program."[155]

Zadora was a devoted disciple of Ferruccio Busoni, performing and recording many of his works. He also was the founder and president of

---

[153] "Michael Zadora, 63, Pianist and Teacher," *New York Times*, 1 July 1946.
[154] Egon Petri and Zadora were both students of Ferruccio Busoni, and they teamed in Europe as duo-pianists often performing Busoni transcriptions.
[155] "Zadora presents A Piano Recital," *New York Times*, 9 November 1943.

the Busoni Society. But Zadora did some of his best playing in Chopin, an example of which is preserved in a 2010 Ward Marston recorded compilation entitled *A Century of Romantic Chopin*. He married late in life, at the age of 61, in Philadelphia into one of the city's aristocratic families, the Biddles. He died two years later in 1946 in New York City.[156]

Ed Barcik Collection

**Maryla Jonasówna (Jonas)** is as little-known today as when she appeared for her Carnegie Hall debut in 1946. On February 25 of that year, friends, ushers, and a few critics were all who occupied the legendary venue's 2,800 seats. The rental of the hall cost a staggering $1,400; but when the recital was over, Jonas became an overnight sensation. The following month she was booked for another concert, and this time Carnegie Hall was packed, five encores were necessary, and many more appearances were to come. Olin Downes wrote, "There is not only room for such a pianist in the front ranks of her profession; there is need of her there."[157]

---

[156] This well-maintained website has a biography of Zadora: www.bach-cantatas.com/Lib/Zadora-Michael.htm, accessed September 12, 2014.

[157] "Miss Jonas Rated as a Great Pianist," *New York Times*, 31 March 1946.

Soon she was contracted for two Chopin recordings with Columbia Masterworks. Subsequently, recordings of Schumann, Schubert, and the little-known seventeenth-century composer Michelangelo Rossi were released.[158]

Jonas was born in Warsaw in 1911. Proclaimed a "wunderkind," she was admitted to the Warsaw Conservatory at the age of eleven in the class of Professor Józef Turczyński. She competed in the first Chopin International Piano Competition at the age of sixteen, and was awarded a prize in the next competition in 1932.[159] She also performed with the Warsaw Philharmonic in Henryk Melcer-Szczawiński's Piano Concerto No. 1.[160]

Her father, mother, husband, and two brothers were killed in a German bombing raid, and she was imprisoned by the Gestapo. A German officer who knew her playing released her, after which she walked 325 miles to the Brazilian Embassy in Berlin. Eventually she was able to escape to Rio de Janeiro where her sister lived. Maryla, who was by that time suffering from very poor health, entered a sanatorium.

Artur Rubinstein discovered her in Brazil and encouraged her to renew her career. She came to New York, and after her triumph at Carnegie Hall, she opened the New York Philharmonic's 1946 season under Artur Rodziński.[161] The following week, she performed at the Academy of Music in Philadelphia. Max de Schauensee, the well-known reviewer of the *Philadelphia Evening Bulletin,* called her "a pianist of quite extraordinary endowments."[162] Unfortunately, her career in America was short. She

---

[158] There has been considerable research on Jonas' career located at http://nettheim. com/jonas/index.html, accessed September 12, 2014.

[159] Fryderyk Chopin Institute, "Maryla Jonasowna," http://en.chopin.nifc.pl/chopin/ persons/detail/id/1601, accessed September 12, 2014.

[160] Melcer-Szczawiński (1869–1928), an important figure in the music history of Poland, was a virtuoso pianist who studied with Moszkowski and Leschetizky and performed throughout Europe. He was also a conductor and composer who held many positions in his lifetime, including Directorship of the Warsaw Philharmonic Society and the Warsaw Conservatory of Music. He was awarded the Paderewski Prize in composition in Leipzig in 1898.

[161] "Music: Touchdown," *Time,* 8 April 1946.

[162] Max de Schaunsee, "Maryla Jonas, Pianist, Displays Artistry in Local Debut," *Philadelphia Inquirer,* 17 October 1946.

contracted a rare blood disorder and died at the age of 48 in New York City.[163]

Courtesy of Arbiter Records

In 1879, also in Kraków, in the suburb of Kazimierz, **Severyn (Severin) Eisenberger** was born. It is extraordinary that in a period of six years this small area of Poland could produce three of the world's greatest pianists (Józef Hofmann, Ignaz Friedman, and Severyn Eisenberger). To add to this extraordinary coincidence, these three families' lives were also musically interwoven throughout the boys' early years. Ignaz Friedman's father was a busy performer on several instruments. Severyn Eisenberger's father was a performer who also conducted a military band. Both of those men played in the Kraków Orchestra conducted by Hofmann's father, Kazimierz. Like

---

[163] "Maryla Jonas, 48, Pianist is Dead," *New York Times*, 5 July 1959. Also see Howard Taubman, "Lady Who Has Lived," *Liberty*, 10 May 1947.

Friedman, Eisenberger traveled to Vienna to complete his studies with Leschetizky, but not before also taking lessons with Flora Grzywińska. Eisenberger debuted in Poland at the age of eight in the Beethoven Piano Concerto No. 2. In Berlin, he studied with Henrich Ehrlich, a student of Czerny who was, in turn, a favorite of Beethoven. Eisenberger's strong Beethoven interpretations were based on that Czerny-Ehrlich connection passed down from the composer himself; he was to perform Beethoven often throughout his career, but despised the label often attached to him as a Beethoven specialist. Chopin appeared frequently on his programs. In Berlin, he performed the Grieg Piano Concerto with the composer conducting.[164]

He arrived in America in 1928 to concertize and settled into teaching positions in Ohio, both in Cleveland and at the Cincinnati Conservatory, where he recorded the Chopin F Minor Piano Concerto with the student orchestra. In 1930, he debuted in New York at Town Hall and, within the next seven months, had performed twice at Carnegie Hall. He was featured by the same artists' management as Josef Hofmann and was admired by many musicians including Ignaz Friedman and Artur Rodziński. He was a regular soloist with the Cleveland Orchestra under Rodziński's direction, playing the first performances there of the Szymanowski *Symphonie Concertante* (Symphony No. 4), and surprisingly gave the first performance of Mozart's Piano Concerto No. 24 in C Minor in that city. The final performances of his career were also in Cleveland with Rodziński conducting the Beethoven *Emperor* Concerto in 1941. He suffered a heart attack and died in New York in 1945. Little of his playing is preserved, but in a description from the noted author and researcher Allan Evans, his playing "embodies the lost musical culture of Central Europe. . . which vanished after the Second World War. . . among the commanding keyboard masters to perform throughout Central Europe and the United States." It is not likely that he ever appeared in Philadelphia, but he was heard regularly on Saturday afternoon WABC radio programs broadcast nationally from the Cincinnati Conservatory.[165]

---

[164] An entire CD of broadcasts from the late 1930s is available on PEARL 9858. Eisenberger's 1938 broadcast of the Grieg Piano Concerto was included as part of that CD ("Grieg and his Circle"). Eisenberger is also well-represented on ARBITER 158.

[165] Evans (2009) 16–17.

National Institute of Fryderyk Chopin

Another pianist whose reputation has endured since his death in 1977 is **Witold Małcużyński.** Born in Koziczyn, near Warsaw in 1914, he eventually studied piano at the Warsaw Conservatory, having first enrolled in law school. Paderewski accepted very few students during his life, but he taught Małcużyński in preparation for the 1937 Chopin International Piano Competition, in which he won third prize. As a member of the Polish Army in France during World War II, he visited Polish military camps until that country fell. He traveled to Argentina, where the Polish conductor Grzegorz Fitelberg arranged a tour of South America for him in 1940. In 1942, he came to the United States, where Yehudi Menuhin helped him settle and Artur Rodziński contracted him as a soloist. He performed with every major orchestra and conductor in America until 1945, when he returned to Europe. Although considered a Chopin specialist, in England in the 1960s he made numerous recordings of many composers from Bach to Rachmaninoff for Angel records. He died in Majorca and is buried in Powązki cemetery in Warsaw.

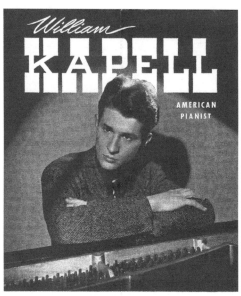

ACADEMY OF MUSIC
Thursday Evening, APRIL 19, 1945 at 8:30
Courtesy of Dave Kapell

In 1953, a flight from Australia was about to land in California, but just three miles short of the runway, it crashed. All nineteen on board were killed, including a young pianist who had just reached his thirty-first birthday. **William Kapell** was the most celebrated young pianist in America at the time and commanded an extraordinary concert fee from a devoted following of audience and critics alike. Willy, as he was known, was born in New York City in 1922 to a Polish mother and a father of Russian-Jewish heritage who owned a bookstore. He studied with Olga Samaroff in Philadelphia and won the Philadelphia Orchestra Concerto Competition, which entitled him to perform with Eugene Ormandy and the Philadelphians in 1940 in the Saint-Saëns Piano Concerto No. 2. In 1941, he performed Paderewski's *Minuet L'Antique* at a Philadelphia Orchestra Youth Concert. The same year, a Naumburg Award led to a debut at New York's Town Hall. He performed and recorded with Stokowski and Rodziński, as well as Ormandy with the Philadelphia Orchestra, Koussevitzky with the Boston Symphony, and Bernstein with the New York Philharmonic. He played with the Philadelphians every year until his death and performed three different concertos on eight different programs in 1942 and 1943. His recording of the Khachaturian Piano

Concerto was an enormous hit, and decades after his death, his playing continues to beguile listeners with his imagination and a sensitivity that clearly offset the aggressive style of Horowitz.[166]

New York Philharmonic Leon Levy Digital Archives

Born in in 1928 McKeesport, Pennsylvania, **Byron Janis** performed in Philadelphia more than 40 times after his debut in the Beethoven Piano Concerto No. 3 at the Academy of Music in 1949. In addition, he did two television appearances with the Philadelphia Orchestra under Eugene Ormandy in 1967. During that time, he was the most acclaimed American classical artist on the international scene. Janis was born to Polish-Jewish parents; his father had changed their name from Jankielowicz to Yankelovich to Yanks. Then Byron, in his professional life, transformed it again from Yanks to Jannes and, finally, to Janis. He attended the Columbia Grammar school with Willy Kapell. He went to the Juilliard School to study under Josef and Rosina Llevinne and Adele Marcus. He then became one of only three students whom Vladimir Horowitz ever

---

[166] A website dedicated to Kapell is well maintained at www.williamkapell.com, accessed September 12, 2014.

taught. At the age of sixteen, he performed with the Pittsburgh Symphony conducted by the fourteen-year-old Lorin Maazel, and made his Carnegie Hall debut in 1948.

He became a valuable emissary for the United States: in 1958, he represented the U.S. at the World's Fair in Brussels, he performed in Cuba just before Fidel Castro marched on Havana, and in 1960 he was invited to be the first American sent to Russia in efforts toward a friendly exchange between the two countries during the Cold War. In St. Petersburg, he gave the first Russian performance of Gershwin's *Rhapsody in Blue*, with Benny Goodman and his band. In France in 1967, he discovered two Chopin waltzes that had been composed in 1832 but were as yet unknown to the world (*Grand Valse Brilliante* in E-flat Major, Op. 18, and *Waltz* in G-flat Major, Op. 70). At that time, it was called "the most dramatic musical discovery of our age."[167] Chopin's music has always been his greatest love and the "find" was "a defining moment in his life." He visited the granddaughter of Georg Sand in Nohant, France, and played Chopin for her on the family's 1849 Pleyel piano. He was also a close friend of Andrew Borey, great-grandson of Ludwika, Chopin's sister, and Janis played at his funeral. When Janis recorded his award-winning Chopin CD (National Public Radio Critics' Choice Award), Andrew Borey and his son were onstage with him.

After a recital at the Reagan White House in 1984, he revealed that painful arthritis was about to shorten his career; he has spent the remainder of his life as a spokesman for the Arthritis Foundation. He took his dramatic and literary skills to Broadway to compose the music for a new musical, *The Hunchback of Notre Dame*. Many awards were bestowed upon his recordings with RCA and Mercury, including the Grand Prix du Disque and Cannes Classical Award. He married the painter Maria Cooper, daughter of the actor Gary Cooper.[168] On March 11, 2015, the Consulate General of the Republic of Poland held a special ceremony in New York City for Janis as a tribute to his "unique contribution to Polish

---

[167] Chopin/Janis, "The Most Dramatic Musical Discovery of the Age," (1978) Envolve Books .

[168] There is a well-maintained website dedicated to Janis at http://byronjanis.com/, accessed September 12, 2014. Also, a Michael Elkin interview for the *Jewish Exponent*, 20 July 2011, www.jewishexponent.com/article/15479/Music_and_the Man.

art and culture through his lifelong personal and professional association with the music of Chopin."

Courtesy of Schnabel Music Foundation

**Arthur Schnabel** (1882-1951) was born in Lypnik, a village in Poland tracing its roots to the 14<sup>th</sup> century, now part of Bielsko-Biała. The town was under the Austrian Habsburg Monarchy when Schnabel was born, but reverted back to Poland after World War I. As a young boy his family moved to Vienna where he eventually became a student of Leschetizky during the same period as the young Polish pianists Ignaz Friedman and Mieczysław Horszowski. In 1898 he moved to Berlin and began his concert career there, developing into the pianist who "invented Beethoven"[169] ; he edited the complete piano sonatas and was the first to perform and record all thirty-two. Schnabel also performed that composer's cello sonatas, violin sonatas and various chamber pieces with the most famous musicians in the world- Huberman, Casals, Piatigorsky, Szigeti, Flesch

---

[169] Schonberg (1963) 401.

and Hindemith, naming only a few. He toured the world and, encouraged by the Impressario Sol Hurok, came to America in the 1920s. Schnabel became a frequent guest of the Philadelphia Orchestra, performing the Brahms Piano Concerto No.1 in 1923 under Stokowski, and later the Beethoven Piano Concertos Nos. 1, 3, 4 and 5, as well as two Mozart piano concertos under maestros Otto Klemperer and Eugene Ormandy. After his second appearance with the Philadelphia Orchestra Schnabel was prompted to say, "I always thought that our European orchestras were good…. however, those of New York, Philadelphia and Boston are much better, indeed on an almost unbelievable level."[170] In Berlin, Schnabel performed Paderewski's Piano Concerto. He then moved to America at the outbreak of WWII and, in 1940, performed with the Philadelphians in Ann Arbor, Michigan at their annual May Festival. When a few years later he became a naturalized citizen of the United States, he secured a teaching position as visiting Lecturer at the University of Michigan. He was also a composer of approximately sixty works throughout his life. His *Rhapsody* for Orchestra enjoyed particular success: it was performed by George Szell and the Cleveland Orchestra, by Dimitri Mitropoulos and the New York Philharmonic, by Paul Kletzki and the Philharmonia Orchestra of London, and then recorded a few days later under the baton of Walter Süsskind. Helen Schnabel, daughter- in-law of Artur, was an excellent pianist who recorded many of his compositions for that instrument. Schnabel died in Switzerland at the age of 69.

People thought of Artur Schnabel as German, and with his severe grey brush-cut and moustache he certainly looked German. But once, when rehearsing a concerto in Warsaw with the conductor Grzegorz Fitelberg, there was a disagreement about a matter of tempo or *rubato*, a difference the maestro attributed to the pianist's Germanness. "Oh no," said Schnabel, "I'm a Polish Jew, just like you."[171]

Beginning in 1932 and for the better part of thirty years, Rawicz and Landauer were the most popular duo-pianist team in Europe, heard regularly on BBC radio broadcasts. **Marjan Rawicz** (1898–1970) was

---

[170] Saerchinger (1957) 242.
[171] Michael Steinberg. Linear note for Phillips "Great Pianists of the Twentieth Century", vol. 89, 456-961-2.

born in Poland and studied in his homeland. He was playing at a resort in Austria to finance his study of law in Kraków when he met Walter Landauer (born in Vienna in 1910). They formed a duo, performing light-classical medleys, and began their successful union over the air in Vienna. They moved to England with their families in 1935. After the war, they toured much of the world, including the United States, and collaborated with Mantovani, both in concert and in the many recordings, including the Warsaw Concerto by John Addinsell. They also recorded Saint-Saens' *Carnival* of the Animals in London with Sir John Barbirolli. Both were also composers and recorded their own works.

**Andrzej Wasowski** was born into a prosperous family in Lwów in 1919. His father owned properties and businesses in Silesia, and his mother, Maria Glińska Wasowska, was Professor of Piano at the Warsaw Conservatory. At the age of four, Andrzej began lessons with his mother; he entered the Conservatory in 1931, studying with Margarita Trombini-Kazuro. He graduated with highest honors in 1939 just as the country was overrun by the Russians. Captured and sent to the Soviet Union, he played 186 recitals there in the next two years, returning to Lwów just before the Nazis took that city. The Germans permitted him to perform concerts to benefit war relief organizations, as long as he did not play Chopin or any other Polish works. He was later consigned to a slave battalion digging trenches, but he escaped to Vienna where he was hidden by friends until the war's end.

After World War II, all the family estates and possessions were confiscated by the Communists, and Wasowski became homeless. He won competitions in Italy and France, and *Time* magazine noted that after his appearances in Rome, Vienna, and Moscow he was called "the greatest Chopin interpreter of modern times."[172] He married Maria Grocholska, and while touring South America, became a Venezuelan citizen. In 1965, he arrived in the United States but could find little concert work and took a teaching position at Oral Roberts University in Tulsa, Oklahoma (1968-1985). In 1966, he played a Chopin recital for the Kosciuszko Foundation in New York commemorating the 1,000th anniversary of Poland's conversion to Christianity, but Wasowski languished in relative obscurity in Oklahoma until his performances in New York City at Carnegie Hall and Alice Tully

---

[172] "War Prodigy," *Time*, 25 November 1946.

Hall in the late 1970s and early 1980s.[173] His subsequent recordings of the Chopin mazurkas for the little-known Concord label are monumental, and the nocturnes received the Critics' Choice Award from National Public Radio.[174] These recordings, not released until years after production, are now available through the Atlantic Recording Corporation. A recital of the *Mazurkas* at Alice Tully Hall was called "one of the most revelatory Chopin recitals in decades."[175] Wasowski did not concertize extensively in America until late in his career. In 1983, he performed a special Chopin program for the Polish Heritage Society in Philadelphia. In 1993, he died in Washington, D.C., where he had made his home and taught privately.[176]

New York Philharmonic Leon Levy Digital Archives

---

[173] F. Warren O'Reilly, "Andrzej Wasowski, a Star at 60," *Washington Times*, 20 February 1984.

[174] Bernard Sherman, "Putting the Dance Back into Mazurka," *New York Times*, 29 June 1997.

[175] William Zarareisen, *New York Daily News*, 10 January 1981.

[176] Bernard Holland, "Andrzej Wasowski; Polish Pianist, 69, Toured as Prisoner," *New York Times*, 29 May 1993.

"Few pianists would consider performing all four Chopin *Ballades* one after another in recital.... but Miss Zaremba has set herself the task.... and there was some lovely playing in them."[177]

In 1982 at age 51, **Sylvia Zaremba** was appearing in New York at Alice Tully Hall, but probably few in the audience realized that she had already debuted in New York—41 years earlier. Zaremba was born in 1931 in Chicopee, Massachusetts, the town which today houses the Polish Center of Discovery and Learning. The Zaremba family and her mother's family, Szot, arrived in America at the turn of the century from Galicia and settled in this region where Poles tended to gather from the 1880s. Sylvia's father became a lawyer. Sylvia was a child prodigy who first studied with her mother and was performing in public by age five. At age seven, she played the Mozart Piano Concerto No. 23 from memory with the Womens' Symphony Orchestra of Boston.[178] The year of her New York debut[179] also included a performance with the Cleveland Orchestra under Artur Rodziński. She was a favorite of Rodziński, who had steered her to attend the Curtis Institute of Music, and while studying there with Isabelle Vengerova, engaged her several times when she was between the ages of 10 and 16. In that same time frame she performed in New York's Town Hall four times. At the age of twelve, she was in Philadelphia performing the Mozart Piano Concerto No. 25 under Eugene Ormandy. She had also performed the Mozart Concerto for Two Pianos at Curtis with fellow classmate Gary Graffman,[180] who was to become Director of the School in 1986. Three years later, she was again in New York performing the Chopin Piano Concerto in F Minor with the Philharmonic under Rodziński.[181] Rodziński's successor, Leonard Bernstein, also included her in his programming. She performed with many more orchestras in

---

[177] Allen Hughes, "Pianist: Sylvia Zaremba," *New York Times*, 14 January 1982.

[178] "Tiny Sylvia Zaremba Pleases Boston Audience," *Miami News*, 9 March 1939.

[179] Olin Downes from the *New York Times*: "It is an astonishment to hear her playing with such complete technical mastery. This was first class playing."

[180] Zaremba and Graffman performed the Mozart Concerto for Two Pianos together as children. Jacob Lateiner, Seymour Lipkin, and Eugene Istomin were also in that class at Curtis.

[181] She repeated the work with the American Chamber Symphony again in Alice Tully Hall some 36 years later.

America including the American Symphony, the Symphony of the Air, and the Chicago Symphony.

In 1945, she played at the White House for President Truman and guests at a diplomatic dinner. In the midst of all this early success, she remained a student of Vengerova at the Curtis Institute and continued to see her long after her graduation in 1947. She was a valued Steinway artist for 60 years and was represented by Sol Hurok Artists' Management. She performed on tours of America, South America, and Europe including a three-week invitational tour of Poland where she performed in recital, on radio and with symphony orchestra. Zaremba's recording of Brahms' Handel Variations and Rhapsodies for Unicorn Records won "The Best of the Month" by HiFi/ Stereo Review, and her recording engineer and producer, John Thornton, recalled her "picturesque Polish phrases" when things did not suit her.[182] In 1966, in a Carnegie Hall concert celebrating Poland's millenium, she performed the Chopin F Minor Piano Concerto with Leopold Stokowski and the American Symphony Orchestra under the sponsorship of the Kosciuszko Foundation. For ten years Zaremba was a judge for the Chopin Piano Competition held at the Kosciuszko Foundation in New York City, and also enjoyed teaching responsibilities at several universities for which she was acclaimed: University of Oklahoma (1953-62), Tulane University (1964-75) and at Ohio State University as Chair of the Piano Department. She retired from OSU in 1995 and passed away in Columbus in 2005.[183]

---

[182] Zaremba papers at Ohio State Libraries University Archives.

[183] "Pianist Sylvia Zaremba Remembered as Grand Player," *American Music Teachers National Association, Inc.*, 1 August 2005. Also see"Deaths: Sylvia Zaremba," *New York Times*, 17 June 2005.

The Juilliard School Archives, Berko-Aspen

**Jacob Lateiner** (1928–2010) was born in Havana, Cuba to Polish parents. A gifted pianist, he first studied with his mother as a child and made his debut with the Havana Philharmonic at age ten, playing the Beethoven Piano Concerto No. 1. Two years later, the family came to the United States to settle in Philadelphia, where both Jacob and his violinist brother Isidor could attend the Curtis Institute of Music. There Jacob studied with Isabelle Vergerova, who had been a student of Leschetizky. In 1944, at age sixteen, Jacob made his debut with the Philadelphia Orchestra, playing Tchaikovsky's Piano Concerto No. 1 and went on tour accompanying Efrem Zimbalist, violinist and Director of the Curtis Institute at that time. After graduating from Curtis in 1948, he made his New York recital debut at Carnegie Hall. He entered the U.S. Army in 1951 and emerged three years later, renewing a career as a soloist appearing with many leading orchestras, among them the New York and Berlin Philharmonics, the Boston, Cleveland and Chicago Symphonies. He received a Grammy award in 1965 for a recording with Piatigorsky and Heifetz, with whom he made five recordings.

Lateiner owned a large collection of manuscripts and first editions that he greatly valued and often consulted before a performance. He taught at the Juilliard School for 44 years.[184] When he died, he was remembered for his uncompromising artistic integrity—as well as his enthusiasm and appreciation of fine wines, Havana cigars, single malts, fresh coffee, and great chefs.[185]

Photo: Christian Steiner

**Misha Dichter** was born in 1945 in Shanghai, China. His parents had escaped Poland just ahead of the Nazis. In 1947, the family moved to Los Angeles, where Dichter began piano at the age of five. He attended the Juilliard School and, in 1966 while still a student, won the silver medal in the Tchaikovsky Piano Competition in Moscow. An international career was launched, complete with appearances in the major musical capitals of the world and recording contracts. He played many times in Philadelphia, beginning in 1967 with the Tchaikovsky Piano Concerto No. 1 under Eugene Ormandy. In 1998, he received the "Grand Prix International Du Disque Liszt" for his transcriptions on the Philips label. He has recorded

---

[184] Parnassus Records, http://www.parnassusrecords.com/our-own-cds/the-lost-art-of-jacob-lateiner/, accessed September 12, 2014.
Juilliard School, www.juilliard.edu/journal/2010-2011/1102/articles/obit-lateiner.php, accessed September 12, 2014.
[185] Margalit Fox, "Jacob Lateiner, at 82; Noted Pianist and Music Scholar," *New York Times*, 16 December 2010.

the Weber-Liszt *Polacca Brilliante*, Addinsell's *Warsaw* Concerto, and Chopin's *Grand Fantasy on Polish Airs*.[186]

Dichter married **Cipa Glazman** while at The Juilliard School. She was born in Brazil to Russian-Polish parents and made her debut at the age of sixteen with the Symphony Orchestra of Brazil. The couple has combined their careers to unite into one of the foremost duo-piano teams of the time. Their repertoire covers all the standards for two pianos, a fascinating array of transcriptions and world premieres written especially for them. In Philadelphia in 1989, they performed both the Mozart Concerto No. 10 for Two Pianos and Saint- Saëns Carnival *of the Animals* with the actress Blythe Danner as narrator. They were awarded the "Recording of the Year" by Music Web International in 2005. They reside in New York City.

Photo: Benjamin Ealovega

**Peter Jabłoński** is "an unusually modest performer,"[187] a pianist who doesn't seem to expect any applause, even after a Liszt *Hungarian Rhapsody*. He was born in Sweden in 1971 and now lives in London. His father was

---

[186] Dichter has a well-maintained website at www.mishadichter.com, accessed September 12, 2014.

[187] Adrian Jack, "Peter Jablonski-Queen Elizabeth Hall," www.independent.co.uk, accessed September 12, 2014.

Polish, and his first teacher in Malmo was Michał Wesołowski.[188] An early interest in jazz began with drum lessons at age five. At eight, he was playing at the Village Vanguard in New York City with jazz greats Buddy Rich and Thad Jones. Piano began at age six, and he went on to study both piano and percussion at the Malmo Academy of Music in Sweden. He performed with the Polish Radio Orchestra; then further study at the Royal Academy of Music in London brought him to the attention of Vladimir Ashkenazy. At age eighteen, he recorded the Gershwin Concerto in F with Ashkenazy and the Royal Philharmonic for Decca Records. They went on to record and win the Edison Award for their performance of the Rachmaninoff *Rhapsody on a Theme of Paganini*. In 1988, he won the Warsaw Autumn Festival Orpheus (Orfeusz) Award for the premiere performance of Wójciech Kilar's Piano Concerto, a work written for him.

A 2002 *Gramophone* award was presented to Jabłoński for his collaboration with Anne Sofie von Otter and Bengt Forsberg on a recording of Cecile Chaminade's music for Deutsche Grammophone. A recording for Altara featured the mazurkas of Chopin, Szymanowski, and Maciejewski. He has performed recitals around the world and teamed with many of the best maestros and orchestras, including the Philadelphia Orchestra in 1995 under Charles Dutoit. At a recital in London's very formal Queen Elizabeth Hall, his attire was quite informal, as is his usual demeanor, and for an encore he offered a jazzed-up version of *Flight of the Bumble-Bee*.[189] A mini-career in conducting has included an appearance with the Kraków Philharmonic.[190] He has also recently teamed up with his brother Patrik to perform works for two pianos.

**Józef Kapustka** was born in Tarnów in 1969.[191] There he began the piano at age three and traveled to Kraków to continue his early education. His further studies took him to the United States, France, and England, and a

---

[188] Jabłoński has a well-maintained website, www.peterjablonski.com, accessed September 12, 2014.
[189] Adrian Jack, "Peter Jabłoński. Queen Elizabeth Hall, London," www.independent. co.uk, accessed September 12, 2014.
[190] Biography for L.A. Philharmonic: www.hollywoodbowl.com/philpedia/peter-jablonski, accessed September 12, 2014.
[191] Kapustka maintains a website, www.jozefkapustka.net, accessed September 12, 2014.

Bachelor of Music from Juilliard (1992), the Grand Prix du Conservatoire International du Musique de Paris (1994), and a Postgraduate Advanced Studies Diploma from the Royal Academy of Music in London (1997). In the United States, he also received the Olga Samaroff Prize in Piano and the Johnson Foundation Award. He was a recitalist at Hunter College in New York under the auspices of the Kosciuszko Foundation, performed in Alice Tully Hall at Lincoln Center, at Carnegie Hall, and was part of the live performance series for WQXR radio. Kapustka's recitals have taken him around the world from the Ukraine to French Polynesia to the "Bach in Rio" project in Brazil. He resides in Paris, where he holds a diploma in French language and culture.

**Paweł Chęciński**, pianist from Łódź, came to the United States in 1971 after winning a Fulbright Grant to study at Juilliard where he received a Doctorate of Musical Arts under Mieczysław Munz. In 1972, he won the Temple University Music Festival Competition. For the American Bicentennial celebration in 1976, the Eucharistic Congress gathered in Philadelphia for a performance in the Academy of Music entitled *A Night with Polish Composers*. Chęciński was the soloist, and Karol Cardinal Wojtyła, primate of Poland, was in attendance. Chęciński received the Szymanowski Medal from Poland, and has been a prize-winner at competitions around the world. He held a teaching position at Pennsylvania State University and was artist-in-residence at Roosevelt University in Chicago.

Courtesy of Ann Schein

In 2010, Ward Marston records created a special four CD collection, *A Century of Romantic Chopin.* Marston chose the best performances of that composer's music beginning with recorded cylinders dating from 1895. **Ann Schein** was included in that compilation.

Ann Schein was trained in her native United States, where she studied with both Mieczysław Munz and Artur Rubinstein. Her first recordings, made when she was 18 and 19 established her as "one of the premiere Chopin pianists of our time". (Ward Marston and Gregor Benko)

Ann Schein was born in 1939 in White Plains, New York, but lived much of her early life in Evanston, Illinois and Washington, D.C. Her mother was a violinist and her father an attorney. Ann's grandfather Louis Schein came with his four siblings to New York and Chicago around 1890. They emigrated from Nowy Sącz (Neu Sandec), Austrian Poland, along with their in-laws, the Amsterdams, from Sędzisów, Poland, and Satoraljauhely, Hungary. The family group had already formed ensembles in Europe, and eventually they made their way to Chicago to play in the Austrian pavilion of the World's Fair: Columbian Exposition of 1893. In

1897, deciding to settle there, they brought over their musician father, Leiser Schein, and mother, Esther Loeffer (originally Lauffer). A family prodigy who preceded Ann was Fanny Amsterdam, niece of Louis. As a very young girl playing the cimbalom, Fanny was a mainstay of the family's "Royal Hungarian Band," which played many society engagements before Fanny was sent back to Budapest to graduate from the Conservatory. The rest of the Scheins went on to help found the Chicago musicians' union along with James Petrillo, and played in musicals, pit bands, chamber groups, and orchestras with their variety of string instruments.

As a young student Ann played for Mieczysław Horszowski and Edward Steuermann, but it was Mieczysław Munz who became her lifelong influence. She was his student in Mexico City where he vacationed and at the Peabody Conservatory of Music in Baltimore. Later in her life, Artur Rubinstein also became an advocate for her career.

**Ann Schein with Mieczysław Munz, courtesy as above**

When she burst upon the scene at the age of nineteen and recorded Chopin, she also embarked on a series of tours arranged by the legendary impresario Sol Hurok, who dubbed her his American "piano-princess."[192] The following year, she performed the Rachmaninoff Piano Concerto No. 3 with Alfred Wallerstein at Lewisohn Stadium before an audience of 4,000.[193] Accompanied by her mother, she performed in Kraków in 1961 and stayed with a relative of her teacher, Mieczysław Munz. Three years later, she performed a recital in Warsaw at the Ostrogski Palace, now the Fryderyk Chopin Museum. That same year in Philadelphia, she performed the Schumann Piano Concerto with the Orchestra under the conductor Joseph Rosenstock at the Robin Hood Dell, the Orchestra's summer home in Philadelphia's Fairmont Park.[194] Throughout her career, she teamed with many of the world's greatest orchestras and conductors in 50 different countries.

Schein also had a long relationship with Stanisław Skrowaczewski, performing the Chopin F Minor Concerto both in Minneapolis and Reykjavik. She was also friends with Artur and Halina Rodziński. Like Rubinstein, Halina was an advocate for her career and was to arrange some important concerto engagements for Schein. In 1980, for the first time in 35 years, New York heard a Chopin Recital Series. Schein presented six all-Chopin concerts, once a month at Alice Tully Hall[195] much appreciated by the respected New York Times reviewer Donal Henahan: "With two such eminent Poles on her side, she moved naturally into the Chopin repertory and enjoyed considerable success . . . she is a splendid musical pianist as well as a precise one."[196]

---

[192] Arts and Leisure, *Aiken Standard*, 17 May 1998.

[193] Allen Hughes, "Music: Ann Schein Bows," *New York Times,* 4 August 1960. She went on to perform this concerto more than 100 times in her career and played it again in Brazil in 2012.

[194] Rosenstock (1895–1985) was born in Kraków. He came to America in 1928 and conducted 248 performances at the Metropolitan Opera in New York and Philadelphia in cluding leading the Met's first perfomance of Berg's *Wozzeck*. He also conducted for the debuts of some of that company's most famous voices. Dena Kleiman, "Joseph Rosenstock, 90, Conductor of Operas," *New York Times, 18* October 1985.

[195] Raymond Ericson, "Ann Schein's Chopin Marathon," *New York Times*, 14 December 1980.

[196] Donal Henahan, "Piano: Ann Schein in All-Chopin Night," *New York Times*, 14 October 1980.

Aiken, South Carolina, where Józef Hofmann had a home with his first wife, Mary Eustis, has held a Josef Hofmann Piano Competition and Festival annually since 1993. In 1998, Schein was the Festival's celebrity judge-recitalist presented by the Maytag Foundation. In her career, she has also enjoyed many collaborative roles. With Kristine Ciesinski she performed Chopin *Songs,* and with Jessye Norman she performed and recorded an album of Alban Berg (Sony, 1995).

In addition to a busy performance career, Ann Schein has been a faculty member of the Aspen Music Festival and has had a presence throughout the world in her master classes from America to China. She joined the faculty of her alma mater, the Peabody Conservatory, in 1980, and in 2012 she was honored with the Peabody Distinguished Alumni Award. She is married to Earl Carlyss, former violinist of the world-renowned Juilliard String Quartet and brother of Gerald Carlyss, former timpanist with the Philadelphia Orchestra. Earl joined Ann on the faculty of Peabody and continued his legacy at the Juilliard School, holding string quartet seminars.[197]

Ruth Slenczyńska Collection, Lovejoy Library,
Southern Illinois University Edwardsville

---

[197] Schein maintains a website, http://annschein.com/biography, accessed September 12, 2014.

**Ruth Slenczyńska** was born in California in 1925 and became one of the twentieth century's most famous piano prodigies who gave her first concert at the age of three. Her father, Józef Slenczyński, was a violinist from Warsaw who came to America by way of New Jersey, then married and settled in the West. He was reportedly a ruthless taskmaster determined to create one of the world's great musicians through a strenuous regimen of practice and study. Józef Hofmann heard her play and arranged for the four-year-old to study at the Curtis Institute. Shortly thereafter, however, her father took her to Europe, where she debuted in Berlin at age six and in Paris at age seven. This little "Mozart" (Olin Downes called her "the greatest piano genius since Mozart") became very popular, and her performances commanded generous concert fees, especially considering her age. At eight, she played her first Town Hall recital, declared "an electrifying experience" by the *New York Times*. At nine she filled in for Paderewski to nationwide press coverage of her success. She was "burned out" by the age of fifteen, however, and she separated from her father, withdrawing from the concert stage. In 1958, she returned to Town Hall and began her career anew with a 56 city tour. A recording contract with Decca Records followed. In 1962, she played the Chopin F Minor Piano Concerto with Eugene Ormandy and the Philadelphia Orchestra. In 1964, she accepted a full-time faculty position at Southern Illinois University at Edwardsville, which allowed her to concertize, and where she remained until 2000.[198] In 1967, she wed James Kerr, a professor of political science at the university. In 1984, her 50th anniversary return to Town Hall in New York City was heralded by John Rockwell in the *New York Times*. Ambassador Romuald Spasowski awarded her Poland's highest civilian award, the Golden Cross of Merit, for bringing the music of Chopin closer to the world.[199] Deutsche Grammophon (DGG) has included Slenczynska's recording of the Chopin *Etudes* from 1957 in their newly released Historic Series.[200]

---

[198] www.siue.edu/~tdickma/RuthBiography.html, at Southern Illinois University website, accessed September 12, 2014.

[199] Richard Nilsen, "Piano Prodigy Ruth Slenczynska Now a Legend at 87," *The Republic*, 14 January 2012.

[200] Biography and CD listing at Ivory Records, www.ivoryclassics.com/releases/71004/, accessed September 12, 2014.

Photo: Lisa Marie Mazzucco

**Emanuel Ax** has been one of the world's most recognized pianists of the last quarter of the twentieth beginning of the twentieth-first centuries.[201] He was born in Lwów in 1949.[202] Both of his parents had survived the Holocaust. At the age of six, Emanuel studied piano first with his father, who was a coach at the Lwów Opera. When he was eight, the family moved to Warsaw, and then went on to Winnipeg, Canada. In New York, Emanuel studied with Mieczysław Munz at the Juilliard School and received a degree in French from Columbia University. He became a U.S. citizen in 1970. His Polish roots make Chopin an obvious choice for Ax, but he has a wide-ranging repertoire, which includes contemporary composers.

---

[201] Official Website for Sony Classics: www.emanuelax.com, accessed September 12, 2014.

[202] Emanuel's father was born when the city was part of the Austro-Hungarian Empire (Lemberg). His mother, Helen, was born when it was again Poland (Lwów). Today it is the Ukraine (Lviv), but the Russians named it L'vov. They considered themselves Polish, and that was the language spoken at home.

His presence in Philadelphia has been frequent, and no pianist has played here as often as Ax since he won the Artur Rubinstein International Piano Competition in Tel Aviv in 1974. In 1979, he was awarded the Avery Fisher Prize. As of 2102, Ax has won seven Grammy Awards, and was nominated for the two Chopin Piano Concertos with Eugene Ormandy and the Philadelphia Orchestra. He performed those Chopin concertos eight times in Philadelphia during his regular stops here.

One of the most endearing pianists ever to grace the instrument, Ax is a popular performer with his orchestral colleagues—and always welcomes the opportunity to play chamber music with them—as well as with the world's great soloists, with whom he frequently performs. In 2010, he performed the world premiere of Thomas Ades's *Mazurkas,* a tribute to Chopin written for Ax and presented at Carnegie Hall. In 2011, he performed his 100th concert with the New York Philharmonic. Ax lives in New York City and in 2007 received an Honorary Doctorate in Music from Yale University. He is a member of the American Academy of Arts and Sciences.[203]

---

[203] This website contains years of reviews and articles from the *New York Times* about Ax: http://topics.nytimes.com/topics/reference/timestopics/people/a/emanuel_ax/index.html, accessed September 12, 2014.

Photo: Peter Schaaf

". . . her return to the concert platform is so gratifying as to make her seem like a brilliant newcomer." – David Patrick Stearns, *Philadelphia Inquirer* 3 October 2010.

A cancerous tumor on her arm had taken **Janina Fialkowska** from the stage, and her reappearance in concert hall and recording studio brought extraordinarily enthusiastic reactions from around the world—this when she was nearly sixty years of age.

"She's back now. . . wrap your ears around the real thing . . . this is high class Chopin playing, deeply felt and demonstrably authentic."[204]

Fialkowska was born in 1951 in Montreal, Canada. Her father, Jerzy, an engineer and Polish Army officer born in Lwów, went to Canada in 1945. At the age of four, Fialkowska began pianos lessons with her mother, and at age twelve, she was performing with the Montreal Symphony. By the age of seventeen, she has received two degrees from the Universite de

---

[204] Norman Lebrecht, "The Lebrecht Report," which appears weekly online at www. scena.org/columns/lebrechtweekly.asp, 16 December 2009.

Montreal, was a prize winner in a Canadian competition, and went to New York to study at the Juilliard School. In 1974 in Tel Aviv, she was a prize winner in the inaugural Artur Rubinstein International Piano Master Competition. (Emanuel Ax from Lwów was also a prize winner). Artur Rubinstein became her mentor, launched her career, and secured for her a lengthy list of engagements—not the least of which was a series of performances in 1976 with the Philadelphia Orchestra in the Chopin E Minor Piano Concerto.

Throughout her career, she has been a champion of Polish composers, from both the nineteenth and twentieth centuries. She performed the North American premiere of Andrzej Panufnik's Piano Concerto and has recorded a large collection of literature by Chopin, Szymanowski, Moszkowski, Koprowski, and Paderewski. The CBS documentary *The World of Janina Fialkowska* won a Special Jury Prize in the 1992 San Francisco International Film Festival. Her latest *Chopin Recital* CD has won great praise and is included on many "best of" classical recommended lists; two more Chopin albums including the *Concerti, Etudes, Sonatas,* and *Impromptus* followed. Fialkowska's made her period instrument debut in Toronto performing the Chopin E Minor Concerto on an 1848 Pleyel piano, a descendant of a Pleyel upon which Chopin would have played in 1830. During the healing process from muscle and nerve damage caused by cancer surgery, she performed all the important concerto compositions written for the left hand with her right hand. Several new recordings are anticipated in addition to her 2011 Liszt CD release, which included a Liszt transcription of Chopin's *Songs*.[205]

---

[205] Fialkowska has a well-maintained website found at www.janinafialkowska.com/, accessed September 12, 2014.

"A class above any other pianist around," —the *London Guardian,* 2005.[206]

"Arguably the greatest pianist of his generation," —the *Los Angeles Times,* 2009.[207]

National Institute of Fryderyk Chopin

Devoted followers of his art would say that Krystian Zimerman is one of the greatest pianists in the history of the instrument. Certainly his prodigious technique, power, and brilliant intellect leave every listener with a profound impression of his interpretations. He was born in Zabrze in 1956 into a musical family and first studied with his father. He attended the Music Conservatory in Katowice, continuing with Andrzej Jasiński who was a leader in the music culture of the city. In 1973, Zimerman won the International Beethoven Piano competition in Hradec Kralove, Czech Republic. Two years later, at the age of

---

[206] Andrew Clements, "Krystian Zimerman," *Guardian,* 14 June 2005.
[207] Mark Swed, "Krystian Zimerman's Controversial Appearance at Disney Hall," *Los Angeles Times,* 27 April 2009.

eighteen, he astounded the world and thrilled the Polish nation when he won the first prize in the 1975 Chopin International Piano Competition. He also won the prize for the best mazurka performance, awarded by Polish Radio.

More than merely a Chopin specialist, however, he has honed his tour programs to stress the music of the city and country of his concerts: Debussy in Paris, Beethoven and Mozart in Vienna, Brahms in Germany, and Bernstein in New York, while never forgetting to put at least one Polish composer on the program, even if only for an encore. His performances are infrequent and highly anticipated. The Polish Festival Orchestra, formed by Zimerman in 1999, toured with the Chopin Piano Concertos and performed in the Salle Pleyel in Paris on the anniversary of Chopin's death. They were then recorded with Zimerman conducting from the piano. He has made more than twenty CDs with DGG.

In 2011, he made his first CD in five years, celebrating the 100th birthday of Grażyna Bacewicz by recording three of her works, two of which are accompanied by Polish artists. Like his compatriot Paderewski, nearly 100 years earlier, he has taken confrontational political postures. He made it clear in 2006 that he would not return to the United States until George W. Bush left office. When he returned for his next U.S. tour in 2009, he lectured from the stage to the audience in Los Angeles, stating his strong opposition to American missiles in Poland, saying, "Get your hands off my country." He has a highly developed level of knowledge in piano construction and always travels with his own Steinway piano, repairing and tuning as needed at each concert site. He serves as his own artist's management and has even been known to drive his own touring truck carrying his Steinway.

Philadelphians have been fortunate to hear Zimerman, since his touring and concert schedule is very infrequent. He has participated in the Philadelphia Chamber Music Society Series and has performed with the Philadelphia Orchestra both in the Academy of Music and Verizon Hall. Highly respected and sought after by Riccardo Muti, the highlight of the 1983 Philadelphia Orchestra season was his performance of the Liszt Piano Concerto No. 2 and again in 1988, the Beethoven Piano Concerto No. 3.[208] He performed the Piano Concerto written for him by Witold Lutosławski on his last visit in 2009.

---

[208] This website contains years of reviews and articles about Zimerman in the New York Times: http://topics.nytimes.com/topics/reference/timestopics/people/z/krystian_zimerman/index.html, accessed September 12, 2014.

Courtesy of Stephane Deneve

One of the outstanding pianists of his generation, **Piotr Anderszewski** was born in Warsaw in 1969 to Polish-Hungarian parents. His father has deep family aristocratic roots in Poland, and his mother was Hungarian, from a family of Jewish Communists. Piotr studied in Paris as a youngster, returned to Poland to study at the Chopin Academy of Music in Warsaw as a teenager, and then received a scholarship to study at the University of Southern California, which his violinist sister, Dorota, was attending. He exploded into world view in 1990 by winning England's most prestigious piano competition, the Leeds, and has since become a regular performer in London. He became a Gilmore Artist in 2002 and was named the Royal Philharmonic Society's "2000 Best" instrumentalist. His repertoire is as interesting as his background, and he has recorded composers from Bach to Szymanowski and, of course, Chopin. When asked if there was music in the house growing up, Anderszewski replied, "my biggest memory.... the Chopin Competition, which in Poland is bigger than football. I remember my aunts and great-aunts arguing about who played the mazurkas better in 1956. They got so angry they wouldn't speak for days."[209]

---

This website has extensive information about Zimerman: http://culture.pl/en/artist/krystian-zimerman?gclid=CIDzu7bz0sACFeRj7Aod3HAAjQ, accessed September 12, 2014.

[209] Ivan Hewett, "Piotr Anderszewski Interview," *London Telegraph*, 20 May 2009.

His love for the music of Szymanowski was acquired rather late. He won the Szymanowski Prize in 1999 and brought the *Symphonie Concertante* (Symphony No. 4) twice to the Philadelphia Orchestra under Charles Dutoit.[210] His solo CD of Szymanowski received the Classic FM Gramophone Award for best instrumental disc of 2006.[211] Three award-winning documentaries about him have been produced, *Piotr Anderszewski Plays the Diabelli Variations* (2001), *Piotr Anderszewski, Unquiet Traveler* (2008), and *Anderszewski Plays Schumann*, which was broadcast on Polish television in 2010. He lives in Paris and Lisbon. His violinist sister, **Dorota**, was educated at Juilliard and was a laureate at several European violin competitions, including the Wieniawski-Lipiński, before becoming concertmaster of the Bordeaux Symphony in France. The two have concertized together and recorded for the Accord label.[212]

Photo: Marco Borggreve

It is very rare indeed when a young classical artist instantly draws the attention and admiration of the world. In the case of then twenty-year-old **Rafał Blechacz**, a towering career was ensured for him when he won all five first prizes in the 15<sup>th</sup> International Chopin Piano Competition in

---

[210] www.culture.pl/baza-muzyka-pelna-tresc/-/eo_event_asset_publisher/eAN5/content/piotr-anderszewski, accessed September 12, 2014.
[211] Andrew Clements, "Tough Customer," *London Guardian*, 14 March 2008.
[212] Anderszewski website, www.anderszewski.net, accessed September 12, 2014.

Warsaw in 2005.[213] He won prizes for best mazurkas, polonaises, sonata, and concerto, as well as the grand prize—an accomplishment never before done. So dominating was his playing that no second prize was awarded, and he became the first Pole in 30 years to gain the first prize. His performing life now took him to whichever musical capital he chose, booked at least two years in advance, with a Deutsche Grammophon recording contract. In 2014, he again jolted onto the scene when he was chosen to receive one of the world's most lucrative musical prizes, the Gilmore Artist Award, which carries with it a bounty of $300,000. The award is presented to a pianist chosen by an anonymous selection committee, which receives and evaluates nominations by music professionals from around the world.[214]

Blechacz was born in Nakło nad Notecią, Poland, in 1985. He studied in Bydgoszcz at the National Artur Rubinstein Music School and graduated from the Feliks Nowowiejski Academy of Music in Bydgoszcz, having studied piano with Katarzyna Popowa-Zydroń. There, he won second prize in the Artur Rubinstein Memorial Competition at the age of seventeen. Prizes in Japan and Morocco preceded the Chopin competition. Blechacz's first recording success came in 2007 with the release of the Chopin *Preludes*. It was awarded the prestigious French prize Diapason d'Or de l'Année. 2010 was a special year of awards for Blechacz. First, he received the Premio Internazionale Academia Musicale Chigiana, presented by a panel of international music critics to young musicians for their artistry. Then *British Gramophone* magazine bestowed the honor "Best of the Year" on Blechacz for his 2010 Chopin anniversary album of Chopin Piano Concertos recorded with Jerzy Semkow and the Royal Concertgebouw Orchestra of Amsterdam. That album also won the Preis der Deutschen Schallplattenkritik. A 2012 album of Debussy and Szymanowski won another *British Gramophone* award and the German Echo Klassik Award for Solo Recording of the Year. The 2013 release of Chopin *Polonaises* brought Blechacz another Preis der Deutschen Schallplattenkritik.

Blechacz is a man of many scholarly interests, and has worked towards a doctorate degree in philosophy at the Nicolaus Copernicus University in Toruń, with a particular focus on the works of Roman Witold Ingarden (1893–1970),

---

[213] http://konkurs.chopin.pl/en/edition/xv, accessed September 12, 2014.
[214] Michael Cooper, "Sneaky Judges Find Their Pianist," *New York Times*, 8 January 2014.

who once taught at the university. He is also writing a book on piano pedagogy with emphasis on the teaching and philosophy of musical expression.[215]

When the young Blechacz won the Chopin International Piano Competition, he received a very warm, congratulatory letter from Krystian Zimerman, the great Polish pianist who was the first-prize winner in 1975 and the last Pole to attain that distinction. They spent several days together, and Zimerman became an important mentor to Blechacz, guiding him through the new micro-universe of agents, recording contracts, and performance venues. As with Zimerman, Blechacz's career is advancing at an unhurried pace, as he fills the endless appeals for his appearance in concert at a well-balanced level that allows him to grow slowly as a great artist and human being.[216]

Photo: Mathias Bothor

"A talent like this comes two or three generations apart." These words were spoken by Pinchas Zukerman after he heard **Jan Lisiecki.** Born in Calgary on March 23, 1995, Lisiecki is the only child of parents who were born in Poznań and Gdańsk. They were both graduates of horticultural

---

[215] Jacek Hawryluk, "Blechacz Philosophy," *Gazeta Wyborcza*, 18 July 2013.

[216] Blechacz has a well-maintained website, www.blechacz.net/en-home. Also see http://culture.pl/en/artist/rafal-blechacz. Both accessed September 12, 2014.

school in Poznań and had a strawberry farm in Poland. In 1988, they moved to Canada and found a place for their trade in Calgary. Although neither parent was musical, Jan began piano lessons at the age of five, and his stellar talent became quite clear—he gave his first performance with orchestra at age nine. He was accelerated four grades in school (skipping kindergarten, then grades 7–9), was declared a piano prodigy, and was jettisoned into a piano career that has brought him great attention.

In the next few years, he won seven international competitions, including being named the youngest-ever recipient in the Orchestre symphonique de Montréal Standard Life Competition and the Canadian National Festival. The appeal of these successes enticed recording companies to pursue the young Lisiecki. Like Krystian Zimerman and Rafał Blechacz, Lisiecki became a recording artist for Deutsche Grammophon, but at the remarkable age of fifteen. In 2010, he opened Poland's 200th birthday celebration of Chopin at the composer's birthplace, Żelazowa Wola. A few months later, his album of Chopin Piano Concertos with the Simfonia Varsovia won the French Diapason d'Or Découverte award. In sharp contrast, a few months later he graduated from high school. His youth is easily forgotten, however, as listeners and music critics marvel at his playing—his respect for musical details and "uncommon maturity." He has attended the Glenn Gould School of Music at the Royal Conservatory in Toronto, studying piano with Marc Durand towards a Bachelor of Music degree.

In 2012, Lisiecki made his first appearance with one of America's major orchestras, the New York Philharmonic, performing the Schuman Piano Concerto. That same year, he was named UNICEF Ambassador to Canada, having already been the National Youth Representative since 2008. In 2013, Lisiecki was named Artist of the Year at the *British Gramophone* awards; the first time an artist from North America has won. [217]Also in that year, for his first appearance in France, he opened the Paris season at the Auditorium du Louvre with a program and internet broadcast that began with two Paderewski compositions and ended with Chopin Etudes. Also in 2013, he received the Leonard Bernstein Award at the Schleswig-Holstein Musik Festival, which supported performances of the Bernstein Symphony No. *2 (The Age of Anxiety)*.

---

[217] www.gramophone.co.uk/awards/2013/young-artist-of-the-year, accessed September 12, 2014.

For his first recording release for Deutsche Gramophone (B0016888-02), Lisiecki chose the Mozart Piano Concertos Nos. 20 (K.466) and 21(K.467), performed with the Bavarian Radio Symphony. In April of 2014, he brought these two concerti to Philadelphia and added another, No. 22 (K.482) for a weeklong Mozart celebration, during which he gave five concerts in three days with the Philadelphia Orchestra under Maestro Yannick Nezet-Sequin.[218] In 2013, Lisiecki's latest release for Deutsche Grammophon, the Chopin *Etudes Op. 10* and *Op. 25* (DG 479 1038), prompted Anthony Tommasini of the *New York Times* to write that Lisiecki "plays like a master [in] technically dazzling performances abound[ing] in musical nuance, color and imagination." Such marvelous exclamations about his playing this early in his career promise music lovers that they can expect an exciting future of Lisiecki performances.[219] Philadelphia presumes a long-term relationship with Lisiecki since he was chosen as soloist to appear with the Orchestra in their 2015 tour of the summer European music festivals.

Courtesy of the Liberace Foundation for the Creative and Performing Arts

---

[218] David Patrick Stearns, "Piano Prodigy Prepares for Mozart Marathon," *Philadelphia Inquirer*, 24 April 2014.

[219] Lisiecki has a well-maintained website, www.janlisiecki.com/Jan_Lisiecki.html, accessed September 12, 2014.

Before dismissing **Władziu Valentino Liberace (1919–1987)** for his musical distortions, flamboyance, gaudy showmanship, extravagance, sentimentality, and glitz—all intended to draw an audience—one should recall a talent who might well have had a career on the concert stage. He was born near Milwaukee to Frances Zuchowski and Salvatore Liberace. The Zuchowski family arrived in America in the late nineteenth century from the environs of Kraków while the Liberaces came from Naples. Both families settled in Philadelphia, where Władziu's brother, George, was born before the family moved to Wisconsin. Władziu showed great musical aptitude at an early age; he began playing at four and was pronounced a child prodigy. At the age of eight he met Paderewski, who was his idol and inspired him for many years, even to the point of deciding to use only his last name, Liberace, as Paderewski had done. Liberace attended the Wisconsin Conservatory of Music and, in 1940, performed the Liszt Piano Concerto No. 2 with the Chicago Symphony in Milwaukee, an accomplishment that any of today's best pianists would admire. Within two years, however, he began to reinvent himself, combining "classics" with "pop" to "put on a show."

Eventually, Liberace became the wealthiest performer in the world. Television, radio, recordings, movies, and concert appearances brought him millions. His final appearances in 1986 were held in New York's Radio City Music Hall. In eighteen performances, he earned $2.5 million. His life has been well documented in several books, film and television specials, and at the Liberace Museum in Las Vegas.

## Collaborative Artists

Sometimes a great pianist devotes the better part of an entire career to accompanying other great musicians, the soloists. That featured artist with whom the accompanist collaborates typically receives all the accolades, and the accompanist must be at ease with the fact that the public usually comes away from a concert remembering only the soloist. The "billed" performer, however, could not have communicated an exceptional musical experience to the audience without a collaborator who complemented his or her abilities, musicality, and sensitivity. The accompanist may even bring his or her own ideas forward into the performance, leading the soloist to yet a higher level of musical interest.

Such was the case with **Leon Pomeraniec (Pommers)**, the leading collaborator of his generation. "They don't make gentlemen like Leon Pommers anymore. Mannes mourns the loss of one of the twentieth Century's great musical partner-artists, pianist, teacher, coach and incomparably elegant friend." —Joel Lester, Dean of Mannes College of Music, June 8, 2001.

Pommers was the longtime accompanist to Nathan Milstein, performing around the world and recording many albums with him. His high degree of sensitivity was also treasured by Erica Morini.[220] They performed together beginning in the 1940s, including to an audience of 6,500 at Lewisohn Stadium in 1952, and they continued their partnership until her final concert 25 years later; he often shared the program with her as soloist. Michael Rabin and Janos Starker also chose Pommers for their recordings. Joseph Szigeti, Ruggiero Ricci, Yehudi Menuhin, Zino Francescatti, Szymon Goldberg, Nathan "Tossy" Spivakowsky, Jean de Rimanoczy, Edith Peinemann, Mikulas Grosz, and Pierre Fournier, the finest soloists in the world, were among his other partners in recital. Some of these most acclaimed performers of the twentieth century could also be the most difficult personalities to accommodate. Pommers' talent for reconciling with a high-strung artist, to whom he was required to often cede control, is a tribute to his uncommon gifts of musical sensitivity.

Leon Pommers was born into a well-to-do Jewish family in 1914 in Pruzana[221] on the Eastern border with Russia. His father was a prominent landowner and owner of a brewery. He was a boyhood friend of Menachem

---

[220] Allan Evans, "Morini in Concert," Arbiter Records liner notes.

[221] Pruzana, from its time under the Polish-Lithuanian Union in the late sixteenth century, was a vibrant Jewish community. The first synagonue dated back to 1463. Under Kings Władysław, Jan Kazimierz, Jan Sobieski III, and Augustus II, Jews lived with few restrictions. They practiced their religion, engaged freely in their occupations, and the town was largely administered by them. In 1795, Poland was partitioned and Russia took control of Pruzhany. After WWI, Pruzana returned to Poland, only to have it revert back to Russian territory after WWII. "Pruzana in Three Encyclopedias," http://cpsa.info/pruzany/pruzhist.htm 1983, accessed September 12, 2014.

Begin (Mieczysław Biegun), the future Prime Minister of Israel.[222] He began the piano at a very young age and at the age of seven was taken to Warsaw to live with relatives who would find him a proper teacher. He went on to study at the Warsaw Conservatory. While he was a student there, Germany invaded Poland. His mother and a sister were lost to the Nazis, but Leon fled Warsaw, then made a hazardous, yearlong escape across Russia, Siberia, Japan, and China, all the while hoping to get to America.[223] He secured passage on the last boat out of Shanghai, which took him to Australia,[224] a week before the Japanese attacked Pearl Harbor. By another stroke of luck, the great Polish pianist Ignaz Friedman was then living in Sydney. Pommers had heard Friedman play in Warsaw, but had never been introduced. Friedman became his teacher, and Pommers remained in Sydney for three months. When he finally departed for Canada, Friedman helped him with introductions. He then made his way to New York City.

Pommers' career was not limited to the violinists and cellists mentioned above—he once performed 30 different sonatas in a year with various performers.[225] In 1943, at one of his first appearances at Town Hall, he worked with the marimbist Dorothy Stockton. In Carnegie Hall, he accompanied a recital of the cantor Miihal Kusevitsky. In the 1950s, he taught and accompanied during the earliest years of the Aspen Music

---

[222] As told by violinist Cecylia Arzewski, whose father was a friend of Pommers.

[223] When he was in Japan, he decided to try to get to Canada and was given a Canadian visa by the Polish Ambassador to Japan. As the threat of war enveloped the entire region, however, travel in now-unfriendly countries was becoming impossible. The only way to get to Canada was through Australia, but passage from Japan was now terminated. Then the only way to Australia was through China. The Polish Embassy together with the HIAS (Hebrew Immigrant Aid Society) paid for his trip, and he arrived in Shanghai but with very little money to continue. Through good fortune, he met a Polish journalist who introduced him to a member of the Shanghai Symphony, and Pommers learned that the orchestra wanted to perform George Gershwin's *Rhapsody in Blue* and was auditioning soloists. He practiced for two days, won the audition, and went on to perform the Gershwin in ten concerts, earning enough to live there for six weeks.

[224] Robert Dumm. Taped interview on January 3, 1989 with Pommers, housed at Stetson University Library, and transferred to text by Jean Wald, Music Specialist and Research Librarian. December 2011- April 2012.

[225] Evans (2009) 192.

Festival. In 1962 at the Jazz at Lincoln Center Festival, he shared the stage with Eddie Burke, Lionel Hampton, Bobby Hackett, and Benny Goodman, not to play Goodman's jazz, but to showcase Goodman's affinity for the classics; Pommers accompanied him in Beethoven's *Clarinet Trio.* At that same time, they recorded the Beethoven and Brahms trios for a CD that also featured the Weber *Quintet* by the Berkshire String Quintet. When that recording was finally released in 1987, it was nominated for a Grammy Award.[226] During his busy career, Pommers was a frequent visitor to Philadelphia.

He never considered himself a pedagogue of the piano, but all who knew him valued him as a gifted teacher for his enthusiastic playing and coaching. He earned advanced degrees in music and became Professor Emeritus of Music at Queens College in New York. His thesis, entitled "Polish Aspects of Karol Szymanowski's Style," remains a useful source on the complexity of that composer's music and his contribution to the musical history of that time in Poland.[227] Pommers left Queens College when mandatory retirement required it, but his teaching career was not over; he then joined the Faculty of Mannes College. He died in New York in 2001.

---

[226] Benny Goodman (1909–1986) was the eighth child of eleven born in Chicago to David Goodman, a tailor from Warsaw, and Dora Rezinski of Kovno (Kaunas), Lithuania. Benny's family was very poor, and his mother had not learned to read or write before coming to the U.S. In America, the Goodman kids learned their instruments at their synagogue, and Benny also took lessons with a member of the Chicago Symphony. In addition to his great fame as the "King of Swing," his interest in classical music was intense. He commissioned Bartok, Hindemith, and Copland to compose for him. His band included the great drummer **Gene Krupa** (1909–1973), who was also born in Chicago, to Anna Orłowski and Bartlomiej Krupa from Poland. Krupa became the most famous drummer of his time and was even the subject of a movie, *The Gene Krupa Story.* Known for his hyper-energetic, flamboyant style, he was to appear many times in Hollywood and has influenced every drummer since that time. In 1973, Goodman and Krupa performed on a concert with the Philadelphia Orchestra at the Saratoga Performing Arts Center in N.Y.

[227] Leon Pommers, "Polish Aspects of Szymanowski's Style," Queens College Graduate Division Thesis, 1968.

National Institute of Fryderyk Chopin

Frequent appearances by Ewa Podleś in Philadelphia have given Philadelphia the opportunity to hear **Ewa Pobłocka,** one of Poland's most distinguished pianists. Although Pobłocka had already amassed a considerable list of solo appearances around the world, it is only as an accompanist that she has been heard in Philadelphia. Pobłocka was born in Gdańsk and studied there at the State Higher School of Music, receiving a diploma with honors in 1981. She had already begun performing recitals with her mother, the singer Zofia Janukowicz-Pobłocka. During postgraduate studies in Hamburg, she won first prizes at important piano competitions in Bordeaux and Vercella. She was a prize winner in the 1980 Chopin International Piano Competition, with a special prize for best mazurkas from Polish Radio. The English Chamber Orchestra, London Symphony Orchestra, Munich Radio Orchestra, and Florence's Orchestra del Maggio Musicale Fiorentino had already recognized her as a world-class soloist.

In solo recital or as a collaborator, Munich, Hamburg, Vienna and Madrid were just a few of Pobłocka's stops around Europe. Tours of Asia brought her to Japan, Australia, Korea, and Singapore. She has been on five foreign tours as soloist with Warsaw's National Philharmonic under Kazimierz Kord. She is Professor at Warsaw's Fryderyk Chopin University of Music. In 2004, she was decorated with the Knight's Cross of the Order of Polonia Restituta by the President of Poland, and was laureate of the annual award of the Minister of Culture. She has made more than thirty recordings covering a very wide range of composers and including the concertos of Panufnik, Lutosławski, Szymański and Mykietyn, as well as the songs of Szymanowski and Karłowicz. She has conducted master classes at the Feliks Nowowiejski Academy of Music in Bydgoszcz, as well as in Calgary and Tokyo.[228]

---

[228] Pobłocka maintains a website, www.poblocka.com/biography.html, accessed September 12, 2014.

# B. SINGERS

When the Metropolitan Opera in New York City opened in 1883, it provided the catalyst for the arrival of Europe's most famous singers. Here was the first appearance of Poland's best contributions to America's opera culture, and on the Met's second night, Marcella Sembrich sang. She was one of the world's great divas and became one of Philadelphia's and the Curtis Institute of Music's greatest assets.

From Poland some of the best singers in all of Europe now arrived, several often gracing the stage at the same time.

> If any opera enthusiast or student of singing were asked to mention a single name of the last 'golden age' the odds would favor his saying: Jean de Reszke. Or he might say the de Reszke brothers. Henry Pleasants[229]

The world's most famous operatic family name was **Reszke**. Jan, Edward and Józefina, together with Wiktor, were born into a wealthy family in Warsaw. Their father, Jan Mieczysław, was a violinist who made a living managing the Saski Hotel and three other properties that he owned on Krakowskie Przedmieście Street. He was also an intense patriot, who fought in the failed 1863 uprising against the occupying Russians, and was exiled to Siberia for five years. Their mother, Emilja Ufniarska, was an amateur singer; she gave lessons to all the children, who sang at the Carmelite Church in Warsaw. They became the most famous family of singers of their time, and Jan and Edward the famous brothers in the history of opera.[230]

---

[229] Pleasants (1966) 256.

[230] Jan Wiktor Kiepura and Władysław Ladis-Kiepura were also a well–known pair of brothers, but Władysław had a lesser reputation outside of Poland.

The Metropolitan Opera Archives, Aime Dupont
**Jean de Reszke as Raoul de Nangis in Giacoma
Meyerbeer's *Les Huguenots* (1891)**

The oldest, **Jan Mieczysław Reszke (1850–1925)**, the "King of Operatic Stage," the "Polish Apollo,"[231] was expected to become a lawyer, and he attended Warsaw University where he received a degree in law.[232] The family never intended for their children to choose singing as a profession, but their talent was quite evident and it was hard to suppress their ambition. Abandoning law at the age of twenty-three, Jan set off to study voice in Turin, Italy with the great baritone, Antonio Cotogni. There he changed his name to **Giovanni di Reschi** and in 1874 he made his debut in Donizetti's *La Favorita* in Venice. He sang throughout Europe as a baritone with moderate success but became convinced that his voice was more natural as a tenor. He studied with Giovanni Sbriglia and after nearly eight years began a careful approach to tenor roles. He was content to accompany his famous siblings Edward and Józefina (now Edouard and

---

[231] "Jean de Reszke, Great Tenor, Dies," *New York Times,* 4 April 1925.
[232] Jacek Gnoinski, "Prominent Poles: Jan Mieczyslaw Reszke," Teatr Wielki Opera Narodowa.

Josephine) around Europe and was very apprehensive about entering the stage again. With the help of his brother and sister, however, he emerged as **Jean de Reszke,** and the three of them sang the very first performance of Jules Massenet's new opera, *Heriodiade.* The audience could be heard chanting, "Vive la Pologne." Jean soon became the idol of Paris. The following year, Massenet composed his opera, *Le Cid* especially for Jean and Josephine and they premiered it at the Paris Opera. Jean was described as the most imaginative singer the world had ever known. In 1891, he became a star at the Metropolitan Opera. He was also a favorite in London and enjoyed a long career at the Royal Opera House at Covent Garden. At Queen Victoria's request, he performed at Windsor Castle with his brother Edouard. They built a genuine friendship with the royal household, and would give a total of seven command performances at Windsor Castle. One of his greatest triumphs took place in Paris when Gounod conducted his own *Romeo and Juliet,* requesting Jean to sing Romeo and adding a new ending to the opera to feature Jean. In London, it was not until the part of Romeo was sung by Jean de Reszke that this opera obtained any real hold upon English audiences.[233]

Reszke bought several properties in Poland: employing a small army of "adoring peasants", he bult a house in Skrzydłów, near Częstochowa, to which he returned each summer to learn new scores. He also built a stud farm and sports stable in Borowno, also near Częstochowa. He married a French woman, died in Nice and is buried in Montparnasse Cemetery in Paris. David Bispham called Jean de Reszke "the finest artist of his generation."[234] After a performance as *Lohengrin*, it was written:

---

[233] "Charles Gounod," www.nndb.com/people/369/000093090/, accessed September 12, 2014.

[234] David Bispham (1857–1921), born in Philadelphia, was the first American baritone to achieve international fame. He wrote a memoir entitled *A Quaker Singer's Recollections*, published by Macmillan in 1920, a valuable source of information regarding singers and repertoire of that era. Bispham sang regularly with the Royal Opera at Covent Garden in primarily Wagnerian roles. He made his American debut when he joined the Metropolitan Opera of New York in 1896 for *Die Meistersinger*. In 1899, he was Alberich in the the first full Metropolitan Opera production of Wagner's *Der Ring des Nibelungen*. He also had a role in the American premiere of the Met's production of Paderewski's opera, *Manru*.

The composite style of Jean de Reszke. . . French elegance of diction and musical phrasing. . . Italian beauty of tone. . . deep sympathy with the German mysticism of the poem and Polish sensibility, a purely German "Lohengrin" now seems deficient in refinement." *New York Times,* February 12, 1902

*Time* magazine of January 1, 1940, reported: "Greatest operatic tenor of the past century was tall, handsome, Polish-born Jean de Reszke, who retired in 1901." The Jean de Reszke era ended as the Enrico Caruso era began. Jean took part in the first American opera recordings but was unhappy with the result and reportedly smashed the masters. Late in his career he chose to undertake Wagnerian roles that undoubtedly shortened his singing life. Nevertheless, his inimitable style left indelible impressions on those accustomed to a typical heldentenor of the German literature.

The Metropolitan Opera Archives, J. Mieczkowski
**Edouard de Reszke as Méphistophélès in**
**Charles Gounod's *Faust* (1892)**

**Edward August Reszke,** basso, was born in 1853, three years after his brother. Like Jean, another career had been chosen for Edward, and he was sent to an agricultural college in Germany. When his father returned from Siberian exile, however, and heard the young man's basso voice, he knew the concert stage was the place for him. He was sent to Italy to study with Giovanni Sbriglia and began using the name, **Edouard de Reszke.**[235] His fame endures as one of the greatest bassos of all time. Like his brother's, Edouard's career took him everywhere. In Paris, Giuseppe Verdi chose Edouard for the role of the King of Egypt for that city's first performance of *Aida,* in 1876. He brought that role to Philadelphia in 1895, one of his many appearances here. On March 29, 1900, Edouard was soloist on the second concert ever given by the newly formed Philadelphia Orchestra in the Academy of Music—a benefit for "Relief of the Families of men killed in the Philippines." A tall, imposing, magnetic presence onstage, he had no basso rival at the Met until Alexander Kipnis and Feodor Chaliapin arrived. Like his brother, he felt a deep sympathy with the Polish peasant. When he sang in America, he was asked if he was conscious of the audience. He replied that "it was his habit to raise his heart and eyes to the utmost gallery, where he knew so many people of his own country were gathered. I thrill with gratitude to know that they are in this free country, where they can carry their heads like aristocrats and look every man straight in the eye. I am proud of their...clothes...watches...their air of prosperity and sturdy independence. I rejoice towards this new country that has transformed the servile peasant into the thinking man." [236]

Eduoard's career did not last as long as his brother's, as his voice did not have the same endurance. He owned an estate in Garnek, Poland. When the failed revolution against the Russians in the Kingdom of Poland began, Eduoard and his family were trapped by the conflict that continued into World War I, becoming prisoners on their property. The two brothers were cut off from one another and never saw each other again. Edouard died there in poverty in 1917.

The last of the three great singers, **Józefina (Josephine),** a soprano born in 1855, had the shortest career. She chose not to appear in America, spending most of her time with the Paris Opera where she enjoyed many successes. She was a favorite of Jules Massenet, and appeared with her two brothers in the first Paris performance of his opera, *Herodiade* in 1884, and singing the

---

[235] Herman Klein, "Edouard de Reszke: The Career of a Famous Basso," *Musical Times*, 1 July 1917.
[236] Leiser (1934) 134-135.

principal role of Sita in the 1887 premiere of Massenet's *La roi de Lahore*. She married a French baron, Leopold de Kronenberg, and retired from the stage performing only at charity events thereafter. For this she was awarded a diamond from the city of Poznań. She died of a heart attack in 1891 in Warsaw at the age of 36, and is buried in Powązki Cemetery.

The Reszkes had two other siblings, **Wiktor**, a talented singer who did not perform professionally, but managed his brothers' estates in Poland, and **Emilja**, who excelled at the piano and could accompany her quartet of siblings.

Jan and Edward appeared in New York so frequently that they were considered regular members of the Metropolitan Opera. In 1888, they sang the first complete performance at the Met of Wagner's *Die Götterdämmerung* with Jean as Siegfried and Eduoard as Hagen. They were conducted by Anton Seidl, who had been an assistant to Wagner in Bayreuth.[237] In Philadelphia, they appeared in multiple performances of Gounod's *Faust*, in which they played the two leading male roles, Doctor Faustus and Méphistophélès. They also appeared together in many other operas around the world. There are no recordings of their vocal art together.[238]

The Metropolitan Opera Archives, Mishkin
**Didur as Boris in Modest Musorgsky's *Boris Godunov* (U.S. premier, 1913)**

---

[237] "Die Götterdämmerung" *Playbill: Metropolitan Opera* February, 2012: 33.
[238] Pleasants (1966) 254–262.

As Eduoard de Reszke was leaving the world's operatic stage, another basso arrived from Poland who would establish himself as one of the foremost of the twentieth century. **Adam Didur** was born in Wola Sękowa in 1874. He studied with the well-known teacher Walery Wysocki in Lwów and then continued to study in Italy. He had already had a heralded career before finally coming to the United States. He was twenty years old when he sang his first Méphistophélès in Gounod's *Faust* in Rio de Janeiro under the first name of **Adamo**; like Edward Reszke, it was to become one of his signature roles. From 1899 to 1903 he sang at the Warsaw Opera, which, because of cultural exchanges between the two countries, became one of the great stages for Italian opera in all of Europe. For the next few years, he was engaged at La Scala and Covent Garden. His first performance in America was in 1907, when Oscar Hammerstein invited him to New York to perform in the Manhattan Opera House he had built just the previous year.[239] At Hammerstein's opera house, Didur appeared as Alvine in *La Gioconda*. *La bohème* followed with the cast of Didur, Enrico Caruso and Marcella Sembrich. He had a long tenure of 25 years with the Met and an impressive list of achievements, which included singing Ramfis in *Aida* for Arturo Toscanini's American debut.[240] He was the Met's foremost basso during most of his career, and sang the first performance in America of *Boris Godunov* at the Met in 1913, sung in Italian and once again

---

[239] Oscar Hammerstein (grandfather of Oscar Hammerstein II, who with Jerome Kern and Richard Rodgers created the greatest Broadway musicals in American history) was a very wealthy man whose fortune enabled him to build opera houses; he built ten in America between 1889 and 1908. He was born in Stettin, now Szczecin, in 1847 and arrived alone in New York City at the age of sixteen. He worked in a cigar factory and moonlighted as a manager in a German theater. Within twenty years he held more than forty patents in the cigar manufacturing industry, and he had acquired the wealth he needed to pursue his interests in theater. Dissatisfied with the Metropolitan Opera's presentations, he built his own Manhattan Opera House to which he invited Adamo Didur in 1907. The following year, he built the Philadelphia Opera House. With a capacity of 4,000, it was the largest theater of its kind in the world. Two years later, however, Hammerstein sold it to New York's Metropolitan Opera, and it became known as the Metropolitan Opera House in Philadelphia. The Met left that opera house and returned to the Academy of Music in 1920. The old Hammerstein building was never again used for opera after 1934.

[240] Harold Taubman, "Toscanini in America," *The Musical Quarterly*, vol. 33, no. 2:178–87.

conducted by Arturo Toscanini. Didur sang an astounding number of world premieres: *La Fanciulla del West (1910)*, *Il Tabarro (1918)* and *Gianni Schicchi (1918)* as well as Humperdinck's *Königskinder (1910)*. Puccini was in attendance for his *La Fanciulla del West*.[241] He sang the American premieres of Tchaikovsky's *Queen of Spades* (1910) and *Eugene Onegin* (1918), Borodin's *Prince Igor* (1915), Rimsky-Korsakoff's *Le Coq d'or* (1918), Franchetti's *Germania* (1908), Mascagni's *Iris* (1908) and *Lodoletta* (1918), Montemezzi's *L 'Amore dei tre re* (1914), Wolf-Ferrari's *Le Donne curiose* (1912), and Umberto Giordano's *La Cena delle beffe* (1926). He also sang in Marcella Sembrich's final performance at the Met, Mozart's *Le nozze di Figaro*. He retired from the Metropolitan Opera in 1933 and returned to Poland, where he became Director of the Kraków Opera. He also became a Professor in Lwów and Katowice and, following World War II, founded and was the Director of the newly formed Silesian Opera in Bytom. After only one year he died suddenly in Katowice in 1946. The directorship in Bytom was taken over by Stefan Belina-Skupiewski.[242] The Adam Didur International Voice Competition is held there in his name.

Didur had two very talented daughters. [243]

---

[241] Giacomo Puccini (1858–1924) was no stranger to America. His opera *Madame Butterfly* was based on a short story by John Luther Long, a native of Hanover, Pennsylvania, who he had met in Philadelphia. *Madame Butterfly's* success was attained only after several years of revisions by the composer, and in 1907, he came to Philadelphia, accompanied by Luther, to attend the second performance of the final, triumphal version of the opera presented by the Metropolitan Opera Company in the Philadelphia Metropolitan Opera House. In 1910, Puccini returned again to New York for the world premiere of his new opera, *La Fanciulla del West*, which had its second performance in Philadelphia, ten days later. Adamo Didur, the Polish basso, sang this premiere as well as two other Puccini first performances.

[242] Stefan Belina-Skupiewski was born in Kiev in 1885 and died in Gdańsk. He was a well-known tenor in Europe who never came to America. He sang the leading role in the premiere of Stravinsky's *Oedipus Rex* in Paris with the composer conducting. He sang *Tristan und Isolde* with Toscanini at La Scala and had performances in opera houses throughout the continent as well as South America.

[243] www.cantabile-subito.de/Basses/Didur__Adamo/didur__adamo.html, accessed September 12, 2014.

Narodowe Archiwum Cyfrowe

**Olga Didur** (1900-1963) sang Verdi's *La Forza del Destino* as well as Mussorgsky's seldom performed *The Fair at Sorochintzy* with the Metropolitan Opera in the 1930–31 season. In the Mussorgsky, she was joined by longtime Met favorite **Ina Bourskaya** (b. **Korzeniowska**).[244]

---

[244] Leon Blaszczyk, "Polish Contribution to the Musical Life of America," *Bicentennial Essays*, 1978: 588. Bourskaya had a very busy career at the Met and also appeared in Philadelphia more than fifty times in more than a dozen different roles.

Library of Congress, Bain Collection

**Ewa (Eva) Didur,** the older of the two, sang often in New York a dozen years earlier. Her first public appearance there occurred in 1918, when she shared a program with the renowned violinist Mischa Elman. Leopold Auer and Madame Paderewski were in the audience and Eva received "a fair riot of cheering after the Russian songs ended."[245] With her father, Eva sang before a crowd of almost 6,000 people at the Hippodrome. She also sang at Polish Night at the City College Stadium, accompanied by the chorus of the Metropolitan Opera.

---

[245] "Eva Didur Wins Throng," *New York Times,* 11 March 1918.

Vladislav Mierzwiński,
slavný polský zpěvák.

At the end of the nineteenth century, the person most responsible for bringing opera to America was the Englishman James Mapleson (1830-1901). He studied at the Royal College of Music in London, went to Italy to study voice, and performed under the name of Enrico Mariani. For twenty years he presented operas in London, then in 1878 he decided to expand his efforts and embarked on a trip to America to establish an opera company in New York that would also perform in Philadelphia and Boston as part of their season. On October 7, 1882, his latest cast arrived on a steamer in New York harbor. His new star, the Polish tenor **Władysław Mierzwiński** was to make his first U.S. appearance.

"I have collected together the best company that has ever been brought to America to sing Italian opera. . . Mierzwiński will make as great a sensation as when Campanini appeared. He has made for himself, in London, a place second to none among the tenors of the operatic stage." James Mapleson, *New York Times*, October 8, 1882

Mierzwiński was born in Warsaw in 1848 and was expected to follow in the steps of his father as a bricklayer. After he began violin lessons and his musical abilities became apparent, his future outside the building trade was secured. He attended the Warsaw Institute of Music and was initially trained to become a baritone. Further studies took him to Italy for several years, but it was at the Paris Opera that he was to make his debut. In 1874, he sang the role of Raoul in Meyerbeer's *Les Huguenots,* one of the most taxing tenor roles in all of the operatic repertoire.

Mierzwiński appeared in Warsaw for the first time in 1881 and was crowned the "króla tenorów," king of tenors. He once again sang Meyerbeer's *Les Huguenots,* as well as *L'Africaine* and *Robert le Diable,* and went from there to success at the Royal Opera at Covent Garden in London, singing with Marcella Sembrich and Jean de Reszke. They were dubbed the "strong Polish group" by the London press.

In America, his debut with the Mapleson Company in 1882 came in the role of Melchtal in Rossini's *Guilliame Tell.* "Brilliant vocal efforts excited the audience to an unusual pitch of demonstrative applause."[246] For his second appearance with the Mapleson Company, Mierzwiński sang Raoul in *Les Huguenots* as he had in Paris. In Philadelphia in January of 1883, he sang Radames in *Aida,* Melchtal in *Guillaume Tell,* and Manrico in *Il Trovatore,* all within six days. Later that season, he performed in *Lohengrin.*

The return of the Mapleson group's well-known regular tenor, Italo Campanini, saw the departure of Mierzwinski. He returned to Warsaw and there teamed with Helene Modjeska (b. Modzejewska) to perform charity concerts; he also continued to sing in Europe, adding Russia to his successes. Unfortunately, at the age of 42, Mierzwiński required throat surgery, the result of which was he was unable to sing for six years. He worked as a hotel porter until 1896, when he emerged again, trying to re-ignite his career in Paris. He was never to be the same, however, and died there in poverty in 1909.

---

[246] "The New Tenor," *New York Times,* 26 October 1882.

Meymen and Co.

**Selma Kronold** (1861–1920), one of the outstanding sopranos of her day, was born in the Catholic Convent of St. Thomas' in Kraków—though her parents were Jewish.[247] She sang and studied with the nuns at the convent but traveled to Germany and Paris to formalize her training. She made her debut at the age of sixteen in Leipzig, singing Agathe in *Der Freischütz*, and began a long professional association with the conductor Anton Seidl.[248]

In 1889 she arrived in New York City. She married Jan Koert, a Dutch violinist in Walter Damrosch's orchestra, and thereafter sang under the name Selma Koert-Kronold, though her marriage was to last for only ten years. Kronold had sung in many of the European musical capitals, mostly in Wagnerian roles, and could easily have adapted to the Metropolitan Opera's repertoire, but at the time the company was dominated by two stars, Lilli Lehmann and Lillian Nordica. She finally made her debut at the Met in 1989 singing Helmwige in *Die Walküre*. She continued to appear occasionally at the Met, but it was with other companies that she

---

[247] James (1971) 349–50.
[248] Seidl was brought to America to succeed Walter Damrosch during the "German period" of the Metropolitan Opera.

achieved fame. In Philadelphia in 1891, she sang the American premiere of Pietro Mascagni's *Cavalleria rusticana,* creating the role of Santuzza with the highly progressive Gustave Hinrichs Opera Company. In 1893, she again sang an American premiere of what was to become the very popular *I Pagliacci* by Ruggiero Leoncavallo, performing Nedda with the Met at New York's Grand Opera House. She also sang the premiere of the lesser-known Massenet opera, *L'amico Fritz.* She went on to introduce many works to the American public. With the Emma Juch English Grand Opera Company, she performed *The Trumpeter of Sackinger* by Victor Ernst Nessler. When the double bill of *Cavalleria rusticana* and *I Pagliacci* played at the Met at the same time as *Tannhäuser,* Kronold moved to the title role of Elizabeth in the Wagner. In two years, she sang more than twelve different roles, from Carmen to Sieglinde, and her career is credited with having sung at least forty-five different characters.

Kronold lived part of her career in Philadelphia. In 1904, she retired from the stage and lived in New York City just outside the walls of the Convent of the Sacred Heart, clinging to the religious teachings she had received as a child in Kraków. She left the notoriety of New York's Metropolitan Opera and the three other opera companies where she had created new roles, deciding to "renounce the world and spend the rest of my life in a convent."[249] Her vows to be become a nun were never fulfilled, but she founded the Catholic Oratorio Society, which became a very active musical organization whose purpose was to create performances as a "means of spiritual elevation." The choral group, which would number some two hundred singers, performed at St. Patrick's Cathedral, and in one of many appearances at Carnegie Hall sang Dvorak's *Saint Ludmila* with the New York Symphony. With her Choral Society, Kronold was often a soloist in an eclectic selection of literature including obscure works such as Theodore Dubois' *Paradise Lost.* She died in New York in 1920.

Selma had a brother, **Hans Kronold** (1872–1922), a cellist also born in Kraków, who became a member of the Metropolitan Opera Orchestra and the New York Symphony Orchestra under Walter Damrosch. He was an active soloist, taught at the New York College of Music, and was the composer of a song cycle and a number of pieces for the cello and the violin.

---

[249] "Kronold Leaves Opera to Live Near Convent," *New York Times,* 3 October 1904.

The Metropolitan Opera Archives, Aime Dupont

**Wiktor Grąbczewski**, using the name **Victor De Gromzeski**, became a member of the Metropolitan Opera in New York in 1893 and, with Selma Kronold, sang the leading role of Silvio in the first American performance of Leoncavallo's *I Pagliacci,* also bringing it to Philadelphia. Two years later, he brought that role of Silvio in *I Pagliacci* to Warsaw. In all, this distinguished baritone sang nine different roles in seventy-six performances at the Met, in addition to several gala concerts.

He was born in 1864 in the town of Dublany on the Belarus border and studied voice in Paris with Jean de Reszke. He completed his studies in Italy, first as a baritone then switching to tenor before deciding that his career would be best as a baritone. He debuted in Milan in *La Traviata* and sang 60 roles in the baritone repertoire. In Paris, he joined the Reszke brothers, Jean and Eduoard, in performances of Gounod's *Romeo e Juliette* and Massenet's *Les Huguenots;* in Philadelphia, he sang *Carmen* and *Manon* in addition to those historic performances of *I Pagliacci*. In 1901, together

145

with Ignacy Jan Paderewski, Grąbczewski was a soloist in the inaugural concert of the Warsaw Philharmonic with Emil Młynarski conducting.[250] In 1914, he became a Director of the Warsaw Opera and the following year was given an emeritus position. He died in Warsaw in 1924.

On February 14, 1902, Paderewski's opera, *Manru,* had its America premiere. The previous year, at the premiere in Dresden, his friends Theodor Leschetizky from Vienna, Joseph Joachim from Berlin, and Marcella Sembrich-Kochańska and Maurice Grau from New York had been in the audience. Grau was the Manager of the Metropolitan Opera, which was planning a series of American performances. In the Dresden performances, the principal role of Ulana was sung by **Janina Korolewicz.** Although Marcella Sembrich was to perform that role in America the following year, Grau was impressed enough with Korolewicz's performance to bring her to New York for other productions. The principal male role of *Manru* was sung by Aleksander Bandrowski. When the opera was later performed in America, Bandrowski had to make his American debut singing the role in English, a considerable challenge for the Polish tenor. The critics in Chicago, Boston, Pittsburgh, Baltimore, and Philadelphia, however, were very enthusiastic about his performance. The conductor for all the American performances was Walter Damrosch, the man who also led Paderewski's debut in New York with the New York Symphony.[251] Five days after that premiere of *Manru* in New York, it was brought to Philadelphia's Academy of Music for its second performance.[252]

---

[250] He had sung in concert with Paderewski in Paris eleven years earlier.

[251] November 17, 1891 in the Saint-Saens Piano Concerto No.4.

[252] Packed, enthusiastic audiences heard this Paderewski work, but it has never had another performance in America. On the very same evening in Philadelphia, while *Manru* was being performed at the Academy of Music, the Imperial English Opera Company was performing *Il Trovatore* a short distance away at the Philadelphia Grand Opera House. Selma Kronold sang *Leonora.*

**Aleksander Bandrowski** was born in 1860 in Lubaczów, on the border with the Ukraine. He began singing minor roles in the Lwów Opera as a baritone. Studying in Milan, he discovered the true character of his voice and switched to tenor. Upon further studies in Vienna, his voice developed into an authentic heldentenor, a Wagnerian specialty. He became a principal tenor in the Frankfurt Opera and performed *Tannhäuser*, *Lohengrin, Tristan und Isolde,* and *Rienz*i, as well as Siegfried in *Der Ring des Nibelungen*. He was well known to Paderewski who selected him for the extensive run of performances of *Manru* that began with its opening at Dresden's Royal Opera on May 29, 1901. The Met's Music Director, Walter Damrosch, decided to engage him in other German operas during that season in New York. Under the name Alexander von Bandrowski, he sang the role of Lohengrin and then Siegfried in *Die Götterdämerung*. In the latter production, Eduoard de Reszke sang the role of Hagen. Von Bandrowski, also appeared in gala concerts with the de Reszkes and Sembrich. After only one season at the Met, he returned to Europe and in 1904 made his home in Kraków. There he worked as a Director in the Kraków Opera and wrote the libretti to the Władysław Żeleński opera, *Stara Basn,* and the Lubomir Różycki opera, *Bolesław śmiał*. He also translated many of Wagner's operatic works into Polish. He died in Kraków in 1913.

Narodowe Archiwum Cyfrowe, Edward Hartwig

Aleksander Bandrowski was the uncle and teacher of **Ewa Bandrowska-Turska.** Born in Kraków in 1894, Ewa was a lyric coloratura who was well known in Europe and eventually enjoyed a greater reputation than her uncle. As a young singer, she was heralded for performances of the *lieder* of Schumann and Schubert in Vienna. Her operatic debut came in Warsaw at the Teatr Wielki in *Faust* as Małgorza (Marguerite). She became a professor at the Kraków and Warsaw Conservatories, and she sang with the opera companies of Lwów and Poznań, but her career was interrupted by a persistent lung disorder that was cured only after a lengthy stay in the Polish mountain resort of Zakopane.

Tadeusz Kassern, Reinhold Gliere, and Alexander Arutiunian all composed works for her. She appeared several times in America in the 1930s; she debuted [253] there with the Cleveland Orchestra under Arturo

---

[253] *Evening Independent,* 13 March 1935.

Rodziński, singing the role of Rosina in their production of the *Barber of Seville*. She also sang solo recitals in other venues. In San Antonio,[254] she charmed the audience with a song recital arranged by the Polish Ambassador to the United States, Stanisław Patek.[255] With the well-known French composer Albert Roussel as accompanist, she toured Europe and America and, just after World War II, appeared in Pennsylvania singing performances of *Halka* with Ladis Kiepura. Her operatic roles took her from Mozart's coloratura lines to Moniuszko's *Hrabina* to Wagner's *Lohengrin*, but she was also adroit with the French art song. She championed the music of Karol Szymanowki and Jan Maklakiewicz.[256] She toured with Szymanowski and sang the premiere of his *Songs of a Fairy Princess* for voice and orchestra.[257] She died in Warsaw in 1979.

---

[254] *San Antonio Light,* 7 April 1938.

[255] At the time, Patek was a lawyer and diplomat of considerable prominence in the evolution of government in Poland. He defended Polish political prisoners before Russian courts in the years before WWI, became an ally of Józef Piłsudski, and then an important delegate of the newly formed Second Republic of Poland. He was a Piłsudski representative at the Treaty of Versailles and Polish envoy to both Tokyo and Moscow where he negotiated for the Soviet-Polish non-aggression pact. He left his position as Ambassador to the U.S. due to illness in 1935. He worked to save Jews in World War II and was killed in the 1944 Warsaw Uprising.

[256] Jan Maklakiewicz (1899–1954) studied in Warsaw and Paris and was the Director of the Kraków Conservatory of Music until his death.

[257] Wightman (1999) 386.

Library of Congress, Bain Collection

**Bella Alten**, one of the most versatile singers in America's "Golden Age" of opera, was born in Zaskaczewo, Poland in 1877. She was a lyric soprano who was equally impressive in both Mozart and Wagner. Alten studied in Europe and was creating a successful career there when at the age of 27 she was engaged to sing at the Metropolitan Opera, and in little more than 10 years she presented an incredible 426 performances with that company. In 1904, in her debut performance at the Met, she sang in *Le nozze di Figaro*. Sharing the stage with Marcella Sembrich in her celebrated role as Susanna, Alten sang the role of Cherubino to such a level of audience approval that she had to repeat the aria, "Voi che sapete".[258] Her career included a number of Metropolitan Opera premieres, including *Hänsel und Gretel*. With the composer Engelbert Humperdinck in the audience she sang the role of Gretel and went on to add more than 70 renditions of that character at the Met, including performances in Philadelphia in three different seasons. With Sembrich as Rosalinde and Alten as Adele, the Met premiered Johann Strauss' *Die Fledermaus* in February of 1905, and five days later it came to Philadelphia. The previous month, Enrico Caruso had joined Sembrich and Alten in *La bohème* at the Academy of Music. In an unusual double-bill, Alten again sang *Hänsel und Gretel* coupled with

---

[258] Kolodin (1953), 196.

*I Pagliacci*: Alten as Nedda and Caruso as Canio. Even though she had performed at least eight Wagner operas and sung at the Bayreuth Festival, Alten also found a home with the Opera Comique companies in Berlin and Vienna, and in America she even did a run on Broadway playing Lady Marian in Reginald de Koven's *Robin Hood*. She married Hermann Deri, a banker from Czechoslovakia in 1912, and they lived most of their married life in Europe, finally settling in London before the outbreak of WWII. Herman, however, passed away in 1941 and Bella went on to outlive her husband by twenty-one years.

Narodowe Archiwum Cyfrowe

Soprano **Janina Korolewicz-Wajdowa** was born in Warsaw in 1876. She studied at the Conservatory of Lwów (Lemberg), profiting from a scholarship from Marcella Sembrich Kochańska. She graduated at the age of seventeen, and debuted at the Lwów Opera in 1893 singing Hanna in *Straszny Dwór* by Moniuszko. She went to Warsaw where she sang principal roles and also traveled to sing at the major musical centers of Europe, including Covent Garden and La Scala. She often used the name **Giannina Wayda** outside Poland. In 1909, she joined the famous Australian opera star Nellie Melba in a 10,000-mile tour of Australia. She then embarked for America in 1911 and became a member of the Philadelphia-Chicago Opera Company. Philadelphia enjoyed her artistry but during her forty-year career she was also twice Director of the Warsaw Opera. She sang as **Jeanne Korolowicz** in six different roles in Philadelphia, including Leonora in *Il Trovatore* and Giulietta in *Les Contes d'Hoffmann*, and performed Radames in *Aida* in Chicago with Nicola Zerola, one of the Met's stalwarts. She also shared an international song recital with Met stars John McCormack, Nicola Zerola, Marguerite Sylva, Wilhelm Beck, and Carolina White. Korolewicz sang the music of Moniuszko, Paderewski, and Moszkowski and arrangements by Niewiadomski.

She returned to Warsaw and directed the Warsaw Opera from 1917 to 1919. Back in America in 1921, she performed her New York debut at Aeolian Hall. In a special concert benefiting the Polish Childrens' Relief Fund, she sang the works of Chopin, Karłowicz, Żeleński, Paderewski, and Moniuszko.[259] Korolewicz sang 70 different roles in her career ranging from coloratura in the operas of Rossini to dramatic soprano in the role of Brünhilde. She again returned to Warsaw and renewed her role as Director of the Warsaw Opera from 1934 to 1936. She died in Kraków in 1955, but is buried in Powązki cemetery in Warsaw.

---

[259] "Sings Polish Folk Songs," *New York Times,* 11 May 1921.

Enrico Caruso, the most renowned tenor of his generation and perhaps the entire twentieth century, considered **Raitza Burchstein (Rosa Raisa)** the greatest dramatic soprano in the world. She was born in 1893 in a ghetto in Białystok, Russian Poland. Although she knew Polish, the majority of the populace of Białystok was Jewish, so the language spoken at home was Yiddish, and the children were required to attend Russian language school. The violent pogroms of 1906 sent many Jews fleeing the country, and in 1907, Raitza traveled to Italy where political refugees had gathered on the Isle of Capri. There her voice was discovered, and her early studies were financially supported by a wealthy Italian family. She attended the Naples Conservatory under the tutelage of Barbara Marchisio.

At the age of 20, she was heard by the conductor Cleofonte Campanini, who invited her to perform for a Verdi centenary festival in Parma. Campanini, who was also the conductor of the Chicago Grand Opera Company, encouraged her to take the stage name Rosa Raisa. He engaged her to sing in America, and for the next 25 years she sustained a brilliant career throughout the world, often using Chicago as her base. For her debut in that city, she sang Aida in a production that was shared with Philadelphia, as for four years the two cities combined their productions as the Philadelphia Chicago Grand Opera Company. In 1914, at the Philadelphia Metropolitan Opera House, often under Campanini, she sang roles in the popular operas *Aida* and *Don Giovanni*, but also added the American premieres of *Cristoforo Colombo* by Alberto Franchetti and *Cassandra* by Vittorio Gnecchi. In that same year, she appeared for the first time at London's famed Royal Opera Covent Garden. She sang Aida with Adamo Didur and Caruso, and Elena in Arrigo Boito's *Mefistofele* with John McCormack, as well as Didur in the title role. In 1918, after her first appearance at Carnegie Hall, one critic compared her to Marcella Sembrich. In 1920, in an extended recital tour of America, she sang for the first time at Philadelphia's Academy of Music.

Raisa often returned to Italy to sing at Milan's La Scala and it was there that she will be best remembered as the singer for whom Puccini created *Turandot*. Under Arturo Toscanini, she sang its world premiere in 1926. In 1924, Toscanini had conducted the world premiere of *Nerone* by Arrigo Boito with Raisa in the role of Asteria. She retired from the stage in 1938 and opened an opera/voice school in Chicago with her husband, the Italian baritone Giacomo Rimini. They had a daughter, Rosa Giuletta Frieda Rimini, with whom Raisa was living when she died in Los Angeles in 1963.

The Metropolitan Opera Archives

The baritone **Johannes Lurié (Juan Luria)** was born in Warsaw in 1862, studied in Vienna and performed with the Stuttgart Opera. In 1890, he joined the Metropolitan Opera in New York and, for his debut, sang the role of De Nevers in the Met's first performance of Meyerbeer's *Les Huguenots*. He also sang the first performances of two now-forgotten operas, *Diana Von Solange* by the German prince Enst II of Saxe-Coburg-Gotha, and *Der Barbier von Bagdad* by Peter Cornelius (first conducted in Weimar by Franz Liszt in 1858). After twenty-five performances in seven Metropolitan operas, he spent the rest of his career in Europe. He sang Wotan in the first Italian performance of *Die Walküre*, appearing under the name **Giovanni Luria**. Singing in Paris and throughout Italy and Germany, he performed operas from Verdi to Richard Strauss. After his operatic career ended, he settled in the Netherlands as a teacher. He was arrested by the Nazis and died in Sobobor in 1943 at the age of 79.

The Metropolitan Opera Archives, E.Chickering
**Lipkowska in Lèo Delibes' *Lakme* (1910?)**

**Lydia Lipkowska** was born in Babino, near Białystok, in 1882. This lyric soprano studied at the St. Petersburg Conservatory and debuted with the Mariinsky Theater in 1906. Her career took her to the Metropolitan Opera in 1909 where she debuted as Violetta in *La Traviata* with Enrico Caruso. She was a guest artist with the opera companies in Boston (1909) and Chicago (1910). In 1911, she appeared in Philadelphia singing *La Traviata, Rigoletto,* and *La bohème* with the Philadelphia-Chicago Opera Company, sang with Stokowski and the Cincinnati Symphony, and added the Royal Opera House in London to her credits.

She was a prosperous woman and had a home in Petrograd. She was in the Soviet Union throughout World War I and managed to escape the Bolsheviks in 1920, coming to America with only the jewels she was able to smuggle out of Russia.[260] She was then signed to a contract with the Chicago Opera Association at the same time as the Polish basso, Edward Lankow.[261] She toured with the *Merry Widow* in 1921 and hoped for a

---

[260] "Russian Singer Who Escaped Reds with Gems Reaches U.S.," *Billings Gazette,* 17 February 1920.
[261] "New Singers for Chicago Opera," *New York Times,* 19 August 1921.

movie career. After a series of concerts in the Far East, she decided to retire from the stage to Romania, where she became a renowned voice teacher. She died in Beirut in 1958 at the age of 75.

The Metropolitan Opera Archives
**Kiepura as Rodolfo in Giacomo Puccini's *La bohème* (1938)**

With the exception of Paderewski and Rubinstein, there was no Polish classical music artist of the twentieth century who achieved more success and wealth than the tenor **Jan Kiepura.** In the years between the wars, Jan had one of the great tenor voices of his time, and thanks to his handsome, movie-star looks, he brought a magnetic charisma to both stage and film that extended beyond the opera theater: a rare artist indeed.

Born in 1902 in Sosnowiec, he came from a poor family with no apparent musical background; his father was a baker. To placate his parents, who wanted him to learn a trade, he studied law at Warsaw University but was also permitted to take voice lessons with Wacław Brzezinski and Tadeusz Leliwa. In 1923, Kiepura made his first public appearance in concert at the "Sfinks" movie theater in Sosnowiec, and that led to being engaged by Emil Młynarski for the role of the highlander (góral) in Moniuszko's *Halka* at the Teatr Wielki in Warsaw. Engaged by Artur Rodziński a year later, he sang his first major role in Gounod's *Faust* in Lwów (Lemberg). After appearing in Warsaw, Poznań, and Gdańsk, notoriety and great popularity soon followed as he took his career outside of Poland.

On September 22, 1926, Kiepura had a triumphant debut in *Tosca* at the famed Vienna State Opera House, singing with Maria Nemeth and then Maria Jeritza. The next month, appearing as Calaf in Puccini's *Turandot,* he received an ovation seldom seen in the world of classical music. On October 22, his appearance in that role caused such a sensation with the audience that Lotte Lehmann, the German diva, delayed the third act by threatening not to go on stage, calling Kiepura a "circus performer."[262] The following year he signed a three-year contract at La Scala, where he appeared under Maestro Arturo Toscanini. He would then sing on the best-known stages in the world, including Budapest, Berlin, Prague, London, Paris, Brussels, and Munich. In 1927, he sang the premiere of Erich Korngold's *Wunder der Heliane.* In 1929, he toured South America and the following year began a long career in film in Germany. He appeared in nineteen films.

Kiepura became prosperous enough that in 1933 he built a hotel, the Patria, in Krynica-Zdrój for the equivalent of $3 million. His every appearance throughout the world, not only in Poland, caused a sensation, and in 1936, his concerts supported the construction of the National Museum in Kraków. Kiepura had begun to sing lighter operatic roles in addition to his more serious engagements and also appeared in film. On the set of one of those films he was making in Vienna, he met a Hungarian singer-actress, Marta Eggerth. They married in 1936 and teamed together many times in movies; they also headed a national and international tour of *The Merry Widow* (*Die lustige Witwe*), the very popular operetta by Franz Lehar, singing it in English, French, German, and Italian. They sang 2,000 performances of the Lehar operetta together and even added a Polish version for a large, enthusiastic audience in Chicago, where Kiepura had performed many times with the Chicago Civic Opera Company. Lehar wrote the music for two more films especially for Marta Eggerth.

On the more serious side again, Kiepura debuted with the Metropolitan Opera in 1938, appeared on tour in Philadelphia, and remained with the company until the end of the 1942 season. After his debut at the Met in *La bohème* on February 10, 1938, Samuel Chotzinoff wrote in the New

---

[262] "Ovation to Kiepura Angers Lehmann," *New York Times,* 23 October 1926.

York Post, "As breezy a star as ever twinkled in an operatic sky, the Polish tenor, personable in dress and figure, injected high spirits into the role of Rodolfo and turned that ordinarily pompous and bombastic poet into a musical-comedy hero". Two months before the Nazi invasion of 1939, Kiepura and Eggerth sang to an audience of twenty thousand in Warsaw's Old Town Square (Stare Miasto) to raise money for the National Defense Fund. The couple was in Paris when war broke out. Because Jan was listed in the Nazi's Lexicon of Jewish Musicians—his mother was Jewish—they returned to New York and did not leave North America until the war was over.

Courtesy of Marjan Kiepura, Patria Music

Shortly after arriving in America in 1938, he performed at a Carnegie Hall concert commemorating Polish Constitution Day of May 3rd, and was very active singing in support of many Allied war relief causes, including Polish and Jewish organizations in America. He sang with the New York Philharmonic led by Artur Rodziński in a concert that included works by Szałowski, Wiechowicz, Moniuszko, and Nowowiejewski, and the New York premiere of Karol Szymanowski's *Symphonie Concertante* (performed by Stanisław Szpinalski, a young piano protégé of Paderewski). A few months later, and just six weeks after the German invasion of Poland, Kiepura had teamed with Artur Rubinstein in the first of a series of nationwide concerts for the relief of Polish refugees performed by many artists throughout America. He added the songs of Karłowicz and Marczewski to his usual repertoire of Polish composers. Kiepura became a U.S. citizen in 1943.

In 1945, the role of Tadeusz Kosciuszko was created for Kiepura by the Warsaw-born American film composer, Bronisław Kaper, in his Broadway musical, *Polonaise*. The musical ran for 113 performances at the Alvin Theater; Kiepura's co-star was his wife, Marta Eggerth.[263, 264] Kiepura's signature song, "Nińon," had been written for him by Kaper while both were still living in Europe; he sang it and recorded it in three different languages. Over his career, he was to appear in a total of twelve musicals in Polish, French, German, or English. In recital, he presented a wide variety of composers and styles often including Moniuszko, Nowowiejewski, Chopin, and Wieniawski. In 1956, after an absence of almost twenty years, Kiepura returned to perform in Poland, visiting Bydgoszcz, Gdańsk, Łódź, Katowice, Poznań, Wrocław, Kraków, Warsaw, and his home in Krynica-Zdrój. Two years later, on a concert tour with his wife, he traveled beyond the Iron Curtain into his former homeland, unaware that his passport had been stolen. To prove that he was Jan Kiepura, he sang his way through the East German checkpoint. Thousands awaited his arrival at Okęcie Airport in Warsaw where he was literally carried off the plane by throngs of adoring Poles.[265]

He was an astute businessman who owned several properties in various countries. He finally settled with his family in Rye, New York, where he died in 1966. His last performance had been that year, in Port Chester, for the Polish American community there.

Kiepura's funeral was held at St. Patrick's Cathedral in New York City. His wife[266] had his body returned to Poland, where another funeral mass

---

[263] Brendan Carroll, "Kiepura & Eggerth," *BBC Music Magazine*, November 1998: 37.
[264] Anne Midgette, "Heard for Eight Decades, Her Voice Doesn't Waver," *New York Times,* 8 August 2005.
[265] "Kiepura Goes to Poland with Voice as Passport," *New York Times,* 9 September 1958.
[266] In 2013, Marta Eggerth passed away at the age 101, having outlived Jan Kiepura by 47 years. Though Europe's "Liebespaar" (Love Pair) had ended in 1966, Marta Eggerth's career did not. She continued to live in Rye, N.Y. where they had settled many years before, and she went on to appear in opera, operetta, on Broadway, and also on television in Europe and America. In 1990, accompanied by their son,

was held at the Church of the Holy Cross (Kościół Swiętego Krzyża), where Chopin's heart is interred; the Warsaw Philharmonic performed or the occasion. Kiepura's remains now rest in the Powązki Cemetery of Warsaw. For his numerous humanitarian efforts and artistic achievements, Kiepura was honored in many European countries and in the United States where he was invited to the White House by President and Mrs. Roosevelt in thanks for his help in the war effort. The Polish government awarded him the "Polonia Restituta" and the "Polish Golden Cross of Merit" ("Krzyż Zasługi"). A monument to Kiepura was erected in Krynica-Zdrój, and the Jan Kiepura Festival takes place there every August.

Jan Kiepura's son, **Marjan,** is a pianist who began studies in the Preparatory Division of the Juilliard School of Music with Jeaneane Dowis and continued coaching with Menahem Pressler. Born in Paris in 1950, where his parents were filming the French thriller *Valse Brillante,* he has himself performed in concert around the United States and Europe. He also accompanied his mother, Marta Eggerth, on tour and at the Teatr Wielki in Warsaw in 1990 and performed again in Poland in 1994. In 1992, he produced a CD, *Jan Kiepura Vol. 1* and *Jan Kiepura Vol 2* for the Pearl label, which includes opera, operetta, and song arrangements of Chopin and Wieniawski, some never heard before. In 2000, he released a highly praised CD of Chopin's music entitled *Images of a Homeland* on the Patria Music label (KIE2000). He also collects books and articles on Chopin and has written articles and held workshops on Chopin's connection to his homeland and the music that was influenced by it. More recently, and due to a special interest in the *mazurkas* of Chopin, he produced and filmed these and other Chopin works at the renowned Mechanics Hall in Worcerster, Massachusetts, in which he performs—and

---

Marjan, she sang at the Teatr Wielki in Warsaw. In 1999, she sang at the Vienna State Opera. After more than eighty years she continued to stun audiences with her talents and shared her knowledge in master classes. In 2002, a two-CD collection was released, entitled *Marta Eggerth: My Life and Song.* It is a compilation of her artistry of 70 years from Lehar to Puccini and includes Chopin *Songs* (Patria Productions KIE3000). In September 2012, at a ceremony at the Consulate General of Poland in New York, President Bronisław Komorowski of Poland awarded a tearful Eggerth the Knight's Cross of the Order of Merit (*Order Zasługi Polskiej Rzeczypospolitej Ludowej*) for her achievements in the artistic world and for her social and charitable works.

speaks about the national character of Chopin's music. These clips are available on YouTube.

Narodowe Archiwum Cyfrowe

Jan Kiepura had a most talented brother, **Władysław Kiepura,** who was also a tenor. Władek was also born in Sosnowiec, in 1904, two years after his brother. He had a distinguished career, but did not reach the level of notoriety of his sibling. His early years mirrored his brother's: he studied with Tadeusz Leliwa, and sang the title role in Gounod's *Faust* in Kraków and in *Rigoletto* at the Lwów Opera. To separate himself from Jan's increasing fame, he began using the name **Władysław Ladis-Kiepura** when he debuted in Hamburg and La Scala. In 1937 he sang the role of Jontek in the film adaptation of Moniuszko's *Halka.* Another Pole, Ewa Bandrowska-Turska, sang Halka in that production. In 1935, he signed a five-year contract with the Hamburg State Opera but World War II intervened, and he traveled to America in 1939.

In New Jersey, Władysław met and married Doris Gzowski, an amateur singer whose parents were from Żywiec and Sochocin. He performed in Moniuszko's *Halka* in New York City at the Mecca Temple in 1940, at

Carnegie Hall in 1952, and at the Manhattan Center in 1955. That year, the Manhattan Center also staged performances of two other Moniuszko operas, *Verbum Nobile* and *Flis* with the Polonia Opera Company under Walter Grigaitis' direction. Ladis-Kiepura recorded for the Odeon and Parlophon record companies and made a recording with his brother, Jan, singing operatic favorites including the music of Moniuszko.[267]

He sang in Philadelphia a number of times. In 1940, to excellent reviews, he appeared as *Mario Cavaradossi* in *Tosca* using the name Laddis Kiepura. The cast of that Verdi opera also included Jerzy (George) Czaplicki and Theodore Czerwinski. In 1941, Kiepura represented Poland in an eleven-nation musical presentation, *Let Freedom Sing*, to benefit the Allies in World War II, and in 1942, he led a group representing the United Nations in Bond Rallies for Poland. Like his brother, Jan, he had the personality and voice to sing the operettas of Franz Lehar and also performed *The Land of Smiles* (*Das Land des Lächelns*). He sang little after the mid-1960s though he outlived his brother by thirty-two years. He owned farms in New Jersey and New York and property in Toronto; he finally settled in Florida where he became a real estate investor. He last visited Poland with his family in 1972; he died in Florida in 1998 at the age of 94.

---

[267] http://ale.gratka.pl/ogloszenie/jan-i-wladyslaw-ladis-kiepura-dwaj-19659323. html?sesja_gratka=422d35047d6c228d5de624f1d78b8b74, accessed September 12, 2014.

ROSA OLITZKA

*Aimé Dupont* ·574·FIFTH·AVENUE· ·NEW·YORK·

The Metropolitan Opera Archives, Aime Dupont
**Olitzka as Amneris in Giuseppe Verdi's *Aida* (1896)**

**Rosa Olitzka** was a contralto born in 1873 in Berlin to Polish parents. She studied there and spent the bulk of her professional career specializing in the German operatic repertoire, in which she was highly acclaimed. She also had a very successful, lengthy engagement with London's Covent Garden Opera, and in Paris she sang the French premiere of Wagner's *Die Götterdämerung.*

Olitzka performed many roles with the Metropolitan Opera in New York. In 1899, she sang in one of the "most important events of the season," Mozart's *Magic Flute* with Marcella Sembrich and Eduoard de Reszke.[268]

In Philadelphia, she sang in *Die Walküre, Tannhäuser, Tristan und Isolde, Lohengrin, Der Fliegende Holländer,* and some of the Italian and French repertoire. Olitzka also had a lengthy relationship with the Opera Company of Chicago, where she sang in that company's first season of 1910. She died in Chicago in 1949.312

---

[268] "Brilliant Opera Season," *New York Times*, 3 October 1899.

The Metropolitan Opera Archives
**Olitzki as Faninal in Richard Strauss' *Der Rosenkavalier* (1940)**

Forty years later, her cousin, **Walter Olitzki** (1899–1949), who was born in Hamburg, also had success in America specializing in the German operas of Wagner and Strauss. In Philadelphia, besides the role of Faninal in *Der Rosenkavalier*, he sang Klingsor in *Parsifal* and Alberich in *Die Götterdämerung*. This basso-buffo became an American citizen, singing for years with the Metropolitan, San Francisco, Chicago, and Philadelphia opera companies. He died of cancer in Los Angeles the same year as Rosa.[269]

---

[269] "Walter Olitzka, 50, Baritone in Opera," *New York Times*, 4 August 1949.

Narodowe Archiwum Cyfrowe, Maurice Seymour (Chicago)
**Czaplicki as Baron Scarpia in Giacomo Puccini's *Tosca* (1939)**

**Jerzy Czaplicki** was born in Warsaw in 1902.[270] A baritone, he attended the Warsaw Conservatory, graduated in 1924, and continued studies in Italy. He married the soprano Luisa Tapales in Milan in 1927. He debuted there in 1928 singing Sylvio in *I Pagliacci* and Alfio in *Cavalleria rusticana* and spent a total of three years there. He then began appearing throughout the rest of Europe, debuting at the Paris Opera in 1931 in *La Traviata*. After the Teatr Wielki was remodeled, Janina Korolewicz—during her second stint as Director—brought Czaplicki into the company to perform *Aida, Don Carlos, Tosca, Faust, Rigoletto,* and *L'Africaine*. When Korolewicz left her position, Czaplicki also departed the Warsaw Opera and began a season with the Lwów Opera in 1936. During that year in Lwów, he sang with one of the world's most renowned singers, the Polish basso Adam Didur, in Tchaikovsky's *Pique Dame*. Czaplicki indulged his interest in tango music, recording Brazilian and Argentine tangos in the 1930s, and in 1937, he made a film in Warsaw titled *Fredek Uszcześliwia Swiat (Freddie Makes the World Happy)*, singing a tango sound track for this musical comedy.

---

[270] Adam Czopek, "Jerzy Czaplicki—zapomniana legenda," *Nasz Dziennik*, 19 August 2002.

Czaplicki arrived in the United States on October 23, 1937, from Hamburg.[271] Using the first name George, he began a five-year career with the Chicago Civic Opera Company, opening their season with Verdi's *Aida*. Expanding his repertoire, he sang Wolfram in Wagner's *Tannhäuser*. and John the Baptist in Richard Strauss' *Salome*. He headlined with many of the great singers of the day: Kiepura, Gigli, Albanese, Kullman, Harshaw, Melton, Pons, and Stevens. In 1940, he made his New York debut at the Mecca Temple with the Polish American Opera Company as Janusz in an especially praised performance of Moniuszko's *Halka* with Ladis Kiepura as Jontek.[272] In 1944, he sang the role of Scarpia in the first performance of Puccini's *Tosca* with the newly formed New York City Opera Company and, later that year, sang that same role with the Philadelphia La Scala Opera Company. Czaplicki also performed with opera companies in San Francisco and Puerto Rico. He returned to Poland in 1964 and was a vocal coach and director of the new production of *Tosca* at the Warsaw Opera. When Czaplicki left Italy in 1931 he separated from his wife. After their divorce in 1943, he married Anna Czernecka, an announcer and commentator for Polish Radio. After a long illness Czaplicki died in Warsaw in 1992.

---

[271] That same day, the child prodigy pianist, Ruth Slenczyńska, and her father, Józef, returned to America, arriving on the *Stefan Batory* liner out of Gdynia. "Ocean Travelers," *New York Times*, 23 October 1937.

[272] "*Halka* Given by Polish Troup," *New York Times,* 19 February 1940.

Courtesy of 2009 Korjus Recordings and Its licensors

Coloratura **Miliza Korjus** was born in Warsaw in 1909 to an Estonian father, a colonel in the Russian Army, and a mother of Polish-Lithuanian nobility. The family moved to Kiev after World War I, and she studied at the Conservatory there, joined the Dumka Chorus of Kiev, and toured the Soviet Union. She moved to Germany and married a physician, Kuno Foelsch. Her career began when she was engaged by the Berlin State Opera. Her performances propelled her to prominence in Europe; she became known as the "Berlin Nightingale" for her amazing high register, and Irving Thalberg of MGM offered her a ten-year movie contract "sight unseen." She went to Hollywood in 1936 and worked in films where she earned an Academy Award nomination for best supporting actress in *The Great Waltz* in 1938. During World War II, she lived in Mexico and made one film there, *Caballeria del Imperio,* then returned to the United States in 1944. She appeared at Carnegie Hall in recital and toured in concert appearances.[273]

She settled in California, and in 1952, she retired from the stage and founded Venus Records, which released a four-CD set of her earlier recordings. She also has made recordings produced in Germany that

---

[273] "Korjus Welcomed at Carnegie Hall," *New York Times*, 23 October 1944.

included songs by Moszkowski and Chopin. She died in California in 1980. At the time, she had begun to learn the Wagnerian repertoire. She was, until the end, greatly admired as an artist and personality.[274]

At about the time that Adam Didur died in 1946, another Polish basso was emerging from Warsaw. Although he was not to achieve the same level of acclaim as Reszke or Didur, **Bernard Ładysz** was quite respected and was highly decorated by the Polish government. He was a particular favorite of Krzysztof Penderecki, whose music brought both of their careers into greater prominence.

Photo: Marta Ankiersztein

Ładysz was born in Wilno in 1922 and studied there in 1940–1941 before entering the Higher School of Music in Warsaw. At the end of World War II, he was a member of the professional group "Artists from the Polish Army." In 1950, he received his first major operatic opportunity when he was engaged by the Warsaw Opera to sing Prince Gremin in Tchaikovsky's

---

[274] "Miliza Korjus, Singer Who Won Acclaim in 'Great Waltz'," *New York Times,* 1 September 1980.

*Eugene Onegin.* He also sang the role of Mefistofeles in *Faust,* always a *tour de force* for a basso. In 1956, he won first prize in the International Voice Competition in Vercelli, Italy. This afforded him the opportunity to perform with some of Europe's most celebrated singers, including Victoria de Los Angeles and Antonietta Stella. In 1959, he recorded *Lucia di Lammermoor* in London for the Columbia label with Maria Callas under the conductor Tullio Serafin. Columbia Records continued to engage him for the Italian and Russian literature. In 1960, he scored his greatest success to date when he sang the dramatic role of *Boris Godunow* with the Warsaw Opera, appearing there again in that role in 1973.

As the music of Krzysztof Penderecki emerged in America, so did Bernard Ładysz. In 1967, in Cologne, Germany, he recorded Penderecki's *Passion According to Saint Luke* with the conductor Henryk Czyż for the Philips label; the world's curiosity for the music of this Polish composer was bringing his work to every corner of the musical world. In 1970, Eugene Ormandy and the Philadelphia Orchestra with Ładysz and soprano, Stefania Woytowicz,[275] performed Penderecki's startling *Utrenja, The Entombment of Christ;* they also gave its first New York performance in Carnegie Hall and recorded the work for RCA. That same year, Ładysz performed Penderecki's *Cosmogonia* at the United Nations. The U.N. Secretary General commissioned the oratorio for the 25th anniversary of the United Nations, and it was first performed in the U.N.'s General Assembly Hall.[276] Ładysz, Zubin Mehta, and the Los Angeles Philharmonic gave the composition its Carnegie Hall debut a short time later.[277]

In 2007 the Hamburg State Opera released an eleven-CD series entitled "Cult Operas of the 70s" (ArthausDVD). Included was Penderecki's opera *The Devils of Loudon,* featuring Ładysz and Tatiana Troyanos, with

---

[275] **Stefania Wójtowicz** (1922–2005) made a rare appearance in America. She was born in Odyniu, studied in Kraków, and died in Warsaw. She won the Bach Competition in Leipzig (1951) and the Prague Spring Competition (1954) and was the first to perform and record the Górecki Symphony No. 3, singing it with many orchestras and conductors. She was President of the Warsaw Music Society for 15 years and sang in a special concert for Pope John Paul II at Castel Gandolfo. She appeared often at the Warsaw Autumn Festival (Warszawska Jesień) concerts and is buried in Powązki cemetery.

[276] "Polish Music at the UN," *New York Times,* 5 March 1971.

[277] "Baton of Mehta Evokes 2 Moods," *New York Times,* 31 October 1970.

Marek Janowski conducting the Hamburg State Opera Orchestra. In 1973, Ładysz recorded Moniuszko's *Halka* in Poland for Harmonia Mundi records. Wiesław Ochman sang as Jontek and Jerzy Semkow conducted a chorus from Kraków and the Radio Orchestra from Katowice. Ładysz has recorded Karol Szymanowski's *Król Roger (King Roger)* and appeared at the Warsaw Autumn (Warszawski Jesień). He has been a recitalist in the United States and often performed with the coloratura Bogna Sokorska, the "Polish Nightingale."[278]

Ładysz also had a film career in Poland, last appearing in the 1999 movie *With Fire and Sword (Ogniem i Mieczem),* his seventh cinematic role. He recorded many popular Polish songs and played Tevye in *Fiddler on the Roof (Skrzypek na dachu).* In 2002, Poland's Minister of Culture presented Ladysz with a Lifetime Achievement Award. In 2008, he was presented with an Honorary Doctorate from Warsaw Conservatory and the following year he was given the Prize of the City of Warsaw.

The Metropolitan Opera Archives
**Kuchta as Senta in Richard Wagner's *Der Fliegende Holländer* (1963)**

---

[278] "2 Warsaw Opera Stars Will Sing," *Oakland Tribune,* 21 February 1967.

**Gladys Kuchta,** whose parents were Polish, was born in 1923 in Chicopee, Massachusetts, but spent the bulk of her life in Germany.[279] She studied in New York at both Mannes College and the Juilliard School before becoming a leading dramatic soprano in Europe. In 1958, she joined the Deutsche Oper in Berlin and remained there for eighteen years. Her Metropolitan Opera debut was in 1961 singing Richard Strauss' *Electra,* and in the next eight years she was to sing eleven more roles in ten other operas with the Met. She appeared in Philadelphia in 1965 with the Philadelphia Lyric Opera Company as Brünhilde in Wagner's *Die Walküre.* The cast included Jon Vickers as Siegmund and Regine Crespin as Sieglinde. The following year, she sang in two concerts with the Philadelphia Orchestra in Wagner and Strauss operatic highlights, and also presented the first peformance in England of Richard Strauss' *Die Frau ohne Schatten.* She performed throughout the world in opera and in recital, and taught in Dusseldorf. She died in Hamburg in 1998.[280]

---

[279] Obituary: Gladys Kuchta. *Independent UK,* 9 November 1998.
[280] "Rosa Olitzka, 76, Once with Opera," *New York Times,* 1 October 1949.

**Marta Wittkowska** came with her family to America from Gdańsk in 1889 when she was five years old and settled in Syracuse, New York.[281] As a young girl, Marta was employed as a maid by a wealthy local family. When they heard her singing, they decided to arrange for her instruction, and she was enrolled at the College of Fine Arts at Syracuse University for two years. She also studied with Emma Thursby in New York City. Further support from another patron allowed her to continue her studies in Milan and Rome. First trained as a coloratura, her voice changed, and she decided to pursue her career as a dramatic soprano.[282] When she returned to America, she was engaged in Philadelphia by the Philadelphia-Chicago Grand Opera Company for several operas in the 1911–12 season. On three successive evenings, she sang Serena in Wolf-Ferrari's *I gioielli della Madonna*, Fricka in Wagner's *Die Walküre*, and Niklausse in Hoffmann's *Les Contes d'Hoffmann*—an uncommon feat by twenty-first century practices.

"Marta Wittkowska's splendid sonorous tones as Waltraute echoed from the mountain heights soaring superior to the sea of sound in the orchestra." Chicago, December, 1911.

She spent eight years with the Royal Opera at Covent Garden in London, first singing Carmen in the Georges Bizet opera, then expanding her repertoire with the dramatic Wagnerian soprano roles of Isolde in Richard Wagner's *Tristan und Isolde* and Ortrud in *Lohengrin*.[283] Back in America, she returned to Syracuse to sing for a Polish-American Bazaar[284] and was engaged by opera companies in St. Louis, Detroit, Boston, and Cincinnati. In New York, she sang another Wagner opera, *Tannhäuser* with Johanna Gadski and Alexander Kipnis. In Chicago, she sang one of the first American performances of the opera *Quo Vadis,* composed by the Frenchman Jean Nouges and based on the novel by the Polish Nobel laureate Henryk Sienkiewicz. In 1927, Wittkowska was again engaged by the Philadelphia Grand Opera Company to sing Amneris in Giuseppe Verdi's *Aida* at the Academy of Music, and also with the Quaker City

---

[281] Lahee (1912) 434–37.

[282] "Marta Wittkowska Now a Soprano," *Syracuse Herald*, 14 September 1913.

[283] "Wittkowska Leads Grand Opera to Columbus Hall," *Circleville* (Ohio) *Herald*, 21 October 1933.

[284] "Marta Wittkowska to Sing at Bazaar," *Syracuse Herald*, 15 October 1920.

Opera Company.[285] She married Arlington Mallery and had a family, settling in Cincinnati for several years, where she had a teaching studio, and together with her husband founded the Columbus (Ohio) Civic Opera Company. Wittkowska retired from the stage in 1937, wrote two novels, composed, and continued to teach. In 1977, at the age of 93, she died at her son's home in Madison, New Jersey.[286]

The Metropolitan Opera Archives, James Heffernan
**Ochman as Turiddu in Pietro Mascagni's *Cavalleria rusticana* (1978)**

The world's most famous Polish tenor since Jan Kiepura is **Wiesław Ochman**, born in Warsaw in 1937. No Polish singer has more recordings to his credit than Ochman (31 by 2011). He sang in San Francisco and Chicago before his engagements with the Metropolitan Opera in New York, and his recorded collaborations from "Live From the Met" with conductors Rostropovich, Abbado, Kubelik, and Karl Böhm provide us with a journal to enjoy his artistry. His 1975 debut in New York in Verdi's *I Vespri Siciliani* was well received by both critics and audiences alike, even those who had heard Richard Tucker, one of the Met's all-time favorites, sing the role of Arrigo for many years. Although his repertoire

[285] "Marta Wittkowska Will Open with Quaker City Opera Company," *Syracuse Herald*, 16 May 1927.
[286] "Mrs. Mallery Dies," *Post Standard* (Syracuse), 25 May 1977.

included Mozart and Italian operas as a lyric tenor, he was to return to the Met for the next sixteen years singing mostly the Slavic roles of Janacek, Tchaikovsky, and Musorgsky. His 1977 performances in *Boris Godunov* were conducted by **Kazimierz Kord.** He shared the stage with **Teresa Żylis-Gara, Teresa Kubiak,** and **Stefania Toczyska,** as well as the Met's most famous: Placido Domingo, Martti Talvela, Elisabeth Soderstrom, Renata Scotto, Paul Plishka, Aage Haugland, James Morris, Justino Diaz, and Sherrill Milnes. Outside of the United States, he recorded Penderecki and Kilar. In 1990, one of his last performance years, he teamed with Leonard Mróz in recording the Szymanowski opera *Król Roger* with Antoni Wit and the Polish State Philharmonic Orchestra for the Naxos label

The Metropolitan Opera Archives, Louis Melancon
**Żylis-Gara as Desdemona in Giuseppe Verdi's *Otello* (1972)**

Soprano **Teresa Żylis-Gara** has had one of the most outstanding careers of any Polish singer in the twentieth century. Born in 1930 in Landwarowa, near Vilnius, she studied in Lwów and in 1953 won the National Competition for Young Singers in Warsaw. Her 1956 operatic debut was in Kraków in Moniuszko's *Halka.* She achieved great fame for the role of Donna Elvira in Mozart's *Don Giovanni,* which she sang at the Paris Opera. She collaborated with the best singers in the best companies in the world, and in 1968, she began a sixteen-year relationship with New York's Metropolitan Opera, singing 232 performances in 24 different roles. In 1970, she sang with Robert Merrill in *La Traviata* to celebrate the baritone's 25th anniversary with the Metropolitan Opera. In 1972, she sang with Raymond Michalski in Verdi's *Otello*. In 1981, Żylis-Gara brought the role of Tatyana in Tchaikovsky's *Eugene Onegin* to Philadelphia, singing with the Philadelphia Opera Company in a production that included Ewa Dobrowska [287] and Leonard Mróz . She recorded works from Bach and Mozart to Strauss and Mahler in both the United States and Europe for EMI, Deutsche Grammophon, Harmonia Mundi, and Erato, as well as on Polish labels. In recital and recording, she included the songs of Chopin, Moniuszko, and Szymanowski. Besides an Honorary Doctorate from the Academy of Music in Wroclaw, Żylis-Gara has received cultural awards from the Polish Government. She has lived in Monaco since 1980.

Metropolitan Opera Archives, Winnie Klotz
**Toczyska as Amneris in Giuseppe Verdi's *Aida* (1994)**

---

[287] Dobrowska appeared again with the Philadelphia Opera Company in 1981. The previous year, she had performed in a very significant Carnegie Hall concert presenting exclusively the music of Szymanowski. The program included the *Stabat Mater, Harnasie,* and the Violin Concerto #1 with Wanda Wiłkomirska as soloist and Tomasz Michalak conducting the New Jersey Symphony.

**Stefania Krzywińska Toczyska,** mezzo-soprano, made her U.S. stage debut in 1979 with the San Francisco Opera in a worldwide live telecast of *La Gioconda* with Renata Scotto and Luciano Pavarotti. Toczyska was born in Grudziądz in 1943. She sang with her mother and grandmother around the house and at Mass but there were no music lessons. It wasn't until she was fifteen years old that anyone paid any serious attention to the talent that lay beneath. She attended the Music School in Toruń, married Romuald Toczyska, a music teacher, and they moved to Gdańsk where she attended the Academy of Music. There she received her first major exposure when asked to sing *Carmen* in Gdańsk at the Baltic State Opera House.

More performances in Gdańsk led to European engagements; then Toczyska performed, toured, and recorded with Riccardo Muti and the Philadelphia Orchestra in connection with a series of CDs of the complete Alexander Scriabin symphonies. In 1981, she made her New York Carnegie Hall debut in Musorgsky's *Khovantschina,* singing the role Marfa with Eve Queler and the Opera Orchestra of New York. Peter Davis of the *New York Times* (March 3, 1981) praised her for capturing so well "all the smoldering sensuality and tortured spirituality of Marfa." In 1988, she made her Metropolitan Opera debut in the same opera, and in the next nine years appeared there in seven different productions,[288] including teaming up with Teresa Żylis-Gara and Leonard Mróz in a recording of the Dvorak *Requiem* with Armin Jordan and the Nouvel Orchestre Philharmonique de Radio France. Recordings with Sir Colin Davis (*Il Trovatore*) and Mstislaw Rostropovich (*War and Peace*) are other highlights in a busy career. Toczyska also recorded the Chopin *Songs* with Janusz Olejniczak.[289]

---

[288] "Opera: Khovanshchina," *New York Times,* 24 February 1988.
[289] "Stefania Toczyska's Operatic Odyssey," *New York Times,* 1 March 1988.

During Martial Law in Poland and the imprisonment of Lech Walesa, the leader of Solidarnosc, the Primate of Poland, Archbishop Jozef Glemp, appealed for Walesa's release. – Warsaw (Reuters) March 14, 1982

The U.S. delegation arrived in Bonn to seek stronger European economic sanctions against the governments of Poland and the Soviet Union for the imposition of Martial Law. - Bonn (AP) March 14, 1982

During this time in the early 1980s when Poland was under Martial Law, the Warsaw Grand Opera staged a production of Verdi's *Il Trovatore*. When the basso, Leonard Andrzej Mróz came onto the stage of the Teatr Wielki, a group of Solidarność activists interrupted the performance with whistling, clapping, and coughing. Mróz had performed at a Polish-Soviet Friendship concert the previous month, and he was accused of collaborating with the military regime. Although the performance continued, the protesters succeeded in drawing attention to this period of hateful subjugation of their freedom.[290]

**Courtesy of Mróz**

---

[290] "Prelate Seeks Walesa's Release," *New York Times,* 14 March 1982.

**Leonard Andrzej Mróz** was born in Warsaw in 1947. At the age of five, he began playing the piano and at seventeen began studying singing. During his studies at the Chopin Academy of Music in Warsaw, he won first prize in 1969 at the Stanislaw Moniuszko National Competition in Wrocław. At the International Vocal Competition in Munich the following year he won a prize as the youngest participant. He made his operatic debut singing Zbigniew in Moniuszko's *Straszny Dwór (Haunted Manor)* at the Teatr Wielki and went on to perform throughout the world during his career. In 1978, he recorded with Mstislav Rostropovich and the London Philharmonic Orchestra the Shostakovich opera *Lady Macbeth of Minsk.*[291] In 1981, he joined Stefania Toczyska in their New York debuts singing Musorgsky's *Khovanshchina* at Carnegie Hall.[292] That same year, he sang Prince Gremin in Tchaikovsky's *Eugene Onegin* with the Philadelphia Opera Company. This was a Metropolitan Opera production in Philadelphia, and he was joined by one of their divas, Teresa Żylis-Gara, as well as Ewa Dobrowska. The following year, he joined Stefania Toczyska and Teresa Żylis-Gara in a recording of Dvorak's *Requiem* with Armin Jordan and the Nouvel Orchestre Philharmonique de Radio France.[293] He recorded Szymanowski's *Król Roger* with Karol Stryja and the Polish National Radio Orchestra for Marco Polo records; the character of Jontek was sung by Wiesław Ochman. With Ewa Podleś' husband, Jerzy Marchwinski, he recorded the songs of Musorgsky and Rachmaninoff and a 1992 series entitled "Music From Six Continents." He recorded an album entitled "Viennese Modern Masters" and one of "Russian Orthodox Church Songs" with Nicolai Gedda. In 1994, he made his conducting debut with the Wrocław Philharmonic and began a teaching tenure at the Academy of Music there.

"The best singing of the evening. . . a real basso cantante, with a smooth voice of unusual size and creamy texture." In 1964, at the first American performance of a concert version of Donizetti's *Maria Stuarda*, that was how **Raymond Michalski** was described by the *New York Times* music

---

[291] EMI Classics CMS 5677762.
[292] "Opera: Khovanshchina," *New York Times*, 24 February 1988.
[293] Erato STU 71430.

critic Harold Schonberg.[294] One month later, Michalski debuted with the Metropolitan Opera in Verdi's *Aida* under Zubin Mehta to further praise from Schonberg. A career that began principally in Philadelphia was at last receiving important recognition.

The Metropolitan Opera Archives, Louis Melancon
**Michalski as Monterone in Giuseppe Verdi's *Rigoletto* (1968)**

Michalski was born in Bayonne, New Jersey, in 1933 and attended the Mannes School of Music in New York, studying with Rosalie Miller.[295] In 1958, while Michalski was still a young singer, Eugene Ormandy engaged him for a Verdi program with the Philadelphia Orchestra in a special pension concert. The following year, the Philadelphia Grand Opera at the Academy of Music engaged him to sing Nourabad in Georges Bizet's *Les pêcheurs de perles,* followed by Giuseppe Verdi's *Aida* in the role of the King. In 1963, for the Philadelphia Opera Society, he joined Joan Sutherland, Nicolai Gedda, and Justino Diaz in a concert performance of

---

[294] Harold Schonberg, "Opera: 'Maria Stuarda,'" *New York Times,* 17 November, 1964.
[295] Jason McVicker on Raymond Michalski, http://listserv.bccls.org/ cgi-bin/wa?A3=ind0003A&L=OPERA-L&E=7bit&P=514646&B=-- &T=text%2Fplain;%20charset=US-ASCII, accessed September 12, 2014.

Vincenzo Bellini's *I Puritani* at the Academy of Music. Two years later, he was singing for the Metropolitan Opera, and before his eleven-year career at the Met ended, he had sung 32 different roles in 301 performances. After his debut in *Aida*, he sang in the world premiere performances of *Anthony and Cleopatra* by the Philadelphia composer Samuel Barber. These performances were not only the premiere of the work but also the grand opening in New York City of one of that city's most famous cultural spaces: Lincoln Center.

Each year Michalski was asked to add more roles of greater prominence to his repertoire, and he collaborated with all of the Met's leading stars: Corelli, Tebaldi, Merrill, Arroyo, Moffo, Kirsten, Talvela, Caballe, Verrett, Tucker, Flagello, Elias, Diaz, McCracken, Vickers, Bergonzi, and Guarrera. He also sang major roles with the Chicago Lyric and San Francisco operas with Tito Gobbi and Leontyne Price, and continued to appear in Philadelphia, including a Mozart *Marriage of Figaro* with the Polish conductor Stanisław Skrowaczewski.

Michalski appeared with many other opera companies in the United States, but unfortunately is only represented on one recording, Handel's *Rinaldo* for RCA. He did participate, however, in numerous Saturday afternoon radio broadcasts *Live From the Met.*

Peter G. Davis wrote in The New Grove Dictionary of American Music: "In terms of vocal endowment, technical security and longevity, he was unequaled among baritones of his generation at the Metropolitan."

The Metropolitan Opera Archives, Sedge LeBlang
**Merrill as Figaro in Gioacchino Rossini's** *il Barbieri de Siviglia* (1955)

His subject was **Robert Merrill,** the great American baritone who was born in Brooklyn in 1917 and who sang with the Metropolitan Opera from 1945 to 1976. Merrill's parents, Abraham Milstein and Lillian Balaban, were wed through an arranged marriage in the Warsaw Ghetto. In the United States, they changed their name to Miller, and their son was born as Moishe Miller. His name was changed again to Morris Miller, and he went by the name of Merrill Miller when he sang on the radio and entertained at the summer resorts of the Catskill Mountains ("Borscht Belt"). Finally, he adopted the name **Robert Merrill** before becoming the Met's leading baritone following the death of Leonard Warren in 1960. He sang virtually every baritone role in the Met's repertoire in 769 performances. He performed for Presidents Roosevelt, Truman, Eisenhower, and Kennedy and sang in nine different programs of operatic highlights with the Philadelphia Orchestra. In 1981 after he had retired from the Metropolitan Opera, he received the University of Pennsylvania's "Glee Club Award of Merit" for his accomplishments to the world of music. After his retirement, he would return to the Borscht Belt to sing on Jewish holidays. He loved baseball, especially the New York Yankees, and beginning in 1969, he regularly sang the "The Star-Spangled Banner" on Opening Day at Yankee Stadium. Merrill died at his home in New Rochelle, N.Y., in 2004—during the first game of that fall's World Series.[296]

Courtesy of Robert Witt

**Anastasja (Nadja) Witkowska** was born in 1928 in Detroit. Her father's family arrived in America from Gdańsk, opened a mens' clothing business, and helped found the St. Josaphat Parish in Detroit. Nadja went to New York City and studied at the Juilliard School. This lyric soprano became a mainstay of the New York City Opera in the 1950s and 1960s; her debut with the City Opera was as Gilda in Verdi's *Rigoletto*. Nadja performed Carl Orff's *Carmina Burana* at the City Opera many times, but also with the Philadelphia Orchestra in 1963 with Hans Schwieger, and again in 1971 with Rafael Frühbeck de Burgos. Beginning in 1972, she sang Gilda in *Rigoletto* for two seasons with the New York City Opera, and a few years later the Queen of the Night in *Die Zauberflöte*, as well as *Die Entführung aus dem Serail* and *La Traviata*. The 1954 production of Mozart's *Abduction* was broadcast by NBC Television. In 1963, she sang

---

[296] "Robert Merrill, a Favorite at the Met for 30 Years, Is Dead at 87," *New York Times,* 26 October 2004.

the first performance of Benjamin Britten's *Midsummer Night's Dream* at the New York City Opera and three years later sang the complete Mendelssohn version of the Shakespeare drama with William Steinberg and the New York Philharmonic. In the summer of 1964, she was heard at the Santa Fe Opera in performances of *Rigoletto*, *La bohème*, and *L'Enfant et les Sortilèges*. Performing Handel's *Messiah* with the Philadelphia Orchestra in three successive seasons added to this most varied career.

On New York's Central Park Mall, she sang Bizet's *Les Pêcheurs de Perles* with the Naumburg Symphony, and for a 1966 NBC telecast from St. Patrick's Cathedral, she sang Poulenc's *Gloria*. In 1971, a special highlight to her career occurred when the Metropolitan Opera engaged her for Lucia in Donizetti's *Lucia di Lammermoor*, joining George Shirley as Edgardo in three performances. In that same Met season, she also sang Marguerite in Gounod's *Faust*. When a Toscanini-Stokowski Memorial concert was held in New York City at St. Patrick's Cathedral on December 4, 1977, Witkowska was soloist with the Metropolitan Opera Orchestra and choirs from St. Patrick's and SS. Peter and Paul's Cathedral (Philadelphia). Two years later, when Pope John Paul II visited New York City and held Mass at St. Patrick's Cathedral, Witkowska sang in the Polish language for the occasion.[297] In 1983, she was honored back home as Woman of the Year in Orchard Lake, Michigan, near Detroit. She continued to reside in New York City after her retirement.

In 1964, when William Procacci campaigned for election to the New Jersey State Senate from Camden, just across the Delaware River from Philadelphia, he depended upon his wife, Rita, to enlist the support of the local Polish-American community—to add to his connections with the Italian community. Through her, he had already become a member of the Polish-American Club. Now he could count on her full-time help because she was retiring, a well-known soprano who had been a member of the New York City Opera and had made many appearances in Philadelphia with a variety of opera companies.[298]

---

[297] Basile (2010) 221.

[298] "Procacci and Cahill Seek Ethnic Votes in First District," *New York Times*, 29 September 1964.

THE COSMOPOLITAN
OPERA COMPANY
SEVENTEENTH SEASON

*Presents*

"CARMEN"

RITA KOLACZ as CARMEN

JUNE 19, 1948

ACADEMY OF MUSIC — PHILADELPHIA

Courtesy of author

**Rita Kolacz,** had a varied and successful singing career for nearly twenty years, performing with some of America's best-known artists. In 1947, as a soprano with Philadelphia's Cosmopolitan Opera Company, she first performed lesser roles in *Il Trovatore, Rigoletto,* and *Carmen.* The following year, she secured the lead role in *Carmen* and went on to sing Leonora di Vargas in *La Forza del Destino* and Suzel in the seldom performed *L'Amico Fritz* of Pietro Mascagni. She sang in other little-known operas: *Lord Byron's Love Letter* by Rafaello de Banfield and *L'Oracolo* by Franco Leoni with the Philadelphia Civic Opera Company.

Kolacz was noticed by Eugene Ormandy who engaged her for his 1953 performances of Mahler Symphony No. 2 at Philadelphia's Academy of Music and New York's Carnegie Hall. He also engaged her for the Philadelphia and New York performances of Beethoven's Symphony No. 9. In 1960, at the Berkshire Music Festival in Lenox, Massachusetts, she sang the world premiere of *The Barrier* by Jan Meyerowitz. It was staged by Boris Goldowsky, longtime Curtis Institute of Music faculty member, and featured George Shirley and Sherrill Milnes.[299] In 1958, she debuted with New York's City Opera under Music Director Julius Rudel and sang both in New York and on tour with them as Countess Almaviva in Mozart's *The Marriage of Figaro.* In 1964 she retired with her husband in Camden.

**Patryk Wróblewski** (b. 1956), baritone, was Grand Prize Winner in the first Rosa Ponselle International Voice Competition and a winner in the Luciano Pavarotti International Competition. This led to performances in the 1986–1987 season of the Chicago Lyric Opera singing in *La Gioconda, Katya Kabanova, Un ballo in maschera,* and *La bohème.* In 1990, he debuted with the Opera Company of Philadelphia in Rossini's *La gazza ladra.* The following year, he made his debut with the New York City Opera singing *I Pagliacci.* For the next five seasons, he sang the operas of Verdi, Puccini, Strauss, Weill, and Rihm at the Santa Fe Opera and recorded Argento's *Casanova's Homecoming* for Newport Classics. In 2004, he sang Umberto Giordano's little-known opera, *La Cena Delle Beffe,* with the Teatro Grattacielo at Alice Tully Hall. He stopped singing professionally, however, and pursued his ambition to become a nurse, working in Texas.

Courtesy of Indiana University Jacobs School of Music, Bloomington

---

[299] "Music: Student Talent," *New York Times,* 5 August, 1980.

For twenty years, **Teresa Kubiak** was one of the world's foremost full-voiced spinto sopranos. Her career was highlighted by singing with the best artists in the world, important appearances in Europe, and a brilliant fourteen years at the Metropolitan Opera in New York. She was born in Łódź in 1937, studied there with Olga Olgina, and made her operatic debut at the Łódź Opera, singing the role of Halka in the Moniuszko opera of the same name. She was then engaged for the Warsaw Opera. She first appeared in America in 1970 at Carnegie Hall in a concert version of the seldom performed opera *Die Königin von Saba* by Goldmark.[300] She had also come to America in that year for a performance of Weber's *Euryanthe* with the Little Orchestra Society at Avery Fisher Hall. In 1971, she appeared at the Glyndebourne Festival in what was to become her signature role, Lisa in Tchaikovsky's *Pique Dame*. The role of Madame Butterfly at Covent Garden was followed by Ellen in Britten's *Peter Grimes* with Jon Vickers.

Kubiak debuted with the Metropolitan Opera in 1973 in Tchaikovsky's *Pique Dame*. "Impressive debut . . . gripping performance" read Donal Henahan's review in the *New York Times* of January 21, 1973. That was the very first performance at the Met of that opera sung in Russian, and **Kazimierz Kord**,[301] in his first season as guest conductor at the Met, led those performances.

---

[300] Available on the Carnegie Hall vintage series # CA344.60.

[301] He would go on to conduct sixty-four performances of six different operas between 1972 and 1988. In Poland, he became principal conductor of the Warsaw Philharmonic in 1977.

Kazimierz Kord courtesy of The Metropolitan Opera Archives

For the first time in 50 years, 1974 saw a presentation of Janacek's opera *Jenufa;* Kubiak was paired again with Jon Vickers and also John Reardon.[302]

In that same year she performed, and made one of the first recordings of Tchaikovsky's *Pique Dame* under Sir Georg Solti at the Royal Opera House in Covent Garden.

In 1975, Kubiak decided to make her home in America, settling in Montclair, New Jersey. She and her husband, Janusz, a cellist, had two daughters, Dorothy and Margaret, but she continued to return for guest appearances at the Łódź Opera.[303]

For the tenth anniversary of the New Jersey Opera, Kubiak appeared in a special performance of *Tosca* with Placido Domingo and Tito Gobbi.[304] Since the Philadelphia Orchestra first introduced the Shostakovich Symphony No. 14 to America in 1971, New York had yet to hear that symphony; with Leonard Bernstein and the New York Philharmonic, Teresa Kubiak performed and recorded the work for Sony.[305] Another historic performance came when she sang Smetana's *Dalibor* with Eve

[302] "Janacek's 1st Major Opera," *New York Times*, 26 September 1985.
[303] "The Kubiaks of Montclair," *New York Times*, 27 March 1977.
[304] "State Opera Raising Its Curtain," *New York Times*, 29 October 1975.
[305] "Music: Death," *New York Times*, 5 December 1976.

Queler and the Opera Orchestra of New York. A new production of Wagner's *Tannhäuser* opened at the Met in 1978 with Kubiak in the lead of Elisabeth, inheriting a role long sung by Leonie Rysanek; Kubiak was a great success.[306] A fundraiser for the Met found her sharing the stage with Jerome Hines, Marilyn Horne, Leontyne Price, Roberta Peters, Sherrill Milnes, Renatta Scotto, and James Morris.[307]

Kubiak sang sixty-two performances at the Met in sixteen different roles. She always clung to her Polish roots and was generous with her support. In 1977, the New Jersey Symphony, under their conductor Tomasz Michalak, held a Polonaise Ball and concert, with the Polish consul general and the cultural affairs attaché at the embassy in attendance. The Janosik Dancers were part of the entertainment, and Kubiak attended, delighting the audience even though she had just sung a performance of *Tosca* at the Met.[308] The following year, the Garden State Arts Center held a Polish Festival as part of their Annual Heritage Series for the support of free concerts, with Kubiak the featured performer. In 1999, long after she left the Metropolitan Opera, she participated in a gala concert for the Polish Cultural Foundation at The Grand Hall on Broadway and a few years later sang in a special Kosciuszko Foundation Chopin concert at Alice Tully Hall at Lincoln Center.

She has held master classes and judged competitions throughout the world. She was awarded an honorary doctorate from the Music Academy of Łódź in 2005. She has served as Professor of Music (Voice) at Indiana University since 1990, and in 2012, she was awarded the Medal Fides Et Ratio from the Warsaw University Association.[309]

## Podleś and family

One of the truly unique voices in the world today belongs to **Ewa Podleś**.[310] Podleś, considered by some followers to be the greatest contralto in the

---

[306] "Tannhäuser," *New York Times*, 15 January 1978.

[307] "Met Opera Stars to Sing," *New York Times*, 26 February 1979.

[308] "A Festive Evening for the State Symphony," *New York Times*, 10 April 1978.

[309] "Teresa Kubiak Recieves Major Polish Award," *Jacobs School of Music Release*, 13 March 2012.

[310] www.podles.pl, accessed September 12, 2014.

world, was born in Warsaw in 1952. Her mother, Juliana, also a Polish contralto she sent her daughter to study at the Warsaw Academy of Music. Podleś went on to win international music prizes in Moscow in 1978 and Rio de Janeiro in 1979. A rare contralto voice of almost unbelievable range with a rich, dark sound, she is able to perform works from Rossini to Mahler. She is also a regular soloist with the Warsaw Chamber Opera.

The Metropolitan Opera Archives

Philadelphians have been fortunate that Podleś has chosen to make frequent appearances as part of the city's Chamber Music Society series. The well-known Polish pianist, Ewa Pobłocka, a laureate of the 1980 Chopin International Piano Competition, has been her partner in Philadelphia, and together they have recorded Chopin, Karłowicz, Moniuszko, Szymanowski, and Lutosławski. Since 2000, Podleś has been touring with the American pianist and first-prize winner of the 1970 Chopin International Piano Competition, Garrick Ohlsson. They have recorded live at Warsaw's Fryderyk Chopin University of Music the songs of Chopin, Prokofiev, and Mussorgsky, and in Wigmore Hall in London they added Szymanowski, Tchaikovsky, and Rachmaninoff to their discography. Podleś' drama in Chopin Songs is especially moving.

She made her debut with the Metropolitan Opera in New York in 1984 in Handel's *Rinaldo* but did not return to the Met for twenty-four years, spending most of her time in Europe. She sang Mahler's *Das Lied von der Erde* with the Philadelphia Orchestra and Verdi's *Don Carlo* with the Philadelphia Opera Company. In 2006, a review of a concert with the Moscow Chamber Orchestra said, "Ewa Podleś can certainly excite an audience. There was so much foot- stomping that the walls seemed to shake."[311] In 2008, in her highly anticipated return to the Metropolitan Opera, she was critically acclaimed for her heart-rending portrayal of the role of Cieca in *La Gioconda* .

Podleś has received Poland's most important prize for cultural activity in music, the Szymanowski Foundation of Polish Culture award, as well as the Order of Polonia Restituta (*Order Odrodzenia Polski*). Podleś has made many recordings ranging from Handel to Ptaszyńska. In 2012, she sang the leading role in Rossini's *Ciro in Babilonia* in an historic new critical edition for the 200th anniversary of the work's premiere. Podleś was honored with the Golden Orpheus - Prestige Prix Lyrique l'Orphée d'Or 2015 - the prize awarded by the Académie du Disque Lyrique in Paris in recognition of her outstanding discographic contribution. When Podleś made her North American debut on July 25, 1982 at the Newport Music Festival in Rhode Island singing a varied program that included Chopin Songs, her accompanist was her husband, **Jerzy Marchwiński.**

Photo: Andrzej Świetlik

---

[311] Thomas Tommasini, "Almost Bringing the House Down with a Rarely Heard Rossini," *New York Times,* 28 February 2006.

Marchwiński was educated at the Chopin Academy of Music, studying piano with Maria Wiłkomirska (see Wanda Wiłkomirska) and chamber music with Kiejstut Bacewicz, brother of Grażyna Bacewicz. An extensive chamber music background has taken him to international music festivals around the world as an official accompanist. He has also collaborated with Maureen Forrester, Regine Crespin, Rita Streich, Teresa Żylis-Gara and violinists Konstanty Kulka and Charles Treger. He is represented on twenty-five recordings and has been in charge of Piano Chamber Music at the Chopin Academy of Music. Podleś and Marchwiński reside in Warsaw. An injury to Marchwiński's right hand ended his performance career, but their daughter, Anna, who has achieved an outstanding career of her own in chamber music and opera coaching, has taken up the role of accompanist for her mother.

Photo: Agnieszka Kłopocka

**Anna Marchwińska** has built a piano career specializing in chamber music. Growing up in Warsaw, she studied at the Warsaw Music University and then continued studies in America at Stanford University and Juilliard, where she also became a vocal coach. She has participated in many festivals around the world and is frequently the vocal coach for the Bregenzer Festpiele in Austria. She lives in Warsaw and is the principal opera coach and head of the music staff at the Teatr Wielki/Opera Narodowa. In 2006,

Anna accompanied Ewa Podleś' solo recital in Philadelphia as part of the Philadelphia Chamber Music Society Series, and has also performed in Carnegie Hall, Alice Tully Hall and the Kennedy Center in Washington, D.C. She has been with the Polish National Opera Company at the Teatr Wielki in Warsaw since 2002.

In the many productions with various opera companies beginning in the 1920s, Walter Grigaitis (see conductors) hired a number of artist-singers for lesser roles, especially in *Aida, Faust,* and the American premier of Mussorgsky's *Khovanschchina*: **Janina Stańska, Thaddeus Górecki, Edward Ryglewicz, Maria Mickita, Philomena** and **Sophia Wysocka, Joseph** and **Valentin Figaniak.** He used some of them in principal roles in the three Moniuszko operas of 1925–28. [312]

The basso, **Valentin Figaniak** (1891–1975), sang in at least two dozen productions in Philadelphia between 1924 and 1938, and he recorded for Victor records with Grigaitis. In 1938 and 1939, his last years of singing in Philadelphia, he performed with the Met's leading tenor, Jan Peerce, in a production of Verdi's *La Traviata*.[313]

## A NEW GOLDEN AGE OF POLISH SINGERS

Since 2006, a number of Polish singers have established themselves in leading roles at the Metropolitan Opera, prompting Eric Myers of *Opera News* to declare in the August 2013 issue that "we may be in a new golden age of Polish singing."

**Mariusz Kwiecień** (b. 1972) from Kraków is a very popular artist. One of the opera world's leading baritones, he is a particular favorite at the Met for his performances of Mozart's *Don Giovanni*. He also has sung the role of the King of Sicily in Szymanowski's *Król Roger* throughout the

---

[312] As of this writing, I can find no biographies of these singers.

[313] Jan Peerce (Joshua Pinus Perelmuth) was born in 1904 on the Lower East Side of Manhattan, New York to Louis and Henya Perelmuth from the Jewish shtetl, Horowetz, Poland. Peerce became one of America's greatest tenors, beginning his operatic career in Philadelphia with the Philadelphia La Scala Opera Company and going on to sing in 347 performances with the Metropolitan Opera Company in New York. He died in 1984 in New Rochelle, New York.

world and recorded it both on CD and DVD with the Paris Opera. "Slavic Heroes," a CD for the Harmonia Mundi label, includes arias from three Moniuszko operas and Szymanowski's opera, and received *Opera News'* "Critic's Choice" designation for 2012. He was also featured on the cover of *Opera News* in September of 2011.

**Piotr Beczała** (b. 1966), a tenor from Czechowice-Dziedzice who made his Met debut in 2006 has also become an international star. He received glowing reviews for his 2010 CD of Slavic arias. The 2012 release of a CD from a Dresden recital prompted the reviewer in *Opera News* to write: "Beczała again works wonders . . . charms the pants off. . ." (July 2012). His recording of Dvorak's *Rusalka* earned him a "Best of the Year Most Valuable Player" from *Opera News* in 2012. He also recorded Szymanowski's *Król Roger* as the shepherd, with Stefania Toczyska as the deaconess and with the Polish National Opera Orchestra under Kacek Kasprsyk from a live broadcast at the Teatr Wielki in 2003. He was featured on the cover of *Opera News* in 2012.[314]

**Paolo Szot** (b. 1969), baritone, has a most interesting background. He was born in Sao Paolo, Brazil to Polish parents who moved there after World War II. At the age of eighteen, he traveled back to Poland by boat for twenty-three days to study dancing at Jagiellonian University in Kraków. A knee injury motivated him to pursue the study of voice, and he began his professional career singing with Śląsk, the Polish National Song and Dance Ensemble. In America, he sang in several productions with NewYork City Opera. In 2008, he made his Broadway debut singing the role of Emile de Becque in *South Pacific*, for which he won a Tony Award, a Theater World Award, and a Drama Desk Award. He debuted at the Met in 2010 in the Shostakovich opera *The Nose*. In January 2013, he was featured on the cover of *Opera News* in connection with a new production of *Die Fledermaus* in which he sang the role of Dr. Falke.

**Andrzej Dobber** (b. 1961), one of Europe's busiest baritones, is from Wiecbork near Kraków. He made his Metropolitan Opera debut in 2007 as Amonastro in Verdi's *Aida*. He also substituted that year for Placido Domingo in *Simon Boccanegra* in Germany under Daniel Barenboim. In 2011, he made one of his thirteen appearances at the Met as Giorgio Germont in *La Traviata*.

---

[314] Scott Barnes, "Peak Form," *Opera News*, September, 2012: 28

Soprano **Adrianne Pieczonka** (b. 1963) made her Met debut in 2004 portraying Lisa in Tchaikovsky's *Queen of Spades*. She sang the 2008 Wagner *Ring* cycle as Sieglinde and recently sang Amelia in Verdi's *Simon Boccanegra* alongside Placido Domingo. All of those operas were also broadcast in HD. A recent recording of Wagner's *Lohengrin* under the directorship of Marek Janowski was reviewed in the October 2012 issue of *Opera News* and described her as "sounding pure and youthful."

Soprano **Aleksandra Kurzak** (b. 1977), born in Wrocław, made her Metropolitan Opera debut in 2004 as Olympia in *Les Contes d'Hoffmann*. Her mother, Jolanta Zmurko, was a successful singer in Poland and her first teacher. Kurzak was a member of the Hamburg Opera before joining the Met and has since sung in all the important opera venues of the world, including the Teatr Wielki in Warsaw. Her CD release for Decca entitled *Gioia* (which includes songs by Stanisław Moniuszko) has been highly acclaimed by the critics. In a 2011 recital at La Scala, she performed the music of eight different Polish composers. Mezzo-soprano Judith Malafronte, writing in *Opera News* (December 2013) praised Kurzak's "masterful technique...... and real musicianship combine in stunning display" at the release of the 2013 CD entitled *Bel Raggio* for Decca Records.

**Edyta Kulczak** (b. 1970), a mezzo-soprano from Sieldce, studied at the Warsaw University of Music before coming to America. She won the Metropolitan auditions in 1999 and has been a frequent artist with the New York Opera, singing 250 performances over a ten-year period.

In 2015, **Amanda Majeski** (b. 1984) became one of the newest additions to the Met's roster of lead singers. Majeska grew up in a "nonmusical" Polish-American family in Chicago, and studied at the Curtis Intitute of Music in Philadelphia. Upon graduation she joined the Lyric Opera Company of Chicago, and was contracted to sing Mieczysław Weinberg's *The Passenger*. She remarked that her parents were really looking forward to hearing her sing in Polish.[315] Her debut with the Metropolitan Opera of New York was in Mozart's *Le Nozze di Figaro* singing the role of Countess Almaviva.

---

[315] F. Paul Driscoll, "Out Late with Amanda Majeski," *Opera News*, March 2015.

Since his 2001 *Carmen* debut in the role of Zuniga at the Metropolitan Opera in New York, basso cantante **Valerian Rumiński** has appeared in twenty-four performances there. Radio and TV broadcasts of Met presentations of *I Puritani* and *Boris Godunov* followed in 2007 and 2011. He then recorded *I Puritani* with Deutsche Grammophon that included Anna Netrebko and John Relyea in the leading roles. Earlier, a Naxos release featured him on a CD, *Night at the Opera*, which also featured other young singers who were making their Met debuts.

Courtesy of Valerian Ruminski

Ruminski was born in Buffalo, N.Y., in 1967. The first of the Ruminskis to arrive in America had been Marcin (Martin) from Dobrzejewice, near Toruń, in 1905. Valerian's early studies took him to the State University of New York at Buffalo. He then attended the Academy of Vocal Arts in Philadelphia, studying with Bill Schuman, teacher of many of the world's great singers, and Louis Quilico, longtime veteran of the Metropolitan Opera. Ruminski went on to receive the Lincoln Center Martin Segal Award and sang in two gala concerts at Lincoln Center after receiving a Richard Tucker Grant.[316] The Marcella Sembrich Prize from the Kosciuszko Foundation was presented to him in New York, and he was to win many

---

[316] Music review, *New York Times*, 16 November 1999.

more competitions and accolades which led to his debut with the New York City Opera in 2000. There he performed the roles of Albert and Brogni in Fromental Halevy's *La Juive* and took those roles to Tel Aviv for performances at the New Israeli Opera. He sang at the 2004 Bard Music Festival as part of "Shostakovich and His World."[317] In 2008, he sang the American premiere of the reconstructed Handel opera *Jupiter in Argos* with the Orchestra of St. Luke's at Avery Fisher Hall.[318]

Ruminski has sung Moniuszko's opera, *Straszny Dwór*, in a production with the Buffalo Philharmonic, and he offers a list of seventy other operas in his repertoire. He is the founder of the Nickel City Opera in Buffalo,[319] and frequently performs at the Marcella Sembrich Museum in Bolton Landing, N.Y. In 1997, he sang in the Marcella Sembrich Voice Competition in Warsaw which was won by the soprano Aleksandra Kurzak, now a Metropolitan Opera favorite. Ruminski and Edyta Kulczak, another favorite of the Met, performed together in New York for the Kosciuszko Foundation's 150th "birthday" concert honoring Marcella Sembrich.[320]

Poland had produced two of the world's most heralded pairs of siblings in the history of opera: Jan and Edward Reszke and Jan and Władysław Kiepura. Would there be another famous pair to compare to them?

## The Ciesinski Family

August Ciesiński came to America in the late nineteenth century and settled in Detroit. He married Frances Bydłowski, and together they had eleven children. One of their sons, Roman Anthony, and his wife, Katherine, did indeed produce one of America's most talented duos in the world of music, but in an environment that one would not have imagined for such extraordinary musicians.

Roman Anthony Ciesinski was born in 1921. He was a World War II war hero who fought in the Battle of the Bulge, survived as a German prisoner of war, and was awarded the Bronze Star and Purple Heart. He

---

[317] Critic's Notebook, *New York Times*, 13 August 2004.
[318] Colligiate Chorale, *New York Times*, 25 April 2008.
[319] Nickel City Opera, *Tonawanda News*, 21 June 2011.
[320] www.valruminski.com/, accessed September 12, 2014.

was an exceptional athlete, enrolled at the University of Delaware, excelled at several sports, and helped the school win the national championship in football in 1947. He coached champion teams in more than one sport and is in the Delaware Sports Hall of Fame—not the typical parent of two musical stars.[321]

The Metropolitan Opera Archives, Winnie Klotz
**Katherine Ciesinski as Niklausse in Jacques Offenbach's *Les Contes d'Hoffman* (1968)**

His oldest daughter, **Katherine Ciesinski**, was born in 1950. She stayed close to home for her education, studying piano and voice and attending Temple University. She then studied at the Curtis Institute with Margaret Harshaw and Dino Yannapolous, who at the time was the head of the Opera Department. By the time she had graduated from Curtis, she had won the Gramma Fischer Award at the Metropolitan Opera National Council auditions, the WGN Auditions of the Air, and first prize in the Geneva International Music Competition. Winning the Philadelphia Orchestra's senior student competition in 1974 rewarded her with a concert

---

[321] www.legacy.com/obituaries/nytimes/obituary.aspx?n=roman-a-ciesinski&pid=152584875, published in *New York Times*, July 17, 2011, accessed September 12, 2014.

of Mozart and Bizet with the Orchestra. This led to many engagements with the Philadelphians under Maestros Ormandy, Ceccato, Leinsdorf, and Penderecki, some taking her to Carnegie Hall. In 1979, she sang the first Philadelphia performance of the Suite from Shchedrin's opera *Not Love Alone* and ten years later sang a New Year's Eve gala with the Orchestra. The previous year, in 1988, Katherine had sung two gala concerts at New York's Metropolitan Opera as a Metropolitan Opera audition winner; she then made her official debut at the Met in *Les Contes d'Hoffmann* in the role of Nicklausse, and sang in later productions of Umberto Giordano's *Andrea Chenier* and Bela Bartok's *Bluebeard's Castle*. In a concert with James Levine, hosted by Beverly Sills for national television, she sang the well-known trio from Richard Strauss' *Der Rosenkavalier* with Kiri Te Kanawa and Kathleen Battle.

The Santa Fe Opera has presented her in repertoire ranging from Claudio Monteverdi to Alban Berg. Surely one of the busiest singers of her day, she brought her mezzo voice to nearly every major musical center in Europe and America. For her recorded performance of Paulina in Tchaikovsky's *Queen of Spades* with Seiji Ozawa and the Boston Symphony (BMG), she received a Grammy nomination. Other recordings include Prokofiev's *War and Peace* with Rostropovich (Erato) and Wagner's *Die Walküre* with Dohnanyi and the Cleveland Orchestra (London/Decca). Her Erato recording of Paul Dukas' *Ariane et Barbe-bleue* won a Gran Prix du Disque in 1984; she also participated in the first digital recording of Handel's *Messiah* (RCA*)*.

Contemporary music is still a part of her repertoire. She has performed with groups such as the Ensemble Intercontemporain in Paris and sung the music of Elliott Carter, Mark Adamo, Paul Nelson, and Tod Machover. Katherine partnered with her sister, Kristine, in a program of Songs by Ned Rorem. The *Renard* Stravinsky Collection (vol. 7) for Naxos includes Stravinsky songs interpreted by Ciesinski.[322] She has been a sought-after teacher throughout the United States for lectures and master classes, and remains a judge for the regional Metropolitan Opera Auditions. She joined

---

[322] Igor Stravinsky, *Histoire du Soldat Suite* / Renard (Craft) (Stravinsky, Vol. 7) 8.557505 Naxos.
Website of the Eastman School of Music, www.esm.rochester.edu/faculty/ ciesinski_katherine/, accessed September 12, 2014.

the faculty of the Eastman School of Music in 2008, after having been on the faculty of the University of Houston. She frequently participates in the International Symposium on Care of the Professional Voice held in Philadelphia and has been elected to the American Academy of Singing.

Photo: Jayme Feary

**Kristine Ciesinski,** born in 1952, has enjoyed the same kind of stellar career as her sister. Kristine also won first prize at the Geneva International Music Competition, just one year after Catherine. She embarked on a career of considerable importance in the opera world of Europe. In Richard Strauss's *Salome,* she had a long tenure in the title role, singing eighteen different productions, principally at the Bayerische Staatsoper in Munich, the Teatro Carlo Fenice in Florence, the Dresden Oper, the English National Opera in London, and the Bellas Artes in Mexico City. She also performed the principal role of Marie in Alban Berg's *Wozzeck* many times throughout Europe as well as at the Teatro Colon in Buenos Aires. The Peter Mussbach production of *Wozzeck* from Frankfurt is available on DVD. She also sang in the BBC film *The Secret Life of Alban Berg.*

Performing often in England, she sang the role Emilia Marty in Leos Janacek's *The Markopoulos Case* at Glyndebourne and joined Sir Simon

Rattle with the City of Birmingham Orchestra in Bela Bartok's *Bluebeard's Castle*. She has performed in Warsaw at the Teatr Wielki, singing Sieglinde in Wagner's *Die Walküre*. This 1988–89 undertaking was part of Poland's first postwar production of the complete Wagner *Der Ring des Nibelungen*. She went on to tour Europe with the Polish National Opera, performing throughout the continent including appearances in Moscow and St. Petersburg as Lady Macbeth in Verdi's *Macbeth*. In Karol Szymanowski's *Król Roger*, she sang the principal role of Roxana in a production in Bremen for the Polish film director Krzysztof Zanussi.

Her early successes in America helped to set up her triumphs in Europe. In Philadelphia after the Geneva Competition, she sang *The Beggar's Opera* (John Gay/Benjamin Britten) with the Pennsylvania Opera Theater and *Rumpelstiltskin* (Joseph Baber) with the Opera Company of Philadelphia. She often sang with her sister, Katherine; they performed together in the Schubert *Mass No. 3* in B flat (D234) at Carnegie Hall and in numerous duo recitals. They were fortunate that their voices blended so well. They performed at the Chamber Music Society of Lincoln Center, Alice Tully Hall, the 92nd St. Y. and the Metropolitan Museum of Art in New York. In Philadelphia, they performed at the Walnut Street Theater with the Concerto Soloists. In 1984, in an historic concert held at the Newport Music Festival in Rhode Island, Kristine sang Chopin songs accompanied by Halina Czerny-Stefańska, winner of the 1949 Chopin International Piano Competition, in her first appearance in America.

Kristine Ciesinski now lives in the United Sates. She was a faculty member of Brigham Young University-Idaho, while also directing the Idaho Falls Opera Theater; in 2011-12 she was a faculty member of Florida State University. She also became a glider pilot/instructor.

Photo: Joe Jenson

The soprano **Susan Narucki** is one of the leading interpreters of contemporary vocal music in the world, having presented over one hundred premieres in opera and concert. She received a Grammy and a Cannes award in 2000 for George Crumb's *Star-Child* ("Best Contemporary Composition") and in 2002 was nominated in the "Best Classical Vocal Performance" category for Elliott Carter's *Tempo e Tempo*. In 2011, she recorded Songs of Charles Ives for New World Records (80680-2).

Narucki was born in 1957. Her grandfather came from Poland and landed in Boston before settling in Bellville, New Jersey. Her father was a silversmith for Tiffany's, and it was not always clear where Susan's interests would take her. At Syracuse University, she majored in film-making and photography. It was when she attended the San Francisco Conservatory, however, that a life of singing became her future. There are few major cities in the United States where she has not performed. She appeared in Philadelphia with the Network for New Music, in New York with the Lincoln Center Chamber Music Society, and with James Levine in the MET Chamber Ensemble. Narucki appeared with the Contemporary Music Players in San Francisco and at the Santa Fe Chamber Music Festival, and has also sung with the Los Angeles Philharmonic (under

Esa-Pekka Salonen), Cleveland Orchestra (Pierre Boulez), and the San Francisco Symphony (Michael Tilson Thomas). She performed and filmed with the Netherlands Opera and sang in Warsaw with the Argo/ Schoenberg Ensemble. There seem to be no limits to her discovery of new music ventures and vital interpretations of exceptional musicianship. She is currently Professor of Music at the University of California at San Diego.

# C. VIOLINISTS

Nicolo Paganini (1782–1840) is often admired as the greatest violinist in the history of the instrument. Chopin and his teacher, Josef Elsner, both heard him perform in Warsaw and became lifelong admirers.[323] Paganini played ten concerts in Warsaw including the coronation of the Russian Tsar at the Warsaw Cathedral. During that period, Poland also produced a native son considered a superstar, **Karol Lipiński**.

Courtesy of Karol Lipiński Music Academy, Wrocław

Lipiński was born in Radzyń, near Lublin, in 1790, and was called the "greatest violinist of the nineteenth century until Paganini," and Poland's most important musician before Chopin. Paganini and Lipiński were friends, and on several occasions played concerts together in Italy and Poland.[324] They were also considered competitors. Paganini, when asked who the greatest violinist was, he replied, "I can't say who the greatest is, but the second is definitely Lipiński."[325] However, it is also clear that they were lifelong admirers of one another.[326] Lipiński also was a composer, arranger, and conductor in Lwów. He died on his estate in Urlow in 1861.

---

[323] Farga (1952) 169.
[324] Pulver (1936) 100–101, 178–79.
[325] Farga, 195.
[326] Sheppard (1979) 199, 388.

Robert Schumann and Henryk Wieniawski both dedicated compositions to him, and the Karol Lipiński University of Music in Wrocław was named in his honor. The International Competition for Young Violinists in honour of Karol Lipiński and Henry Wieniawski takes place in Lublin every three years. The extraordinary 1715 Stradivarius violin known as the "Lipinski" is today owned and performed on by the American violinist Frank Almond.

It has also been said that the greatest violinist after Paganini was **Henryk Wieniawski**. Leopold Auer, the teacher of Heifetz, Elman, and Milstein, reminiscing about the Wieniawski he had known and heard fifty years earlier, said:

> Wieniawski was one of the greatest masters of his instrument in any age. He fascinated his audience with an altogether individual talent, and he was as entirely different from any of the other violinists of his day in outward appearance as he was in his manner of playing. Since his death no violinist has seemed able to recall him.[327]

Archives of Musical Society of Musical Studies of Henryk Wieniawski, Poznań

Wieniawski was born in 1835 in Lublin and died too soon at the age of 47, having suffered ill health for a number of years. He came into a musical

---

[327] Schwarz (1983), 225.

family: his mother was a professional pianist; an uncle was a musician living in Paris and friend of Chopin. He entered the Paris Conservatoire at the age of eight and at age eleven received the First Violin Prize (Premier Prix de Violon). He had also began composing, and became a travelling virtuoso, touring at the age of sixteen with his fourteen-year-old pianist brother, **Józef.** In 1860, Anton Rubinstein convinced the twenty-five-year old Wieniawski to move to St. Petersburg where Rubenstein was reestablishing a Conservatory of Music. Wieniawski lived and taught there for twelve years and helped to develop a school of violin-playing which his successor, Leopold Auer, could then build upon. For two years starting in 1872, he toured the United States with Rubinstein. They appeared in Philadelphia at the Academy of Music as part of a grueling tour that consisted of 215 concerts in 60 cities. The Philadelphia appearance was billed as "The Greatest Concert Combination on Record."[328] He returned to Europe and took a position at the Brussels Conservatory after the death of Henri Vieuxtemps. Although there was much that he disliked about the Russian state and its oppression of Poland,[329] he returned frequently; he died in Moscow in 1880, but is buried in Powązki cemetery in Warsaw (see Józef Adamowski).

Wieniawski's catalogue of compositions numbers about fifty, many of them shorter works, but the violin concertos and etudes are required playing for all aspiring professional violinists. Many of those compositions display his nationality: mazurkas, kujawiaks, polonaises, and a rondo alla polacca. The International Henryk Wieniawski Violin Festival Competition, the oldest music competition in the world, is held every five years in Poznań. It began in Warsaw in 1935, the one-hundredth anniversary of his birth. **Adam** Wieniawski, nephew of Henryk and Józef was Director of the Chopin Music School in Warsaw at that time.[330]

In Central and Eastern Europe, the late nineteenth century saw the beginning of the greatest emergence of brilliant violinists the world had ever

---

[328] Armstrong (1884) 269. See also Marion (1984) 87.

[329] Julian, another brother, took part in the failed 1863 Polish Uprising against the Czar.

[330] Schwarz (1983) 218–226. Maria Pilatowicz, "Polish Composers: Henryk Wieniawski," *PMC* 1999. www.usc.edu/dept/polish_music/composer/wieniawski._html, accessed September 12, 2014.

heard. From the street musicians and klezmer bands of Warsaw,[331] whose musicians could not even read music, to the privately trained musicians from a culture that respected their talents, great young players were always emerging. The everchanging political situation of Poland, however, made it difficult for the "systematic cultivation of musical art";[332] musicians traveled to Berlin, Vienna, or St. Petersburg to expand their training. Polish and Russian violinists then began to arrive in America, where they were to dominate the performance landscape of this country and much of the world for many years to come. Almost all these violinists were Jewish. No instrument in the Jewish culture held such prominence as the violin for it was the best choice to communicate the sorrow and yearning of the cantor. Being a first-class violinist was a means of escaping the subjugation of the czars, a path to a new life. These musicians often went to other European countries first, to make a reputation for themselves before coming to America. Once in America, almost all made it their lifelong home.

Leopold Auer, to whom Wieniawski passed the violin leadership at the St. Petersburg Conservatory, produced the greatest group of Russian violinists ever to come to America. His teaching confrere in Berlin, Carl Flesch, also brought to America an amazing group of Polish prodigies.

Leopold Auer and Carl Flesch were Hungarian Jews by birth and both taught in their later years at the Curtis Institute of Music in Philadelphia.

**Carl Flesch** was born in 1873. He experienced modest success as a soloist and chamber player, but it was his brilliant teaching, launched at the beginning of the twentieth century, to which so many young future Polish stars gravitated. During his teaching tenure in Berlin, Flesch's Polish "prodigies" included Stefan Frenkel, Szymon Goldberg, Bronisław Gimpel, Roman Totenberg, Henryk Szeryng, and Ida Haendel.[333] Most of these had begun their studies with **Mieczysław Michałowicz**, a valued teacher

---

[331] David Arben, a violinist born in Warsaw in 1927 who is included in this book, tells of hearing violinists all over the city during his childhood. Even his father's barber had a violin hanging on the wall and would pull it down to play at every opportunity. Carl Kleis, "David Arben Interview," *Philadelphia Orchestra Archives*, 14 October 1998.

[332] Van der Straetan (1933) 378.

[333] Schwarz (1983) 343–350.

in Warsaw, but each traveled to Berlin to continue under the tutelage of Flesch. All became international headliners, and most ended their careers in the United States. Add to this group the pupils Flesch taught while at the Curtis Institute for several years (1924–1928) and this violin teacher produced "perhaps the most important body of executant-pedagogues in existence" (Yehudi Menuhin, in his Preface to Flesch's book, *Violin Fingering*).

In 1928, at the age of 84, **Leopold Auer** followed Carl Flesch at the Curtis Institute (1928–1930). Auer was born in 1845 and came to America in 1918 after teaching at the St. Petersburg Conservatory for nearly fifty years. He was succeeded at the Conservatory by Paweł Kochański, just as Auer, himself, had succeeded Henryk Wieniawski. The Russian Revolution of 1917 scattered teachers and students alike to foreign lands, but already his former students, Jascha Heifetz, Mischa Elman, Efrem Zimbalist, and Nathan Milstein had established themselves in America. His Warsaw-born student Alexander Hilsberg (see Stokowski) had secured the concertmaster chair with the Philadelphia Orchestra by the time that Auer immigrated. Hilsberg eventually inherited Auer's seat on the faculty at Curtis.[334]

## THE POLISH PRODIGIES

**Stefan Frenkel** (see **Concertmasters of the Metropolitan Orchestra** for photo), born in Warsaw in 1902, was the oldest of this group of Carl Flesch's Polish students. As with all of these stellar artists, his career took him around the world. After Berlin studies with Flesch, Frenkel joined violinist Szymon Goldberg (see below) as co-concertmaster of the Dresden Philharmonic. He appeared as soloist with that orchestra and in Poland. He was a close and admiring friend of Kurt Weill and performed the premieres of Weill's Concerto for Violin and Wind Orchestra and his Concerto for Violin and String Orchestra. Hindemith, Bartok, Toch, and

---

[334] When in 1926 he officially became the "oldest young citizen" of this country, Auer was heralded at a reception in New York City by an entourage that included Józef Hofmann, Aleksander Lambert, Ignace Friedman, Sigismond Stojowski, Ignacy Paderewski, Paweł Kochański, and Walter Damrosch. "Prof. Auer Celebrates American Citizenship," *New York Times,* 13 December 1926.

two other Poles, Tansman and Rathaus dedicated sonatas and chamber works to him. He also toured the Soviet Union with Bela Bartok.

Frenkel is well known for his arrangement of Weill's *"der Dreigroschenoper" (The Threepenny Opera)* for violin and piano. He taught at the Hochschule fur Musik in Berlin but had to relinquish that position with the rise of the Nazis. Frenkel then became concertmaster of the L'Orchestre de la Suisse Romande in Geneva, his last post in Europe. In 1936, he moved to New York City and became concertmaster of the Metropolitan Opera for four years, spending summers as concertmaster of the Santa Fe Opera and Rio de Janeiro Opera. He taught privately in the Philadelphia area and at Princeton University for four years. In 1944, he became a U.S. citizen, and he died in New York City in 1979.[335]

University of Adelaide Archives' Series 312, Maude Puddy Collection

**Szymon Goldberg** taught violin at Curtis late in his life.[336] He was born in Włocławek in 1909 and first studied with Mieczysław Michałowicz in Warsaw. His family moved to Berlin in order for Szymon to become a student of Carl Flesch. His performance debut was in Warsaw at the age of twelve, and he became concertmaster of the Berlin Philharmonic under

---

[335] J. S. Locketz, "In Memoriam: Stefan Frenkel," *Journal of the Violin Society of America*, vol. 5, no. 1 (Winter, 1978–79): 162–163.

[336] Schwarz (1983) 343–344.

Wilhelm Furtwängler at the age of twenty. At that time, he also became part of a trio with Emanuel Feuermann and Paul Hindemith. In 1934, however, the orchestra was obliged to dismiss all Jewish players, and he came to America.

Goldberg made his Carnegie Hall debut in 1938 and toured with pianist Lili Kraus. While on a tour of Asia during World Was II, he was taken prisoner and interned by the Japanese in Java for three years. Resuming his career, he settled in the United States, became a citizen in 1953, and for fifteen years taught in the summers at the Aspen Music School. At the same time, he also started a new passion: Music Director and conductor of the Netherlands Chamber Orchestra (1955–1979). He led this chamber orchestra on extensive tours of Europe and the United States. In 1967, he performed the Brahms Violin Concerto with the Philadelphia Orchestra at the Saratoga Performing Arts Center in Saratoga, New York. At the age of 89, he took over leadership of the New Japan Philharmonic in Tokyo and married the Japanese pianist, Miyoko Yamane. They made their home in Philadelphia from 1981, when he began to teach at the Curtis Institute, until his death (in Japan) in 1993.[337]

---

[337] Margaret Campbell, "Obituary: Szymon Goldberg," *Independent.co.uk*, 16 August 1993.

Courtesy of Totenberg family

One of the most respected violinists in the last 75 years, **Roman Totenberg** was born in Łódź in 1911 and died in Boston at the age of 101 having been on the faculty of Boston University for many years.[338] In 1981, he was chosen Artist Teacher of the Year by the American String Teachers Association. As a child prodigy he had studied in Warsaw with Michałowicz and, at age eleven, debuted with the Warsaw Philharmonic.[339] After receiving a gold medal at the Chopin Conservatory, Totenberg went to Berlin to also study with Carl Flesch (who had recently returned from Philadelphia). He won the Mendelssohn prize there with Arturo Balsam in 1931. At the Paris Conservatoire, his studies continued with Jacques Thibaud and Alfred Cortot, and then made his British and American debuts in 1935. He toured South America with Artur Rubinstein and spent two years touring with Karol Szymanowski as his accompanist. He eventually played in every major city of the world, soloed with most of the world's great orchestras, and performed at the White House for Franklin and Eleanor Roosevelt. Totenberg performed in Philadelphia, accompanied by Oscar Levant,

---

[338] Bruce Weber, "Roman Totenberg, Violinist and Teacher, Dies at 101," *New York Times,* 8 May 2012.
[339] Schwarz (1983) 347.

and again years later for a 1986 benefit at the city's Ethical Society. He introduced the Penderecki *Capriccio* for Violin and Orchestra to Boston and also the Szymanowski Violin Concerto No. 1 to that city under Pierre Monteux.

He performed with many of the Polish maestros: Artur Rodziński, Grzegorz Fitelberg, Witold Rowicki, Jan Krenz, and Antoni Wit. With Leopold Stokowski he performed a specialty of his, the Violin Concerto by Samuel Barber. In 1978, he became the Director of the Longy School of Music in Boston. In 1998, Totenberg visited Poland once again to give a master class and in the year 2000 was awarded the Order of Merit of the Republic of Poland. His daughter Nina is familiar to all who have listened to National Public Radio since 1975.

The New York Philharmonic Leon Levy Digital Archives, Jacques Aubert-Phillips

In 1918, the brilliant violinist **Henryk Bolesław Serek (Szeryng)** was born in Żelazowa Wola, the birthplace of Chopin.[340] Later in life, he made his home in Mexico, and became a naturalized citizen there in 1946. He first studied piano with his mother in Poland, but when his interest in the

---

[340] Henryk Szeryng website, www.henrykszeryng.net/, accessed September 12, 2014.

violin emerged, Bronisław Huberman encouraged the family to take him to Berlin to study with Carl Flesch.

Szeryng spoke no less than seven languages and, after the invasion of Poland in World War II, enlisted in the Polish Army in exile. He joined the staff of General Sikorski, the head of the Polish Government in London, to help relocate refugees escaping to Latin America. They found homes for 4,000 Polish refugees in Mexico in 1941. In addition, Szeryng performed 300 concerts for Allied troops throughout Asia, Africa, Europe, and America.

Following the war, he was invited to organize the string department at the University of Mexico where he spent the next ten years. When he and Artur Rubinstein rediscovered each other, however, they convinced impresario Sol Hurok to introduce them once again to the international scene and their touring began. Szeryng was a frequent visitor to Philadelphia, playing many concerts over twenty years with the Philadelphia Orchestra directed by conductors from Ormandy to Skrowaczewski. On one of those occasions, he performed the Bach Concerto for Two Violins with David Arben, the Orchestra's assistant concertmaster, also a native of Poland. Szeryng conducted those performances from his soloist's position. The Szymanowski Violin Concerto No. 2 also had a performance with Szeryng and the Philadelphians in 1981. The accolades for Szeryng's many recordings include two Grammy and two Grand Prix du Disque awards. He is generally regarded as Flesch's greatest student.[341]

---

[341] Schwarz (1983) 348–50.

Archives of Musical Society of Musical Studies of Henryk Wieniawski, Poznań

The youngest of this group of Flesch's Polish prodigies is **Ida Haendel**, born in 1923 in Chełm. She took up the violin at the age of three and a half and studied with Estera Greenbaum Spiro. At age seven, she was admitted to the Warsaw Conservatory to study with Mieczysław Michałowicz. After winning first prize in the 1933 Bronisław Huberman Competition in Warsaw, she was awarded a prize in the very first Wieniawski Violin Competition of 1935. Her family moved to England in 1937, and Ida went on to study with Carl Flesch in Berlin. During World War II, she toured and played for British and American factory workers and, in 1991, as a British citizen, was awarded the Commander of the Order of the British Empire (CBE).

Haendel was well known for her playing of the Sibelius Violin Concerto, earning high praise from the composer himself and winning the Sibelius Prize in 1982. She lived in Miami, Florida and spearheaded the Miami International Piano Festival.[342] In 1982, Ida Haendel was honored as one of the great violinists selected to play in Tel Aviv for the Huberman Centenary. In 2005, she played the Beethoven Triple Concerto

---

[342] http://miamipianofest.com/artists/haendel.html, accessed September 12, 2014.

with Mischa Maisky and Martha Argerich and the Philadelphia Orchestra in Saratoga, N.Y. She was present at a special ceremony held in Poznań in 2006 during the Wieniawski International Violin Competition for the renaming of the Poznań Airport to the Henryk Wieniawski airport.

Archives of Musical Society of Musical Studies of Henryk Wieniawski, Poznań

**Bronisław Gimpel** was born in 1911 into the founding family of the Yiddish Theatre of Lemberg (Lwów). He and his two brothers, **Jakub** and **Karol,** all became well-known musicians.[343] Bronisław started violin and piano with his father, was accepted to the Lwów Conservatory on violin at age eight, and made his first public performance there playing the Mendelssohn Violin Concerto.[344] He continued studies at the Vienna Conservatory, performing the Goldmark Violin Concerto with the Vienna Philharmonic at the age of fourteen. In 1928, he began studies in Berlin with Carl Flesch but remained with him only one year because he proved

---

[343] Jacob (1906–1989), a pianist, studied with Eduard Steuermann, and participated in the very first Chopin International Piano Competition in 1927. Karol (1890–1942) was killed by the Russian NKWD.
[344] Schwarz (1983) 345–47.

himself to be difficult to control. Nevertheless, Bronisław was a prize winner in the first Wieniawski Violin Competition in 1935.

Otto Klemperer brought Gimpel to the Los Angeles Philharmonic as concertmaster and there he became a U.S. citizen, volunteering and fighting with the American Army in World War II. After the war, The ABC Radio Symphony in New York engaged him as concertmaster, and he formed a very popular trio in New York with John Mannes and Luigi Silva. In 1962, at the Warsaw "Springtime" Festival, the director of the Polish Concert Agency decided to organize a group composed of Poles with two or three players of dual citizenship from Poland and the United States. The group was called the **"Warsaw Quintet" (Kwintet Warszawski).** To form the group, Bronisław Gimpel joined the pianist **Władysław Szpilman.**[345] To fill out the quintet, they added **Tadeusz Wroński,**[346] violin, **Stefan Kamasa,**[347] viola, and **Aleksander Ciechański,**[348] cello.

---

[345] Władysław Szpilman (1911–2000) was a friend born in Sosnowiec. He is famous for having the Steven Spielberg movie *The Pianist* based on his World War II experiences.

[346] Tadeusz Wroński (1911–2000) was born in Warsaw and became a great teacher at Indiana University with many published teaching methods to his credit.

[347] Stefan Kamasa (b. 1930), the distinguished violist in the quintet, studied in Warsaw with Wroński and after his tenure with the Quintet continued his career at the Warsaw Academy of Music. Penderecki, Baird, and Bacewicz all wrote concertos for him, and he made the first recording of the Penderecki.

[348] Aleksander Ciechański (1927–2012) graduated from the Kraków Academy of Music, performed as a soloist in Poland, and was principal cellist of the National Philharmonic of Poland. He eventually took a position with the St. Louis Symphony and joined the faculty of St. Louis Conservatory. He died in Florida.

Courtesy of Andreas Szpilman

The "**Kwintet Warszawski**" played in Philadelphia in October of 1967.[349] The headline in the Evening Bulletin read, "Warsaw Quintet Superlative," and the reviewer went on to say that "they did their country proud with some pretty superlative playing." Bronisław, with his brother, Jakub, made his home in Los Angeles but concertized often in Europe. Both Jakub and Bronisław died in Los Angeles; Bronisław, in 1979, just days before they were to give a joint recital. He was often called Bronisław II, since he followed another great Polish violinist named Bronisław Huberman.[350]

> I am a Pole, Jew, free artist and a Pan-European. In view of these characteristics I have to consider Nazism as my mortal enemy. The issue is not about the concerts or the Jews; it is about the most fundamental principles of our European culture, about personal freedom liberated from the fetters of the caste system and racism. I cannot

---

[349] Władysław Szpilman website, www.szpilman.net/, accessed September 12, 2014.
[350] "Jakob & Bronislaw Gimpel Archives," www.gimpelmusicarchives.com/, accessed September 12, 2014.

conclude this letter without giving vent to my deepest pain caused by the factors which temporarily moved me away from Germany. I experience this pain all the more so as a friend of my German friends, as an interpreter of German music and someone who misses the German audience a lot.[351] Bronisław Huberman.

Courtesy of Joan Payne

Such was the response of **Bronisław Huberman** to an invitation to perform in Germany in 1933. "Among the great violinists of the twentieth century," Huberman was born in 1882 in Częstochowa, the son of a Jewish lawyer, and surely the greatest inspiration to the "Polish prodigies" who followed him. He also first studied at the Warsaw Conservatory with Mieczysław Michałowicz, the highly regarded violin teacher who began many a Polish-born violinist's education. At the age of nine, he played for Joseph Joachim in Berlin and, at fourteen, he performed the Brahms Violin Concerto with the composer in attendance and received his deep appreciation and gratitude. Brahms proposed writing a *Fantasy* for him, but died before its undertaking. Although Berlin could have seemed hostile territory to these "Polish prodigies," they undoubtedly would have been encouraged to follow Huberman's successful example to continue their studies in that important musical center when their time arrived.

---

[351] The Bronislaw Huberman Archives, AMLI Central Library for music and dance, Tel Aviv.

In that same year, 1896, Huberman came to America and made his Carnegie Hall debut. He taught at the Vienna State Academy between the two wars, and his tours brought him to Philadelphia many times. His first appearance with the Philadelphia Orchestra occurred in 1921, performing at the Academy of Music with Richard Strauss conducting his own Violin Concerto. In the ensuing years Philadelphians heard him in the Beethoven concerto with Stokowski, the Brahms with Klemperer, and the Tchaikovsky with Ormandy. His performance and full teaching schedule in Germany ended in 1933 with the emergence of the Nazis. He assembled persecuted Jewish musicians from Europe and formed the Palestine Symphony in Tel Aviv. It later became the Israel Philharmonic, and Arturo Toscanini conducted its first performance in 1936.[352] Huberman transcribed a number of Chopin pieces for the violin, spent World War II at his home in Switzerland and died there in 1947, a year before the creation of the state of Israel. Huberman has been described by some as the most individualized violinist ever recorded.

A fascinating story about his Stradivarius violin:

Before 1936, Huberman's principal instrument for his concerts was the 1713-vintage Stradivarius "Gibson," which was named after one of its early owners, the English violinist George Alfred Gibson. It was stolen twice. In 1919, it was stolen from Huberman's Vienna hotel room, but recovered by the police within three days. The second time was in New York City. On February 28, 1936, while giving a concert at Carnegie Hall, Huberman switched the Stradivarius "Gibson" with his newly acquired Guarnerius violin, leaving the Stradivarius in his dressing room during intermission. It was stolen by a New York nightclub musician who painted the violin with black polish and kept it for the next half century. Huberman's insurance company, Lloyd's of London, paid him 30,000 dollars for the loss in 1936. The thief went on to become a violinist with the National Symphony Orchestra in Washington, D.C., and performed with the stolen Stradivarius for many years. In 1985, he made a deathbed confession to his wife,

---

[352] David Grundschlag (1914–1996) was one of the first members of Huberman's orchestra who became a member of the Philadelphia Orchestra from 1959 to 1984. He was born in Drohobycz (Galicia) Poland and studied in Vienna and Berlin. Huberman convinced him to leave Germany and join his Palestine Symphony in 1936. He was buried in Israel.

Marcelle Hall, that he had stolen the violin. Two years later, she returned it to Lloyd's and collected a finder's fee of $263,000. The black polish did not damage the instrument, and it underwent a 9-month restoration by J&A Beare Ltd., in London. In 1988, Lloyd's sold it for $1.2 million to British violinist Norbert Brainin. In October 2001, the American violinist, Joshua Bell, purchased it for $4,000,000. In 2009, Joshua Bell performed the Brahms Violin Concerto in Huberman's birthplace, Częstochowa, in a homecoming for the great Polish artist's long-lost Strad.

In 2012, the city of Częstochowa renamed its orchestra the Bronisław Huberman Philharmonic in honor of their native son. The newly rebuilt Philharmonic Hall sits on the site of a former synagogue that was destroyed by the Nazis in the war.[353]

Curtis Institute of Music Archives
**Temianka wth Carl Flesch at the Curtis Institute of Music**

One of Carl Flesch's students at the Curtis Institute of Music of whom he was especially proud was **Henri Temianka**. Born in Scotland in 1906 to Polish parents, he studied in Holland and Berlin. While continuing his studies in Paris, the Polish conductor and friend of the family, **Ignaz**

---

[353] Schwarz (1983) 309–315.

**Neumark,**[354] introduced Temianka to Flesch. Temianka played for him, and two days later, Flesch took him on the next ship to America to attend the Curtis Institute in Philadelphia. In addition to his studies with Flesch, Temianka also pursued conducting with Artur Rodziński, a skill he was to use later in life.[355] He was one of the first graduates of the Curtis Institute in 1928 and one of the first recipients of a school-sponsored solo tour of Europe, performing in eleven different countries.[356]

After graduation and touring, he returned home to England. At that time, the Wieniawski Violin Competition, then in Warsaw, was new, and Temianka had no inclination to try it since he didn't even know the literature required, but Polish pianist **Leopold Muenzer** [357] was insistent that he compete. He catapulted to fame when he won third prize in that first Wieniawski competition of 1935 (behind Ginette Neveu and David Oistrakh). That success resulted in his being offered the concertmaster chair with the Scottish Orchestra under George Szell and, later, the same position with the Pittsburgh Symphony under Fritz Reiner. In 1940, Bronisław Huberman engaged him as conductor of the newly formed Palestine Symphony which consisted entirely of Jewish refugees from Central and Eastern Europe. With them he conducted a concert in a Moslem Benefit tour of Egypt sponsored by King Farouk to support victims of a Turkish earthquake.[358]

---

[354] Ignaz Neumark (1888–1959) was born in Płock. In 1919, he became the second conductor of the Oslo Philharmonic. Temianka saw him often in the European centers of Berlin, Warsaw, Paris, Venice, and Amsterdam. Neumark became conductor of the Scheveningen Orchestra in Holland until the outbreak of WWII, when he narrowly escaped the Nazis and came to New York City. He barely survived in the U.S., depending on friends for financial help until after the war when the Netherlands again welcomed him as a prominent conductor. He died there.

[355] Schwarz (1983) 350–351.

[356] Viles (1983) 82.

[357] Born in Lwów in 1901, Muenzer spent much of his career in England. He was not reluctant to perform Szymanowski piano pieces there and in turn, took the John Ireland Piano Concerto to Lwów together with Elgar's *Dream of Gerontius*, (in a Polish translation by his wife). He is believed to have been killed by the Nazis in 1942.

[358] Joseph M. Levy, "Jewish Orchestra in Moslem Benefit," *New York Times*, 2 May 1940.

Back in the United States, Temianka was a popular soloist, appearing with many orchestras in America, including in Philadelphia under Dimitri Mitropoulus at the Robin Hood Dell. In 1945, Elizabeth Sprague Coolidge sponsored Temianka's performances of the complete Beethoven violin sonatas at the Library of Congress. The following year he settled in California to found a new chamber group, the Paganini Quartet. Mrs. William Andrews Clark, the wealthy widow of the U.S. Senator from Montana, purchased two violins, a viola, and cello, all Stradivarii that had once belonged to Paganini, for the quartet's sole use. They had great success and notoriety touring throughout the United States for twenty years. In 1947, they were honored for the industry's best recording of the year for the Beethoven *"Razumovsky"* String Quartets, opus 59. Temianka also performed all the Beethoven and Bach Violin Sonatas in recital. He took Professorships at California State University at Santa Barbara in 1960 (joining Stefan Krayk) and at Long Beach in 1964. He formed and conducted the California Chamber Symphony in 1960. The Ensemble was based at Royce Hall, on the UCLA campus.[359]

Library of Congress, Bain Collection

---

[359] "Henri Temianka Is Dead at 85," *New York Times*, 10 November 1992.

**Samuel Dushkin** was another student of Carl Flesch who pursued his discipline in New York City. Dushkin was born in Suwałki, Poland, in 1891 and studied in Paris before arriving in America. He made his U. S. debut with Walter Damrosch and the New York Symphony in 1924, and performed again in 1928 under Maurice Ravel. In 1925, he played the first performance of a *Short Story* for violin and piano by George Gershwin. His close association with Igor Stravinsky, however, brought Dushkin the most enduring musical legacy.[360] He played the world premiere, the U.S. premiere, and the first recording of Stravinsky's Violin Concerto. In 1932, he also performed this work in Philadelphia, Washington, and Baltimore with Stokowski and the Philadelphia Orchestra on a program that also included Grzegorz Fitelberg's *Polish Rhapsody*. The Violin Concerto was also done as a ballet choreographed by Balanchine, with Dushkin as concertmaster and soloist. He brought many of today's "standards" to the public for the first time: works by Ravel, Prokofiev, and Martinu.[361]

He was a close friend to Stravinsky, and they toured together as a duo, with Stravinsky at the piano performing arrangements of many of his own compositions: excerpts from *le Rossignol, Petrouchka,* and *Firebird,* as well as his *Divertimento* based on Tchaikovsky themes.[362] Dushkin often embraced an eclectic recital program that might include *Brazilian Dances* by Darius Milhaud, *Ripples* by Musorgsky, or *Palestinian Song* by Paul Kirman, in addition to the usual Wieniawski *Polonaise*.[363] He also performed Szymanowski's *Fountain of Arethusa* from *Król Roger*. Dushkin owned two Stradivarius violins, a Guadagnini and a Guarneri *del Gesu* that is now played by Pinchas Zukerman. Dushkin died in New York City in 1976.[364]

---

[360] Christopher H. Gibbs. "One of the most fruitful partnerships to emerge in the 20th Century was between Igor Stravinsky and Polish-American violinist Samuel Dushkin." *Philadelphia Orchestra Playbill,* November 2014, 34.

[361] Schwarz (1983) 514–517.

[362] Olin Downes, "Igor Stravinsky and Dushkin Play," *New York Times,* 26 January 1937. Harold Taubman, "Dushkin Presents Stravinsky Work," *New York Times,* 1 April 1941.

[363] "Dushkin Gives Novelties," *New York Times,* 19 January 1925.

[364] "Samuel Dushkin, 82, Violinist and Introducer of New Works," *New York Times,* 26 June 1976.

The Juilliard School of Music Archives

**Paweł (Paul) Kochański** was one of the most beloved violinists of the twentieth century: "he was the greatest, most profound musician amongst today's celebrated violinists."[365]

His life was cut short by cancer at the age of 47, but the impact of this amazing musician on the world of music can perhaps be best conveyed by naming the honorary pallbearers for his funeral in New York City: Arturo Toscanini, Serge Koussevitzky, Frank and Walter Damrosch, Jascha Heifetz, Vladimir Horowitz, Fritz Kreisler, Leopold Stokowski, and Efrem Zimbalist. A tribute to him at the Juilliard School of Music was attended by 1,500.[366]

Kochański was born in Odessa in 1887, and his family soon moved to Warsaw where he was taught by the famed violinist/conductor, Emil Młynarski. When Młynarski founded the Warsaw Philharmonic in 1901, he summoned Kochański, only fourteen years old, to be concertmaster. (His brother, **Eli**, was a cellist in the orchestra.) The pianist Artur Rubinstein was a very close friend throughout their lives. They first toured together as teenagers in Poland, then in London. Kochański taught at the Warsaw Conservatory for two years beginning in 1909, and in 1913, he succeeded Leopold Auer as Professor of Violin at the St. Petersburg

---

[365] Wightman (1999) 355.
[366] "Musicians Mourn Paul Kochanski," *New York Times*, 15 January 1934.

Conservatory. In 1921, when both were 34 years old, Kochański and Rubinstein come to the United States together with Karol Szymanowski. Kochański made his American debut with Walter Damrosch and the New York Symphony in 1921.[367] In 1922, the two again performed together, this time at Philadelphia's Academy of Music.[368] They paired in concert many times during their careers. Kochański's first performance at the Academy of Music with the Philadelphia Orchestra was, improbably, the Vivaldi Concerto in A Minor conducted by Richard Strauss in 1921.[369] He also performed concertos by Beethoven, Brahms, and Szymanowski with Stokowski in 1923 and 1924. Kochański gave the first performance in America of the Szymanowski Violin Concerto No. 1 with Stokowski and the Philadelphians at Carnegie Hall.[370] Rubinstein and Kochański continued touring many countries extensively and played the premiere of the Szymanowski Violin Sonata in Warsaw and also the first performance of the Bloch Violin Sonata No. 1.

Kochański and Szymanowski also concertized together.[371] "Violinist Gives Audience Great Pleasure" was the headline when Kochański introduced Stravinsky and Szymanowski transcriptions for the first time. In Paris, the three of them were introduced to many of the city's great artists, including Pablo Picasso, Pierre Monteux, and Igor Stravinsky, who dedicated a *Firebird* violin transcription to Kochański and gave him sole performing rights for two years to his *Suite Italienne*.[372] In 1928, he shared a recital with Sigismond Stojowski at New York's Town Hall performing the works of Paderewski, Wieniawski, Szymanowski, and Stojowski.[373]

---

[367] "Paul Kochanski Appears," *New York Times*, 15 February 1921.

[368] Marion (1984) 209.

[369] Richard Strauss conducted several weeks with the Orchestra in 1921, but it was not his first appearance with the Philadelphians. That occurred in 1904 conducting his own music.

[370] Olin Downes, "The Philadelphia Orchestra," *New York Times*, 3 December 1924.

[371] Szymanowski dedicated his First Violin Concerto to him, and Kochański wrote the cadenza. In 1926 when Kochański returned to America for another concert tour, he brought with him Szymanowski's new Symphony No. 3 scheduled to be performed that season with the New York Symphony. "Kochański Here with New Work," *New York Times*, 30 September 1926.

[372] "Recital by Kochański," *New York Times*, 31 October 1926.

[373] "Polish Artists in Recital," *New York Times*, 20 April 1928.

Kochański assisted Sergei Prokofiev in the composing of his first violin concerto. He was to premiere the Szymanowski Violin Concerto No. 2, for which he wrote the cadenza in New York City, but was too sick to complete the task. (His successor at Juilliard, Albert Spalding, performed it the year after Kochański's death) He taught at Juilliard for his last 10 years. The National Museum in Warsaw contains the Paweł Kochański Manuscript Collection. He had also begun to compose later in his brief life.[374] The Polish Ministry of Culture and National Heritage funded the purchase of his written creative work from Sotheby's in New York in 1988.[375]

In remembering Kochański after his death in 1934, Dr. John Erskine, Dean of the Juilliard School, said, "Magnificent as his playing and teaching here were, I think he was a bigger man than we had yet realized. His influence and his fame were only beginning. Had he lived, I believed he would have distinguished himself in compositions, to which his attention was turning."

Near the end of World War II, in April of 1945, a Nazi cattle car was transporting Jewish prisoners from Flossenburg to Dachau concentration camps in Germany. The train was strafed by an Allied plane and was disabled. Unfortunately, half of the prisoners were also killed. The survivors were forced on a march to Dachau, but after about a week, the guards decided to abandon them when they heard that the Allies were closing in. The prisoners scattered, and a seventeen-year-old boy was left alone, without food, money, or anywhere to go. His entire family had been murdered by the Germans, and all that he had known in Warsaw, his birthplace, had been destroyed. He found some raw potatoes in a field and cooked them over a fire he built fueled by a bag of German Reichsmarks that had been abandoned at a bank when the Germans fled the approaching Allies. But the war was not yet officially over, and fear of being discovered was always a threat. He slept anyplace he could find to remain undetected. He had spent the entire war in concentration camps, sure to be murdered at some point, but when circumstances were at their worst, music saved his life.

---

[374] Among other works, he composed a violin caprice entitled *Flight*, dedicated to Charles Lindberg.

[375] Tyrone Greive, "Kochanski's Collaborative Work as Reflected in His Manuscript Collection," *PMC*, vol. 1, no. 1 (Summer 1998).

Specifically, the violin saved his life. Three years earlier, as a fourteen-year-old in Budzin, he had been saved by an officer who pulled him from his turn at the firing squad because the boy had played the violin for him and his mistress in their quarters.

That boy was **Chaim Arbeitman (David Arben).** He is a Polish Jew born in Warsaw in 1927 at a time when the streets were alive with music and especially the violin. Chaim even remembered his father's barber pulling a fiddle off the wall and playing it for his customers. At an early age his family knew they had an exceptional child. Chaim was attracted to and always imitated the violin. His father, a tailor, took him to Warsaw's most famous teacher, Mieczysław Michałowicz, to be tested. At the age of seven, Michałowicz's assistant went to his house and practiced with Chaim for two hours every day except the Sabbath, and once a week he had a lesson with Michałowicz. Before the year was out, he was playing a recital at the Chopin Academy.

When Chaim was nine years old, his father took him to hear the great violinist Ephraim (Efrem) Zimbalist, who was touring in Warsaw playing the Beethoven Violin Concerto with the Warsaw Philharmonic under the conductor Grzegorz Fitelberg. It made an enormous impression on him. Who could have guessed, however, that the lives of Chaim Arbeitman and Efrem Zimbalist would intersect some day at the Curtis Institute of Music? Who could have predicted any future at all from the inside of a concentration camp? After his liberation in the middle of Germany, he wandered for nine months; he managed to make his way to Munich, often paying his way with a currency much more valuable than Reichsmarks, cigarettes given to him by American soldiers. Chaim recalled the first time he saw an American G. I. and his first non-white, when a huge black man popped out of the hatch of a U.S. tank and offered him help.

In Munich, he resumed his studies and in 1946 won an audition with the Bavarian Radio Orchestra (Symphonieorchester des Bayerischen Rundfunks). At that time, Leonard Bernstein came to Munich and conducted two benefit concerts with Chaim and other musicians who were camp survivors. Bernstein, who had been a student at the Curtis Institute, wrote a recommendation for him to the Philadelphia school, which he hoped to use one day. But before Arbeitman could consider going to the United States, he studied at the Mozarteum in Salzburg and smuggled his way into Geneva, applying for a ten-day visa to enter the Geneva International Music Competition in 1948. He was able to remain and attended the Geneva Conservatory, studying with Michel Schwalbe,[376] who went on to become the famed concertmaster of the Berlin Philharmonic—a Polish-born Jew in a Von Karajan orchestra! Chaim won the Virtuoso Prize at the Geneva Conservatory and performed solos with the L'Orchestre de la Suisse Romande. He also went on a solo tour of Germany accompanied by Michael Taube.[377] In 1949, Arbeitman sailed to America on an American battleship designated for immigrants; he arrived in Boston and then traveled to Detroit, where he connected with Arbeitman families that he had never met. To the dismay of his new family, however, Chaim's ultimate goal was Philadelphia--to study with Efrem Zimbalist at the Curtis Institute of Music, the only reason he had come to America, and now Zimbalist was not only the violin teacher but also the Director of the Curtis Institute. Chaim auditioned and was accepted, and graduated from Curtis in 1954. He shared his graduation recital with one of Curtis and Philadelphia's most famous musicians, the soprano Anna Moffo.

---

[376] Michel Schwalbe was born in Poland in 1919 and graduated from the the the Warsaw Conservatory in 1931 under Moritz Frenkel. He was very highly regarded by all the great conductors and held the concertmaster chair of the Berlin Philharmonic under Ernest Ansermet and Herbert von Karajan. He recitaled and conducted in Japan and Europe, including Poland. He also recorded with Stanisław Skrowaczewski and L'Orchestre de la Suisse Romande.

[377] Michael Taube was a successful piano accompanist who recorded with Emanuel Feuermann, but he was also a very fine conductor. He was born in Łódź and led many orchestras in Germany including an eighteenth-century chamber orchestra in 1933 Berlin during a Hitler-tolerated period of Kulturbund Deutscher Juden (Cultural League of German Jews). Before and during WWII, he was both soloist and one of the first conductors of the newly formed Palestine Symphony, leading many premieres in Israel and commissioning works by Israeli composers. He was a citizen of Palestine and held a British passport. He also led an orchestra of displaced persons in Germany and was a conductor of the Berlin State Opera.

Courtesy of Rebecca Jackson

At that time, Mischa Mischakoff, who had come to America through the Warsaw Philharmonic, was the concertmaster of the Detroit Symphony and was in Philadelphia as guest soloist. Mischakoff heard Chaim play and brought the graduating Arbeitman back to Detroit, where he became a U. S. citizen and played with the Detroit Symphony for one year. He then auditioned for George Szell and won a position with the Cleveland Orchestra, spending four years in the first violin section in Cleveland. During that time, he changed his name from Chaim Arbeitman to **David Arben**.

Through a special arrangement initiated by Josef Gingold, the concertmaster of the Cleveland Orchestra, Arben was given the opportunity to perform the Mendelssohn *Violin Concerto* with George Szell and the Cleveland Orchestra—a very rare occurrence for a section player. When the Cleveland Orchestra made a tour of Iron Curtain countries in 1957, Arben was kept from the Polish part of the tour because the orchestra did not know how the Polish Communist government would treat a visiting performer with a U.S. passport but "born in Poland."

Courtesy of Rebecca Jackson

In 1959, he became a member of the Philadelphia Orchestra, rising to the position of Associate Concertmaster and retiring thirty-four years later in 1993. He did not return to Warsaw until fifty-six years after the destruction of his family. In 1997, while the Philadelphia Orchestra was on tour in Poland, Arben was invited to speak and play at a special televised ceremony arranged by Steven Spielberg's Shoah Foundation at the Synagogue Związek Gmin Wyznaniowych Żydowskich, the very synagogue where his father had taken him as a boy and the only Synagogue partly standing after the destruction of Warsaw.

He has subsequently toured the world telling his story of the hate and intolerance he experienced. May 12, 2012, was declared "David Arben Day" in Santa Cruz, California, and for two days' concerts were given in his honor, including the world premiere of *Haim* for narrator and chamber ensemble by Polina Nazaykinskaya. Similar festivals dedicated to Arben have taken place at Yale University and the Gildenhorn-Speisman Center for the Arts in Rockville, Maryland. His support of Polish music was always evident in Philadelphia as he played the U.S. premiere of the Andrzej Panufnik Violin Concerto in 1986, and he also played the Szymanowski Violin Concerto No. 1 with Christoph Eschenbach. He shared the stage with Henryk Szeryng in a performance of the Bach

Concerto for Two Violins, and on other occasions performed the concertos of Mendelssohn and Mozart. In 1989, in his last solo appearance with the Philadelphians, he performed the Bruch Violin Concerto with the Polish maestro Witold Rowicki. Arben also performed and taught at the Casals Music Festival in Puerto Rico which, at that time, was under the directorship of Krzysztof Penderecki.

Courtesy of Larry Grika

A violinist in the Philadelphia Orchestra for forty-one years (1964–2005), **Larry Grika** was born in Chicago in 1932. His parents had lived in Warsaw. His mother, Celia, was born there, and his father, Sam, was from Parczew. They met after coming to America in the 1920s, married, and settled in Chicago. Celia played in two mandolin orchestras; Sam became a businessman. Larry grew up on the West Side and participated in a strong arts program at school (many high schools had orchestras of one hundred or more players), studying with Sam Arron, and was a member of and soloist with the Chicago Youth Orchestra in Orchestra Hall.

He continued his violin studies with Paul Stassewich, a student of Leopold Auer, and received Bachelor's and Master's degrees (1954 and 1955) from the Chicago Musical College of Roosevelt University. He won the Oliver Ditson Award in violin, and was concertmaster throughout all his years in high school and college. He also studied chamber music with Alexander Schneider of the Budapest Quartet. Grika was in the Chicago Opera Company Orchestra while still in college. He played in the U.S. Army Band at Fort Meyer, Virginia, and worked towards a Doctoral degree at Catholic University in Washington, D.C.

After leaving the Army, Grika led a varied life, first joining the faculty of Antioch College in Yellow Springs, Maryland, for three years. Then he participated in the Aspen Music Festival, studying with Robert

Mann of the Juilliard Quartet. He also played the Casals Music Festival in Puerto Rico and the Santa Fe Opera during the summers. Before Philadelphia, he played in the Cincinnati Symphony under Max Rudolf for two years. He was then invited to join the Philadelphia Orchestra by Eugene Ormandy in 1964 and, fifteen years later, became the planner for Ormandy's 80th birthday celebration in Philadelphia. He was a member of the Board of Directors of the Philadelphia Orchestra for three years and has been a negotiator for many Philadelphia Orchestra members' contract deliberations. He was also the catalyst and inspiration for Riccardo Muti's memorable return to Philadelphia for a benefit concert in 2005. Larry is a highly sought after private teacher and as an adjunct professor at Temple University and Rowan University. He holds regular master classes for the Philadelphia Youth Orchestra and is on the faculty of the Philadelphia International Music Festival.

**Isidor Lateiner** (b. 1930) was born in Havana to Jewish parents who had emigrated from Poland. Lateiner showed exceptional musical talent at a very early age, giving concerts when he was only five years old. He came to the United States with his family when he was ten and, like his brother Jacob, was awarded a scholarship to the Curtis Institute in Philadelphia and graduated one year before his brother in 1947. Also like his brother, at the age of fifteen he debuted with the Philadelphia Orchestra under Eugene Ormandy, playing the Mendelssohn Violin Concerto. He then made his first appearance in New York City in 1956 performing at Town Hall in what was to become a regular occurrence. His career also took him throughout the United States, and in Europe, he performed with many orchestras including the Berlin Philharmonic and the Concertgebouw Orchestra of Amsterdam. He resided in Amsterdam and continued as a soloist and chamber music partner until his death in 2005.

**Leon Zawisza,** was born in 1915 in Camden, New Jersey, across the Delaware River from Philadelphia and the Curtis Institute. He first attended the Combs College of Music in Philadelphia before being accepted to Curtis to study with Alexander Hilsberg and Efrem Zimbalist, the Russian violinist and future Director of the school. He graduated in 1936, after which his career took him first to the Minneapolis Symphony and then to the Cleveland Orchestra. During World War II, he conducted General Douglas MacArthur's military band, the "Manila Symphony." He went on to become Concertmaster of the Indianapolis Symphony and its Assistant Conductor, directing the orchestra many times in eleven years. He also purchased the 1718 *Marquis de Riviere* Stradivarius violin from Zimbalist.[378] He played and recorded with the Felix Galimir Quartet. One of the quartet's other members was Karen Tuttle, another graduate of Curtis (1948) who went on to teach viola there for nearly thirty years. Zawisza then moved to New York City where he became the first staff conductor at the Radio City Music Hall, a position he held for thirty years. He died in 1993.

The International Henryk Wieniawski Violin Competition is held in Poznań every five years. In 1967, the very first Polish violinist to win First Prize in the competition was **Piotr Janowski,** only sixteen years old at the time. He was born in Grudziądz, Poland in 1951 and after winning the Wieniawski, as a recipient of a Kosciuszko Foundation scholarship, Janowski attended the Curtis Institute of Music and won the Philadelphia Orchestra Competition for all instruments. It rewarded him with appearances with the Orchestra, in which he performed the Mozart Violin Concerto No. 4. He made his New York debut four years later in 1971 at Alice Tully Hall. "Janowski plays with...technique and mature musicianship of someone twice his age" read the review by Theodore Strongin of the *New York Times*.[379]

---

[378] Mark Stryker, "Playing a Rembrandt: Strads Set the Standard," *Detroit Free Press*, 29 December 2002. The violin was originally purchased by Mary Louise Curtis Bok. Zawisza eventually sold it to Daniel Majeske, who was to become the concertmaster of the Cleveland Orchestra and was also a graduate of the Curtis Institute (1950). The instrument was passed on to his son Stephen, a former violinist in the Cleveland Orchestra and another Curtis graduate (1975).

[379] Theodore Strongin, "Janowski is Heard in Violin Recital," *New York Times*, 23 April 1971.

Archives of Musical Society of Musical Studies of Henryk Wieniawski, Poznań

Janowski was dedicated to more than the standard composers that one would associate with a Wieniawski winner. He premiered works by many American composers: David Diamond[380], John Harbison, Sidney Hodgkison, John Eaton, and Burt Levy as well as Grażyna Bacewicz in Poland at the Warsaw Autumn Festival (Warszawska Jesień). When a special concert was presented by the American Symphony at Carnegie Hall in honor of the recently deceased Polish pianist Witold Małcużyński, the program included three prize winners from Poland: Janowski performing the Beethoven Violin Concerto, Piotr Paleczny playing the Chopin F Minor Piano Concerto, and Jacek Kasprzyk conducting Richard Strauss' *Don Juan* and Krzysztof Penderecki's Dream of Jacob.[381]

---

[380] Raymond Ericson, "Bernstein Leads Works…and a Diamond Premiere," *New York Times,* 3 April 1976.

[381] Joseph Horowitz, "3 Polish Musicians in Tribute," *New York Times*, 20 May 1978. Piotr Paleczny (b. 1946) won the third prize in the 1970 Chopin International Piano Competition and has appeared in the U.S. a number of times since then, and he continues as a judge for the Chopin Competiton held in Warsaw. At that time, Jacek Kasprzyk was the conductor of the Polish Radio National Symphony Orchestra. He had won third prize in the 1977 Karajan Competition in Berlin.

Janowski also won the Naumburg Competition in New York in 1980 with the New Arts Trio. [382] He collaborated with many of the greatest players, orchestras, and conductors in the world. Master classes and chamber music festivals took him everywhere. During his career, he was accompanied by Horszowski, Balsam, and Peter Serkin, and performed for the Polish Heritage Society in Philadelphia. Janowski and Emanuel Ax also performed a concert for the Kosciuszko Foundation in New York City. He died in London in 2008 and is buried in Powązki cemetery in Warsaw. [383]

When **Stefan Krajkeman (Krayk),** 1914–1999, passed away in 2000, his obituary read:

> Virtuoso violinist, World War II ace fighter pilot, a Polish national tennis champion, winner of an international violin competition, master teacher, and television actor-these disparate personalities all combined into a single remarkable colleague and friend, Stephen Krayk, Professor of Music as UCSB from 1950 to 1977.

University of California: In Memoriam, 2000.

---

[382] "Two Chamber Groups Win '80 Naumburg Awards," *New York Times,* 9 April 1980.
[383] Joanna Maklakiewicz, "Piotr Janowski," *Polskie Centrum Infomacji Muzycznej,* 2009.

Courtesy of Steven Krayk

Stefan Krajkeman (Krayk) was born in Warsaw. At the outbreak of World War I, his father took the family to Russia, then Sweden, then Denmark to escape the war. After returning to Poland, his father became prosperous in leather manufacturing. As a teenager, Krajk became an exceptional tennis player and was chosen for the Polish National Team at the Davis Cup in London. Stefan and his brother studied or, better said, tinkered on the violin with the clear understanding that they would pursue other livelihoods. His brother became a chemist, and Stefan was sent to France to study law at the Sorbonne. The more he studied law, however, the more his interest in the violin increased. He incensed his father with his change of heart but he was permitted to aspire to the violin, studying with France's most famous artist, Jacques Thibaud, at the *Ecole Normale de Musique*. He traveled to Berlin for further studies with Carl Flesch who was then in Baden-Baden, and his father bought him a Stradivarius violin for the sum of 5,000 pounds. Krayk later became Flesch's assistant.

Krayk returned to Poland in 1938, put the violin in safekeeping, and during the Nazi invasion of 1939, flew with the Polish Air Force. His plane crashed, and he escaped into Yugoslavia, making his way through Europe to Lisbon where he was able to gain passage to London. In 1940, he arranged with the Polish Underground for his parents' escape as the

Nazis swept through Europe (his father was Jewish). In London, he played concerts for Polish Relief and then joined the United States Army Special Services in charge of concerts, performing for many thousands of troops, and married an English woman, Sydney. By this time, he had acquired several languages that he was to put to use throughout his life. After the war, he came to America and was engaged as a member of the Philadelphia Orchestra in 1946. That same year, thanks to his three years in the U.S. Army, he was able to become a U.S. citizen in unusually short time.

Krayk was not to make a career in Philadelphia, however. He taught at Oberlin College in Ohio for two years where his son, Stephen, was born and then made his way to California. There he became a member of the Paganini String Quartet, newly formed by Henri Temianka. The Paganini Quartet was so named because they had been given a set of Stradivarius instruments that once belonged to Paganini. The instruments were placed in the Quartet's hands through the generous patronage of Mrs. William Andrew Clark, who wanted to see a new American string quartet formed. (Oddly, the group spoke French during rehearsals.) The Quartet's first performance sensation came when they played all the Beethoven String Quartets at the Library of Congress, which was followed by a recording contract with RCA Victor Records. The Krayks became lifelong residents of California when Stefan joined the faculty of the University of California at Santa Barbara in 1950, heading the string department. He sold his Stradivarius violin so that he could bring his parents to America, and they lived the rest of their lives in Santa Barbara. Stefan, however, did bring his family back to Philadelphia to visit his first residence in America and its most famous landmark, the Liberty Bell.

Krayk was a founder of the Santa Barbara Symphony in 1953 and was its concertmaster until 1983. He also toured with the Fine Arts Trio, which included a concert in London at St. Martin-in-the Fields in 1971. He was a well-respected pedagogue; the first president of the American String Teachers Association; and published a book, *The Violin Guide*.[384] During his tenure with the Philadelphia Orchestra, he wrote an article for *Etude* magazine describing Carl Flesch's teaching methods. Later, from 1987 to 1994, his lifelong dabbling in acting in local productions led him to a brief career in television and film, playing minor roles with a number

---

[384] "Fiddler in the Sky," *Etude*, December 1946.

of the day's well-known actors. He founded the Bear Valley Music Festival in California, taught privately for the last twenty-two years of his life, and frequented the tennis court. He was buried in North Dakota, the home of his last wife, Barbara.

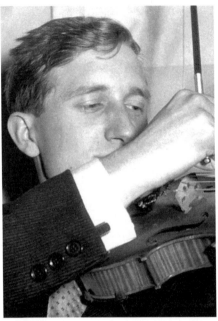

Archives of Musical Society of Musical Studies of Henryk Wieniawski, Poznań

**Tomasz (Thomas) Michalak** was very active and especially successful in the culture belt of America's east coast as both a violinist and a conductor. Michalak was born in 1941 in Kraków and at the age of 10 went to Warsaw to continue violin studies. At sixteen, already an accomplished performer, he appeared as violin soloist with the Warsaw Philharmonic, and the following year he was silver medalist at the International Violin Competition in Moscow. In 1962, he was a prize winner at the Wieniawski Competition in Poznań. He came to the United States the following year to continue his training at the Curtis Institute with Ivan Galamian. He played with the Philadelphia Chamber Orchestra, toured with the Philadelphia Orchestra as a substitute musician, and performed for the Kosciuszko Foundation in New York in 1965.

He added conducting to his studies at Curtis and, at the age of 27, became Assistant Music Director of the Chamber Symphony of

Philadelphia and also led the Ballet Russe de Monte Carlo on a tour of South America.[385] His conducting career in America included the Northeastern Philharmonic and assistant conducting the Pittsburgh Symphony, as an Exxon Affiliate Artist. In 1971, while conductor of the Utica Symphony, he received the Koussevitzky Prize in conducting at Tanglewood. The following year, as conductor of the Orchestral Society of Westchester's "Summer of Music on the Hudson" at the Lyndhurst Estate in Tarrytown, he made his first conducting appearance in the New York area to good reviews.[386] He led a program that included the violinist Aaron Rosand. "A sensitive musician,"[387] his most important position was as Music Director of the New Jersey Symphony from 1977 to 1983. Under his leadership, the orchestra introduced a wide ranging repertoire to its audiences. He conducted one of Wanda Wiłkomirska's first performances in the United States of the Szymanowski Violin Concerto No. 1. The remainder of the Szymanowski program included the *Stabat Mater* and *Harnasie*.[388] He performed as violin soloist at the Marlboro Music Festival with Pablo Casals and conducted both American and Polish orchestras in recording. He died of a heart attack at the young age of 45 in Newark, New Jersey.[389]

---

[385] "Michalak, Native of Kraków, Utica Symphony Conductor," *Polonia Gazette*, September 1968.

[386] Thomas Sherman, "Michalak Conducts Orchestral Works at Site by Hudson," *New York Times*, 24 July 1972.

[387] Campbell (1988) 274.

[388] Peter G. Davis, "Music: All Szymanowski," *New York Times*. 16 March 1980.

[389] "Thomas Michalak," *New York Times*, 12 July 1986. Also see Daniel Webster, "Thomas Michalak, 45, Conductor," *Philadelphia Inquirer*, 12 July 1986.

The Metropolitan Opera Archives, Louis Melancon

In 2010, when **Henryk Kaczka (Kaston)** died in New York City, *Strad* magazine, the string player's leading monthly publication, reprinted a lengthy interview that had been conducted with him five years earlier. The preface read, "acclaimed bow maker and jeweler," but his life of one hundred years encompassed many other accomplishments and triumphs.[390] He was born in 1910 in Piotrków Trybunalski, Poland, an ancient town founded in the thirteenth century near Łódź. It also had the misfortune, however, of being the site of the first wartime ghetto built for Jews in 1939. Fortunately for Kaston, he had left Poland in 1937 for studies in France.

Beginning at the age of eight, Henryk Kaston studied the violin in Poland with his father and grandfather. At age fifteen, he began accompanying silent movies. Two years later, serving some youthful impulse, he joined the circus as an acrobat. This early departure was not to be a career, however, and he returned to violin studies in earnest in Paris. He studied with Georges Enesco and became friends with Wanda Landowska and Ignacy Paderewski.

When World War II broke out, he joined a Polish Cavalry Unit in the French Army. He was to lose his mother, father, sister, and three brothers to the Nazis. In 1940, the Emergency Rescue Committee from America

---

[390] Stewart Pollens, "Remembering Henryk Kaston," *The Strad*, July 2005.

was formed to save artists from the Nazis, and the following year Kaston and his wife were brought to New York— their son was born aboard the ship to America.[391] Very soon after arriving, in 1942, Kaston was hired by Artur Rodziński for the Cleveland Orchestra. (Early results of his many hobbies included a new bow he designed, which Fritz Kreisler endorsed, and a miniature model of a violin, 1-3/4 inches long, made of ivory and using four strands of Artur Rodziński's hair for strings. Later, he would patent an inflatable, collapsible umbrella.[392]) After two years in Cleveland, however, he moved to New York and became a member of the Metropolitan Opera Orchestra.[393] He spent the next thirty-five years there, made many appearances in Philadelphia, and recalled the opening of the new hall at Lincoln Center in 1966—also the tragic collapse of Leonard Warren in 1960, the only time in Met history that an opera was cancelled.

He began working part time at the Wurlitzer store repairing bows, became an expert on the bows of the Frenchman, Francoix-Xavier Torte, and began making his own copies of these extremely valuable bows. With Jascha Heifetz, he developed and patented the "Heifetz mute." He was a longtime collector of not just violins and bows, but violas, cellos, mandolins, citterns, guitars, hurdy-gurdies, viols, harpsichords, tools, and more. A collection of 86 instruments, known as the Schambach-Kaston Collection, was lent to Hamilton College, Yale University, and the Metropolitan Museum of Modern Art. It was eventually purchased by Suntory, the Japanese brewing and distilling company.

Kaston also had a highly successful career as a jeweler. Lily Pons, Rise Stevens, Dorothy Kirsten, Luciano Pavarotti, and other great artists from the Met used or owned his brooches or cufflinks for Met productions. Salvador Dali even commissioned him to do a series of surrealist designs in jewelry, and Kaston accompanied Dali to the Teatro Fenice in Venice to help with the set for the Ballet de Gala. He designed the plaque presented to

---

[391] The ERC was founded by Varian Dry, an American humanitarian who relocated from France to the U.S. artists, musicians, writers, intellectuals, and others who were at risk from the Nazis.

[392] "Inflation Spreads to Umbrella in Baloon-Like Plastic Model," *New York Times*, 24 January 1953.

[393] "Finger Flick on New Violin Bow Changes to Chords," *Waterloo Daily Courier*, 24 February 1944. Also see "He Fiddles at Met, Heart at Carnegie," *New York Times*, 13 December 1951.

Pope John Paul II by the Paderewski Foundation and the plague presented to the New York Philharmonic by the city of New York in 1952. In 2002, the Metropolitan Museum of Modern Art showed a group of his bowls and jewels in the Andre Mertens Galleries of Musical Instruments.

Through most of her career, **Wanda Wiłkomirska** has been one of Poland's most well-known and beloved native-born violinists. There are very few of the world's most important concert stages that have not hosted her talents. Born into a family of musicians in 1929, she first studied the violin with her father, Alfred, then attended the Łódź Academy of Music under Irena Dubiska, graduating in 1947. At the Ferenc Liszt Music Academy in Budapest, she continued with Ede Zathureczki, and later with Henryk Szeryng in Paris. In Warsaw, Tadeusz Wroński prepared her for the 1952 Wieniawski International Violin Competition in Poznań, at which she won the Silver Prize. (Igor Oistrakh was awarded the Gold—his father, David, chaired the judges' committee.) Years later Wiłkormirska became the Chairwoman of that committee and a longtime jurist of the competition.

Archives of Musical Society of Musical Studies of Henryk Wieniawski, Poznań

Thanks to further prizes that she was awarded in Geneva, Budapest, and Leipzig, those successes brought her acclaim from within both Poland and abroad. A long association with the Polish maestro Witold Rowicki took her to America in 1961 for her debut in Carnegie Hall. There she performed with the Warsaw Philharmonic in the Szymanowski

Violin Concerto No. 1 which became one of her specialties. In 1955 she performed at the inauguration of the newly built Philharmonic Concert Hall in Warsaw and was given the same privilege for the new Philharmonic Halls in Rzeszów, Sczeczin, and Wałbrzych. Although she has played and recorded much of the standard repertoire, she has had a very strong commitment to Polish contemporary composers. Wiłkomirska did first performances of Penderecki, Bacewicz, Baird, A. Błoch, Bargielski, Bujarski, Maciejewski, and Kotoński.

Sol Hurok, America's most famous impresario, heard her play and added her to his artists' list, introducing her to audiences across America and Canada. She made annual concert visits to North America, often playing on the East Coast. She toured America with Stanisław Skrowaczewski and the Minneapolis Symphony and also performed with two of the Philadelphia Orchestra's maestros, Leopold Stokowski and Wolfgang Sawallisch. She performed the Szymanowski Violin Concerto No. 1 with the New Jersey Symphony under Tomasz Michalak's direction.

Wiłkomirska completed twelve recordings with the Connoisseur Society record company. Two of the albums won awards: Best of the Year in 1972 and Grand Prix du Disque in 1974. She made many additional recordings with DGG, Philips, Naxos, EMI, and Polskie Nagrania.[394] In 1976, she played the inaugural concert of the new Barbican Hall in London, performing the Britten Violin Concerto with the London Symphony under Sir John Barbirolli. In 1973, Wiłkomirska was the first violinist to perform in the newly built Sydney Opera House. Thus began a long relationship with Australia where she performed often and since 1999 has spent part of each year teaching at the Sydney Conservatorium of Music and the Australian National Academy of Music in Melbourne. Wiłkomirska also performed and recorded in a piano trio, the Wiłkomirska Trio, with her sister, **Maria**, a pianist, and her brother, **Kazimierz**, a cellist/conductor. She left Poland in 1982 while it was under martial law and taught in Germany. The Polish government has since recognized her with many honors for her countless artistic achievements. In 2006, as part of the 13th Wieniawski International Violin Competition, she returned to the site of her first international triumph, Poznań, for a dedication ceremony

---

[394] www.angelfire.com/scifi2/rsolecki/wanda_wilkomirska.html, accessed September 12, 2014.

renaming the city airport the Henryk Wieniawski Airport. Ida Haendel, another prize winner from the very first competition also attended.[395]

"I have heard a very great solo violinist named **Adam Han-Gorski**.. amazingly great technique and beautiful emotional tone and phrasing.. you will be deeply impressed by this young artist." Leopold Stokowski, 25 March 1971.

Courtesy of Han-Gorski

This praise comes from a letter written to Arthur Judson Management in New York, the organization that supported Stokowski early in his career in Philadelphia. Han-Gorski's career had already taken him to three continents: born in Lwów in 1940 and saved from the Nazis by a Christian family, he studied in Tel Aviv and California and then performed as first violinist in one of America's great orchestras, the Cleveland Orchestra. At the time of Stokowski's letter, Han-Gorski chose to leave George Szell's orchestra to become assistant concertmaster of the Minneapolis Symphony

---

[395] Sigrid Harris, "Interview with a Famous Violinist: Wanda Wiłkomirska," *Classical Music*, 25 November 2007.

under Music Director Stanisław Skrowaczewski. In Poland, his mother was an administrator of the Silesian Philharmonic under Jan Krenz, and Skrowaczewski had been a frequent guest there. After five years, he decided to experience Europe again and, for the next twenty-five years, was concertmaster of the Vienna Radio Symphony, soloed throughout Europe and Asia, and learned to speak seven languages. He also formed, conducted and was soloist for the *"I Virtuosi di Vienna."* On one of his touring stops in Philadelphia, he purchased a Balestrieri violin from the dealer William Moennig, one of America's best-known violin authorities. Han-Gorski can be seen on the *Great Performers Series*: "Violinists On Film," performing with Heifetz, Rubinstein, and Piatigorsky.[396]

Photo: J. Henry Fair

**Leila Bronia Josefowicz,** one of America's brilliant young violinists, was born in Toronto in 1977. Her mother is a geneticist, her father, a physicist who plays the guitar. Leila started in the Suzuki system of violin and played the Bruch Violin Concerto at the age of eight. At the age of ten, she appeared on TV on a Bob Hope Tribute program introduced by Lucille

---

[396] www.hangorski.com/Adam_Han-Gorski,_Violinist/History_%26_Legends. html, accessed September 12, 2014.

Ball. Her family moved to Philadelphia so she could begin attending the Curtis Institute at age thirteen. She received a high-school diploma from Philadelphia's Masterman School and a Bachelor of Music degree from Curtis at the same time. As a teen, she was already performing with great orchestras in America—Philadelphia, Chicago, Cleveland, and Los Angeles, as well as Montreal and Toronto.[397] At sixteen, she made her Carnegie Hall debut and at seventeen, she signed a recording contract with Philips Classics and received the Avery Fisher Career Grant.[398] Her profession now has taken her to every part of the world, including performances in 2009 of the Prokofiev Violin Concerto No. 1 with the Warsaw Philharmonic under Antoni Wit.

She has a close affinity for many contemporary composers including Adams, Knussen, Ades, and Salonen, combining today's originals with the standards. With the New York City Ballet, she premiered in a new venture playing the Salonen Violin Concerto to the choreography of Peter Martins with the composer conducting. By 2015, she had performed in Philadelphia on more than twenty occasions and was named the artist-in-residence with the Philadelphia Orchestra for that season.[399] Two of her recordings have received the Diapason d'Or award. She plays on a 1724 Guarneri *del Gesu* violin. In an interview in the UK, she explained that to give herself a break from all those "small black dots," she runs and has taken up kick-boxing. In 2012, she gave birth to her first child.[400]

**Nikolaj Znaider (Znajder)** was born in Denmark in 1975 to Polish-Israeli parents.[401] He first studied at the Royal Danish Academy of Music in Copenhagen and then moved to New York to continue his training at The Juilliard School with Dorothy Delay; he considers the pedagogue Boris Kirschner of the Vienna Conservatory as his mentor. Winning First Prize at the Carl Nielsen Violin Competition and First Prize at the Queen

[397] Lynne Walker, "Leila Josefowicz: The Allure of the Violin," *Independent*, 19 April 2005.

[398] Philip Anson, "Portrait of a Woman with Violin," *La Scena Musicale*, vol. 4, no. 5, 1 February 2000.

[399] Amy Bryant, "My Day on a Plate: Leila Josefowicz," *Telegraph*, 17 January 2011.

[400] Leila Josefowicz website, www.leilajosefowicz.com/Home, accessed September 12, 2014.

[401] http://imgartists.com/artist/nikolaj_znaider1, accessed September 12, 2014.

Elizabeth Competition in Brussels brought notoriety that thrust his career onto the international scene. In 2003, a recording for RCA which included a Wieniawski *Polonaise* and arrangements of two Chopin *Nocturnes* earned the Editor's Choice of *Gramophone*. His personal discovery of the Szymanowski Violin Concerto No. 1, which he considers "one of the great works of the early twentieth century" inspired him to add it to his repertoire and give performances throughout the world.[402] In 2005, he performed it in Philadelphia with Vladimir Jurowski and subsequently the concertos of Tchaikovsky, Brahms, and Prokofiev (No. 2). He has included conducting in his pursuits and was appointed Principal Guest Conductor of the Mariinsky Theater under Valery Gergiev in St. Petersburg. Znaider performs on the "Kreisler" 1741 Guarneri *del Gesu* violin on loan from The Royal Danish Theater.

Photo: Chris Lee

In 1972, one of Poland's most accomplished young violinists joined the New York Philharmonic. **Hanna Lachert,** born near Warsaw in 1944, was a child prodigy, beginning piano at age three, performing at age five,

---

[402] Harriet Smith, "Music That Changed Me," *BBC Music Magazine*, May 2003.

and asking for violin lessons at age eight. Her mother, Hanna Lachertowa (1910–1998), was a well-known pianist and much traveled pedagogue who brought her teaching methods to conferences all around Europe, Toronto, Tunisia, and New York. Before arriving in America, Hanna studied at the Lyceum Muzyczne with violinists Tadeusz Wroński and Zenon Brzewski and continued her education at the Warsaw Conservatory. Her solo career in Europe was interrupted in 1969 when she came to the United States to study with Bronisław Gimpel and received a Masters of Music as his graduate assistant at the University of Connecticut.

Winning a position in a major orchestra like the New York Philharmonic carries a heavy load of about 150 concerts a year including tours to other cities around the world and, of course, Philadelphia. Lachert, however, has also sustained a very active solo career: a recital at Carnegie Hall, a feature for Polish Television, appearances with Zubin Mehta and Pierre Boulez, and recording the complete violin works of Szymanowski and the Karłowicz Violin Concerto. She has performed under the Polish maestros Jerzy Maksymiuk, Antoni Wit, Karol Stryja, and Stanisław Wisłocki. As a champion of contemporary music, she has had numerous pieces written for her.

Lachert has a composer-pianist brother, Piotr, [403] with whom she performs and has recorded his music. In 1993, Hanna came to Philadelphia as concertmaster touring with the musical *The Secret Garden,* as her son, Yaniv, now a conductor in New York City, sang the leading role of Colin in that production. In 1992, the Paderewski Medal from the American Society for Polish Music was presented to her at the Polish Embassy in Washington, D.C. She was instrumental in bringing the last two winners of the Chopin International Piano Competition, Rafał Blechacz and Yulianna Andeeva, to America. Her husband, Piotr Segal, is a luthier and instrument maker, and Hanna plays one of his violins, made in 1982. She

---

[403] Born in 1938, Piotr de Peslin Lachert is a composer, pianist, chamber musician, performer, director, producer, actor, writer, poet, music journalist, and professor. He has lived and worked in five countries, creating an artistic legacy in each place. The Lachert Foundation was established in 2007 in Brussels in order to document and promote Lachert's musical and literary work. He lives in Pescara, Italy. www.lachertfoundation.eu/, accessed September 12, 2014.

writes often for the publications "Ruch Muzyczny" and "Nowy Dziennik." She retired from the New York Philharmonic in 2012.

**Isaac Stern** (1920–2001), who "in his prime was considered one of the great instrumentalists of the twentieth century" was born in Krzemieniec, Poland, during the Bolshevik Revolution and the Polish-Soviet Wars (1919–21). The implementation of Woodrow Wilson's "Fourteen Points" at the end of World War I helped to initiate intense fighting between Poland and Russia over territories granted to a renewed Poland. Though Isaac Stern's parents considered themselves Russian, after the Treaty of Riga, the city of Krzemieniec became Polish at the time of Isaac's birth and remained fairly stable until World War II. At the end of that war, the Soviets reestablished their own borders, and it became Kremenets in the Ukraine. The small city of Krzemieniec with its large Jewish population has a long history going back to the tenth century and was part of the powerful Polish-Lithuanian Commonwealth. Juliusz Słowacki, the great Polish Romantic poet, was born there and a museum in his honor opened in 2002. [404]

In 1960, Stern's leadership was largely responsible for saving America's most famous concert venue, Carnegie Hall, from demolition. He was then

---

[404] Allan Kozinn, "Violinist Isaac Stern Dies at 81," *New York Times,* 23 September 2001.

named its first President and in 1997, after leading another effort to renew its support, the main performance hall was established as the Isaac Stern Auditorium and the street on which it stands was renamed as Isaac Stern Place.

Stern performed and recorded many times with Eugene Ormandy and the Philadelphia Orchestra. The Wieniawski Violin Concerto No. 2 was one of the first during Ormandy's forty-four-year tenure as Music Director to be recorded for Columbia Records with Stern as soloist. He delivered the commencement address to the 1989 graduating class of the Curtis institute of Music.

- **From Boston to Philadelphia**
- **The Adamowski Family**

One of the most important musical Polish American families of music was the **Adamowski** family. Paderewski considered them his family and often planned his tours around a holiday in Boston, where they lived most of their lives. **Tymoteusz** (1858–1943) and **Józef** (1862–1930) Adamowski were born in Warsaw; both studied at the Warsaw Conservatory at very young ages, and both came to Boston shortly after the Boston Symphony Orchestra was founded.

courtesy of the Boston Symphony Archives

**Timothee**, as he was called, studied with Apolinary Kątski in Warsaw and Joseph Lambert Massart at the Paris Conservatory before coming to America in 1878. He toured the United States with soprano Clara Louise Kellog and coloratura Emma Thursby, eventually became the concertmaster of the Boston Symphony, and had the distinction of having soloed with them on 82 occasions between 1884 and 1908. He also was a very popular conductor of the Boston Pops Orchestra (1891-1894; 1903-1907); one newspaper account called him the "Idol of the Pops" and said, "No social affair was complete without the Adamowskis."[405] Frequent guest conducting appearances took him abroad, including to Warsaw. He married Gertrude Pancoast of Philadelphia in 1903 and is buried in the West Laurel Cemetery near Philadelphia.[406] Gertrude was a presence in many philanthropic ventures and was a strong supporter of the Paderewski Fund for Polish Relief in New York during World War II. Timothee was also a published composer of violin pieces and Polish Dances.

Library of Congress

---

[405] Bronislas Jezierski, "The Adamowskis Musicians and Patriots," *PAS*, vol. 5, no. 1/2 (Jan.–Jun. 1948): 19
[406] Gertrude Pancoast came from a long line of famous Philadelphia physicians. Her grandfather Dr. Joseph Pancoast was one of the founders of the Jefferson Medical School.

**Josef,** though a cellist, also studied with the violinist Kątski in Warsaw and made his first solo appearance there in 1883. He added study at the Moscow Conservatory with cellist Wilhelm Fitzenhagen.[407] When Henryk Wieniawski died in Moscow in 1880, Josef Adamowski was given charge of transporting his remains back to Poland. He joined the faculty of the Kraków Conservatory for two years before coming to the United States. In 1889, he became principal cellist of the Boston Symphony and one of the founders of the orchestra's pension program. He also became an editor of G. Schirmer's Library of Musical Classics. Like his brother, he and his family had close friendships with other well-known Polish artists, including Sembrich and the Stojowskis. In 1896, Josef married the pianist **Antonina Szumowska** in Warsaw and they remained together until his death 34 years later.[408]

**Antoinette**, as she was called, had studied with Michałowski and Paderewski, to whom she was related.[409] She performed throughout Europe and came to America in 1895 and married Josef the following year in Warsaw. Antoinette played with the Boston Symphony and toured with Walter Damrosch's New York Symphony before becoming a member of the faculty of the New England Conservatory in 1902. During World War I, she tirelessly sought aid for war victims in Poland and eventually raised more than $300,000 for the cause. In 1924, she was decorated by the Polish government with the Officer's Cross of the Order of the Polonia Restituta (*Order Odrodzenia Polski*), presented to her by Paderewski.[410]

---

[407] Campbell (1988) 77.

[408] "Joseph Adamowski dies at 67," *New York Times,* 9 May 1930.

[409] Paderewski had married her mother's sister; Antoinette was the only female pupil he had ever taught.

[410] "Mme. Adamowska, Concert Pianist," *New York Times,* 19 August 1938.

Library of Congresss

Both brothers, Timothee and Josef, appeared in Philadelphia. The Adamowski String Quartet had as second violin, Emanuel **Fiedler** (b.1860), born in Neu Sandec (Nowy Sącz), Poland, and **Max Zach** (b. 1864), a violist born in Lemberg (Lwów) who also became a conductor of the Boston Pops (1896-1902). [411]

On occasion, Paderewski joined the Quartet in concert, but the quartet eventually disbanded and Timothee, Josef, and Antoinette formed the famed Adamowski Trio, performing thirty times a season. They remained in the Boston area, and all three became faculty members of the New

---

[411] Emanuel and his two brothers, Bernard (b. 1878) and Gustav (b. 1872), were all violinists in the Boston Symphony. Emanuel was the father of the future conductor Arthur Fiedler. Max Zach went on to become the conductor of the St. Louis Symphony. www.stokowski.com, accessed September 12, 2014.

England Conservatory. They were very active in raising money through their Polish Relief Fund concerts at the time of World War I.[412]

Josef and Antonina had two children, a son, **Tadeusz,** and a daughter, **Helenka. Tadeusz ("Ralf")** was born in Switzerland, graduated from Harvard, and was a hockey star for the Polish National Team in the 1928 Olympics. He worked as an agent for General Motors in Warsaw. **Helenka (Helen)** was an American silent film actress and humanitarian who was the founder of the U.S. Committee for UNICEF and was that organization's President from 1953 to 1978. She also founded the Paderewski Fund for Polish Relief in 1941 and served as a fundraiser for the American Red Cross at the same time. Helene married Guido Pantaleoni, a lawyer who was killed in World War II. Guido and Helenka were grandparents of the actress **Téa Leoni.**

Courtesy of Diana Burgin

Another outstanding musician who spent his career in Boston was violinist **Richard Burgin.** Born in Warsaw in 1892 to Moisey (Movsha) and Ronia (Raska) Krzyzowska, he began his training with Jakob Winiecki, a first violinist of the Warsaw Philharmonic. Burgin moved into Winiecki's home,

---

[412] "Adamowski Trio to Play for Polish Relief Fund," *Harvard Crimson*, 17 January 1916. Bronislas Jezierski, "The Adamowskis Musicians and Patriots," *PAS*, vol. 5, no. 1/2 (Jan.–Jun. 1948): 14–32.

living and studying with him for six months. He went on to study with Izidor Lotto, Professor at the Warsaw Musical Institute and concertmaster of the Warsaw Opera (Teatr Wielki). At the age of eleven, he performed with the Warsaw Philharmonic. Deciding that a solo career was not to his liking, he became the concertmaster of the orchestras of Warsaw (only Paweł Kochański held that position at a younger age), Oslo, Stockholm, and Helsinki. Pierre Monteux invited him to become concertmaster of the Boston Symphony in 1920, where he remained for forty-two years, a tenure surpassed in America only by Raymond Gniewek of the Metropolitan Opera in New York. [413] When Koussevitzky took over leadership of Boston, Burgin performed the American premiere of the Prokofiev Violin Concerto No. 1. He owned the only known Guarnerius violin to be made entirely of beechwood. In 1934, he was appointed assistant conductor of the Boston Symphony Orchestra and in 1943, its associate conductor. He led the Boston Symphony some 350 times, including tours of the United States, Japan, and Australia.

Burgin was a ranked chess player and a compulsive gambler, who appeared disheveled and was notoriously absent-minded, but also greatly admired and respected by both his colleagues and Koussevitzky.[414] Jasha Heifetz and he had a warm musical relationship. Burgin married the well-known violinist Ruth Posselt, and in 1949 they toured Poland (where he conducted the Warsaw Philharmonic with Posselt as soloist), Finland, and Norway.[415] They also recorded with the Cambridge Early Music Society. As conductor of Boston's Zimbler Sinfonietta, he brought the ensemble to Philadelphia. He retired to Florida, where he formed the Florestan Quartet with his wife and joined the faculty of Florida State University. He died in 1981.

---

[413] Heiles Mischakoff (2007) 46–50.
[414] Dickson (1969) 27–28, 142.
[415] Ruth Posselt was also a member of the Bel Arte Trio together with violist Joseph dePasquale and cellist Martin Hoherman (see other instrumentalists).

# Concertmasters of The Metropolitan Opera Orchestra (1936-2000)

**Stefan Frenkel** (1936-1940) - see Polish prodigies above for biography.

The Metropolitan Opera Archives

**Hugo Kolberg** (1942-1944), was born in Warsaw in 1898 and was known to have studied with Bronisław Huberman before holding the position of concertmaster with orchestras in the European cities of Oslo, Paris, Copenhagen, Berlin (sharing the position with Szymon Goldberg) and in America with the orchestras of Pittsburgh (Reiner) and Cleveland (Rodziński). He then became concertmaster with the Metropolitan Opera Orchestra for two years. After a return to the Pittsburgh Symphony, Bernstein invited him to serve as guest concertmaster and soloist with the New York Philharmonic in 1947. Besides the standard solo violin literature, he brought the little-known violin concertos of Walter Piston and Nicolai Lopatnikoff to the stage. He finally settled in Chicago to become concertmaster of the Chicago Opera and head the violin department at the Chicago Musical College. He passed away in Hempstead, Long Island, New York in 1979.

The Metropolitan Opera Archives, Louis Melancon

**Felix Eyle** (1945-1957), was born in Lvov, Poland in 1899 and was a member of the Vienna Philharmonic and Buxbaum String Quartet before coming to America in 1928. In 1930, he performed a Town Hall recital in a "Teutonic-Slavic" program that included Szymanowski *Myths, Three Poems for violin and piano, op. 30.* Artur Rodziński brought him to the Cleveland Orchestra as Assistant Concertmaster for twelve seasons beginning in 1933, but when Rodziński left Cleveland, Eyle took the position of Concertmaster with the Metropolitan Opera Orchestra, continuing there for twelve years until the arrival of Raymond Gniewek, at which point Eyle became Personnel Manager of the Orchestra (1957-1970). For another thirteen years he taught violin in Hamilton, New York at Colgate University, and died of a heart attack in 1988. He owned the "Alma Guadagnini" violin.

In an interview for the *New York Times* with Anthony Tommasini in January of 2000, James Levine, longtime Music Director of New York's Metropolitan Opera Company, said, "The single luckiest thing that happened to me since I have been at the Met is that Ray Gniewek was the concertmaster." These words were spoken concerning the impending retirement of **Raymond Gniewek**.[416] For Gniewek's final concert at Carnegie Hall with James Levine, which is available on YouTube, he performed the "Intermezzo" from Jules Massenet's *Thaïs* to stunning, lengthy approval from both audience and Orchestra.

The Metropolitan Opera Archives

---

[416] Anthony Tommasini, "Cheers from the Pit Accompany a Coda," *New York Times*, 18 May 2002.

Gniewek was born on Long Island in 1931 and became the concertmaster and youngest member of the Metropolitan Opera Orchestra in New York at the age of twenty-six, and for the next 43 years he performed more than 115 different operas. His father was from Rzeszów, Poland, and the family lived in Philadelphia during Raymond's early years as his older sister Cecilia, a pianist, studied at the Curtis Institute (1940 graduate) with Vengerova. They were a poor family, and Raymond's mother, whose parents were from Lwów, worked cleaning the offices of the Curtis Publishing Company. His father's brothers came from Poland and also settled in the Richmond section of Philadelphia.

Gniewek began his music studies on the piano at the age of three, and at the age of five performed on the local Polish radio station. Playing the piano ended when, at age eight, he began the violin. He attended the Eastman School of Music in Rochester, New York, and became a member of the Rochester Philharmonic under Erich Leinsdorf at the age of nineteen. Gniewek performed the Karłowicz Violin Concerto with the Detroit Symphony a few years later. He went on to solo many times with the Metropolitan Opera Orchestra and others. At the age of 34, after nearly 1,700 performances as concertmaster of the Met, he finally made his New York recital debut at Town Hall. His sister, Cecilia Gniewek Brauer, accompanied him. "Impeccable.. the superlatives come tumbling over each other" were the words used in the *New York Times* review to describe Gniewek's artistry.[417]

He also excelled at chamber music and collaborated with James Levine in concert. After retirement from the Met, at Levine's invitation, he taught at Tanglewood and Verbier, Switzerland. He has also served as concertmaster for Opera Nomori in Tokyo at the invitation of Seiji Ozawa. He appeared in concert, as a collaborating artist, with his wife, the former Metropolitan Opera soprano Judith Blegen (Curtis Institute, 1964). They divided their time between Plymouth, Massachusetts, and Naples, Florida, where Gniewek continued to play the Opera Naples and the Chamber Concert Series.

---

[417] Richard Freed, "Raymond Gniewek Gives Violin Recital," *New York Times,* 4 April 1966.

**From Poland to Israel**

For twenty-three years, **Cecylia Arzewski** held the position of concertmaster in three of America's best orchestras. Born in Kraków in 1948, Cecylia wanted to play the piano like her father Stanisław (b.1914, Warsaw), pianist for the Kraków Philharmonic, but Cecylia's destiny was to be a violinist. She began at age five studying with **Eugenia Umińska.**[418] In 1957, with the help that Isaac Stern provided to many Jews, her family made their way to Israel and setled in Tel Aviv. There, Cecylia studied with the Hungarian violinist, Odeon Partos (1907–1977). After three years, they arrived in America, and Arzewski attended the Juilliard School where she studied with Ivan Galamian. At the New England Conservatory in Boston, she studied with her most important mentor, Joseph Silverstein, 1950 graduate of Curtis and faculty member since 2000. Her orchestral career began with the Buffalo Philharmonic in 1969, but after only one year, she won a position in the Boston Symphony Orchestra and spent the next seventeen years there.

Courtesy of Cecylia Arzewski

---

[418] Umińska (1910–1980) was a violinist and also the rector of the Kraków Music Academy for two years. She prepared the works of many Polish composers for publication for PWM (Polskie Wydawnictwo Muzyczne) and was also the first to perform many of them.

In 1978, she was a winner of the International Bach Festival in Washington, D.C., and several years later she rose to the position of Assistant Concertmaster of the Boston Symphony Orchestra. She made many appearances with the Bostonians in Philadelphia and performed the Wieniawski Violin Concerto No. 2 under Arthur Fiedler. While on a European tour with Boston in 1985, her father joined her, and together they returned to visit Kraków for the first time in many years.

Music Director Christoph von Dohnanyi enticed Arzewski to the Cleveland Orchestra with the position of Associate Concertmaster in 1987, but three years later, she left to become solo Concertmaster of the Atlanta Symphony under Yoel Levi. Robert Spano took over the reins in Atlanta in 2001 and made a number of highly acclaimed recordings that either were nominated for or won Grammy Awards, including a Rimsky-Korsakoff *Scheherazade* with Arzewski as soloist (Telarc CD #80568). She retired from the Atlanta Symphony in 2008, but not before performing the Wieniawski once again, this time with Zdenek Macal in Philadelphia. With the orchestras of Boston, Cleveland, and Atlanta, she performed more than a dozen concerti from Bach to Berg.

In 2007, Arzewski had the privileged distinction of giving a solo performance for His Holiness, The Dalai Lama, at the ceremony awarding him the Presidential Distinguished Professor from Emory University. She has been a member of the Georgian Chamber Players and has recitaled in France and Belgium. Cecylia's brother, Michael (Mieczysław), is a retired music teacher, having studied with Edward Steuermann and Mieczysław Munz at the Juilliard School on a Rubinstein Scholarship. Cecylia's husband, Paul Lennard, is Director of the Neuroscience and Behavioral Biology Program at Emory University. Arzewski's lifelong devotion to Bach led her on a project that she considers her legacy: the six monumental *Sonatas and Partitas* for solo violin by Johann Sebastian Bach. That dream recording, "J.S. Bach: Sonatas and Partitas," was released in 2012 as a double CD on Bridge Records and duly acclaimed.[419]

---

[419] Mark Gresham, "Former ASO Violinist Cecilia Arzewski Releases CD," *Arts Atlanta*, 15 June 2012.

Photo: Lisa Marie Mazzucco

As Jascha Heifetz was generally recognized to be the greatest violinist of his time in America, the same label could be placed upon **Itzhak Perlman**. For at least forty years he has been the highest achieving violinist in the business and easily the most visible. His parents, Chaim and Shoshanna, came from different parts of Poland and immigrated to Palestine in the 1930s. They met and wed there and worked on a kibbutz. Itzhak was born in 1945 in Tel Aviv after the family had moved there and Chaim had opened a barber shop. Classical music on the radio was a significant presence in the family; they discovered Itzhak's ear for music at the age of two and a half, and found that the violin is what he wanted to play. Unfortunately, a wave of the paralytic disease poliomyelitis struck Tel Aviv in 1949 and left the four-year-old Itzhak crippled for life.[420]

The paralysis of his legs, however, did not deter him from his passion, and he began violin lessons at the Tel Aviv Academy of Music. Israel chose Itzhak to represent the country on the *Ed Sullivan Show* when he was thirteen years old, and his performance was the centerpiece of a two-month tour of the United States with the *Caravan of Stars*. That led to his

---

[420] It was not until 1955 that Jonas Salk was to develop a vaccine against the disease.

education at the Juilliard School and a Carnegie Hall debut in 1963 playing the Wieniawski Violin Concerto No. 1. By then, his family had moved to New York and needed financial help, and the Zionist Organization of America and Isaac Stern stepped in to aid them. The Leventritt Award in 1964 sent Itzhak on a coast-to-coast tour of thirty American cities, launching a career that has not been equaled by any violinist since.

It would be difficult to find a musical center in the world that has not seen and heard Perlman. In 1987, he accompanied the Israel Philharmonic on a concert tour that included Warsaw. In addition to his many stops in Philadelphia, both as recitalist and soloist with the Orchestra (fifty times since 1965), he began a new pursuit in the 1990s and conducted performances with the Philadelphia Orchestra. Fifteen Grammy awards for solo, instrumental, and chamber playing, honorary doctorates, and television appearances from Carnegie Hall to Sesame Street have made him an immensely popular artist who glows from the moment the violin touches his chin. Presidents Clinton and Reagan have presented him the National Medal of the Arts and the Medal of Liberty, and he played at President Obama's Inauguration in 2009. He performs on the "Soil" Stradivarius violin that once belonged to Yehudi Menuhin. Perlman often toured as a duo with our next artist, Pinchas Zukerman.[421]

---

[421] Perlman official website, www.itzhakperlman.com/about/, accessed September 12, 2014.

Photo: Cheryl Anne Mazak

**Pinchas Zukerman** was born in Tel Aviv in 1948 to parents who had emigrated from Poland. He studied with the same teacher as Perlman and when the two performed together, it was as if their two instruments had a similar soul. Zukerman has surely been considered one of the foremost performers on not just the violin but also the viola for at least thirty years of the twentieth century. He performs on the Samuel "Dushkin" Guarneri *del Gesu* violin of 1742, and since 1970 he has performed with the Philadelphia Orchestra forty times. Like Perlman, Zuckerman also took up the baton, but his conducting responsibilities have extended much further. He has been Music Director of the St. Paul Chamber Symphony and presently is Music Director of the Ottawa National Arts Centre Orchestra (until 2015). He also serves as Principal Guest Conductor of London's Royal Philharmonic Orchestra. In 1999, he founded the National Arts Centre Young Artists Program. He also has been music director of the summer festivals of the Dallas and Baltimore Symphonies. He has won two Grammy Awards and received twenty-one other nominations. In 1983, President Ronald Reagan presented Zukerman with the National Medal of the Arts in a ceremony that also included another recipient of that honor, Poland's Nobel Prize–winning poet, Czesław Miłosz.

# D. OTHER INSTRUMENTALISTS

In 1938, an English reviewer wrote in *The Strad* magazine, "I do not think there can any longer be doubt that Feuermann is the greatest living cellist, Casals alone excepted… the Wieniawski of the cello." Artur Rubinstein declared him the "greatest cellist of all time."[422]

Courtesy of Dr. Klement Hambourg, www.hambourgconservatory.ca

**Emanuel Feuermann** was born in 1902, in Galicia, Austrian-occupied Poland, just outside of Lemberg (Lwów). His hometown of Kolomyja had been founded in the thirteenth century and had a long history of conflicts against the Turks, Cossacks, and Austrians. King Jan III Sobieski, Poland and Europe's hero of the 1683 Battle of Vienna against the Turks, built a synagogue there to honor his lieutenant, Jan Samuel Chrzanowski—but at the beginning of the twentieth century, Kolomyja was under Austrian

---

[422] Brinton Smith, "The Physical and Interpretive Technique of Emanuel Feuermann," Thesis (D.M.A), Juilliard School of Music, 1998, www.cello.org/theses/smith/chap1. htm, accessed September 12, 2014.

rule, and life for the Poles, including the Galician Jewry, was better there than in other parts of Poland; today, Kolomyia is in the Ukraine.

The Feuermann family was intensely musical. The patriarch, Maier, played the cello and violin, and there were great expectations for Sigmond (Zygmunt), Emanuel's very talented older brother who played the violin. Moriz Rosenthal persuaded Felix Weingartner, the conductor of the Vienna Philharmonic, to use the two in performance. In 1914, Emanuel and Sigmond performed the Brahms Double Concerto with the Vienna Philharmonic under Weingartner. It had been seventy years since a child that young—the violinist Joseph Joachim at the age of twelve—had played with the Vienna Philharmonic.[423] Munio, as Emanuel was called, made his solo debut that same year performing the Haydn D Major Concerto, again with the Vienna Philharmonic and Weingartner. Munio then went to Leipzig to study with the famous cellist and teacher Julius Klengel. Feuermann served for four years as Professor of the Berlin Hochschule,[424] becoming the world's greatest example of the German School of cellists. During his time at the Hochschule, he formed a trio with Paul Hindemith and Josef Wolfstahl, later replaced by Szymon Goldberg. He performed the complete sonatas of Brahms and Beethoven with Artur Schnabel in Moscow and played the Brahms Double Concerto with Carl Flesch. When the Nazis came to power, his contract was canceled, and Bronisław Huberman[425] helped him escape to Palestine; after a short period there, he spent most of the remainder of his life in America. He applied for citizenship in 1938.

Feuermann's recordings with Heifetz and Rubinstein are still treasured today. He greatly valued his partnership with Leopold Stokowski and the Philadelphia Orchestra, making his first recording of the Bloch *Schelomo* and collaborating in a Chinese Relief concert in 1940. His first performances with the Orchestra were in the Brahms Double Concerto with Joseph Szigeti.[426] He also performed several times with the Philadelphia Orchestra

---

[423] Unfortunately, mental illness kept Sigmund from developing a career.

[424] At seventeen he had been Professor at Cologne University; only one of his students was younger than he. Ginsberg (1983) 224.

[425] Feuermann was playing in a trio with Huberman and Artur Schnabel.

[426] www.allmusic.com/artist/emanuel-feuermann-mn0001371379, accessed September 12, 2014.

under Eugene Ormandy. He began teaching at the Curtis Institute in 1941. His very last concert performance was with Ormandy and the Philadelphians playing the Dvorak Cello Concerto. He died shortly afterwards at the age of 39 of peritonitis after a routine operation.

Courtesy of Diana Burgin

**Martin Hoherman** joined the Boston Symphony in 1953 as assistant principal cello and at the same time as principal cellist and frequent soloist with the Boston Pops Orchestra. He held both positions until 1982. He was born in Warsaw in 1912 and spent the years leading up to World War II in Poland. He began music lessons at age five and went on to study cello with Eli Kochański (brother of the well-known violin soloist, Paweł.) At twelve, he performed a concerto with the Warsaw Philharmonic, and a few years later he became a member of that orchestra; he also became principal cellist and conductor of Warsaw Radio.

When Germany invaded Poland, Hoherman fled to England, joined the British Army, and served as a member of the ENSA (Entertainments National Service Association), an entertainment group for allied troops that performed in Egypt, India, Ceylon, and Burma. After the war ended in Europe, he performed recitals in London and the British Isles but then returned to Ceylon since he had developed a fascination with their culture.

Hoherman stayed for three years and became Director of Western Music for the Colombo Broadcasting Company. He also trained promising young cellists, for some of whom he arranged further studies in England. He also began composing, mostly children's songs, and frequently performed on Radio-Ceylon.

When he went to Boston, his ability to work easily with children continued with the Boston Pops through its youth programs and recordings.[427] He wrote lyrics for and was soloist in Saint-Saens' *Carnival of the Animals;* his performance, in reissue, is paired with Eugene Ormandy and the Philadelphia Orchestra in *Peter and the Wolf* (RCA: CD # 1132287, Catalog # 68131). It seems there was no end to his range of instruments: he knew the banjo, sax, mandolin, celesta, clarinet, accordion, and double bass, and was called on by the Orchestra to play them as needed. In his book *Gentlemen, More Dolce Please*, Harry Ellis Dickson wrote: "name the instrument, Hoherman will play it. And if he can't, give him a few hours' practice time."[428]

On a 1979 tour of China with Seiji Ozawa and the Boston Symphony, Hoherman learned a Chinese stringed instrument, the ban-hu, for a special performance in Peking of the Chinese ballet *The White Haired Girl*. Harold Schonberg, the critic for the *New York Times* on tour with the orchestra, reported that the concert had to be stopped as the screams of the 18,000 in attendance went up for Hoherman.[429] He also collected stamps and coins, liked photography, painted in oils, and repaired watches. He was on the faculty of the Berkshire Music Center from 1976 to 1981. Before Boston, he had spent three years teaching at the Bornoff School of Music in Winnepeg, Manitoba. He also performed in the Bel Arte Trio with Joseph dePasquale (longtime principal viola of the Philadelpha Orchestra) and Ruth Posselt (wife of Richard Burgin). Hoherman died in 1998 in Boca Raton, Florida.

---

[427] Hoherman biography for Boston Symphony provided by Barbara Perkel, Assistant Archivist, 1 December 2011
[428] Dickson (1969) 9.
[429] Harold Schonberg, "18,000 Hear Bostonians' Finale in Peking," *New York Times*, 20 March 1979.

Courtesy of Gina Kapuscinski

Cellist **Richard (Roman) Kapuściński** was born in 1921 in Milwaukee, Wisconsin. His father, Wincenty Roman Kapuściński, arrived at Ellis Island from Poland in 1905. Although Richard was the only child to become a professional musician, he was born into an intensely musical household where one could hear the piano, cello, trumpet, banjo, accordion, or horn played by one member of the family or another. As a teenager, Richard studied for one year in Cleveland with Leonard Rose before deciding to attend the Curtis Institute in Philadelphia under the tutelage of Felix Salmond, who had been Rose's teacher when Rose himself was attending Curtis. While still in school in Philadelphia, Kapuscinski played in the WPA (Works Project Administration) Youth Orchestra; and became principal cello of the Philadelphia Opera Company. In 1943, he left Curtis after only three years and embarked on a much-traveled career, first joining the Cleveland Orchestra as assistant principal cello under George Szell. He then also became the head of the cello department at the Cleveland Music Settlement. Five years later, in 1948, the principal cello position in the Baltimore Symphony lured him to that city, where he also taught at the Peabody Conservatory. During his years in both Cleveland and Baltimore, Kapuscinski was a member of the LaSalle String

Quartet.[430] But a few months after the ensemble's 1955 New York debut at Town Hall, he decided to part company with both the quartet and the Baltimore Symphony.

Kapuscinski moved to Boston where he was a most active teacher and performer, taking a position in the cello section of the Boston Symphony. He played the Boccherini Cello Concerto in B flat with the Boston Pops under Arthur Fiedler and formed the Boston Arts Quartet and Gabrieli String Trio. On the faculty of Boston University's School of Fine and Applied Arts, he taught cello and chamber music. Kapuscinski was also chairman of both the Contemporary Music Society of Boston and the Boston Arts Association.[431] During the Boston Symphony's 1966–67 season, under Music Director Seiji Ozawa, Kapuscinski took part in an historic exchange with the Tokyo Philharmonic; he and his family lived in Tokyo for a year, during which he played with the Tokyo Philharmonic and organized informal English classes for the Japanese orchestra musicians.[432]

After 12 years in Boston, Kapuscinski moved back to Cleveland, not as a member of the Cleveland Orchestra but to accept a professorship at Oberlin College. He spent the rest of his life there, as a vital member of the school. He fulfilled all his ambitions as a teacher, chamber music performer, conductor, and mentor to the many young musicians whose lives he and his wife, Lucy, touched. He was an inspiration and role model to those students. When Oberlin adopted co-ed dormitories for the first time, he and Lucy even lived in a newly created residence apartment with

---

[430] The LaSalle String Quartet was an important chamber group from 1946 to 1987. Performing on donated Amati instruments, they were formed by their first violinist, Walter Levin. The Quartet specialized in the music of the "Second Viennese School," composers in the tradition of Schoenberg, Berg, and Webern. They were in residence at the College of Music of Cincinnati but performed in a wide array of concert sites throughout the U.S. and Europe. They also brought the music of Alexander Zemlinsky into the light, recording all four of his string quartets and winning the Deutsche Schallplattenpreis. A recording of the late Beethoven quartets won them a Grand Prix du Disque. They also premiered the Lutoslawski String Quartet, and their work continues to be studied by the many string quartets that have followed.

[431] Thanks to Bridget Carr, Archivist, Boston Symphony, 9 February 2012.

[432] Raymond Erickson, "Four Tickets in Boston-Tokyo Swap," *New York Times,* 9 July 1967. Also see Robert Trumbull, "Bostonians' Link to Tokyo In Peril," *New York Times,* 27 May 1967.

practice studio and acted as house directors. He founded a faculty string quartet and, as a recitalist, performed not just at Oberlin but also in a Carnegie Hall recital in 1971. He was described as "an intellectualist," and his playing as "nicely detailed and elegantly articulated."[433]

Kapuscinski continued to return to Massachusetts in the summer to perform with the Berkshire Chamber Players at Tanglewood.[434] He was important in establishing the symphony orchestra at Oberlin, conducting it and expanding his efforts outside of Oberlin as Music Director of the Philharmonia, an orchestra for advanced high-school students in northern Ohio. He took a leave of absence in the 1970s to travel through Europe, from England to Hungary, visiting various conservatories and studying the best-known cello pedagogues. With students like Steven Isserlis and Rhonda Rider, one can include Kapuscinski among those illustrious pedagogues. He died in Oberlin in 1991.[435]

The stories of so many of the musicians in these pages are spellbinding. It is not possible for most people living in a privileged society to imagine the hardship through which one could not just survive but actually become one of the world's leading musicians. **Leszek Zawistowski (Leshek Zavistovski)** is no different. He was cellist with the Metropolitan Opera in New York City for 36 years, but how he got there is a volume in itself and is documented in his memoir, *Children and Fish Don't Talk.*

---

[433] Peter Davis, "Richard Kapuścinski Gives Cello Recital," *New York Times,* 15 March 1971.

[434] Raymond Erickson, "105 Years Later," *New York Times,* 7 July 1968.

[435] Thanks to Luisa Hoffman, Oberlin College Archives, 6 February 2012.

Courtesy of Leshek Zavistovski

He was born in Warsaw in 1938 on Good Friday, April 15. He came from an affluent family, which would have seemed to offer peace and security, but the world that was Europe was changing quickly; in 1939 there was to be nothing but anxiety for everyone living between the two neighbors, Germany and Russia. Poland was about to be overrun from both east and west. Leszek's parents had studied in Warsaw; his father was a specialist in French antiquities, and his mother was an artist who had studied at the Academy of Fine Arts. She was also of Czech-Polish-Jewish background and came to Poland because that country more than anywhere else in Europe offered the best life for a Jew. When World War II struck, Leszek's father fought in the AK (Armia Krajowa) of the Polish Resistance against the Nazis, presuming the family would be safe in the East—until the Russians decided to claim Polish territory. To evade the Russians, the family came to Warsaw, but the Nazis captured Leszek's older brother, Henryk. Even though his mother's family had converted to Catholicism years earlier, Henryk was still a Jew in the eyes of the Nazis and was sent to Auschwitz where he was murdered. Their mother escaped and went to Jasna Góra in Częstochowa and survived the war there working in the monastery. With his father in the AK and mother in the monastery, Leszek was entrusted to whomever could take care of him. When the Russians captured Polish territory, Leszek was considered an orphan and the responsibility of the Russian army. His mother did eventually find him after the war, and they returned to Warsaw and lived in terrible poverty like everyone else after the total destruction of that city, then under the rule of the Communists. His father fought the entire war; helped in the Warsaw Ghetto Uprising and in the American cleanup of the death camp Ohrdruf, a part of Buchenwald. However, he was captured by the Russians as he was returning to Warsaw. The KGB put him into a gulag and relentlessly searched for any surviving members of the Polish Resistance, considering them enemies of the new Communist regime. He was eventually released, but because of years of separation, Leszek really didn't meet his father until he was ten years old.

Zawistowski's musical life began in earnest when he was nine and began to study with the Warsaw Philharmonic's principal cellist, **Tadeusz Kowalski**. He went on to receive a Master's Degree from the Warsaw Academy of Music[436] and won the Polish Youth Music Competition in 1958. Mstislaw Rostropovich came often to Warsaw, and the young Zawistowski played for his master classes. Rostropovich wanted to bring him to Moscow for further studies, but Leszek declined and took a position with the Warsaw Philharmonic in 1959 as the orchestra's youngest member. He was present when Leopold Stokowski came to Warsaw and conducted the orchestra in Mussorgsky's Pictures at an Exhibition. He also became a member of the newly-formed Musicae Antiquae Collegium Varsoviense and the Warsaw Chamber Opera.

With their music director, Witold Rowicki, the Warsaw Philharmonic toured the East Coast of America in 1961, including Philadelphia. On their next tour in 1964, while in New York City, Leszek Zawistowski defected to the United States. With the help of Stanisław Arzewski (father of violinist Cecylia Arzewski), he was granted political asylum and received a student visa at Juilliard and remained there for two years. He became a substitute musician with the Metropolitan Opera Orchestra and at Radio City Music Hall. He also performed the Chopin Sonata for Cello in recital with Mieczysław Munz, who no longer taught piano at the Curtis Institute or the Peabody Conservatory, having chosen to spend his last years at Juilliard. In 1965, Zawistowski became a founding member of the Vaghy String Quartette, and they recorded the Shostakovich String Quartet No. 8 and the Mozart *K. 465*. They also performed with soprano Adele Addison for the Polish Cultural Foundation. Halina Rodzińska arranged an audition for Zawistowski with Leopold Stokowski, and he was hired

---

[436] His classmate was the brilliant violinist Tomasz Michalak.

as the Associate Principal Cellist in Stokowski's newly-formed American Symphony Orchestra. Stokowski also signed his immigration papers, acting as his "godfather." Basia (Barbara) Hammerstein, Polish-born wife of Oscar Hammerstein II, took an interest in Leszek and arranged for an apartment for him to stay in. It belonged to the famous bandleader/composer Luther Henderson, who declared that Paderewski was his piano inspiration. Leszek's rent was to help Henderson copy parts for his various commitments. Having never seen a black person in Poland, Leszek was now introduced to the nation's most famous: Duke Ellington, Lena Horne, and Harry Belafonte. He then auditioned for the New York Philharmonic, but before Leonard Bernstein could make a decision, Zawistowski won a position at the Metropolitan Opera, and he remained there for 36 years, performing in Philadelphia on at least two dozen occasions. Now prosperous, when it came time for him to find his own bachelor pad, a brownstone duplex near the Met, Halina Rodzińska once again stepped in and helped him acquire some hand-me-downs from Nela and Artur Rubinstein who were moving to another place in New York City.

Zawistowski married the violinist Toni Rapport, also a member of the Metropolitan Opera Orchestra, and they both performed at the Aspen Music Festival in Colorado. In 1969, they formed the Bergson Trio with pianist Martin Katz. In the same year they became two of the original artistic founders of the Newport Music Festival in Rhode Island, formed as a summer season for Metropolitan Opera musicians and singers.[437]

Upon becoming a U.S. citizen in 1973, Leszek Zawistowski changed the spelling of his name to Leshek Zavistovski. In 1978, Toni and Leshek founded the Newport Opera Festival. They brought in some of the world's foremost artists, and Piotr Janowski and the Warsaw Chamber Opera were on the playbill. The Warsaw Chamber Opera was sent by the Polish

---

[437] The Newport Music Festival had considerable significance to several Polish artists: Ewa Podleś' first appearance in North America was here in the summer of 1982 with her husband, Jerzy Marchwinski, as her accompanist. Bella Davidowich and Halina Czerny-Stefańska who had shared the first prize in the 1949 Chopin International Piano Competition appeared here as a duo piano team in 1984. Czerny-Stefańska, in her first appearance in America, also accompanied Kristine Ciesinski in Chopin *Songs* and Carol Wincenc, flutist, in Chopin's *Variations on a Theme by Rossini*. Raymond Gniewek, the Metropolitan Opera's longstanding Concertmaster, was also a part of a string quartet with Zawistowski and Tony Rapport.

Government, and programs included a wide range of late eighteenth-and early nineteenth-century operatic repertoire from little known Italian composers to Moniuszko and Kamieński. With Artur Balsam and Roman Totenberg, a trio was organized, which performed at the Kościuszko Foundation in New York City for a gala event honoring Artur Rubinstein. Leshek and Toni moved to Santa Fe, New Mexico, in 2002. Leshek became a successful, commissioned sculptor, and for several years he and Toni also formed a specialized travel-arts organization, Zara Arts International.

The cellist, **Mstislaw Rostropovich (Roztropowicz)**, one of the greatest, most revered and honored instrumentalists of the last hundred years, also has a Polish background. His father, Leopold Roztropowicz, was of Belarussian-Polish noble ancestry from a family palace in Skotniki, Masovian Voivodship. Leopold was a talented cellist and the first professional musician in a family that had produced musicians for generations. He studied with **Aleksander Wierzbiłłowicz**, a Pole who was the cello professor at the St. Petersburg Conservatory.[438] Mstislaw, born in 1927, was a prodigy who learned the cello at a very early age and also studied piano, conducting, and composition with Shostakovich and Prokofiev at the Moscow Conservatory. One of the twentieth century's most recognized instrumentalists, he received honors and awards from dozens of countries throughout the world and appeared in Philadelphia many times as a soloist, beginning with his historic visit in 1959. At that time, he was accompanied by Shostakovich, another musician of Polish background. Rostropovich also taught at the Curtis Institute in the 1990s.

He performed no less than 100 premieres in his solo career, including the works of Lutosławski and Penderecki. In 1967, he gave a series of eight concerto concerts at Carnegie Hall. In two-and-one-half weeks, he completed the astounding accomplishment of playing 34 concertos

---

[438] Wierzbiłłowicz studied in Warsaw and then St. Petersburg, eventually becoming the Professor of Cello there after Karl Davidov. He also returned to Warsaw often to perform in a trio with pianist Aleksander Michałowski, and violinist Stanislas Barcewicz. Both were Poland's best-known musicians and teachers. Wierzbiłłowicz was also a friend of Tchaikowsky and helped him with orchestrations.

by 20 different composers.[439] He was also an excellent pianist who often accompanied his wife, the Russian soprano Galina Vishnevskaja. He added conducting to his resume later in life when he became Music Director of the National Symphony in Washington, D.C., and began guest conducting most of the major orchestras in the world, including Philadelphia. Rostropovich died in 2007.

Indiana University Jacobs School of Music, Bloomington

In 2010, **Stephen Wyrczyński** was appointed Professor of Viola and head of the String Department at the Indiana University Jacobs School of Music.[440] Wyrczynski was born in 1966 in New Jersey to family from Warsaw and Rzeszów. His father played piano, accordion, and bass in polka bands from his teenage years. Stephen attended Juilliard and the Curtis Institute before becoming a member of the Philadelphia Orchestra for 18 years. He performed in Warsaw at the Teatr Wielki and was the Philadelphia Orchestra's spokesman to the Polish audience. Wyrczynski holds an artist-faculty position at the Aspen Music Festival and has taught at both the Peabody Conservatory and Mannes School of Music. He has become a very active chamber music player, collaborating with today's

---

[439] Cowling (1975) 174.
[440] http://info.music.indiana.edu/sb/page/normal/1605.html, accessed September 12, 2014.

leading soloists, such as Joshua Bell, Sarah Chang, Pamela Frank, Edgar Meyer, and Dawn Upshaw. He regularly conducts master classes and seminars throughout the United States and Canada.

**Virginia Majewski,** violist, was born in Texas in 1915 and died in California in 1995.[441] She graduated from the Curtis Institute of Music in 1935, having studied with Max Aronoff. She also became Aronoff's student assistant and chamber music coach. She was a busy and highly-respected player, even from her earliest days as a student in Philadelphia. She performed Alexander Tansman's *Triptyque* with the Curtis Chamber Music Ensemble in 1936 at Town Hall in New York City.[442] She also performed the Mozart *Symphonie Concertante* with Eudice Shapiro and Fritz Reiner for radio broadcast in Philadelphia and New York (WABC). In 1939, Stokowski wrote a letter of introduction for her to Pierre Monteux and Eugene Ormandy, saying "I have never heard such wonderful playing with such a large and beautiful tone."[443]

Majewski eventually moved to California, where she began a long career as solo viola in the studios, recording for at least ten different labels and at MGM, where her solos for films often garnered her a listing in the final credits. She was one of the first women studio musicians to be recognized in this way.[444] She came into the lives of most Americans not just through the movies but also by way of her recording collaborations with popular greats from Frank Sinatra, Ella Fitzgerald, and Count Basie to the American Art Quartet. Majewski also performed and recorded with Heifetz and Piatigorsky,[445] and made several recordings with the guitarist Laurindo Almeida.[446]

---

[441] "Virginia Majewski: Violist for Glendale Symphony," *Los Angeles Times*, 18 October 1995.

[442] Olin Downes, "Curtis Ensemble in Varied Program," *New York Times*, 25 March 1938.

[443] University of Pennsylvania Rare Book and Manuscript Library, Stokowski Papers, Ms. Coll. 381.

Daniel (1982) 922–23.

Stokowski collection, University of Pennsylvania .

[444] www.discogs.com/artist/Virginia+Majewski accessed September 12, 2014.

[445] RCA LDS 6159.

[446] Capitol P 8546, 8571, 8582.

Boston Symphony Archives

The brilliant principal horn of the Boston Symphony Orchestra from 1972 to 1997 was **Charles Kavalovski (Kawalowski),** long admired for his consistency and discipline on this most treacherous of solo instruments. The beauty of his playing can be enjoyed on his many recordings. But Kavalovski had a brilliant career *before* the horn! He earned a Bachelor's degree in mathematics, a Master's of Business Administration, and a PhD in nuclear physics, and became a full professor of physics by the age of 35. During his academic career, he was a member of the physics faculties at the University of Washington in Seattle, Eastern Washington State University in Spokane, and the University of Lowell in Massachusetts; he was also a Research Associate at MIT, where he worked on their proton cyclotron.

Kavalovski was born in 1936 to Kazimierz Kawalowski and Elvene Philipesek. Kazimierz had come from Warsaw to America with his mother, Ewa, in 1913; upon arrival at Ellis Island, their name was inadvertently altered to Kavalovski. Elvene's ancestors had come from Twardawa in Silesia.[447] Both families settled on farms in Minnesota, but Kazimierz

---

[447] Charles's sister, Charlotte, went to Warsaw and hired a genealogist who made a detailed history of the family in Poland, most of it obtained from the Church of the Holy Cross (Kościół Świętego Krzyża.).

and Elvene found their way to the Minneapolis-St. Paul area for work: Kazimierz at the Swift meat packing company and Elvene as a caretaker for a local family.

Kazimierz and one of his brothers played the accordion, and Elvene played the piano. They married in 1935 and had five children, all of whom attended private Catholic schools. Though the family had limited means, a second-hand grand piano graced their living room, and all the children were required to learn to play. For Charles, the oldest, the piano was not a happy experience. One day, his mother brought home an instrument in a case and told him, "If you concentrate on 'this' you can give up the piano." Charles at first said, "It's a deal" and then discovered a French horn in the case. Two of his siblings also later played the horn, another sang, and the fourth played the organ, but none chose music as a profession. In all, these five children amassed fifteen college degrees, but Charles was the only one for whom a degree would never have been necessary for a position like the principal chair in the world-renowned Boston Symphony.[448] During his educational work on his many non-music degrees at the University of Minnesota, he continued his interest in the horn. He was largely self-taught, but also occasionally studied privately with members of the Minnesota Orchestra. He formed a woodwind quintet with colleagues from the Physics Department and became a substitute player with the Minneapolis Symphony (now the Minnesota Orchestra).

While still on the faculty in Spokane, Washington, Kavalovski decided to try out his skills in finding a symphony orchestra job and took a leave of absence from his teaching position. His success was electrifying. He won auditions for the Denver Symphony, the San Francisco Symphony, the Portland Symphony (now the Oregon Symphony), and the Montreal Symphony, all within a year. He decided to play in Denver for one year, during which time he won the principal horn position in Boston. During his tenure as principal French horn in the BSO he also was a member of the faculties of Boston University and the New England Conservatory. For the Musical Heritage Society, he recorded an album entitled *Twentieth Century Music for the Horn*. In 1992, he had a disastrous fall from his roof, landing on his head and fracturing the back of his skull. Through great luck and

---

[448] Thomas Cowan, "Profile Interiew with Charles Kavalovski," *The Horn Call*, November 1976: 61–67.

personal determination, however, he reclaimed his solo chair in the Boston Symphony just three months later and continued in that post until August 1997, when he retired from the orchestra after its Tanglewood season.[449]

Returning to his roots, Kavalovski settled on a farm in Minnesota with his wife, Margo Garrett.[450] But he also free-lanced, played substitute first horn with the Minnesota Opera, and joined the horn faculty of the University of Minnesota's School of Music. With the Westwood Wind Quintet, he embarked on a fourteen-CD project, recording the complete quintets of Anton Reicha for Crystal Records. He also started restudying physics and has since decided that he'll probably be a student all his life.

Courtesy of David Zauder

In 1944, no one could have imagined that a sixteen-year-old boy imprisoned in Auschwitz for a year and a half and forced to make an infamous death march from that camp would become one of America's foremost trumpet

---

[449] William Scharnberg, "A Tribute to Charles Kavalovski," *The Horn Call*, February 1998: 35–41.

[450] Kavalovski's wife, Margo Garrett, is a well-known pianist and pedagogue. She has been recital and recording partner to a large number of classical singers and instrumentalists, including Philadelphia's own Benita Valente (Curtis 1960) and long-time Curtis Institute faculty member and violinist Jaime Laredo (Curtis 1959).

players. **David Zauder** was born in Kraków in 1928.[451] His father was a tailor who was also a drummer for the Yiddish Theater; his mother made costumes for the productions there. As a boy, David loved to go at noon to the main square of the town and listen to the trumpet player perform the mournful call from the tower of St. Mary's Church (*Kościół Mariacki*).[452] Before David could even aspire to musical training, the Nazis occupied Kraków, and the family was confined to the ghetto there until they were all sent to Płaszów, just outside Kraków.[453] Both of David's parents died there before he was sent to Auschwitz, Sachsenhausen, and finally Flossenburg in 1944.

After the Allies liberated Europe, Zauder worked for the Seventh U.S. Army in Frankfurt, shining shoes in a barber shop and having his first experience with a trumpet—Frank Bond, a G.I. from Georgia, let him play on his trumpet every chance he got. Through the Red Cross, Zauder was able to make contact with an aunt in Detroit who sent him a ticket for passage to America; he arrived in 1946. Detroit was home to a famed trumpet player and band leader, Leonard B. Smith, who took an extraordinary interest in Zauder, which was to propel his life and career. Because of his lack of English, the eighteen-year-old was placed in the fifth grade, but he was a brilliant student and quickly excelled enough for Leonard Smith to arrange a scholarship for him to the New York Military Academy in Cornwall, N.Y. By then he had begun serious training on the trumpet and was under the tutelage of some of America's best player-teachers, including Harry Glantz, who had briefly been first trumpet in the Philadelphia Orchestra.

Zauder eventually entered the U.S. Army and spent four years as a member of the United States Military Academy Band at West Point. When he left West Point, he spent two years touring the country as first trumpet

---

[451] This year of birth is not for certain. The date that Zauder uses is the first of two that the Nazis listed for him. 1931 is the other.

[452] A legend from the thirteenth century, the Tartar invasion of 1241, tells of the call of a trumpet, called the *hejnal,* as sounding the alarm to the town that the Tartars were attacking. The call was abruptly ended when a Tartar arrow struck the trumpeter. Today that call is performed four times an hour, twenty-four hours a day in all four directions, and can only be performed by a member of the Fire Brigade (strażak), who were entrusted with the duty beginning in the late nineteenth century.

[453] Płaszów was the Nazi work camp used in the Steven Spielberg film *Schindler's List.*

with Arthur Fiedler's Boston Pops Orchestra, after which he embarked on a most extraordinary 39-year tenure with the Cleveland Orchestra.[454] During that time, he earned a business degree from Case Western Reserve University, which he put to good use as personnel manager of the Cleveland Orchestra, while he continued to maintain the highest level of playing. He taught at the Cleveland Institute of Music for seventeen years. In 1997, the Musical Arts Association of Cleveland bestowed upon him its Distinguished Service Award. In 2008, General Norman Schwarzkopf, Commander in Chief of Central Command Forces in Operation Desert Shield (1990-91), made Zauder an honorary member of the 1956 graduating class of West Point for all his lifelong accomplishments and especially for his musical support during Schwarzkopf's cadet days that coincided with Zauder's. Zauder died in Colorado in 2013.[455] His daughter, Karen Zauder, established a website telling the story of his Holocaust experience at www.standupsters.com.

Photo: Justina Piernik

It is not likely that a tubist would be considered a major influence in *avant garde* music, but in the case of **Zdzisław Piernik**, one can only marvel at the challenge for innovation that he presented to Polish composers. He

---

[454] Frank Kaderabek, "The Worst of Times...The Best of Times," *ITG Journal*, March 2005: 6–14.
[455] Grant Segall, "David Zauder," Cleveland.com/obituaries, 16 April 2013.

inspired originality in no less than Krzysztof Penderecki, who composed the *Capriccio* for Solo Tuba for him, which Piernik performed for the first time in 1980 at the Warsaw Autumn (Warszawska Jesień). It quickly became the most frequently performed piece of new twentieth-century music written for the instrument. Piernik also gave the first performance of Henryk Górecki's *Aria* at the Aspecte Salzburg Festival in 1987.

Piernik was born in Toruń in 1942 and, of course, did not start on the tuba but first played the trumpet; he also played the double bass in the jazz band. His solo career on the tuba was launched in 1970, when he won first prize at the Third National Festival of Young Musicians in Gdańsk. In the midst of the oppression of the cold war, he performed in underground clubs or anywhere else he could, and made several recordings. He became a member of the National Philharmonic Orchestra in Warsaw but spent most of his time performing recitals and inspiring commissions to expand the repertoire for his instrument. In addition to recitals throughout Europe, he has performed in Mexico and Japan. Piernik's renditions of old masterworks transcribed for his instrument have been recorded and have received worldwide distribution. He has appeared on television and been frequently heard on radio throughout Europe. Piernik is a longtime member of the faculty of the Chopin Academy of Music in Warsaw. In 1983 he participated in the International Tuba Conference, held in the United States at the University of Maryland, where he performed in a recital with this writer, tubist of the Philadelphia Orchestra. Piernik introduced a new work by the Polish composer Witold Szalonek, startling the audience with both its originality and performance. In 1987, he welcomed the Philadelphia Orchestra to Warsaw when they performed at the National Theater (Teatr Wielki) on a European tour.

Indiana University Jacobs School of Music, Bloomington

Although **Elżbieta Monika Szmyt**, Professor of Harp at Indiana University, came to America in 1987, she has maintained close contact with Poland and each year returns as a soloist or teacher. She was born in Warsaw in 1962 and first studied piano at the Wieniawski Primary School of Music with Ewa Orwicz. She began the harp at age fifteen with Poland's best known harpist, **Alina Baranowska**, first studying at the Elsner School of Music, followed by a Master's degree at the Chopin Academy of Music. At the same time, she also earned a Master's degree in clinical psychology from Warsaw University. She then came to Indiana University, working towards an Artist Diploma and, in 1991, was offered a teaching position at the world famous Jacobs School of Music. Every two years, she returns to the Elsner Conservatory in Warsaw to conduct international harp master classes. She has premiered the major harp concertos of Gliere and Ginastera with the Warsaw Philharmonic and the Rodrigo *Aranjuez* Concerto with the Kraków Philharmonic. She played a special recital at St. Matthew's Cathedral in Washington, D.C., in memory of Pope John Paul II. Szmyt has performed and lectured all over Europe, Canada, Japan, and the United States, also performing at the World Harp Congresses in Denmark (1993) and Prague (1999). Her research interests include pedagogy and the psychology of music. She released a solo CD entitled *Rhapsody* and is on the board of the International Harp Competition. A master class at the Curtis Institute of Music brought her to Philadelphia in 2011.[456]

Courtesy of Ursula Kwasnicka

**Urszula Kwaśnicka (Ursula Kwasnicka)**, harpist, was born in Szczurowice, Poland, in 1943. She started her musical life on the piano at the age of five, began harp studies in the fifth grade, and credits Ewa Węgrzyniak as her inspiration on the harp. She attended the School of Music in Bytom and, from 1959 to 1961, while attending school, she became the harpist with the Silesian Opera in Bytom. Her paternal grandfather had come to America in 1904 and worked as a tailor in New York City. In 1962, Urszula came to America with her family. Her musical talents were immediately recognized, and she received a full scholarship to study with the French-American harpist Marcel Grandjany at the Manhattan School of Music. While still a student there, Ursula was a busy soloist and recitalist throughout the United States. She studied there from 1962 to 1968, receiving both a Bachelor of Arts and a Master of Arts. In 1966, she won First Prize in the second American Harp Society Competition; her reward was a Carnegie

---

[456] Indiana University website for Szmyt, http://music.indiana.edu/precollege/year-round/harp/faculty.shtml, accessed September 12, 2014.

Hall recital.[457] "Miss Kwasnicka coaxed a remarkable variety of sounds from the solo harp, and her zestful playing gave the music precisely the right blend of fun and fantasy," *New York Times*. Kwasnicka was also a member of Leopold Stokowski's American Symphony. When Grandjany, who also taught at the Juilliard School of Music, died, Kwasnicka joined the Juilliard faculty for one year.

In 1968, she became a member of the Honolulu Symphony and the following year received a fellowship from the French government to pursue her career in France. She studied harp with Pierre Jamet, professor of the Conservatoire Superier in Paris. In 1970, she was a prize winner at the International Harp Competition in Israel, and the following year she held her solo recital debut in France at the Salle Gaveau in Paris. While in Paris, she met Marta Ptaszyńska, and the outcome of their collaboration was the composition *Jeu Parti* for harp and vibraphone, which was first performed at a special concert at Bennington College in Vermont. That same year, she went to Poland and gave recitals at the Academy of Music in Warsaw and at her alma mater, the School of Music in Bytom. Kwasnicka returned to the United States in the summer of 1971 and joined the Syracuse Symphony Orchestra as principal harpist. During her tenure at Syracuse, she performed Mozart's Concerto for Flute and Harp and Debussy's *Danses sacrée et profane*.

Kwasnicka was on the faculty of Hamilton College. Her son, Mark G., is an avant-garde composer whose compositions Ursula has performed several times, and her daughter, Agatha, is a social worker who speaks several languages including Polish and Mandarin.

When the 2007 Metropolitan Opera season began, Music Director James Levine chose to open the year with Gaetano Donizetti's *Lucia di Lammermoor*, and with it presented a challenge for Natalie Dessay, the great French soprano who was to star in the role of Lucia. Donizetti's concept for some of the vocal writing in the "mad scene" for the character of Lucia included the accompaniment of a glass armonica, an instrument rarely used to supplement or substitute for the traditional flute, but originally intended by the composer. Dessay, however, had never performed this

---

[457] Robert Sherman, "Ursula Kwasnicka…is Heard," *New York Times,* 21 October 1968.

version at the Met. [458] Levine knew that this would be a bit different for her, but he was also quite certain of its artistic success since, after all, he had one of the great sopranos in the world, and for the playing of this uncommon instrument he had in his own orchestra a virtuoso and one of only "fifteen or sixteen" professional glass armonica players in the world.

**Cecilia Gniewek Brauer** joined the Metropolitan Opera Orchestra in 1972 as an associate with the Orchestra playing the celeste; toured with them as pianist, and in 1993 became their official keyboard artist. In 1990, she also began a career on the glass armonica, and made history when she first played that instrument at the Met, using it in a run of ten performances of *Lucia de Lammermoor* in 1992. Many performances followed, and then, more than thirty years after that first opera, she added three new productions with the armonica: Richard Strauss' *Die Frau ohne Schatten* in 2013, Dimitri Shostakovich's *Lady Macbeth of Mtsensk* 2014 and Bela Bartok's *Bluebeard's Castle* in 2015.

Cecilia Gniewek (b.1924) came to Philadelphia from Long Island, New York with her brother, Raymond, the long-standing concertmaster of the Metropolitan Opera Orchestra, when they were children so that Cecilia could study at the Curtis Institute of Music with one of Leschetizky's most

---

[458] Anthony Tommasini. "Resonance Is a Glass Act For a Heroine on the Edge". *New York Times.* 5 October 2007.

famous students, Isabelle Vengerova. Cecilia's father was from Rzeszów and the family first settled in Detroit. Cecilia graduated from Curtis in 1940. In 1947, she was a finalist in the Naumburg competition and signed a contract for a solo concert tour sponsored by the National Music League, but after only two years gave up that concert career to marry and raise a family; content to teach and perform as a guest artist in the area of Long Island. She also accompanied her brother's triumphant Town Hall solo recital debut in 1966, and also joined him at the Newport and Caramoor Music Festivals.

Quite unpredictably, at the age of 61, although she had given up the rigors of concert touring 35 years earlier, Cecilia decided to challenge herself again, and entered the Young Artists Association International Piano Competition, and was a finalist in the over 33 category, of which there wasn't anyone close to her age.

For another career, however, she really didn't learn about Benjamin Franklin's 1861 invention, the glass armonica, until she was 67 years old, watching a television show featuring an armonica player who fascinated her, and she decided to learn to play it. Not the easiest instrument to master, and declaring that the instrument was truly a "diva", Cecilia recalls, "Here I could play the Tchaikovsky and Rachmaninoff piano concertos, but I was so happy when I could play 'Yankee Doodle' on the armonica".[459] Subsequently, she has been a busy artist and lecturer: her appearances have included the National Archives, the Franklin Institute, Metropolitan Museum of Art, Independence National Park, and the Carnegie Museum. She has also been a guest on the History Channel, CBS and Japanese TV, and, of course, she is always prepared for the next opera.

---

[459] Laura Sanchen. "Armonica Virtuoso". *CIM Overtones* Spring 2015.

# E. CONDUCTORS

The role of the modern conductor is a comparatively recent development. In a simpler age of music when a small group got together to play or sing, they just needed someone to start them and maintain their tempo with the tapping of a foot, the snap of the fingers, or the waving of a hand. "In the fifteenth century it was custom for somebody in command of the Sistine Choir to beat with a roll of paper."[460] As string-dominated groups became the norm, the first violinist became the "leader" using his bow and body language. The keyboard player was added as co-conductor when ensembles grew larger. With the emergence, however, of the large, modern orchestra in the mid-nineteenth century, the role of the conductor attained considerable prominence. Now the literature of the Romantic composers required the assembling of perhaps a hundred or more players, to bring one cohesive interpretation of the composer's intentions to the listening audience. Much more than just the beating of a rhythm was needed. The symphony orchestra had developed into the most expressive and powerful of instruments and now the conductor also had to draw the public into the concert hall with his interpretation and charisma. I have already introduced America's greatest example, Leopold Stokowski.

The best European orchestras, such as the ones in London, Paris, and Vienna, were forged in the early years of the nineteenth century. Our American orchestras, with the exception of the New York Symphony under Walter Damrosch, were organized some fifty to eighty years later, and so it was reasonable to expect that America's first conductors would be drawn from Europe. Today, even with the rise of America's orchestras to the highest status, envied by the world, that preference for European leaders often continues—to the dismay of the American-trained conductor. As I have discussed in previous chapters, the structure and early years of the Curtis Institute of Music, the Philadelphia Orchestra, and the Philadelphia Grand Opera were determined by three Polish maestros, Leopold Stokowski, Artur Rodziński, and Emil Młynarski. Stokowski's departure in 1940 from the musical arena in Philadelphia left a void in the presence of conductors from Poland for about twenty years. The long siege

---

[460] Schonberg (1967) 26.

of Russian Communist domination after World War II made it difficult for Polish musicians to take their art to the rest of the world, although in the 1960s, some Polish artists made their way out.

Unfortunately, some of Poland's best known conductors, **Robert Satanowski, Juliusz Wertheim, Roman Chojnacki, Antoni Wit, Andrzej Markowski,** and **Agnieszka Duczmal** never directed in America.

Others, **Jerzy Semkow, Jacek Kasprzyk, Kazimierz Kord, Jerzy Maksymiuk, Daniel Sternberg, Karol Stryja, Grzegorz Nowak, Stanisław Wisłocki,** and **Zygmunt Noskowski** have conducted in the United States but never in Philadelphia.

Previously mentioned violinists **Tymoteusz Adamowski, Richard Burgin,** and **Szymon Goldberg** had highly successful conducting careers in the United States.

Poland's most famous composers, **Krzysztof Penderecki, Witold Lutosławski,** and **Andrzej Panufnik,** were also skilled conductors, comfortable leading orchestras throughout the world in music other than their own.

The early years of "Grand Opera" in Philadelphia were blessed with some of the world's greatest singers. Sembrich, the Reszkes, and Didur had been here and conquered America. The conductors who would lead their profession as opera conductors had to wait another decade to make their impact. Artur Rodziński and Emil Młynarski emerged in the 1920s through the Curtis Institute to develop an opera identity for Philadelphia. But at that same time, another man worked to build the longevity of opera in Philadelphia and America.

Though barely remembered today, **Władysław (Walter) Grigaitis** was a conductor of the Philadelphia La Scala Grand Opera Company, the Pennsylvania Grand Opera Company, the Century Grand Opera Company, the Apollo Grand Opera Company and the Florentine Opera Company in Philadelphia. In New York, he conducted the French-Italian Opera Company and Polonia Opera Company (1940-1953). He was also the longtime Director of Philadelphia's Paderewski Choral Society. In Philadelphia Grigaitis conducted more than a dozen different operas between 1927 and 1929, including *Aida, La Traviata, Faust, Tosca,*

*La Gioconda, Otello,* and the historic American premiere of Modest Musorgsky's *Khovanschchina.* Between 1916 and 1927, he recorded for Victor Records, accompanying the Polish bass Valentin Figaniak, playing violin in a trio and composing, conducting, and arranging Polish choral works. He was also devoted to bringing the music of the Polish composer Stanislaw Moniuszko to the public. In 1925, he directed Moniuszko's *Flis,* with members of the Philadelphia Orchestra and the Polish Choral Society at Philadelphia's Metropolitan Opera House. The Polish-American Opera Company was formed in 1934 to resurrect a performance of Stanisław Moniuszko's *Halka,* held at the Scottish Rite Temple on Broad Street in Philadelphia with the Polish-American Opera Company. Four years earlier, in 1930, in New York City Grigaitis conducted *Halka* with the Polish Opera Company under the patronage of Tytus Filipowicz, Polish Ambassador to the United States. Moniuszko would very likely never have had a presence in the history of opera in Philadelphia had it not been for Grigaitis.

Władysław Grigaitis was born in 1880 (?) in Riga, Lithuania, received his music education at the Warsaw Conservatory and studied engineering at the University of St. Petersburg. [461] He arrived in the United States in 1905 and settled in Philadelphia. In 1936, he attempted the creation of a National Grand Opera, whereby through the American Opera Guild, opera chapters would be formed throughout the country, all contributing to local productions of operas staffed only by Americans and sharing the productions with other companies. Unfortunately, the venture was not successful.[462]

When the Warsaw Opera House (Teatr Wielki) was reopened after World War II, the first performance was of Moniuszko's *Verbum Nobile.* To commemorate the event, Grigaitis scheduled the same work in Philadelphia in the same year with the Polish-American Opera Company.[463] Grigaitis had previously performed *Verbum Nobile* in 1928 with the newly formed Pennsylvania Grand Opera Company at the Academy of Music. Added to

---

[461] Anna Iwanicka-Nijaniowskahttp://www.polmic.pl/index.php?option=com_mwosoby &id=1108&view=czlowiek&litera=8&Itemid=6&lang=pl. Accessed July 6, 2015.

[462] Frank Shea, "Move for National Grand Opera is Sponsored in United States," *Altoona* (Penna.) *Mirror,* 4 January 1936.

[463] November 21, 1928, *Verbum Nobile,* Academy of Music, American premiere.

the 1946 program of this one-act opera were songs by Paderewski, arranged by Grigaitis, and excerpts from Moniuszko's *Halka*.[464] Grigaitis went on to schedule *Halka* at Carnegie Hall in 1952 with Ladis Kiepura as *Jontek* and in 1955 at the Manhattan Center also with Kiepura. He continued to teach voice and piano and conduct the Paderewski Choral Society until his death in Philadelphia in 1957.[465] In 1962, his son, Walter Jr., teamed up with Artie and Harold Singer to form the Manchester Music Co.

Narodowe Archiwum Cyfrowe, Benedykt Jerzy Dorys

**Grzegorz Fitelberg** was one of the most important Polish musicians of his time. He was a talented violinist, a composer of note, and also best friend and advocate to Karol Szymanowski. It was his conducting career, however, that was to have the greatest impact on Polish music

---

[464] March 12, 1946, *Verbum Nobile*, Town Hall, Paderewski Choral Society. The program also featured Paderewski's *Songs of a traveler*, arranged for orchestra by Walter Grigaitis; Polish songs with Alfred Orda, soloist; and choruses from Moniuszko's opera, *Halka*.

[465] "Walter K. Grigaitis," *New York Times*, 17 November 1957.

in the twentieth century. He was born in 1879 in Latvia to a Russian officer and Polish mother. The family settled in Warsaw, and at the age of twelve, Fitelberg began studies at the Warsaw Conservatory—violin with Stanisław Barcewicz and composition with Zygmunt Noskowski. In 1896, he joined the Warsaw Opera Orchestra as a violinist and a few years later became a member of the Warsaw Philharmonic. In 1898, he won the Ignacy Jan Paderewski Composition Competition Prize for his Sonata in A minor for violin and piano, and in 1901 he won the Count Zamoyski Competition in Warsaw for his Trio in f Minor for violin, cello, and piano.

In 1904, Fitelberg conducted his first concert with the Warsaw Philharmonic, premiering his own Symphony No. 1; a few years later he became that orchestra's chief conductor. It was the formation of the "Young Poland" (Młoda Polska) group[466] and the Young Polish Composers' Company (Spółka Nakładowa Młodych Kompozytorów Polskich), however, which can be counted among Fitelberg's greatest achievements. His championing of Polish music and Polish composers was to continue throughout his career and brought inspiration to many young talents. He conducted most of the first performances of music by Szymanowski and his friend, Lubomir Różycki. After World War II, he worked in Paris, conducting the Ballets Russes of Sergei Diaghilev, and led the premiere of Stravinsky's *Mavra*. He returned to Warsaw, where he once again resumed his post with the Warsaw Philharmonic and founded the Polish National Radio Orchestra. He conducted the premiere of Szymanowski's *Stabat Mater* in 1928.

He remained in Warsaw until war broke out in 1939. At that time, he conducted in Rio de Janiero and Buenos Aires, at the Teatro Colon, before traveling to the United States. Between 1942 and 1945, Fitelberg found work touring throughout America conducting the Ballets Russes de Monte Carlo, which could not perform in Europe during this period. He joined with America's most famous Polish musicians to form the Polish Musicians Committee to provide war relief to Poland. In 1944, the committee arranged a special Festival of Polish Music that was presented by the New York Philharmonic with Fitelberg as conductor.

---

[466] "Młoda Polska" members were Karłowicz, Szymanowski, Różycki, Szeluto, and Fitelberg, sponsored by Prince Władysław Lubomirski.

Leopold Stokowski and the Philadelphia Orchestra programmed the first American performances of his Polish *Rhapsody* in 1921 and again in 1932. Returning to Poland in 1947, he settled in Katowice and relocated the Polish National Radio Orchestra to that city from Warsaw. He was also Professor at the State High School of Music. Fitelberg and his Katowice orchestra premiered Lutosławski's Symphony No. 1 in 1948. Fitelberg died in Katowice in 1953.[467] Since 1980, Katowice has held in his honor the Grzegorz Fitelberg Polish National Competition for Composers and the Grzegorz Fitelberg International Competition for Conductors.

**Józef Aleksander Pasternak (Josef Pasternack)** was born in Częstochowa in 1881. His father and grandfather were bandmasters who started him on the violin at age four. He studied at the Warsaw Conservatory (now the Fryderyk Chopin University of Music in Warsaw) beginning at age ten, concentrating on piano and composition but eventually learning every instrument in the orchestra except the harp. At fifteen, he came to America with his father and two brothers. They all worked in hotel bands, Josef became a U.S. citizen and was hired by the Metropolitan

---

[467] "Grzegorz Fitelberg, Polish Conductor, 74," *New York Times,* 25 June 1953.

Opera in 1902. He was first a violinist, then the principal viola, and finally, Arturo Toscanini engaged him as his assistant conductor in 1909. He conducted the Bremen Opera in 1911, but returned to the Met that same year and resumed his position as assistant conductor. He had now become a respected guest conductor and led two of the best orchestras in America—Boston and Chicago.[468]

It was Pasternack's position as conductor in the early years of the recording industry, however, that had been of the most interest to Stokowski while he was Music Director of the Philadelphia Orchestra. In 1916, Pasternack became the Music Director of the Victor Talking Machine Company in Camden, New Jersey, just across the river from Philadelphia. That company eventually became RCA Victor, and Pasternack conducted more than 2,000 pieces as Music Director.[469] It was a most convenient location both for Stokowski's experiments and Pasternack's leadership. Pasternack introduced Marian Anderson to Philadelphia with the Philadelphia Philharmonic Orchestra and directed her recordings and those of many of the world's most famous artists: Caruso, Kreisler, and Heifetz, to name just three. He was a frequent conductor in the 1930s in the early years of the newly formed Robin Hood Dell concert series in Philadelphia's Fairmont Park. He also composed for the radio and motion pictures. Pasternack died in 1940, having spent his last years conducting orchestras for live radio shows on NBC.

---

[468] Many sources credit Pastenack with having conducted the Chicago Symphony, but the Symphony has no information in their Archives, which may be due to the fact that their record-keeping in the early twentieth century may not be complete.
[469] http://adp.library.ucsb.edu/index.php/talent/detail/17138/ Pasternack_Josef_conductor. Accessed May 2, 2015.

Courtesy of Stanisław Skrowacweski

In 1960, to celebrate the 150<sup>th</sup> anniversary of Fryderyk Chopin's birth, the Polish government dispatched six musicians throughout the world to represent their country in this celebration of their greatest composer. **Stanisław Skrowaczewski** was one of those chosen and the only conductor among the group. On February 24, 1960, a special concert was held in the General Assembly Hall at the United Nations in New York City. Introduced by Dag Hammarskjold, Secretary-General of the United Nations, Skrowaczewski conducted members of the New York Philharmonic and pianist Adam Harasiewicz (another of the six Polish emissaries) in a program including the music of Chopin and Skrowaczewski. He had already been to America, making a very successful debut and was about to experience even greater triumphs both in the United States and abroad.

Stanisław Skrowaczewski was born in Lwów in 1923 into a cultured, privileged family. He spoke French fluently as a boy, began the piano at an early age, and at eleven he debuted on Polish Radio Lwów. He soon began composing and conducting. Two years later, he had both performed and conducted the Beethoven Piano Concerto No. 3 with a small orchestra from the Lwów Musical Association. During a German bombing raid in World War II, his hands were injured, ending his aspirations of a piano career. However, his other two abundant talents were to take him on his lifelong musical jaunt.

After the War and into the 1950s, Skrowaczewski conducted the orchestras of Wrocław, Katowice, Kraków, and Warszawa and composed for several Polish films. During that time, he also spent two years studying composition in Paris with Nadia Boulanger. In 1948, he conducted L'Orchestre Philharmonique de Radio France in his composition *Ouverture 1947*,[470] and the Paris premiere of the Shostakovich Symphony No. 5. He joined the avant-garde performance group "Zodiaque."

In France, he introduced many newer works to Parisian audiences and began a lifelong friendship with fellow Pole Paweł Klecki, who exerted considerable influence on Skrowaczewski's musical growth. In 1953, he won the second prize of the Koussevitzky Musical Foundation in Liege, Belgium. (Elliott Carter won first prize for his String Quartet.) In 1956, in Italy, he won the Santa Cecelia Prize for conductors and was invited to conduct in America by George Szell. He conducted the Cleveland Orchestra in 1958 in a program that included the first American performance of Witold Lutosławski's Concerto for Orchestra, now a classic of the twentieth century. In the next season, he presented a concert with the popular Berlioz *Symphonie Fantastique*.

"The conducting of Stanisław Skrowaczewski, guest with the Cleveland Orchestra at Severance Hall last night, left one spellbound, transfixed and electrified. The young Polish conductor is one of the greatest we have heard."[471]

For the next forty years, Skrowaczewski became one of America's foremost conductors, leading every major orchestra and always mentioned as a candidate for Music Director when a new position opened up. In 1960, he was appointed Music Director of the Minneapolis Symphony, now called the Minnesota Orchestra. The opening concert of his first season was a sensation.[472]

---

[470] The *Ouverture 1947* had won second prize to Panufnik's *Nocturne* in the Karol Szymanowski Competition in Warsaw, and he had already won the French Radio Award for his *Cantique de Cantiques*.

[471] Herbert Elwell, *Cleveland Plain Dealer*, 18 December 1959.

[472] "Minneapolis Hails Its New Conductor," *New York Times*, 6 November 1960.

"Skrowaczewski made the Minnesota Orchestra into one of America's great ensembles."[473]

In 1956, in the post-Stalin thaw of the Communist government Skrowaczewski participated in the revolutionary "Warsaw Autumn Festival" (Warszawska Jesień) in Poland. He conducted a program of his own composition, *Musica At Night,* and the music of Zafred, Perkowski, and Stravinsky, with Nadia Boulanger in attendance. That same year, he took the Warsaw Philharmonic (now the National Philharmonic of Warsaw) to the Brussels World's Fair, where he conducted them in Moniuszko, Chopin, and Lutosławski, and then to London where Roman Totenberg joined them in a performance of the Szymanowski Violin Concerto No. 1.

Skrowaczewski's tenure in Minnesota has brought many accolades both to the orchestra and to him. The Kosciuszko Foundation commissioned Górecki's Symphony No. 2, *Copernicus,* for the 500th anniversary of the birth of Nicolaus Copernicus, which was premiered by Skrowaczewski in 1973. The previous year, they played the U.S. premiere of Lutosławski's Cello Concerto with Mstislaw Rostropowich. Skrowaczewski was also an advocate of America's composers, performing the music of Gunther Schuller, George Antheil, Peter Mennin, William Schuman, Alan Jay Kernis, Adrienne Albert, Helen Zwilich, Joan Tower, and others.

"Skrowee" as he was affectionately called in "Philly," used Philadelphia as his most frequent guest stop in America. Since Skrowaczewski and Eugene Ormandy had both been music directors of the Minnesota Orchestra, they had much in common, and Ormandy called on Skrowaczewski many times in Philadelphia. He took the Philadelphia Orchestra on an eleven-concert tour of South America in 1966, the West Coast and Mexico in 1979, and has guest conducted the orchestra well over one hundred times. In 1970, he conducted Copland's *Lincoln Portrait* with Marion Anderson as narrator. The world premiere of his Violin Concerto, commissioned by the Old York Road Committee for the Philadelphia Orchestra, took place in Philadelphia in 1985 with concertmaster Norman Carol as soloist. He was also Philadelphia's composer-in-residence for the summer season of the Saratoga Performing Arts Center in 1988.

Skrowaczewski also has been a strong presence at the Curtis Institute of Music, conducting the Curtis Institute Symphony Orchestra in rehearsal

---

[473] Harold Schonberg, "Music: Skrowaczewski," *New York Times,* 15 April 1970.

and concert in programs that have included his compositions. In 1998, they performed the premiere of his revised Concerto for Orchestra and in 2003, Gary Grafmann, then director of the Curtis Institute, performed as soloist in the world premiere of Concerto *Niccolo* led by Skrowaczewski. A 1976 Kennedy Center Friedheim Award winner, he was nominated for a Pulitzer Prize in both 1997 and 1999. He has been much decorated by the Polish government. Many Lutosławski and Szymanowski works were scheduled by him, some for the first time in America. In 1970, he led the American premiere of Krzysztof Penderecki's *The Devils of Loudon* at the Santa Fe Opera. That same year he conducted Mozart's *Magic Flute* both at the Metropolitan Opera in New York and in Philadelphia. *Le nozze di Figaro* in Philadelphia in 1974 was the last fully staged opera that he conducted. In 1978, at the International Festival of Orchestras in Carnegie Hall he led the New York premiere of Penderecki's Violin Concerto with Isaac Stern as soloist. When Skrowaczewski left the Minnesota Orchestra in 1979, he planned to devote more time to composing. ("I'm a slow writer, extremely critical of myself.")

His conducting career has taken him far and wide since Minneapolis. He returned to Warsaw in 1981 to conduct the Warsaw Philharmonic, an orchestra he has known for fifty years, but one he had not conducted since his "escape" from Poland twenty years earlier. He has directed in Poland many times since his tenure in Minnesota came to an end. In 1997, when the Philadelphia Orchestra was performing in Warsaw's Teatr Wielki, Skrowaczewski was also conducting the National Philharmonic at the Filharmonia.

"He is not regarded as a Bernstein or Karajan, in this super-league of conductors, and yet he is one. But it takes a long time to understand this point, until you learn to respect all of his features, because he doesn't impose anything on you." –Krystian Zimerman, 2009.

In 1983, Skrowaczewski became Music Director of the Halle Orchestra for seven years, taking them on a tour of America for the first time and on a triumphant trip to Poland. His Bruckner recordings have received a Gold Medal from the Mahler-Bruckner Society. His reverence for the music of that composer won for him the Directorship of the Saarlaendischer Rundfunk Orchestra, where he recorded all the Bruckner Symphonies and won the Cannes 2002 Award for Best Orchestral Recording of an

18th/19th Century Orchestral Work; he also recorded all the Beethoven and Brahms symphonies with them. Always challenged by new works, in 2003 he led the NPRSO (National Polish Radio Symphony Orchestra of Katowice) at Paris' Theatre du Chatelet in Penderecki's Symphony No. 5, Lutosławski's Symphony No. 4 and Szymanowski's Three Fragments of Poems of Kasprowicz with Ewa Podleś. He was also revered as the Director of the Yomiuri Nippon Symphony Orchestra in Japan from 2007 to 2010.

Throughout his life, Skrowaczewski has maintained a high level of physical fitness. An avid mountain climber and coach of his sons' soccer teams, he has always remained in the best of shape and health, allowing him to carry a vigorous schedule even well into his nineties. Since 1960, Skrowy has lived in America just outside of Minneapolis, and he is Conductor Laureate of both the St. Paul Chamber Symphony and the Minnesota Orchestra. Another tour of Europe, in 2012, took him back to Poland, where he conducted a new composition, his Music for Winds. Also in April of that year, in a ceremony following his performance of the Bruckner Symphony No. 8 in Minnesota, he was awarded the Kilenyi Medal of Honor from the Bruckner Society of America.[474]

(In an interesting twist of musical interest, his sons, Paul and Nikolas, in their early years, founded the rock electronica groups Psykosonik and Basic Pleasure Model.)

---

[474] Website maintained by the Musical Associates of America, www. musicassociatesofamerica.com/roster/skrowaczewski/skrowaczewski_biography. html, accessed September 12, 2014.

University of Adelaide Archives' Series 312, Maude Puddy Collection

**Paweł Klecki (Paul Kletzki)** spent all but a few years of his life in Europe. Born in Łódź in 1900, he studied violin with Emil Młynarski at the Warsaw Conservatory and philosophy at the University of Warsaw. He was a member of the Łódź Philharmonic for three years but departed for Berlin in 1921. He studied composition with Arnold Schoenberg and wrote the bulk of his compositions during this time in Germany. Wilhelm Furtwangler supported his work and invited him to conduct his Violin Concerto with the Berlin Philharmonic in 1928. In 1933, the Nazi Party ordered all of his published music destroyed, and he fled the country. (His parents and sister were killed in the Holocaust.)

He then secured leadership of the Kharkov Philharmonic in Russia, only to be expelled after two years due to Stalin's eviction of Poles. Kletzki fled to Italy, taught there, and was invited by Arturo Toscanini to take part in the opening concert of La Scala in 1946, where he conducted Antoni Szałowski's *Overture*. His conducting career flourished after World War II, and he recorded the Chopin Piano Concerto No. 2 with the pianist Witold

Małcużyński and the Philharmonia Orchestra of London. He became a Swiss citizen in 1949 and went on to lead two Swiss orchestras, the Bern Symphony and Orchestre de la Suisse Romande. In 1954, he led the Israel Philharmonic in their first recording.[475]

His first appearance in America was in 1957, and the following year he conducted the Philadelphia Orchestra in four performances in Philadelphia and also for his first appearance at Carnegie Hall. He was Music Director of the Dallas Symphony for three years and then returned to Poland for a short period to guest conduct and record with the Warsaw Philharmonic.[476] He also led them at the Montreux Festival in Switzerland. Kletzki died suddenly in 1973 while conducting the Royal Liverpool Philharmonic Orchestra. In 2003, the Dallas Symphony began a project to bring Kletzki's surviving music back to prominence, uncovering and preparing his scores for recording both in Dallas and Sweden for BIS Records. A University of North Texas professor of piano recorded the recovered Kletzki Piano Concerto in D Minor in Russia, and it was considered for a Grammy Award in 2011.[477]

---

[475] Mahler Symphonies No.1 and No.9 as well as Schoenberg's *Verklaerte Nacht* for Columbia Records.

[476] The Classical Music Group, Naxos, maintains this website, www.naxos.com/person/Paul_Kletzki_26103/26103.htm, accessed September 12, 2014.

[477] David Flick, "UNT Professor's Recording of Concerto Once Believed Lost, May Win Grammy," *Dallas News*, 12 February 2011.

Narodowe Archiwum Cyfrowe

The Polish conductor **Witold Rowicki** brought a Wójciech Kilar composition, *Krzesany*, to the Philadelphia Orchestra for his first appearance with them, in 1987. Rowicki, whose true surname was Kałka, was born in 1914 and studied in Kraków. During the Nazi occupation, he was a member of the symphony orchestra in Kraków, playing violin and viola. When the war ended, he became head of the music section of Polish Radio in Katowice in southern Poland. There he founded the Polish Radio Orchestra, now the Grand Symphony Orchestra of Polish Radio and Television.

In 1950, Rowicki moved to Warsaw and brought a newly re-formed National Philharmonic to life. (The orchestra had lost 39 of its 71 players during the war.) At the first performance of the newly restored Teatr Wielki in Warsaw, he conducted Moniuszko's *Straszny Dwór*. Witold Lutosławski dedicated one of the twentieth century's most respected compositions, his Concerto for Orchestra to Rowicki. He first brought the Warsaw National Philharmonic to America in 1961 with Wanda Wiłkomirska as soloist; she was also in the United States for the first time. Over the years of Rowicki's tenure, it was to be one of several trips to America. Wiłkomirska performed the Karłowicz Violin Concerto in 1964 on a similar tour. In 1974, the music of Szymanowski, Bogusławski, Stravinsky, and Mozart was performed with Konstanty Kulka as soloist. Except for a three-year leave of absence in the mid-1950s, Rowicki served as its artistic director and conductor until relinquishing the position in 1977. After leading another European tour with the Warsaw Orchestra he took a two-year position (1983–85) as Artistic Director of the Bamberg Symphony in Germany. He made many recordings, but regrettably, many are no longer available.[478] After his death, recordings were enthusiastically reviewed in 1990 by Mark Swed of the New York Times, who called Rowicki the "greatest of all Lutosławski conductors."[479]

When he conducted the Philadelphia Orchestra in 1987, Rowicki traveled with his teenage granddaughter who helped him with English. He conducted again for seven concerts in Philadelphia in 1989, engaging David Arben as soloist in the Bruch Violin Concerto. Rowicki was then engaged to conduct the Szymanowski Violin Concerto No. 1 in the next season, but died in Poland at the age of 75 shortly after returning from Philadelphia.[480] He was honored with many awards and prizes from the Polish government and received the French Grand Prix National du Disque. He was also a composer of approximately fifteen compositions and won the award of the Polish Composers Union in 1962.

**Marek Janowski** routinely guest conducts in America and recently held joint directorship of the Pittsburgh Symphony. Janowski was born in Warsaw in 1939[481] and was educated in Germany. Janowski's father disappeared in Poland during World War II, and his mother moved to Wuppertal to be with family there. Over his career, he has been music director to many orchestras in Germany, Switzerland, France, England, and Monte Carlo, but early on, opera was his specialty. Krzysztof Penderecki's opera, *The Devils of Loudon*, received its world premiere and first recording with Janowski and the Hamburg State Opera in 1969. He has a huge discography of recordings; he made the first digital recording

---

[478] The Classical Music Group, Naxos, maintains this website, www.naxos.com/person/Witold_Rowicki/53540.htm, accessed September 12, 2014.

[479] Mark Swed, "Recordings: The Consistency of a Career Illuminated," *New York Times*, 18 February 1980.

[480] "Witold Rowicki, 75, Polish Conductor Dies," *New York Times,* 3 October 1989.

[481] Intermusica maintains this website, www.intermusica.co.uk/artists/conductor/marek-janowski/biography, accessed September 12, 2014.

of the complete *Der Ring des Nibelungen* for RCA with Staatskapelle Dresden, concluding the cycle in 1983. He then came to America, making his U.S. debut in San Francisco. There followed his debut in 1984 at the Metropolitan Opera of New York in Strauss' *Arabella*. Two years later, he came to Philadelphia for a series of successful guest conducting appearances. He continues to center his conducting pursuits in Europe, and undertook the huge task of recording live all the Wagner operas with the Berlin Rundfunk Symphony Orchestra.[482]

Courtesy of Stefan Koziński

On December 8, 1962, William Smith, assistant conductor of the Philadelphia Orchestra, led the Orchestra in a concert for young people. On the program was the world premiere of *A Children's Suite*. Any premiere by the Philadelphia Orchestra is a rare privilege, but this was especially noteworthy because this composition was written by a nine-year-old boy, the winner of the Orchestra's composition contest.

That boy was **Stefan Koziński**, a conductor, composer, arranger, pianist, organist, and opera coach. He was born in Wilmington, Delaware,

---

[482] The Classical Music Group, Naxos, maintains this website, www.naxos.com/person/Marek_Janowski/43291.htm, accessed September 12, 2014.

in 1953. His grandparents, Bronisław Koziński and Stefania Szeptunoska, came to America around 1915, and here they raised their twin children, David and Amelie, both of whom became music teachers. David was particularly gifted musically and composed nearly 100 compositions including a march based on the state song of Delaware. He also reset many Polish Christmas Carols for four-part *a cappella* mixed chorus in English translations for the American market, and published those as well as many compositions through the Theodore Presser Company.

Stefan's father, David, married Eleanor Brock, and Stefan and David Paul were their sons. Eleanor, her father, and her two sisters were also musicians, as was Eleanor's Italian brother-in-law, Mario Trezza, from whom Stefan drew much early encouragement.

At the age of four, Stefan began studying piano and experimented with nearly every instrument of the orchestra. At age nine, he won the Philadelphia Orchestra Children's Composition Contest, which entitled him to a performance of his *Suite No. 1*. At thirteen, he conducted the Delaware Symphony in the world premiere of his *Elegy for Orchestra*, and at eighteen, he debuted as piano soloist with Arthur Fiedler and the Boston Pops, performing the Ravel Piano Concerto in G. That same year, he performed a solo organ recital at the Cathédrale de Notre-Dame de Paris. He spent the academic year 1973–74 in Paris studying with Nadia Boulanger, with whom he had begun studies in the summer of 1969. Boulanger called Kozinski "one of the most gifted musicians I have ever met." In late 1974, the Lili Boulanger Award for Composition was presented to him by Aaron Copland and Elliott Carter.

In America Kozinski graduated summa cum laude from Princeton in 1976. In 1978, he received a Masters of Music in composition from Juilliard as a student of Vincent Persichetti, aided by a scholarship from the Kosciuszko Foundation of New York. While attending Juilliard, he performed a recital at Carnegie Hall in honor of Nadia Boulanger's ninetieth birthday. The program included some of his compositions and was well received by Raymond Ericson of the *New York Times*.[483] In February 1978, he made his conducting debut at Carnegie Recital Hall directing a chamber orchestra in the music of Stravinsky, Poulenc, and

---

[483] Raymond Ericson, "Piano Recital Honors His Teacher," *New York Times,* 19 September 1977.

Ravel as well as his own *Octet* for Strings, Winds, and Harp. He also collaborated with Katherine Ciesinski in a performance of Poulenc's *Huit Chansons Polonaises/Osiem Pieśni Polskich*, written in a latter-day Chopin style in both French and Polish.

In 1994, Kozinski made his first organ recording for GM Recordings, entitled "the Grand German Organ Tradition" (GM 2064), produced by Gunther Schuller and including Reger's rarely heard Symphonic Fantasy and Fugue, op. 57. Some years later, a portion of the album was broadcast on National Public Radio's Pipe Dreams.

As a conductor Kozinski has led many orchestras, including the Detroit, Edmonton, Calgary, Delaware, and New Orleans Symphonies. In Spokane, where he was Associate Conductor of its symphony orchestra for 10 years, his *SymFunnies* concerts broke box office records and were repeated under his direction by many other orchestras, including the Stadtsorchester Aachen in Germany. His *Odyssey* for Orchestra was commissioned by the Washington State Centennial and premiered in Spokane on the day of that Centennial, November 11, 1988. His career has also taken him around the world; as Music Director of the New York International Tour of Gershwins's *Porgy And Bess*, he conducted no less than 375 performances of that opera. He performed twice as a guest conductor with the Radio Philharmonic Orchestra of Hannover (Germany) and has recorded with the Czech Radio Symphony of Prague.

His compositions number more than 85, and he was much sought after for his arrangements, which range from Civil War–era spirituals for the Harlem Spiritual Ensemble to an orchestra reduction for 45 players of Richard Strauss' *Salome* for the Shreveport Opera. For a 2012 production of Daniel Catan's *Il Postino* in Philadelphia, the Center City Opera commissioned Kozinski to provide a chamber orchestra reduction of the opera. For the fall semester 2007–08, he was on the faculty of the University of the Arts in Berlin. Since 2008, Kozinski was primarily a coach for the Theater der Freien Hansestadt Bremen, and died of a heart attack there in 2014.[484]

Stefan's brother **David** is a gifted artist and poet, five of whose poems Stefan set to music between 2005 and 2007. German mezzo-contralto

---

[484] Bonnie L. Cook, "Stefan Kozinski, a composer, conductor., and arranger", *Philadelphia Inquirer*, 23 December 2014.

Daniela Kappel sang the premiere of three of those songs in Germany in March of 2008.

Photo: Evin Thayer

In 2005, as part of a tour of the United States, **Mariusz Smolij** led the Wrocław Philharmonic at Philadelphia's Kimmel Center. Smolij was born in 1962 in Siemianowice Śląskie near Katowice. He studied at the Academy of Music in Katowice before coming to America in 1986, touring as violinist and founding member of the Penderecki String Quartet. He attended the Eastman School of Music and earned a Doctorate in 1996. The American Symphony Orchestra League in New York had named him to the prestigious list of the most promising conductors in America.

Smolij has led a busy life, conducting more than one hundred orchestral concerts on five continents. He has frequently conducted the highly acclaimed Sinfonia Varsovia, including a performance at Carnegie Hall. He was conductor of the New Jersey Symphony from 1994 to 1997, held a faculty position at Northwestern University in Chicago from 1996 to 2000, and was resident conductor of the Houston Symphony from 2000 to 2003, while holding the same post with the Wrocław Philharmonic.

For Naxos records, he recorded with the Budapest Symphony Orchestra.[485] Among the composers he has put on disc with the Poznań Philharmonic are orchestral works of Panufnik and Szeligowski. He has also been the conductor of the Sinfonia Juventus Orchestra in Warsaw. In 2005, as part of the Wrocław Philharmonic's tour of America that included Philadelphia, he conducted Wojciech Kilar's *Missa pro Pace* at St. Patrick's Cathedral in New York City.[486]

Photo: Michael Ventura

When the Music Center at Strathmore in Rockville, Maryland, was built, a new orchestra was formed. It was to become the National Philharmonic of Washington, D.C. Its founder was **Piotr Gajewski**.[487] Gajewski was born in Warsaw in 1959, began piano studies at age four, but came to America in

---

[485] Smolij personal website, www.mariuszsmolij.com. Also, the Music Group, Naxos, maintains this website, www.naxos.com/person/Mariusz_Smolij_30677/30677.htm, accessed September 12, 2014.

[486] The work was written in 2000 to celebrate the Warsaw Philharmonic's 100th anniversary, and the city of Wrocław used it in 2005 to commemorate its 50th year.

[487] The National Philharmonic maintains this website, www.nationalphilharmonic.org/Content.aspx?ModuleID=31, accessed September 12, 2014.

1969 to study at the Preparatory Division of the New England Conservatory. He attended Carleton College in Minnesota and came under the influence of the Minnesota Orchestra's Music Director, Stanisław Skrowaczewski. He spent time with Max Rudolf, the conducting teacher at the Curtis Institute, went to Tanglewood on a Leonard Bernstein Fellowship, and won the Leopold Stokowski Conducting Competition in New York City. He has led orchestras throughout the world, conducting often in both the United States and Poland. In 2010, Gajewski conducted the Warsaw Philharmonic in the first Polish performance of Aaron Copland's *Lincoln Portrait* with Krzysztof Zanussi as narrator in the Polish language. He is on the faculty of George Washington University in Washington, D.C., and was a jurist for the 2012 Fitelberg International Competition for Conductors in Katowice, Poland.

**Jacques (Jacob) Singer** was born in Przemyśl, Poland, in 1910. His father, Majer, was a rabbi/cantor and orchestral conductor who brought his family to America as war refugees after WWI and in 1921 they settled on the East Coast, in New Jersey.

Courtesy of the Dallas Symphony

Jacques' violin studies had begun in Poland at a very young age, and he made his New York debut at the age of fifteen in Town Hall. The family moved to Philadelphia when Jacques attended the Curtis Institute of

Music, studying with Carl Flesch. When Jacques went on to study with Paul Kochański and Leopold Auer in New York, his sister, **Bronja** (b. 1918) was admitted to Curtis as a pianist, studying with David Saperton and she graduated in 1938.[488] In 1930, Stokowski hired Jacques as a Philadelphia Orchestra violinist- the youngest member of that section. During his eight-year tenure, Stokowski took an interest in Singer's conducting aspirations. In 1935, he asked Singer to direct the Orchestra in rehearsal and subsequently engaged him in 1936 to lead his youth orchestra.

Singer had adopted many of Stokowski's practices and, in 1937, the Maestro recommended him for the position of Music Director with the newly organized Dallas Symphony, which lead to a lifetime of conducting positions. His great success with the Dallas Symphony was cut short by World War II; most of the orchestra enlisted, as he did. As Private Singer, he received three battle stars for serving in the Pacific theater. After three and a half years in the army, he led a summer series in New Orleans and tried to raise funds for a Veterans' Orchestra but was unsuccessful. He then went to Canada where he became Music Director of the Vancouver Symphony (1947–51) and also organized the British Columbia Philharmonic. He spent two years in New York City conducting Broadway pit orchestras and conducted three orchestras in Israel—Israel Philharmonic, Haifa Symphony,[489] and Jerusalem Radio Orchestra. In 1954, he began an eight-year tenure as Music Director of the Corpus Christi (Texas) Symphony Orchestra. During this time, guest conducting in South America brought him considerable notoriety and acclaim.

---

[488] Bronja ("Bessie") married the great American pianist, Sidney Foster (1917-1977), whose parents were from Russia and Poland. Foster was admitted to the Curtis institute of Music as a ten-year-old by Józef Hofmann in 1929, and in 1941, he was the first winner of the Leventritt Award. He was also a soloist with the Dallas Symphony under the direction of his brother-in-law, Jacques Singer. Bessie and her husband were both faculty members of the Jacobs School of Music at Indiana University.

[489] The first symphony concert ever held in Nazareth was presented by Singer and the Haifa Symphony. The concert for the Arab public featured Milhaud, a Martin Luther chorale, Sibelius, Beethoven, Palestrina, Dubensky, and Israeli composer Marc Lavry. "First Strains of Concert Music Stir the Air of Ancient Nazareth," *New York Times,* 11 May 1953.

After conducting in London, he secured a post leading the Portland Symphony Orchestra, now the Oregon Symphony, where he remained for ten years.[490] After that, he again moved to New York City and conducted the American Symphony but ended his career at Northern Illinois University, where he and his wife, Leslie, an accomplished pianist, were faculty members. Jacques Singer died in Manhattan in 1980.[491]

Courtesy of Gregory Singer

Two of their children, Marc (b. 1948) and Lori (b. 1957) became successful actors. Gregory, Lori's twin, is the founder and Music Director of the Manhattan Symphonie and is the owner of Gregory Singer Fine Violins in New York City.

---

[490] "Orchestra Tour of Oregon is Set," *New York Times,* 25 August 1963.
[491] "Jacques Singer, 70, Dies; Led Orchestra in West," *New York Times*, 12 August 1980.

# F. COMPOSERS

Midway through the twentieth century, there rose out of Poland an extraordinary quartet of composers who altered the direction of music and influenced the technique of many who were to follow: first, Andrzej Panufnik and Witold Lutosławski, then Krzysztof Penderecki and Henryk Górecki. They had very different styles and personalities but all shared a strong national passion that withstood the subservience of Communism and the horrific weight of war. Their efforts emboldened a generation into an inventive and often groundbreaking period of musical composition.

For many years previously, there had been little in the music of Polish composers that was imported by the rest of the musical world. After Chopin, the catastrophe of history for the next 150 years was to create conditions completely unfavorable to cultural growth of any kind, making it "impossible for a single, organic national tradition to develop," according to Karol Szymanowski.[492]

There emerged Stanisław Moniuszko (1819–1872), a composer of operas that have great importance for Poland, though they made little impression on the history of music internationally. The names Żeleński (1837–1921) and Noskowski (1846–1909), bright talents and influences on their generation, are virtually unknown outside Poland. The impact of Wieniawski and Paderewski were as soloists; there is little interest in any of their compositions other than those they composed for their instrument.

Around the dawning of the twentieth century, a "Young Poland" movement of composers supported by Prince Władysław Lubomirski would begin exploration for a new form of expression to fill that vacuum. Most prominent were Karol Szymanowski (1882–1937), Lubomir Różycki (1884–1953), Mieczysław Karłowicz (1876–1909), the composer/conductor Grzegorz Fitelberg (1879–1953), and with a lesser contribution, Apolinary Szeluto (1884–1966). But significant recognition of the Polish composer was still to wait for decades of dedication through the trials of two world wars and circumstances difficult to imagine by those who have never lived under artistic subjugation and suppression.

---

[492] Wightman (1999) 20.

As previously stated, in the years after Chopin, the light of recognition shown very dimly on Polish composers living in their partitioned country, but that was not the case for **Moritz Moszkowski** and **Xaver Scharwenka** who lived in Germany.

Born in Breslau (now Wrocław) in 1854 of Jewish background, **Maurycy (Moritz) Moszkowski** was educated in Berlin and spent most of his life living and teaching there. However, he always claimed Polish nationality, and his earliest student attempts at composition clearly showed the national traits of his Polish contemporaries, Paderewski and Scharwenka and he composed his Piano Concerto in E major for Josef Hofmann. Moszkowski was also one of Europe's most successful piano virtuosi, however, after performing became difficult for him in his thirties due to overtaxed muscles and nerves, his compositions brought him prosperity. The Spanish Dances, in particular, written for both solo and piano four-hands earned him great notoriety, but he also published mazurkas, polonaises, and a krakowiak.[493] Unfortunately, he lost his money during World War I and lived in poverty at the end of his life.

---

[493] Aimee Wood, "Moritz Moszkowski," *Etude*, January, 1900.

Carnegie Hall Archives

While he was hospitalized in Paris, a group of fifteen of the most renowned piano soloists in America, assisted by Walter Damrosch, gave a benefit concert for Moszkowski in 1924 at Carnegie Hall. Among the participants were Ignaz Friedman, Alexander Lambert, and Zygmunt Stojowski. They raised a total of $13,275 including purchasing an annuity that would provide an annual income of $1,250 for him. Moszkowski was not to benefit from their generosity, however, as he died before medicine could arrive for him.[494]

---

[494] Aldrich (1941) 690–692.

**Xaver Scharwenka**

The **Szarwenka, originally Czerwanka? (Scharwenka)** brothers were born in Samter (Szamotuły before 1793 and after 1919)—**Philipp** in 1847 and his brother, **Xaver,** in 1850. They were born into a Bohemian family, but their mother was a Pole and her ethnic spirit was always evident in their music.[495] They both had early instruction in Posen (Poznań) and like Moszkowski, went to Berlin to attend the Kullak Academy of Music. Xaver founded the Scharwenka School of Music in Berlin in 1881. Philipp joined him teaching theory and composition, and when Xaver went to America to found another branch of his school in New York, Philipp became the co-director in Berlin.

Both were well-respected pedagogues but Xaver was to become the better known and one of the premier pianists of his generation, recognized as an important interpreter of Chopin. Some piano rolls of his playing exist from 1910. He made his first solo piano performance tour of the United States in 1891, and he was to cross the Atlantic a total of 26 times on concert tours in the U.S. and Canada. His 25 Polish Dances, particularly opus 3, no.1, were very popular, producing considerable income for him, and his Piano Concerto No. 1 in B flat minor was often performed; Moriz Rosenthal played it in Philadelphia at the Academy of Music in 1897.[496] In 1910, Scharwenka performed his Piano Concerto No. 4 in F minor with

---

[495] Jaroslaw Zielinski, "Poles in Music," *PMC*, vol. 5, no. 2 (Winter 2002).
[496] Marion (1984) 126.

Gustav Mahler leading the New York Philharmonic in New York. In 1996, Gramophone magazine voted that concerto the Record of the Year for the CD recorded by Stephen Hough and the City of Birmingham Orchestra. In 2000, Hough performed with the Philadelphia Orchestra under Neeme Jarvi. Philipp's *Moment Musical* for contra-bassoon and Orchestra was performed in 1934 by Ferdinand del Negro and the Philadelphia Orchestra.

**Nikolaj Myaskovsky** was born in 1881 near Russian-occupied Warsaw in the military frontier town of Novogeorgiyevsk (Modlin Fortress),[497] now, Twierdza Modlin. His father was an engineer in the Russian army and he was educated by his stepmother, a singer with the St. Petersburg Opera. His music is not often played today, but Leopold Stokowski and Artur Rodziński performed the American premieres of his symphonies Nos. 5, 6 and 10. During the tenure of Eugene Ormandy, his Symphony No. 21 was played more than a dozen times. In 1941, he was awarded the Stalin Prize in music for his Symphony No. 21, but in 1948, under Stalinist repression, his music was banned from the concert halls of the Soviet Union.[498] Political uncertainty in Europe and the possibility of an improved livelihood in America lured composers to this country, and many found refuge here.

---

[497] Located in the town of Nowy Dwór Mazowiecki on the Narew River at the confluence of the Wisła, the Fortress traces its existence to "The Deluge" of 1656 when the Swedes invaded Poland and built a military camp there. It was later incorporated into the Russian Empire and heavily constructed by a Dutch engineer in their employ. During the existence of the Duchy of Warsaw, the Poles were allied with Napoleon Bonaparte who increased the size of the Fortress to defend against the Austrians. The Russians defeated the French, and again it returned to their hands until after the WWI. The Fortress then under the control of Poland was one of the last to fall to the Germans in WWII. It was then used as an airfield by the Luftwaffe. It has now been developed as an additional airport for Warsaw. See www.3rzeki.pl/en/The-Modlin-Fortress, accessed September 12, 2014.

[498] www.myaskovsky.ru/?id=32, accessed September 12, 2014.

Library of Congress Bain Collection

The greatest Polish composer after Chopin is clearly recognized to be **Karol Szymanowski** (1882–1937). As Lutoslawski's praise illustrates (. . . "His significance is immense. . ., see below), it is impossible to calculate the immense influence he had on the liberation of creativity for Polish composers in his and succeeding generations. He turned down a position at the Moscow Conservatory [499] and instead chose to accompany his good

---

[499] **Heinrich Neuhaus** was the connection to the Moscow Conservatory. The Soviet pianist and pedagogue deserves mention here since he was a cousin (his grandmother was a Szymanowska) and close friend of Karol Szymanowski, as well as his sister, **Stanisława** Szymanowska, a singer (who was the first Roxana in his opera, *Król Roger*), and Karol's brother, **Feliks,** a pianist. Born in the Ukraine in 1888, he studied piano with Leopold Godowsky in Vienna, was a dear friend of Artur Rubinstein, and became the Soviet Union's most famous teacher at the Moscow Conservatory with pupils like Sviatoslaw Richter, Radu Lupu, and Emil Gilels. Polish culture was prominent in his life, however, and he could recite large portions of Mickiewicz's epic poem, *Pan Tadeusz,* from memory; was a strong promoter of Szymanowski's music; and was a jury member of the Chopin International Piano Competition. His piano teaching method stressed his connections to the guidelines given by Chopin, and the introduction to his well-known *Piano Method* was written by Zbigniew Drzewiecki, Warsaw's famous piano pedagogue and one of the founders of the Chopin International Piano Competition. Neuhaus offered Szymanowski a

friends Kochański and Rubinstein on a concert tour of the United States. He did not, however, spend much time in this country and never visited Philadelphia. He became Director of the Warsaw Conservatory in 1927 but lived much of his life in Zakopane. Virtually every violinist, pianist, and conductor profiled in this book performed his music.

Julliard School Archives

**Zygmunt (Sigismond) Stojowski** was born in Strzelce in 1870.[500] He studied composition in Kraków with Władysław Żeleński, and his mother operated a music salon visited by Anton Rubinstein, Paderewski, Rosenthal, and the young Hofmann. In a personal autograph book, she amassed one hundred signatures and notes from world-famous musicians. At age 17, Stojowski was sent to the Paris Conservatory and Sorbonne University

---

teaching position in Moscow, but he already had already purchased a steamer ticket to accompany Rubinstein and Kochański to America in 1921. Neuhaus never left Russia, traveling only to Warsaw and Prague in his last 40 years. He died in Moscow in 1964.

[500] There is some dispute with that date because the calendar used by the Russians in this occupied land would not have been the same for the Poles.

to continue his studies. In Paris, Stojowski became friends with Peter Tchaikovsky who dedicated the score of his Symphony No. 4 to him in gratitude for his help with translations during rehearsals for the work's premiere in Paris. (Stojowski had an exceptional aptitude for languages.) His composition teacher in Paris, Leo Delibes, had a special affinity for Poland[501] and wanted to adopt Stojowski so that he could enter the Prix de Rome competition as a French citizen—though that never happened. In 1891, a concert of Stojowski's music by the Orchestre Colonne brought notoriety that launched great demand in Europe for both his music and for Stojowski as a solo performer. In 1898, his Symphony in D Minor had its first performance in Leipzig after winning the Paderewski Prize for composition. Arthur Nikisch conducted the work in Berlin and it became the first published symphony by a Polish composer.[502]

Stojowski came to America in 1905, hired to be in charge of the Piano Department of a new school in New York City, The Institute of Musical Art—later to become the Juilliard School. Frank Damrosch (father of Walter) had interviewed Stojowski for this position in Paris. In America, he became a well-respected teacher, performed recitals throughout the country, and appeared with many of the country's best orchestras. The New York Philharmonic played an entire concert of just his music. He performed the American premiere of his Piano Concerto No. 1 with the Metropolitan Opera Orchestra under Joseph Pasternack. Paderewski recorded Stojowski's music and performed his *Chant d'amour, Op. 26, No. 4* on his American concert tours. Josef Hofmann performed his *Caprice-Orientale, op. 10 no. 2* throughout his career.[503] His pieces were popular at the time, but as happens during the evolution of music history, Stojowski's deeply-rooted Romanticism was largely left behind in the rapidly changing world of twentieth-century musical composition.

---

[501] Delibes collected Polish folk tunes and stories for his operas and ballets, and his final work, an unfinished "drama lyrique," *Kassya (Kasia),* utilized those Polish folk elements. It was completed by Jules Massenet and premiered in 1893, two years after Delibes' death.

[502] William Armstrong, "Sigismond Stojowski and His Views on Piano Study", PMC, Winter 2002.

[503] The Paderewskis were godparents to his son Ignatius. Marcella Sembrich and Josef Hofmann were godparents to his son Alfred.

Karol Szymanowski had clearly caught the attention of the world as the next Polish composer of note, so performing and teaching rather than composition provided a living for Stojowski. In 1911, he gave a series of five concerts to show the development of the literature for the piano from the early eighteenth century.

In the early twenty-first century, however, Stojowski's piano music has enjoyed renewed attention through the help of the excellent English pianist Jonathan Plowright, who developed a special interest in the Polish romantics and has recorded Stojowski for Hyperion records.[504] One of the first compositions that Stojowski wrote in America, the *Fantasie* for Trombone and Piano (1905), has enjoyed great popularity, and has often been included in the trombonists' repertoire, as well as transcribed for other instruments.

Leaving the other schools at which he taught, Stojowski opened his own music studio in New York and became a U.S. citizen in 1938. After World War II, he founded the American Council of Polish Cultural Clubs,[505] from which developed vibrant chapters that still exist in the major cities of America, including Philadelphia. Stojowski sustained a full schedule of instruction until his death in 1946, developing many well-known pianists, including Oscar Levant and Arthur Loesser (brother of the Broadway composer, Frank Loesser).

---

[504] Music for Piano, CDA67437 and CDA67314.
[505] Wytrwal (1977) 325.

William and Gayle Cook Music Library, Indiana University Bloomington

Because he was a composer, a conductor, a critic, hosted his own radio show, was a member of the NBC Orchestra and a lecturer at Columbia University, it is difficult to categorize **Tadeusz Jarecki**. He came from a highly accomplished musical family, well known in Poland for two hundred years, but he was the only one to settle in the United States.

His grandfather **Józef** (1818–1871) had been a classmate of Chopin at the Warsaw Conservatory with Josef Elsner. His father, **Henryk** (1846–1918), was a student of Moniuszko and a longtime conductor of the Lwów Opera who conducted Sembrich-Kochańska, Kruszelnicka, Korolewicz, and Bandrowski. He taught composition to Raoul Koczalski, and had begun at Warsaw's Teatr Wielki as a double bass player. Tadeusz Jarecki's sister, **Benigna** (d. 1953), was also a composer and wrote books for children, winning the 1930 Warsaw National Prize for *Wonders and Enchantments of My Childhood.*[506] A brother, **Felix** (1888–1948), was an opera coach in Paris; many American singers sought his help.[507]

---

[506] "Mme. Jarecka-Maurin," *New York Times,* 26 September 1953.
[507] "Felix Jarecki," *New York Times*, 31 March 1948.

**Tadeusz** (1889–1955) was born in Lwów. He first studied there with his father and with the composer Stanisław Niewiadomski. He furthered his education in Moscow and Germany before coming to America for the first time in 1917. He won the Berkshire Festival first prize for his String Quartet, op. 16, an award of $1,000 provided by Mrs. Elizabeth Sprague Coolidge (the first of many awards given to musicians from this important patroness). He returned to Poland for two periods, 1918–20 and 1932–35, and he was decorated by the Polish Government in 1937 before making the United States his permanent home.

He worked for NBC radio in New York as an orchestrator and was conductor for the program *The Composer's Hour.* In 1925, Stokowski and the Philadelphia Orchestra performed the premiere of Jarecki's *Poeme Symphonique: Chimere,* op. 26. His works were premiered by the Columbia Chamber Orchestra, and in Carnegie Hall the young Polish-American pianist Irene Dąbrowski performed his *Mazurkas* in her debut.[508] He was also included in concerts of new works in the Copland-Sessions Concerts of Contemporary Music in New York. Jarecki guest conducted frequently in Europe, including the orchestras of London and Berlin. He directed the opera in Stanisławów, Poland, and in London during World War II he founded The Musicians of Poland, an organization for Polish composers and performers to champion the works of contemporary Polish musicians. In 1946, Jarecki took a teaching position as lecturer at Columbia University in New York City.

Tadeusz' wife, the American **Louise Llewellen Jarecki**, studied voice with Marcella Sembrich. She was reputed to be an eloquent interpreter of young Polish composers, including Szymanowski and Morawski. She also studied in Paris at the Schola Cantorum, was a Paris correspondent for the publication *Musical America,* and also contributed to newspapers and other magazines in the United States. She sang for fifteen years in Europe with many orchestras and Polish opera companies. When she and Tadeusz left Poland, they took posts with the Ministry of Information of the Polish Government-in-Exile. She had a great interest in Polish traditional arts,

---

[508] "Audition Winner Heard," *New York Times,* 29 November 1949.

filming them, creating weavings, and lecturing to educational groups.[509] She also wrote a book, *Made in Poland: Living Traditions of the Land.* She sang for President Wilson at the White House and performed at the Congress of Mid-European Nations in Philadelphia.[510]

Tadeusz Jarecki died in 1955, one year after his wife, Louise. The Jarecki archives are housed at Indiana University. They include compositions by Tadeusz, Louise, and Henryk.[511]

**Karol Rathaus**, "an American composer of Polish origin. . . unmistakable in his affinity to the Polish tradition, both in rhythm and melody: the German expressionism of the 1920s, and in certain scores dealing with Jewish topics, he drew on Judaic intonations, mixing East European and Near-Eastern influences."

Queens College Archives

[509] "Noted Weavers Speak Tomorrow at Eliot Exhibit," *Portsmouth* (NH) *Herald*, 9 August 1949.

[510] "Louise Jarecka, 74, Singer and Writer," *New York Times,* 8 March 1964.

[511] http://library.music.indiana.edu/collections/jarecki/jarecki.html, accessed September 12, 2014.

This is how his good friend and principal biographer Boris Schwarz described Rathaus. Born in 1895 in Tarnopol, Poland (now Ternopil, Ukraine) he left Poland at the age of eighteen and spent the rest of his life in various locales: Vienna, Berlin, Paris, London, Hollywood, and finally New York. He built an impressive career in Europe; all the major conductors were programming his music, and the success of his film scores earned him a substantial living. Walter Gieseking introduced his Third Piano Sonata to the League of Composers in 1930. As ominous clouds had formed over Europe, however, he hoped that Hollywood would make a place for him because he realized that Europe was about to displace him. Arriving in America in 1938, he found that trying to work in Hollywood was too great an adjustment—as his recognition here as a composer was not as it was in Europe. He was happy to secure a professorship of composition at Queens College in New York, where he remained until his death at the age of 59.

During World War II, Rathaus became part of the Polish Musicians' Committee, which raised money to send relief packages to Polish musicians in western Europe and held concerts that were broadcast to Europe through the State Department. The committee members also included Fitelberg, Horszowski, Huberman, Rubinstein, Małcużyński, Landowska, and Stojowski. During this time, Rathaus cultivated his interest in the Polish cause by composing *Polonaise Symphonique, Gaude Mater Polonia, Mazurka,* and also Three Polish *Dances,* which he dedicated to Paderewski. Artur Rodziński had commissioned the *Polonaise Symphonique,* and it was given its first performance in 1944 with the New York Philharmonic. On a 1940 Philadelphia Orchestra concert, two of Rathaus' songs were sung by Dorothy Maynor (Mainor).[512]

In 1944, Rathaus was invited to serve on the MENC (Music Educators National Conference) Committee on Contemporary Music in the U.S. This distinguished group included Henry Cowell, Samuel Barber, Aaron Copland, Morton Gould, Ferde Grofé, Howard Hanson, Otto Luening, William Schuman, William Grant Still, and Virgil Thomson. Rathaus was also on the advisory board of the Fulbright Award. He became a U.S. citizen in 1946, embracing his new home—even writing music for commercials

---

[512] Dorothy Maynor was a well-known soprano and the first African-American woman to serve on the Board of the Metropolitan Opera.

to earn extra money. In 1952, the Metropolitan Opera commissioned him to restore the orchestration of Musorgsky's *Boris Godunov* to its original version.

Upon his death in 1954, Queens College dedicated a new concert hall, the Karol Rathaus Hall, and a Karol Rathaus Memorial Association began awarding a composition prize in his honor.[513]

Tansman Festival Archives, Łódź, Poland

**Aleksander Tansman** was born in 1897 in Łódź. He grew up in a highly cultured environment with his father, Mosze, and mother, Anna Gurwicz, in which he learned French, Russian, English, and German as well as his native Polish. He began piano lessons at age five and studied piano, harmony, and counterpoint at the Łódź Conservatory until the age of eighteen. In 1915, he went to Warsaw to study composition and counterpoint and pursued Law and Philosophy at the University of Warsaw.

In 1919, Tansman won Poland's first composition prize, the Grand Prize of Poland, which enabled him to travel to Paris to further his career in Europe's most vibrant musical capital. While there, he wrote the very first article in French about Karol Szymanowski and met Ravel, Milhaud, Ibert,

---

[513] Boris Schwarz, "Karol Rathaus," *Musical Quarterly*, vol. 42. no. 4 (October, 1955): 481–495. Martin Schussler, "Karol Rathaus," *PMC*, vol. 6, no. 1 (Summer 2003).

Honneger, and Roussel. When George Gershwin visited Paris, Tansman escorted him around the city and helped him with the orchestration of *An American in Paris.*

Serge Koussevitzky, to whom Tansman dedicated two of his compositions, championed Tansman's music and brought him to Boston to perform the American premiere of his Piano Concerto No. 2 in 1927. Paderewski also came to America to be present for those performances. Philadelphia was to have a Tansman premiere also—the first U.S. performance of his Viola Concerto took place in 1939 with Eugene Ormandy leading the Philadelphia Orchestra and Samuel Lifschey as soloist. The *Overture Symphonique* also had its U.S. premiere in Philadelphia, in 1929 with Leopold Stokowski. The *Toccata* and Four Polish *Dances*, which draw from all the Polish dance forms—mazurka, oberek, and kujawiak—were also heard frequently. In 1932, Tansman made his first return to Poland and performed the premiere of his Third Piano Sonata in Warsaw. Upon his second return, in 1936, the government's anti-semitism, stemming from Hitler's Germany, forced him to renounce his Polish nationality and he became a French citizen in 1938. In 1940, he composed his *Rhapsodie Polonaise*, dedicated to the defenders of Warsaw. The following year he came to the United States again, joining colleagues who also had to leave Europe during this time. He won the Elizabeth Sprague Coolidge Medal for "Eminent Services to Chamber Music" in 1941.

Tansman moved to Los Angeles and helped to support himself by writing film scores; he was nominated for an Academy Award for his score of the 1946 movie *Paris Underground.* He also composed hundreds of piano pieces for young students.[514] After the war, he returned to France where he gained great popularity and saw his works performed all over Europe. In 1967, he made his first postwar appearance in Poland. Ten years later, festivals in his honor were being held, the Polish government bestowed its highest honors on him, and the Łódź Academy of Music awarded him the Doctor Honoris Causa. He died in Paris in 1986. In a June 1983 letter, Tansman wrote, "It is obvious that I owe much to France, but anyone who has ever heard my compositions cannot have doubt that I have been, am and forever will be a Polish composer."

---

[514] Summy-Birchard Music, Princeton, N.J., 1955, 1961.

Narodowe Archiwum Cyfrowe, Antoni Sitkowski

**Jerzy Fitelberg**, son of one of Poland's most important musicians of the twentieth century, Grzegorz Fitelberg, was born in Warsaw in 1903 and died in New York City in 1951. In addition to training with his father, he also studied in Berlin and Paris before coming to America in 1940. Jerzy was a much more prolific composer than his father, recognized in America with the 1936 Coolidge Award[515] and a prize from the American Academy of Arts and Letters in 1945. His Violin Concertos were presented at the ISCM (International Society of Contemporary Composers) Festivals of 1932 and 1937. Artur Rodziński performed his music in New York and Europe, and the Copland-Sessions Concerts of Contemporary Music included him in their programming. In 1949, his *Suite* for Organ was sponsored by the Pennsylvania College for Women in Philadelphia, and in 1951, he received a commission from the Koussevitzky Music Foundation. He completed the new work, *Concertino Da Camera* for Violin and Piano, two days before his death. A Fitelberg film score could be heard at the National Holocaust Museum in Washington in a World War II film entitled *Poland, The Country and the People*.

---

[515] "Fitelberg Winner of Coolidge Prize," *New York Times,* 15 January 1937.

Composer, instrumentalist, dancer, choreographer, music director and inventor. . . all this in a student who was to enter the medical profession, **Lucia Długoszewski.** Born in Detroit in 1931[516] to Polish immigrant parents, she studied piano at the Detroit Conservatory of Music and majored in pre-medicine at Wayne State University while also taking courses in physics. Ultimately, she decided to abandon medicine, moved to New York City, where she studied composition with Edgar Varese and began a long career of composing experimental music. She developed and designed more than one hundred instruments including a "timbre piano,"[517] and became a skilled percussionist. Every combination of wood, metal, ivory, plastic, and other materials held the potential for new sounds. With the help of the sculptor Ralph Dorazio, she built an orchestra consisting of a hundred percussion instruments. Even though she wrote for large ensembles, her music could be surprisingly sensitive and delicate. The New York Philharmonic, conducted by Pierre Boulez, commissioned her composition *Abyss and Caress*, and in 1977, she became the first woman to receive the Koussevitzky International Recording Award for her Fire Fragile Flight, the center piece in the repertoire of the Philadelphia Ensemble Orchestra of Our Time.[518]

Also a dancer, Długoszewski composed for the Erick Hawkins Dance Company, and then married Hawkins and became choreographer for the company. She believed strongly in live music and never permitted recorded music to be used in performance with the troupe. When Hawkins died, she became the Director of the company. She died in New York in 2000.[519]

---

[516] Biographers have also cited 1925 and 1934.

[517] Dlugoszewski's timbre piano was an open instrument in which any number of objects could be placed on or through the strings.

[518] In 1967, it became the Orchestra of Our Time, based in New York City and continued to commission works from Dlugoszewski.

[519] Jennifer Dunning, "Lucia Dlugoszewski, 68, Composer; Directed Hawkins Dance Company," *New York Times,* 13 April 2000. Also see "Eleanor remembers Lucia Dlugoszewski," http://musicmavericks.publicradio.org/features/interview_dlugoszewski.html, accessed September 12, 2014.

Narodowe Archiwum Cyfrowe

**Tadeusz Zygfryd Kassern** was born in Lwów in 1904. He studied music and law in Poznań and, upon graduation, worked as an attorney for the Polish Treasury Office. But before World War II, he was also known as one of Poland's "six great young composers."[520] During the Nazi occupation, he continued to compose, but had to withdraw into hiding, and most of his output was lost during this period. After the war, he returned to a government position, this time as a Polish cultural attaché in New York City. In the next few years, amid Communist Party purges and defections, he became the senior representative of the Polish government and, as such, was Acting Consul General and cultural delegate to the United Nations. He himself decided to seek asylum in America, and renouncing his Polish citizenship, he left his post to try to make a living in New York City.

The U.S. Government initially denied his application for citizenship, and he attempted suicide in 1955. He enlisted Leopold Stokowski's help in his attempts to support his family. He did become a U.S. citizen the following year, and he secured a commission for an opera from the Koussevitzky Music Foundation. The work was *The Annointed*, based on a play by Jerzy Żulawaski about a seventeenth-century false prophet. He did manage to have his music performed around the country. The New York

---

[520] "Kassern is Dead; Composer was 53," *New York Times,* 3 March 1957.

Philharmonic played his Concerto for String Orchestra and the well-known critic, Olin Downes, was quite complimentary. He made an orchestration for Chopin's E Minor Piano Concerto, and wrote instructional music for the piano, namely 12 Easy Pieces, Candy Music Book and the Teenage Piano Concert, all published by G. Schirmer Music. He also taught on the faculty of the Third Street Music School Settlement in New York. In 1957, he died at the age of 53.

**Andrzej Panufnik** was born in Warsaw in 1914. His mother was an exceptional though non-professional violinist, and his father was a scientist-engineer who also built violins throughout his life.[521] Andrzej's parents were not enthusiastic about their son's pursuit of a music career until as a sixteen-year-old he composed some very popular foxtrots that brought him some income. He entered the preparatory division of the Warsaw Conservatory studying percussion and in 1932 became a full-time student. When he graduated in 1936, he conducted the Warsaw Philharmonic in his Symphonic Variations at the laureate's concert. Also included on the program were his classmates Witold Lutosławski and Witold Małcużyński.

After graduation and military service, Panufnik received a year's grant to study at the Vienna Academy of Music with the conductor Felix Weingartner. He also lived in Paris and London, but was in Warsaw on September 1, 1939 when war was declared. Leading a precarious day-to-day existence, he formed a duo-piano team with Witold Lutosławski, playing cafes and underground gatherings with their compositions and arrangements of all kinds of repertoire. Unfortunately, all except Lutosławski's Paganini Variations were lost in the war. Family members lost in Auschwitz and the Warsaw Uprising in 1944, together with the destruction of all his compositions, left Panufnik with nothing as he faced a new order under Russian Communism. In Kraków, he was appointed Music Director of the newly formed Kraków Philharmonic and composed for Polish State Film Productions, a mostly distasteful assignment because of the Russian politics it involved.

In 1946, Panufnik was appointed director of the Warsaw Philharmonic. Performers, a concert hall, and an administration all had to be assembled.

---

[521] His "Polonia" violin was awarded to Ginette Niveu, the first-prize winner of the very first Wieniawski International Violin Competition.

Many first performances of his compositions were given by that orchestra. This allowed him to also become the State's principal composer of Polish Music and permitted him the occasion to travel in Europe to exhibit the "Polish School." In 1950, he was chosen Vice-President of the Music Council of UNESCO together with Arthur Honneger. The Minister of Culture in Poland considered this an honor, but would not allow Panufnik to attend any conferences or visit the Council's headquarters in Paris. Even as his work was hailed in the West, the Russian Minister of Culture, Zhdanov, was denouncing Panufnik's latest efforts as alien to Socialism. In 1954, through considerable danger and effort, he escaped to London, where he was greeted by a special branch of the British Foreign Service. He did not return to Poland until near the end of his life 36 years later.

Panufnik's music was welcomed in America, first championed by Stokowski in 1949 when he conducted his Tragic Overture, and then his Symphony of Peace in 1955. Stokowski also later premiered his Universal Prayer in New York's Cathedral of St. John the Divine. And although he was to receive many commissions from the most important musical centers in the United States, America never offered him the security that England did, remaining there until his death. Stokowski even sent a representative to England when Panufnik fled Stalinist Poland to bring Panufnik to America, but had no success. In 1957, Panufnik held a one-year position as Music Director of the Birmingham Symphony. The Kosciusko Foundation in New York under the leadership of Stephen Mizwa commissioned his *Sinfonia Sacra* (Symphony No. 3) in 1963. Stokowski had hoped to conduct the premiere, but it was first performed in Monte Carlo, and some years later, Panufnik conducted a recording of the work with that same orchestra. Throughout the world, honors were bestowed upon him, including "knighthood," and in the 1970s, his music began a period of acceptance in Poland as well. 1986 saw the first performance of his Violin Concerto in America performed in Philadelphia by David Arben, Associate Concertmaster of the Philadelphia Orchestra, who was also born in Warsaw. In 1990, he finally returned to Poland to conduct his music at the Warsaw Autumn Festival. After his death, Lech Wałęsa [522] awarded him

---

[522] Lech Wałęsa was an electrician who co-founded Solidarity (Solidarność), the first trade union in the communist bloc that was instrumental in drawing international attention to Poland's plight to rid itself of Russian domination and establish free

the Knight's Cross of the Order of Polonia Restituta. Although he was an exile and did not return to Poland for many years, his compositions often included and commemorated people and events of the Polish national soul.

Photo: Camilla Jessel Panufnik frps, panufnik.com

**Panufnik's return to Poland in 1990 brought him together again with his dear friend, Witold Lutosławski (on right)**

In 1913, **Witold Lutosławski** was born in Warsaw, one of three boys, into a successful and highly cultured family. During World War I, in an attempt to escape the advance of the German Army, the family went to Russia and was trapped there during the Bolshevik Revolution, and Witold's father was executed by the Russians. In Warsaw, between the wars, Lutosławski studied violin and piano, composing pieces for both instruments while studying composition with Witold Maliszewski, who had studied with Rimsky-Korsakoff. He combined music with the pursuit of mathematics at the University of Warsaw. In 1824, he heard the Polish

---

elections. Wałęsa was the first recipient of Philadelphia's Liberty Medal, awarded to him on the 4th of July in 1989 and that same year he received the Presidential Medal of Freedom from then President Ronald Reagan.

premiere of Szymanowski's Symphony No. 3 (Song of the Night) and was stunned at his first encounter with modern music. Although he was never to copy Szymanowski's style, Lutosławski's respect for him was clear.

"[Szymanowski] undertook a most difficult task: the transplanting of modern West European music into Polish soil. His significance is immense; without him a whole generation of composers would be impossible to imagine."[523]

In 1932, Lutosławski's Dance of the *Chimera* was performed by the Warsaw Philharmonic. The German invasion of 1939 ended any plans he had to study outside Poland. He fought in the Polish Army and was captured and then escaped to Warsaw, which was at the time Russian territory. When the non-aggression pact between Russia and Germany was canceled, his brother, Henryk, died at the hands of the Russians. Lutosławski survived the remainder of the war playing in a duo-piano team with Andrzej Panufnik. Of the many arrangements and original compositions they wrote, only Lutosławski's Variations on a Theme of Paganini survives. Unlike Panufnik, Poland was Lutosławski's home for the rest of his life, where he lived with his wife and ailing mother in a tiny Warsaw flat. While Panufnik was to be erased from memory by the Communists when he left Poland, Lutosławski was to be hailed as Poland's greatest composer.

With the death of Stalin in 1953 and emergence of Władysław Gomułka [524] in 1956, the suppression of cultural ideas temporarily subsided, and the Warsaw Autumn Festival began. Handfuls of Polish composers emerged like plants after the first sign of spring. This annual Festival offered Poland a place for composers to try their new works and to hear what the rest of the world had to offer. Even after another Communist crackdown on artistic freedom, Warsaw Autumn could not be stopped. For the remainder of his life, Lutosławski received honors too many to enumerate—at least a dozen honorary doctorates and countless awards

---

[523] Jacobson (1996) 14.

[524] Władysław Gomułka (1905-1982) was the First Secretary of the Polish Communist party who convinced Nikita Khrushkev, head of Russia's Communist party, to ease some of the conditions on Poland's workers after deadly riots in Poznań in the "October Revolution" of 1956.

from every country in Europe as well as the United States. In 1984, the first Grawemeyer Award from the University of Kentucky was presented to Lutosławski. The cash award of $150,000, the largest of its kind ever granted to a Polish composer, was then donated by him to help establish a fund to allow Polish composers to study abroad. Continuing commissions and conducting appearances took him around the world of music, and it was clear that Lutoslawski was considered one of the great composers of the twentieth century. Like Górecki, Penderecki, and Szymanowski, his music evolved throughout his creative life; folk elements always persisted joined by experiments in the twelve-tone system and aleatoric music, the music of chance. He was a respected conductor and appeared twice with the Philadelphia Orchestra. In 1987, he directed a complete concert of his music, featuring his Symphony No. 3. For a special performance of Polish music, Krystian Zimerman played Lutosławski's Piano Concerto, which was written for him. A small, soft spoken man, Lutosławski exhibited a beautiful warmth and intelligence, disguising the great passion and intensity that stirred in his performances.

At the same time that Panufnik, Lutosławski, Filar, and Małcużyński were attending the Warsaw Conservatory, there was another very talented pianist in their class, **Hillary Koprowski**. Koprowski also became a composer later in life, however, he was, above all, a world-renowned scientist living in Philadelphia. Born in Warsaw in 1916, he started piano at five and attended the Conservatory at age twelve, receiving a degree in 1939. At the same time, he finished a medical degree at the University of Warsaw. As Poland was being squeezed by Germany and Russia, dividing the country between them, the Koprowski family was able to make their way to Rome in 1940. There, Koprowski pursued scientific research in virology and also earned a music degree from Santa Cecilia Conservatory. The war, however, continued to drive him from place to place, first to France, then Spain, then Portugal. He was finally able to secure passage to Brazil where a large community of Poles was welcomed. He taught piano there until he secured a research position through the Rockefeller Foundation.

He came to the United States in 1944 and has lived most of his life in Philadelphia as a world renowned research scientist, heading the Wistar Institute of the University of Pennsylvania from 1957–91. Among his many achievements in the world of science, he developed the first live polio vaccine. He performed on the piano throughout his life and also studied composition. His piano music has been recorded by Janina Fialkowska and his chamber music performed at the Curtis Institute of Music. He held memberships and positions in many world health organizations and was the author of hundreds of scientific publications. Honors came to him from around the world throughout his life, including the Order of Merit (*Order Zasługi Rzeczypospolitej Polskiej*) from the President of Poland. He also received his American home town's most prestigious prize, the Philadelphia Award.[525]

Carnegie Hall Archives, Pete Checchia

**Krzysztof Penderecki** has been a revolutionary composer who became one of the most influential figures of the European avant-garde in the twentieth century. In his early works, he invented a new language of sounds and methods for notating them, and his influence was felt throughout the

---

[525] Stacey Burling, "Hilary Koprowski, 1916–2013," *Philadelphia Inquirer*, 14 April 2013. Also, Margarit Fox, "Hilary Koprowski, Who Developed First Live-Virus Polio Vaccine, Dies at 96", New York Times, 20 April 2013.

world. Later in his career, he left his mark on the American film score that drew other composers, young and old, under his influence. Appearing in the United States many times, and particularly Philadelphia, he has conducted the Philadelphia Orchestra both in Philadelphia and New York City and has had performances of his commissions and premieres here conducted by himself, Eschenbach, and Ormandy. Eugene Ormandy was the first in Philadelphia, and one of the first in the West, to champion his work. The Philadelphians performed the U.S. premiere of *Utrenja* in 1970 featuring baritone Bernard Ładysz and soprano Stefania Wójtowicz.

Penderecki was born in 1933 in Dębica, twenty years after Panufnik and Lutosławski, and although his early years spanned WWII and the Holocaust, his life developed more smoothly than theirs in a post-war period. Though the Pendereckis had to endure a new distress, Communism, Krzysztof's parents (Tadeusz and Zofia) were able to foster his musical enthusiasm and provide him an education without significant incident from Poland's Minister of Culture. In 1951, he studied violin and music theory at Kraków's Jagiełłonian University. In 1954, he attended the Academy of Music in Kraków where he first began studies to become a concert violinist but after one year concentrated instead on composition. Graduating with highest distinction, he became a composition teacher at the Academy in 1958 and also taught a course in Polish Renaissance music at a theological college in Kraków. As with all Polish composers of that time, he endured threats of expulsion by Polish authorities since the themes of liberty and oppression often influenced his work. However, the "Khrushchev thaw" of artistic expression, which began in the late 1950s, would ultimately bring him the freedom to introduce his form of invention into composition. In 1959, he submitted his works to a competition organized by the League of Polish Composers and won first, second, and third prizes. In 1960, he composed *Threnody to the Victims of Hiroshima*, which brought him international attention—and a recording by the Philadelphia Orchestra with Eugene Ormandy in 1969. The Philadelphians also took the work on a short tour of America to include Carnegie Hall and then its first performance in Lisbon, Portugal.

Penderecki held a position at Yale University in the 1970s, and has won three Grammy awards and the 1992 Grawemeyer Prize from the University of Kentucky. Featured in several movies, his music has been used by the well-known American director Stanley Kubrick in *The Shining* (1980) and by the French filmmaker Alain Renais in *Je t'aime, Je t'aime* (1968). His life has included more awards, laurels, commissions, performances, conducting engagements, and directorships than can be listed. He was also Director of the Casals Music Festival in Puerto Rico. It is astonishing that he has found time to compose at all. He has a body of works numbering at least one hundred, and has written more for large ensembles than any other Polish composer of his time. Following his avant-garde days of the 1960s and 70s, Penderecki's music entered a post-Romantic stage which can be heard in the score of Andrzej Wayda's 2007 film, *Katyn*. The Curtis Institute of Music appointed Penderecki as composer-in-residence for the 2013–14 year. His wife, Elżbieta Solecka, whose father was principal cellist of the Kraków Philharmonic, is very active in international causes and they have lived just outside of Kraków.

Of the four composers mentioned, **Henryk Górecki** (1933–2010) would surely have been the least well-known outside of Poland for most of his career.[526] That was true until a recording of his Symphony No.3, *Symphony of Sorrowful Songs* astounded the world; it was *Gramophone*'s best-selling CD in 1993. That symphony did what no classical piece had ever done before, topping the million mark for sales and even competing on the Pop charts in Britain. David Zinman, who directed the recording, also conducted it with the Philadelphia Orchestra and the visiting Polish soprano, **Elżbieta Szmytka**.[527]

Górecki was part of the Polish avant-garde of the 1950s and 60s. His orchestral work *Refrain* won a UNESCO International Rostrum of Composers prize in Paris in 1967. His music during that period was vastly different from later in his creative life, when Górecki adapted more traditional Polish music and explored Poland's history in that music. His Symphony No. 3 occupies a part in this transition.

---

[526] Jacobson (1996) 165–206.

[527] Szmytka studied in Kraków and sings mostly in Europe. A particular favorite of Simon Rattle, she recorded Roxana in Szymanowski's *Król Roger* with Rattle and the City of Birmingham Symphony Orchestra with Thomas Hampson as the King. She has also been chosen to work with Pierre Boulez, Wolfgang Sawallisch, Claudio Abbado, Georg Solti, and Neville Mariner.

Górecki was born in Czernica, southern Poland, and he graduated from the State Higher School of Music in Katowice in 1960. Eight years later, he joined the faculty and became its Provost for several years. In 1979, it became the Karol Szymanowski Academy of Music. The many accolades, awards, and honors that he received from around the world were never enough to draw him out of southern Poland for very long. He once called himself an *odlutek*, a recluse. It did not help that he suffered from crippling ill health for all of his life.[528]

Courtesy of Mikołaj Górecki

Henryk Górecki's son, **Mikołaj**, has also become a composer and shows many spiritual inspirations similar to his father in his compositions. After studying with the elder Górecki at the Karol Szymanowski Academy in Katowice, Mikołaj came to America and received a Doctorate in Composition at Indiana University, was lecturer at McGill University in Montreal, and now teaches in Laredo, Texas. He has had his compositions played at Avery Fisher Hall and at Lincoln Center in New York.

---

[528] Allan Kozinn, "Henryk Górecki, Polish Composer, Is Dead at 76," *New York Times,* 12 November 2010.

**Anna** Górecki, Mikołaj's sister, is a successful pianist and lives in Katowice. She has recorded her father's Concerto for Piano and Strings with the Amadeus Chamber Orchestra. She is married to the Polish guitarist, Wójciech Stańczyk.

Courtesy of Jerzy Sapieyevski

**Jerzy Sapiejewski (Sapieyevski)** was born in Łódź in 1945 and has spent most of his life as a composer in America, having arrived in 1967. He came from a very creative family. His father was an engineer and inventor, and his brother, Roman, who worked for the Bose Corporation, invented noise-silencing headphones. Jerzy first studied at the Music School and Conservatory in Gdańsk but was interested in taking his music interests and compositions into less well-explored realms, so he came to the United States to learn more about American music, especially jazz. He attended the Temple University Festival at Ambler and took master classes at the Aspen Music Festival given by the French composer Darius Milhaud, who himself had been influenced by American jazz. In 1968, Sapieyevski received a Koussevitzky Fellowship to Tanglewood, where he studied with Gunther Schuller. After earning a Master's degree from Catholic University in Washington, D.C., he won a position at American University as Professor of Performing Arts in 1975. He is also founder and artistic

340

director of *New Century Music,* an organization offering music and multimedia services for arts and education.

Sapieyevski has written for many forms of expression, including incidental music for Shakespeare, and has combined classical and jazz music in a multimedia setting. "The distinctive voice of his compositions finds its inspiration from the American spirit of George Gershwin, the innovation of Philip Glass and the spontaneity of improvisation of Keith Jarrett and Dave Brubeck." His chamber compositions have been performed well beyond the environs of Washington. In New York, his music has been heard at Carnegie Hall, Merkin Concert Hall, and the Weill Recital Hall at Carnegie Hall. He has combined his compositional ideas with readings by the Polish actress Anna Dymna, and with paintings by Fujimora and Alexander Kaletski. He has a very large body of compositions published by the Theodore Presser Publishing Company in Philadelphia. In 2005, the Polish Ambassador presented Sapiejewski with the Knight Cross of the Order of Merit of the Republic of Poland. He regularly returns to Poland to perform or hear his music. He was married for eleven years to the writer Anne Spencer Lindbergh, eldest daughter of the aviator pioneer. Sapieyevsky set many of her poems to music. She died in 1993. Their son, Marek (b.1977), a singer-musician and actor, lives in New York City.[529]

---

[529] http://musichappens.com/contact/StaffBios/staffbios.htm, accessed September 12, 2014.

Courtesy of Marta Ptaszyńska

Since 2005, **Marta Ptaszyńska** has held the Sulzberger Professor of Composition chair at the University of Chicago. Previously, she held professorships at Indiana University, Northwestern University, University of California at Berkeley, and Bennington College in Vermont. Since arriving in the United States in 1972, Ptaszyńska has had a very distinguished career as a composer, instrumentalist, and teacher. Born in Warsaw in 1943, she studied composition and percussion at the Academies of Music in Warsaw and Poznań. Witold Lutosławski, with whom she studied privately, was her mentor. In 1974, she received an Artist Diploma degree in percussion from the Cleveland Institute of Music and is acclaimed as a virtuoso percussionist. She performs as a soloist and as a chamber player throughout the world and co-founded the International Percussion Workshop in Bydgoszcz, Poland, in 1986.

Ptaszyńska has received commissions for her compositions from the Cleveland Orchestra, the Chicago Symphony, BBC of London, the Polish Chamber Orchestra, and the Sinfonia Varsovia. Her children's opera, *Mister Marimba*, is a great favorite of the National Opera in Warsaw, where it has been performed more than one hundred times. Her Holocaust Memorial Cantata was first performed in Chicago in 1992 and then recorded in Warsaw under the baton of Yehudi Menuhin in 2001. She has a very large body of works published in Poland and the United States, principally by

Theodore Presser in Philadelphia. Her awards and grants from around the world are too numerous to mention but include the Officer Cross of Merit from Poland and multiple ASCAP awards in the United States. She co-founded the American Society of Polish Music in New York, was President of the Circle of Young Composers of the Union of Polish Composers in Poland, and serves on the Board of the International Alliance of Women Composers. She has been a guest lecturer at Swarthmore College and has had her music performed in Philadelphia by Orchestra 2001. In 2011, she received the Polish Composers' Union Award.[530]

Although the reader may be surprised to find the inclusion of Stravinsky and Shostakovich in this book, I find their backgrounds too interesting to exclude.

**Igor Stravinsky (Strawiński) (1882–1971)** came from a Russified branch of Polish Strawińscy: well known and numerous. His grandfather was a Polish speaking Roman Catholic [531] and even though Igor could not speak Polish, he understood and enjoyed hearing the language of his grandfather.[532] *Time* magazine named him one of the one hundred most influential people of the twentieth century. In Paris, his collaboration with Nijinsky, also of Polish parentage[533] and the Ballet impresario, Diaghilev, created sensation after sensation. After Paris, Stravinsky was to spend most of his life in Los Angeles and became a United States citizen in 1945. Stravinsky conducted the first performance of the violinist Pawel Kochanski with the Philadelphia Orchestra in 1921 and conducted a concert of his own music for the first time at the Academy of Music in

---

[530] www.usc.edu/dept/polish_music/composer/ptaszynska.html, www.presser.com/Composers/info.cfm?Name=MARTAPTASZYNSKA,music.uchicago.edu/page/marta-ptaszynska, all accessed September 12, 2014.

[531] Wightman (1999) 224.

[532] Belanger (1982) 93.

[533] **Vaslav Nijinsky (Wacław Niżyński),** often called the greatest dancer of the twentieth century, was born to Polish parents, Tomasz Niżyński and Eleonora Bereda, also dancers. His sister, Bronisława, was the head of the Polish Ballet in Paris in 1932 and formed a new company in Warsaw in 1937, only to end with the advance of WWII.

1925. He also conducted the Orchestra in 1947; and in 1953 and 1964 he took the Orchestra to New York, Washington, D.C., and Baltimore.

Russia's greatest composer since Igor Stravinsky, **Dimitri Shostakovich (Szostakowicz)** (1906–1975), was indeed of Polish stock. He was born in St. Petersburg but he came from a Lithuanian and Polish Roman Catholic background in Belarus. His grandfather Bolesław Szostakowicz was a Polish revolutionary in the failed January Uprising against the Russians of 1863–64. He was exiled to Siberia where he was interred with others arrested for their complicity in the attempted assassination of Czar Alexander II. When his exile expired, he remained there and became a successful banker. His son, Dmitri Bolesławowicz Szostakowicz, was born there. His grandson was also born there and became the famous composer, Dimitri. At a young age, it was difficult for him to pretend the political zeal necessary to survive in a Marxist empire. His first Symphony in 1926, at the age of nineteen, had the score signed with his original Polish spelling, Szostakowicz. In 1927, he entered the First International Chopin Piano Competition in Warsaw, and although he was not a prize winner, he was recognized with "distinction". Whether his defiance was broken, he chose to cooperate or became truly Russified, that original Polish spelling never appeared again on his next fourteen symphonies. Stokowski gave that Symphony No. 1 its premiere outside of Russia that same year with manuscript music that could only be smuggled in at that time. In 1959, the greatest classical musical event in Philadelphia and probably the whole of the United States occurred: the arrival of Shostakovich, Rostropowich and a large contingency of Soviet artists to Philadelphia. This was the first Soviet group of international stature to ever come to America during the cold war, with Shostakovich the centerpiece. Under his supervision, Ormandy and the Philadelphians played and recorded his Cello Concerto with Rostropowich. They also presented this program for students two day later.

Several other esteemed **Polish composers** are also worth mentioning. Though they never traveled to Philadelphia their music has had some presence in the city. Their music would undoubtedly be better known had they not been isolated in the Eastern Bloc, cut off from the developments of Western culture.

**Grażyna Bacewicz** (1913–1969) whose music is often infused with a compelling rhythmic energy, was also a very talented violinist and pianist who premiered some of her own compositions. In 1995, her String Quartet No. 4 was recorded by Philadelphia's excellent Wister Quartet. Her Piano Sonata No. 2, which received its first performance with her at the piano, was recorded by Krystian Zimerman for DGG.

**Kazimierz Serocki** (1922–1981) wrote many compositions for various ensembles, but it is his works for trombone(s) which are considered standard literature for that instrument in the United States. Serocki was the one of the founders of the Warsaw Autumn Music Festival (Warszawska Jesień).

**Antoni Szałowski** (1907–1973) had his *Overture* performed by the Philadelphia Orchestra in 1939, conducted by Nadia Boulanger, the first woman to conduct the Philadelphia Orchestra)

## Composers For Film

The "Golden Age" of Hollywood began around 1930 with the newly developed method of processing and recording sound on to photographic film.[534] America's great studios became firmly established and dominated the world in film production; no one watched more movies than Americans. The giant corporations of the industry, Warner Brothers, MGM, Paramount, RKO, and Fox were all founded by immigrants from Eastern Europe,[535] and their directors engaged an impressive group of

---

[534] Jozef Tykociński-Tykociner (1877–1969) was the first to demonstrate a motion picture with a soundtrack—the result of his research at the University of Illinois in 1921. He was born in Włocławek and had joined the faculty at Illinois as its first research Professor of Engineering in 1918.

[535] Warner Brothers: Harry, Albert, Sam, and Jack Warner were born Hirsz, Aaron, Szmuel, and Itzhak Wonskolaser near Ostrołęka in Russian occupied Poland.
MGM: Samuel Goldwyn was born Szmuel Gelbfisz in Warsaw. Louis B. Mayer was born Lazar Meir in Minsk, Russia.
Paramount: Adolph Zukor (Cukor) was born in Ricse, Hungary.
RKO: David Sarnoff was born in Uslyany, Belarus.
Fox: Joseph Schenck was born in Rybinsk, Russia. William Fox was born Wilhelm Fried in Tolcsva, Hungary.

composers from around the world to write for their films: Max Steiner and Erich Wolfgang Korngold from Austria, Franz Waxman from Silesia (now Poland), Dimitri Tiomkin from Russia, and Miklós Rózsa from Hungary were the most prominent and respected composers who wrote the scores for some of America's most memorable movies. Bronisław Kaper, who arrived from Warsaw in 1937 and had a long career in Hollywood, could also be included in this select list, as well as Victor Young, who spent much of his youth in Poland.

It wasn't until the 1960s that the first director from Poland, Roman Polański, directed his first film in America, and with it brought attention to the Polish school of film, which had begun with Andrzej Wajda in the 1950s and was previously little known in the United States. Through Polański's film scores, Krzysztof Komeda was introduced to America.

In today's movie industry, the work of many Polish directors is well known.[536] In addition to Polański, Krzysztof Zanussi, Agnieszka Holland, Krzysztof Kieslowski, Andrzej Wajda, Janusz Kaminski, and Andrzej Bartkowiak have acclaimed films to their credit, and these directors' first impulse was to choose the scores of Polish composers. Polish-American directors such as Gore Verbinski, Andy and Larry Wachowski, Aaron Spelling, Alan Pakula, and Billy Wilder chose American composers who were working regularly in Hollywood.

---

[536] Martin Scorcese, one of the most important filmmakers in cinema history, has long been an admirer of Wajda and Polish films. In 2014, a collection of 21 Polish films from the Communist era (1957–87) toured North America under the title "Martin Scorcese Presents Masterpieces of Polish Cinema." Fifteen of those films were shown in Philadelphia.

Courtesy of Bobbie Fromberg

Before and during the Golden Age of film, **Victor Young,** was America's most prolific composer, writing music for 350 scores, from silent films to many of America's classics. He holds the record for 22 Academy Award nominations before finally winning an Oscar for the 1956 film *Around the World in Eighty Days*. The award was bestowed posthumously in 1957. He was a mentor to another of Hollywood's great film composers, Henry Mancini, who once said that Young could shake a melody out of his sleeve in a moment's notice. Young was one of the first composers to use original music in film.

He was born Abe Young in Chicago in 1899 into a musical family. His father, Wulf Jabłoń, was born in Warsaw and changed his name to William Young when he came to the United States. He was a singer with the Joseph Sheehan Opera Company and his son, Abe, began the violin at the age of six. When Abe's mother died four years later, he and his sister Helen, a pianist who was two years younger, were sent to Warsaw to live with their grandfather Berel Segal. They were enrolled at the Warsaw Conservatory where Victor studied with **Izydor Lotto,** who had taught Richard Burgin and Bronisław Huberman. He received a diploma in 1918 signed by the

347

Director of the Warsaw Conservatory, **Stanisław Barcewicz**, who himself was an equally famed violinist. At the Conservatory he met his future wife, Rita Kinel, who he married in Hollywood in 1922. He also studied piano in Paris with Isidor Philipp before making the journey back to America.

His violin debut with the Warsaw Philharmonic was a great success and a wealthy banker gave him a 1730 Guarnerius *del Gesu*, which he played for the rest of his career. He was a member of the Warsaw Philharmonic for two years, and continued studies and concertized, often with Helen, throughout Europe. While in Russia, he was arrested and interned for several months before escaping back to Warsaw—thanks to the help of a Russian officer who admired his talent—only to be captured by the Germans who detained him until World War I ended.

Finally, he made his way to America with Helen in 1920. They first went to Chicago, where Abe changed his name to Victor and slowly began to build a career, dividing his time in those first years between Chicago and New York City. In his career, he worked as a violinist, a conductor, arranger, and composer for silent films, radio, vaudeville, musicals, casinos, dance bands, and in television. He wrote his first popular song in 1928, "Sweet Sue" recorded by Tommy Dorsey, and continued to compose many popular songs, including "Stella by Starlight," "When I Fall in Love," "Love Letters," and many more that endure today. He conducted and performed on radio in New York City and recorded with the Paul Whiteman Orchestra.

Young settled in California, joined Paramount Pictures in 1936, and in 1938 received his first Academy Award nomination for the original score for *Army Girl.* He became Paramount's chief composer. He often wrote for several films at the same time and composed his original scores to Sam Goldwyn, Republic, Columbia, and Mike Todd Pictures. Major films of Cecil B. DeMille and John Ford featured his music. On two occasions, he received four Academy Award nominations in one year (1940, 1941), a Golden Globe Award in 1952 for the score to *September Affair* and a Primetime Emmy in 1955. For the film classic *Shane*, he wrote a love song entitled *Varsovienne*, a traditional, graceful Polish dance. His feel for Polish folk songs was often evident in his music. He died of a cerebral hemorrhage in Palm Springs, California, at the age of 57. He had kept his Guarnerius *del Gesu* violin on display in his house, but at the time of his death it was stolen and has never been recovered. Rita, his wife of thirty-five years, died six years later. Young's Oscar is on display at the Boston Public Library, and many of his scores and possessions are housed at Brandeis University. In 2014, a special concert of the music of Victor Young and Wójciech Kilar took place at UCLA's Fowler Library, sponsored by the Los Angeles Offices of the Polish Council.

The 1951 film, *The African Queen*, starring Humphrey Bogart and Katherine Hepburn is one of the great classics of the film industry, selected for preservation in the United States National Film Registry with the Library of Congress. The composer for this film was **Allan Gray**, virtually unknown in America. In 1902, he was born **Józef Żmigród** in Tarnów, Małopolskie Poland (then Galicia, Austro-Hungarian Empire). He was highly educated in Germany where he was a composition student of Arnold Schoenberg and a piano student of Rudolf Breithaupt along with Claudio Arrau. He first composed for the German "talkies" and was considered a "serious" composer. He moved to England, changed his name to Allan Gray and became one of the busiest composers for English films in the 1930s and 40s. He died there in 1973 in the village of Chesham Bois.

Although filmed with two of America's best known actors and directed by the equally famous American Director, John Huston, *The African Queen* was an English production.[537]

One of the least known film composers, is also the most interesting. **Krzysztof Komeda** was born in Poznań in 1931 but lived in Częstochowa. He was born Krzysztof Trzcinski, but used Komeda as a stage name to avoid tangling with the Communist government while he pursued his love of jazz. As an eight-year-old prodigy studying violin at the Poznań Conservatory, he envisioned a career as a soloist. The war, however, forced him to change direction and in 1956, he became a doctor specializing in otolaryngology. All the while, however, he continued to nurture his interest in popular music, especially jazz piano. He teamed up with a former schoolmate and began mixing with the best jazz players in Poland, playing in the "catacombs" of jazz underground. (This form of music was banned

---

[537] Alexander Gleason, "Allan Gray", http://www.powell-pressburger.org/Reviews/Gray/Gleason.html. Accessed July 20, 2015.

under Communism of the early 1950s.) They all emerged and performed at the 1956 Sopot Jazz Festival. Komeda became the most important figure in the history of jazz in Poland and influenced many European groups that were to follow. His success and reputation as the leader of his jazz group continued until his death in 1969. The Komeda Sextet was the first modern jazz ensemble in Poland. In 1960, Komeda began composing for film with Andrzej Wajda (*Niewinni czarodzieje* aka *Innocent Sorcerers*) and Roman Polański (*Nóż w wodzie* aka *Knife in the Water).* He eventually composed for three dozen movies. He came to America in 1968 with Roman Polański to compose for the films, *Rosemary's Baby* and Buzz Kulik's *The Riot.* Since 1995, the Komeda Jazz Festival has been held annually in Słupsk to promote young artists.[538]

**Zbigniew Preisner** "is Poland's leading film composer and........one of the most outstanding film composers of his generation."[539] He was born Zbigniew Antoni Kowalski in Bielsko-Biala in 1955 and studied history and philosophy at Jagiellonian University in Kraków. For much of his creative life he has chosen to remain in Kraków to work with his favored recording team of musicians and equipment. Most Americans would know him best from Agnieszka Holland's film, *The Secret Garden* and *When a Man Loves a Woman* directed by Luis Mandoki, starring Andy Garcia and Meg Ryan. But his greatest international acclaim would come from his collaboration with the great Polish filmmaker, Krzysztof Kieślowski. *Dekalog, The Double Life of Veronique* and the Three *Coulors* films, *Blue, White* and *Red* brought both Kieślowski and Preisner international success. A three cd set of the soundtracks of those films was released in France where Preisner is a member of the French Film Academy.

In America, Preisner received the Los Angeles Critics Association Awards in 1991, 1992 and 1993 for Kieślowski film scores, as well as *At Play in the Fields of the Lord, Damage* and two more Agnieszka Holland films, *Olivier, Olivier* and *Europa, Europa.* He also received Two Golden Globe Award nominations from Hollywood, as well as The Silver Bear Award from Germany, two Cesar Awards from France and the International

---

[538] Official Komeda website, www.krzysztofkomeda.com, accessed September 12, 2014.

[539] http://www.preisner.com/. Accessed July 20, 2015.

Eurasia Film Festival Award. Numerous accolades also came to him in his native country from both the recording and film industry, as well as an Award from the Polish Minister of Foreign Affairs and a Medal from the Mayor of Kraków.

The early years of his compositional output were centered on his work in film, however, since the 1990s, he has created a number of large works performed throughout the world. A trip to the Yad Vashem Museum in Jerusalem, accompanied by Krzysztof Kieślowski inspired his 2013 composition Diaries of Hope, based on texts written by Polish children who perished in the Holocaust. A performance of that work held at the Barbican in London, and conducted by Preisner scored an "historic triumph" that "will forever remain uplifting".[540] A new album of music for symphony orchestra, Ten Pieces for Orchestra, was released in 2015, and in the same year his film score accompanied the release of the Chinese film, *Lost and Love.*

**Wójciech Kilar, courtesy of Polskie Wydawnictwo Muzyczne**

---

[540] Krystyna Zavish, "Innocence Shines Amid the Horrors of Death Camps". *Morning Star*, 16 October 2013.

**Wójciech Kilar's** musical output is about equally divided between his work for the film industry and his other compositions. Born in Lwów in 1932, he has composed for the films of Kieślowski, Zanussi, Wajda, and Polański. In 1992, he won an ASCAP Award for his music for Francis Ford Coppola's *Bram Stoker's Dracula* (1992). He also provided original music for Roman Polański's *The Pianist* (2002). Steven Spielberg used his *Exodus* for the film *Schindler's List* (1993). As part of the Polish avant-garde of the 1960s, he also composed a large body of serious works. Witold Rowicki conducted his *Krzesany* with the Philadelphia Orchestra in 1987, and his *Missa Pro Pace* was performed for Pope John Paul II at the Vatican in 2001. It was again performed in 2005 at St. Patrick's Cathedral with the Wrocław Philharmonic as a tribute to the Pope who had recently died. In 2011, to commemorate the terrorist attacks on New York City, a performance of his September Symphony was played by the National Philharmonic in Warsaw under the auspices of the U.S. Ambassador to Poland. Kilar received the Boulanger Foundation Award in Boston in 1960 and the Alfred Jurzykowski Foundation Prize in New York in 1984.[541] He died in Katowice in 2013.

This next composer, born in Warsaw in 1902, was also to make his fame in the film industry—but in America, where a fortune could be made. When **Bronisław (Bronislau) Kaper** arrived in America at the age of 35, he had already completed scores for thirty films in Poland, Germany, England, and France. He also composed Jan Kiepura's signature song, *Niñon*, while both were in Europe. He was discovered in France by Louis B. Mayer, head of MGM Studios, and encouraged to move to America.[542] By the time he died at the age of 81, Kaper had written more than one hundred scores for Hollywood.[543] The American actor, George Peppard, when responding to accolades for a particular extended scene from the film *Home From The*

[541] Jan Jacob Bokun, "Wojciech Kilar," www.usc.edu/dept/polish_music/composer/kilar.html, accessed September 12, 2014.

[542] Metro Goldwyn Mayer studios was a partnership between Samuel Goldwyn, born Sam Gelbfisz in Warsaw to a Hasidic Polish family in 1879, and Louis Mayer, born Lazar Meir in Dymer, Ukraine in 1884

[543] www.allmusic.com/artist/bronislaw-kaper-mn0000624071, accessed September 12, 2014.

*Hill* for which he received "best supporting actor", said, "People are always saying what a fine piece of acting it was. Actually, I didn't do anything but walk and stare ahead. All the acting was done by Kaper".[544]

Narodowe Archiwum Cyfrowe
**In Paris, on the far left stands Bronisław Kaper; his wife
Bronisława in the middle with Jan Kiepura.**

In Warsaw, Kaper began the piano at the age of six and was soon composing. At the Warsaw Conservatory, he studied piano, theory, and composition, while also pursuing a course in law at Warsaw University. He went to Berlin, where many musicians from Poland had gone before him, to further his career. He composed concert music and popular music for cabarets and movies, sometimes using a pseudonym to avoid the rising anti-Semitism in Germany.

In his long and very successful career in the United States, Kaper received many awards, including an Academy Award for the film *Lili* in 1953. This was not to be the last of his many Academy Award nominations for both scores and songs in the movies. His personal favorite film scores were *Mutiny on the Bounty* (1962), nominated for an Oscar, and Joseph Conrad's (born Josef Teodor Konrad Korzeniowski) *Lord Jim* (1965). He also scored the long-running TV series, *The FBI*. On Broadway, he produced the music for *Polonaise* (1945), which starred Jan Kiepura and his

---

[544] Cooke (2008), 123.

wife Marta Eggerth. Kaper also did orchestrations for another of the film industry's most famous composers, Erich Korngold, and Kaper's tune for the undistinguished 1947 movie *On Green Dolphin Street* became a jazz classic when Miles Davis recorded it in 1959. He composed little in his last twenty years, but he did become a board member of the Los Angeles Philharmonic. Although he was not a member of the Polish Musicians' Committee, he contributed generously to its activities.[545]

Photo: Szymon Kaczmarek

**Jan Kaczmarek receiving an Academy Award from John Travolta**

In 2005, **Jan A.P. Kaczmarek** won an Academy Award for his score to *Finding Neverland.* Kaczmarek was born in Konin in 1953, and has worked in the United States since 1989. Composition was not his first pursuit. He received a degree in law from the Adam Mickiewicz University in Poznań before performing and composing, however, became for him like a religion, allowing a freedom of expression he could not otherwise capture in those

---

[545] Joseph Herter, "The Life of Zygmunt Stojowski," *PMC*, vol. 5, no. 2 (Winter 2002): 28.

political times in Poland. Intense study with the great avant-garde director Jerzy Grotowski was a major turning point in his life. He formed the "Orchestra of the Eighth Day" (Orkiestra Ósmego Dnia), toured Europe, and came to the United States to perform in New York City. In the group of three musicians, Kaczmarek played a Fischer fidola, an obsolete form of zither, mixing folk songs, hymns, and pop music in a form of minimalism and wailing that was intended to remind us that "political repression exists even on the eighth day."[546] They recorded four albums for Flying Fish Records in Chicago.

As a composer in America, Kaczmarek quickly drew the attention of *Newsday* and the *New York Times* for his scores for the theater in Chicago, Los Angeles, and the New York Shakespeare Festival. Many popular films such as *Unfaithful* and *Total Eclipse* (Agnieszka Holland, director) preceded *Finding Neverland,* and his success continues. Kaczmarek has set up an institute in Poland, the Instytut Rozbitek, inspired by the Sundance Institute, as a center for the development of film, theater, and music that is intended to serve a convergence of European artists. He is also the founder and Director of the Transatlantyk-Poznań International Film and Music Festival, which began in 2012, and includes music, master classes, theater events, and cinema of all varieties from around the world. Kaczmarek has also produced his own films, collaborating with the Polish cinematographer Janusz Kamiński, himself a two-time Grammy Award–winner (i.e., *Hania* in 2007).[547] In 2015, he was awarded the Knight's Cross of the Order of Reborn Poland (*Krzyż Kawalerski Orderu Odrodzenia Polski*) from the President of Poland, Bronisław Komorowski "for his outstanding artistic achievements and promotion of Polish culture."[548]

---

[546] Tim Page, "Concert: 8th Day Orchestra," *New York Times,* 16 November 1982.
[547] Kaczmarek website, www.jan-ap-kaczmarek.com, accessed September 12, 2014.
[548] "Culture Ambassadors awarded". Polskie Radio Dla Zagranicy. 7 February 2015.

Photo: Marcin Oleszczyk

**Abel Korzeniowski** is another recent arrival who, like Jan Kaczmarek, has found considerable acclaim in film and theater and made his impression on America. Also like Kaczmarek, his success was limited to Hollywood. In 2004, Korzeniowski was entrusted with the task of composing a new score to the monumental 1927 German silent movie *Metropolis*. He penned a score for a 90-piece orchestra, chorus, and two vocal soloists. Two years earlier in Poland, he received the Ludwik Award in Kraków for his music to the play *Kafka*. He wrote the music for the documentary *Evolution*, which won a Golden Gate Award at the San Francisco Film Festival, and in 2005, Russia awarded him the Best Composer at their Golden Knight International Film Festival. Best Score for the 2009 film, *A Single Man*, and Best Dramatic Score for Madonna's *W.E.* in 2011 were just two other awards of recognition he received for his creative output that year. In 2013, he won the Fireworks Award for best composer and the Reel Music Award together with the Filmtracks Award and International Film Music Critics Award for best film score, *Romeo and Juliet*.

Korzeniowski was born in Kraków in 1972 and studied composition at the Music Academy of Kraków with Krzysztof Penderecki and became an assistant in the Department of Composition in 1999. His composition for orchestra, *Hypnosis*, was premiered in Berlin with Penderecki conducting the Sinfonietta Cracovia. It was also broadcast on Deutsche Radio. Since 2006, he has spent most of his time in the United States, living in Los Angeles.[549]

**Leo Kempinski** came to America and settled in Philadelphia in 1908. He was born in what is now Nowa Ruda in 1891. He studied in Breslau (now Wrocław) and at the Juilliard School in New York (then the New York Institute of Music). Starting in 1923, he wrote for silent movies. When the "talkies" came to the screen, he composed for B-films and thrillers. He wore many hats in America. A devout Catholic, he was a church organist in Philadelphia and composed religious songs and hymns that were performed regularly throughout the United States. During World War II, he conducted the radio program *The Army Hour* and composed patriotic songs while working as an editor for a music publisher. He also composed for the TV series *The Catholic Hour*. Leo Kempinski and his Continental Orchestra recorded for Columbia Masterworks in the 1940s and could be regularly heard on radio in New York City and across the nation. He served as staff arranger, composer, and conductor for NBC. He died at his summer home in Hampton, Connecticut, in 1958.[550]

---

[549] Korzeniowski website, www.abelkorzeniowski.com, accessed September 12, 2014.
[550] "Leo Kempinski, a Composer, 67," *New York Times*, 27 May 1958.

# REFERENCES

**Abbreviations used in the text and footnotes:**

**CIM** Curtis Institute of Music.

**CIMA** Curtis Institute of Music Archives.

**MOA** Metropolitan Opera Archives.

**PAS** *Polish American Studies*, a publication of the Polish American Historical Association (PAHA).

**PR** *Polish Review*: publication of the Polish Institute of Arts and Sciences of America (PIASA).

**PMC** Polish Music Center at the University of Southern California.

**PMJ** *Polish Music Journal*, the online publication of the Polish Music Center (PMC).

**Suggestion for Further Reading and Study:**

The International Chopin Piano Competition in Warsaw has a history of both the competition and the competitors online at http://konkurs. chopin.pl/en.

A discography of Chopin's music recorded before 1979 is provided in James Methuen-Campbell's book, *Playing Chopin* (1981).

The International Wieniawski Violin Competition has a history of both the competition and the competitors online at http://www.wieniawski. com/ivc.html.

John Curtis, "A Century of Grand Opera in Philadelphia," *Pennsylvania Magazine of History and Biography*, vol. 22, no. 2 (1920).

A history of opera performances in Philadelphia is online at http:// hamilton.francocorelli.nl/ph/ph1.pdf.

*Grove Dictionary of Music and Musicians* is the leading source in the English language, and the various editions can provide an interesting history to both biographies and topics: 1904–10, ed. J.A. Fuller; 1927–28, ed. H.C. Colles; 1955, ed. Eric Blom; 1980, ed. Stanley Sadie; 2000, ed. Stanley Sadie.

*Cyclopedia of Music and Musicians* (1956).

*Baker's Biographical Dictionary of Musicians* (2001).

The Polish Music Center at the University of Southern California has a vast array of sources: scholarly articles, news of interest related to Polish music both in the U.S. and abroad, and it publishes online, www.usc.edu/dept/polish_music/general/PMC_05.html.

Polish Music Information Center (Polski Centrum Informacji Muzyczny) is a source from Poland for biographies of musicians and information regarding their music. Some are translated into English, www.Polmic.pl.

*Polski Słownik Biograficzny* (PSB; Polish Biographical Dictionary) is a Polish-language biographical dictionary, comprising an alphabetically arranged compilation of active persons before the year 2000. The Dictionary, published incrementally since 1935, is a work in progress. Its completion is expected about 2030.

Roman Solecki maintains a website with a list of Poles, including their biographies and sources online, Prominent Poles, www.angelfire.com/scifi2/rsolecki/.

The University of Maryland Piano Archives.

Naxos Records and particularly Arbiter and Marston Records have recordings, biographies, images and period histories of Polish musicians spanning more than one hundred years. Hyperion Records is also a good source for recordings and liner notes of seldom performed and recorded older works of Polish composers. Bach Cantatas Website, http://www.bach-cantatas.com/, also has an interesting mix of recordings and bios, though eclectic and predominantly German.

The website IMDb.com is the major source for information on films, both American and foreign.

# APPENDIX

## POLISH PRONUNCIATION GUIDE

In the summer of 2007 I was in Kraków, attending Jagiellonian University and studying Polish language and history. Jagiellonian University (Uniwersytet Jagielloński) is the second oldest university in middle Europe, dating back to 1364. Kraków has Europe's largest town square, a well-preserved *Stare Miasto* (Old City) encircled by historical sites, gardens, museums, restaurants, shops and small concert halls that make up an area known as the "Planty." In the summer with an influx of often more than a 100,000 students, the Stare Miasto in Kraków is a very vibrant place to be and one that I enjoyed visiting both day and night.

One such evening while taking in the sights, sounds, smells and tastes of this special place, I was surprised to run into the American actor Roy Scheider (*Jaws*) and his wife. They were also enjoying strolling amid all the energy that the square offered. I struck up a conversation with them and learned that he was in Kraków filming the movie *Iron Cross*, a World War II thriller set in Poland in 1939. They asked me why I was there, and I told them that I was studying the language, etc. At that, Mrs. Scheider rolled her head skyward and proclaimed, "Polish is like reading an eye chart."

Yes, the collision of consonants that make up the Polish language can seem incomprehensible. Their pronunciation is indeed daunting to the tongue that is not Slavic.

Once the sounds and combinations are learned, however, the language is quite consistent, especially the vowels. One won't have to cope with a *u* that can vary, as in the English "put," "putt," and "cute," or different vowel combinations that result in the same sound, as in "bare," "bear," and "fair."

Also, with very few exceptions, the accent is consistently on the penultimate syllable.

## VOWELS:

**a** = ah, as in father
**e** = is the same in English, as in get
**i** = ee, as in glee
**o** = the sound of ought
**u** = the sound of too
      **other** vowel sounds:
**j** = y, as in yellow
**y** = i, as in itch

Of course, it couldn't be without some complications. Polish also uses two inflection marks that affect **a, e** and **o:**

**ą** = a nasal combination like gar<u>con</u> in French.
**ę** = a nasal en
**ó** = exactly the same as <u>u</u> (too).

## Vowel combinations:

**aj** = eye
**ej** = the sound of hey! without the h.
**oj** = the sound of oy, as in boy
**ia** = the sound of ee-ah
**ie** = the sound of ee-yeh

## Non-vowel sounds:

**c** = ts, as in its. Górecki= Goo <u>rets</u> kee, Rowicki= Ro v<u>eets</u> kee
**ć,cz** = ch, as in church. Toczyska= To <u>chis</u> kah, Roztropowicz= Roz tro
      <u>po</u> veetch
**ci** = chee, as in cheese . Kwiecień= Kwee <u>eh</u> chee-ain

**ch** = like the start of hah. Kochańska= Ko <u>haa-een</u> skah.

**dź, dzi** = the sound of j, as in jeans. Rodzinski= Ro <u>jean</u> skee. Zdzisław= <u>Zgee</u> swaaf

**g** = get

**j** = as in yodel

**l** = like English, as in look

**ł** = wuh.

**n** = like English, as in nice

**ń** has a singing quality to it depending on the vowel it follows: koń= oneeyeh.

Kwiecień= Kwee <u>eh</u> cheeayn. Kochańska= Ko <u>haa-eens</u> kah.

**r** is rolled like in the romance languages: arividerci

**rz** = the sound of azure or measure. Krzywicki= Kshii <u>veets</u> key. Zarzeczna= Zah <u>zetch</u>- nah

**s** = same as English, **except**

**si** = shee. Zanussi= Zah <u>new</u> shee

**sie** = sheh. Siekierka= Sheh kee <u>ehr</u> kah

**ś**= sh sound. Podleś= <u>Pod</u> lesh. Zamość= <u>Zah</u> moshch

**sz** = sh sound. Horszowski= Hore <u>shov</u> skee

**szcz** = sh plus ch. Szczegulski= Shcheh <u>gool</u> skee

**w** = v, in English, but often as f at the end of a syllable. Lutosławski= Loo to <u>swaaf</u> skee. Wanda= <u>Vaan</u> dah

**z** = like English, as in zoo

**ż, ź** = both like (*soup du) jour*, but ż is pronounced higher in the palate.


<u>**Some of the names:**</u> In this reference, ___ indicates the accented syllable.


Arzewski= Ah <u>zev</u> skee

Chęciński= Hehw <u>cheen</u> skee.

Beczała= Beh <u>chaa</u>wah

Chęciński= Hehw <u>cheen</u> skee

Ciesinski= Cheh <u>sheen</u> skee

Didur= <u>Dee</u> doo(e)r

Długoszewski= Dwoo go <u>shev</u> skee

Fitelberg= <u>Fee</u> tell berg

Gdańsk= Gdinesk (like to dine)

Grąbczewski= Gromb <u>chev</u> skee

Kiepura= Kee-eh <u>poo</u> rah

Kuchta= <u>Kooh</u> tah

Łabuński= Wah <u>booyeen</u> skee

Lutosławski= Loo to <u>swaaf</u> skee

Małcużyński= Mow tsoo <u>zeen</u> skee.

Michalak= Mee <u>hah</u> lock.

Mieczysław= Mee-eh <u>chih</u> swaaf.

Mróz= Mrooz

Penderecki= Pen deh <u>rets</u> skee

Pobłocka= Po <u>bwots</u> kah.

Reszke= <u>Resh</u> keh

Siekierka= Sheh kee-<u>ehr</u> ka

Smolij= <u>Smo</u> lee-ee.

Stokowski= Sto <u>kov</u> skee

Szmyt= Shmit

Szymanowski= Shih maa <u>nov</u> skee

Zarzeczna= Zahr <u>zech</u> nah

Zawisza= Zah <u>vee</u> shah

Zdzisław= <u>Zgee</u> swaaf

# BIBLIOGRAPHY AND SUPPLEMENTAL READING

Adami, Giuseppe, ed. *Letters of Giacomo Puccini*. George G. Harrap & Co., 1931.

Affron, Charles, and Mirella Jona Affron. *Grand Opera*. University of California Press, 2014.

Aldrich, Richard. *Concert Life in New York*. G. P. Putnam's Sons, 1941.

Andrews, Jack. *Samuel Yellin, Metalworker*. Samuel Yellin Foundation, 1982.

Ardoin, John, ed. *The Philadelphia Orchestra, A Century of Music*. Temple University Press, 1999.

Arian, Edward. *Bach, Beethoven, and Bureaucracy*. University of Alabama Press, 1971.

Armstrong, W. G. *A Record of the Opera in Philadelphia*. Porter & Coates, 1884.

Auer, Leopold. *My Long Life in Music*. Frederick A. Stokes Co., 1923.

Barker, Revel. *Crying All the Way to the Bank*. Revel Barker Publishing, 2009.

Barrett, James R. *The Irish Way: Becoming American in the Multiethnic City*. Penquin, 2012.

Basile, Salvatore. *The Extraordinary Story of Music at St. Patrick's Cathedral*. Fordham University Press, 2010.

Behrman, Carol. *Fiddler to the World*. Shoe Tree Press, 1992.

Belanger, Richard J. *Wiktor Labunski: Polish American in Kansas City, 1937-1974*. Teachers College, Columbia University: University Microfilms, 1982.

Blackman, Charles. *Behind the Baton*. Charos Enterprises, 1964.

Blaszczyk, Leon. *Polish Contribution to the Musical Life of America*. Bicentennial Essays, 1978.

Bolek, Rev. Francis. *Who's Who in Polish America*. Beaver Printing, 1940.

Brook, Donald. *Masters of the Keyboard*. London: Rockliff, 1946.

Brymora, Mariusz M, .ed. *400 Years of Polish Immigrants in America 1608–2008*. Warsaw: Exlibiis, 2008.

Bukowczyk, John. *And My Children Did Not Know Me*. Indiana University Press, 1987.

Burgwyn, Diana. *Seventy-Five Years of the Curtis Institute of Music*. Stinehour Press, 1999.

Burton, Humphrey. *Leonard Bernstein*. Doubleday Dell, 1994.

Campbell, Margaret. *The Great Cellists*. Victor Gollancz Ltd., 1988.

Chasins, Abram. *Leopold Stokowski*. Da Capo Press, 1979, pp. 158–59.

Cooke, Melvyn. *A History of Film Music*. Cambridge University Press, 2008.

Cowling, Elizabeth. *The Cello*. Scribner 1975.

Cripe, Helen. *Thomas Jefferson and Music*. University Press of Virginia, 1974.

Curtis, John. *A Century of Grand Opera in Philadelphia*. Pennsylvania Historical Society, 1920.

Czekanowska, Anna. *Polish Folk Music*. Cambridge University Press, 1990.

Damrosch, Walter. *My Musical Life*. Scribner, 1930.

Daniel, Oliver. *Stokowski, A Counterpoint of View*. Dodd Mead, 1982.

Davies, Norman. *Heart of Europe*. Clarendon Press, 1984.

Delgado, Imelda. *An Intimate Portrait of Sidney Foster*. Hamilton Books, 2013.

Dickson, Harry Ellis. *Gentlemen, More Dolce Please!* Beacon Press, 1969.

Dubal, David. *Reflections from the Keyboard*. Summit Books, 1984.

Evans, Allan. *Ignaz Friedman*. Indiana University Press, 2009.

Ewen, David. *The World of Twentieth-Century Music*. Prentice-Hall, 1970.

Farga, Franz. *Violins and Violinists*. Camelot Press, 1952.

Fay, Laurel. *Shostakovich*. Oxford University Press, 2000.

Filar, Marian, and Charles Patterson. *From Buchenwald to Carnegie Hall*. University of Mississippi Press, 2002.

Flesch, Carl. *Carl Flesch*. Da Capo Press, 1979.

Galazka, Jacek, and Albert Juszczak. *Polish Heritage Travel Guide*. Polish Heritage Publications, 1992.

Gerson, Robert. *Music in Philadelphia*. Theodore Presser, 1940.

Gershunoff, Maxim, and Leon van Dyke. *It's Not All Song and Dance.* Limelight Editions, 2005.

Gillespie, John and Anna. *Notable Twentieth-Century Pianists.* Greenwood Press, 1995.

Ginsberg, Lev. *History of the Violoncello.* Paganiniana Publications, 1983.

Golab, Carol. *Polish Communities of Philadelphia, 1870–1920.* University of Pennsylvania, 1971.

Graydon, Neil, and Margaret Sizemore. *The Amazing Marriage of Marie Eustis and Josef Hofmann.* University of South Carolina Press, 1965.

Greenebaum, Linda Schein. *Elizer's Troupe: Scheins in America, 1890–1999.* Common Wealth Printing, 1999.

Halecki, Oscar. *A History of Poland.* David McKay Co., 1976.

Handlin, Oscar. *The Uprooted.* Grosset and Dunlap, 1951.

Harris, Frederick Edward, Jr. *Seeking the Infinite.* BookSurge, 2011.

Hayes, Gerald. *Musical Instruments and Their Music, 1500–1750.* Oxford University Press, 1976.

Heiles Mischakoff, Anne. *America's Concertmasters.* Harmonie Press, 2007.

Hines, Dixie, and Harry Hanaford. *Who's Who in Music and Drama.* H. P. Hanaford, 1914.

Horszowski Costa, Bice. *Miecio, Remembrances of Mieczyslaw Horszowski.* Genova: Erga Edizioni, 2002.

Huneker, James. *Chopin, The Man and His Music.* Dover Publications, 1966.

Ikonnikov, Alexei. *Myaskovsky: His Life And Work.* Greenwood Press, 1946.

Itzkoff, Seymour. *Emanuel Feuermann, Virtuoso.* Kronberg: International Kammermusik-Academie, 1995.

Jacobson, Bernard. *A Polish Renaissance.* Phaidon Press, 1996.

James, Edward and Janet, and Paul Boyer, eds. *Notable American Women 1607–1950.* Belknap Press, 1971.

Janis, Byron. *Chopin, A Most Dramatic Discovery.* Evolve Books, 1978.

———. *Chopin and Beyond.* John Wiley, 2010.

Kellogg, Charlotte. *Paderewski.* Viking Press, 1956.

Kingman, Daniel. *American Music, A Panorama.* Schirmer, 1979.

Kolodin, Irving. *The Story of the Metropolitan Opera, 1883-1950.* Alfred A. Knopf, 1953

Lahee, Henry. *The Grand Opera Singers of Today.* L. C. Page and Co., 1912.

Landowska, Wanda. *Landowska on Music*. Stein and Day, 1981.

Larue, C. Steven. *International Dictionary of Opera*. Saint James Press, 1993.

Lebrecht, Norman. *The Maestro Myth*. Birch Lane Press, 1991.

Leiser, Clara. *Jean de Reszke*. Greenwood Press, 1934.

Lenz, Wilhelm von. *The Great Piano Virtuosos of Our Time from Personal Acquaintance*. Da Capo Press, 1973.

Lieberman, Richard. *Steinway & Sons*. Yale University Press, 1995.

Lipton, Elizabeth. *From One Day to Another*. Madrid: Ediciones Facta, 2011.

Lukowski, Jerzy, and Hubert Zawadzki. *A Concise History of Poland*. Cambridge University Press, 2001.

Marion, John Francis. *Within These Walls*. Academy of Music Restoration, 1984.

Methuen-Campbell, James. *Chopin Playing*. Taplinger Publishing Company, 1981.

Mintzer, Charles. *Rosa Raisa*. Northeastern University Press, 2001.

Mitchell, Mark, and Allan Evans, eds. *Moriz Rosenthal in Word and Music*. Indiana University Press, 2006.

Mizwa, Stephen. *Great Men and Women of Poland*. Macmillan, 1967.

Newcomb, Ethel. *Leschetizky as I Knew Him*. Da Capo Press, 1967.

O'Connell, Charles. *The Victor Book of the Symphony*. Simon and Schuster, 1935.

Opperby, Preben. *Leopold Stokowski*. Midas Books, 1982.

Owen, H. Goddard. *A Recollection of Marcella Sembrich*. Thiggs Color Printing Corp., 1950.

Paderewski, Ignace, and Mary Lawton. *The Paderewski Memoirs*. Scribner's, 1939.

Panek, Waclaw. *Kiepura. Brunetki, Blondynki*. Wydawnictwo Polskie w Wołominie, 2000.

Panufnik, Andrzej. *Composing Myself*. London: Methuen, 1987.

Pekacz, Jolanta T. *Music in the Culture of Polish Galicia*. University of Rochester Press, 2002.

Peyser, Joan. *Bernstein, A Biography*. Beech Tree Books. 1987.

Pleasants, Henry. *The Great Singers*. Simon and Schuster, 1966.

Pommers, Leon. "Polish Aspects of Szymanowski's Style." New York: Queens College Graduate Division Thesis, 1968.

Porter, Cecelia Hopkins. *Five Lives in Music*. Illinois University Press, 2012.

Potocka, Countesse Angele. *Theodore Leschetizky*. The Century Company, 1903.

Pulver, Jeffrey. *Paganini*. Herbert Joseph Limited, 1936.

Pyron, Darden Asbury. *Liberace*. University of Chicago Press, 2000.

Rimm, Robert. *Hamelin and the Eight*. Amadeus Press, 2002.

Robinson, Paul. *Stokowski*. Lester and Orpen Limited, 1977.

Rodriguez-Peralta, Phyllis White. *Philadelphia Maestros*. Temple University Press, 2006.

Rodzinski, Halina. New York: Charles Scribner's Sons, 1976.

Rosen, Charles. *Piano Notes*. Penguin, 2002.

Rubinstein, Arthur. *My Many Years*. Knopf, 1980.

———. *My Young Years*. Knopf, 1973.

Rybczynski, Witold. *My Two Polish Grandfathers*. Simon and Schuster, 2009.

Sachs, Harvey. *Rubinstein, A Life*. Grove Press, 1995.

Saerchinger, Cesar. *Artur Schnabel*. Dodd, Mead & Company, 1957.

Samson, Jim. *The Music of Szymanowski*. Kahn and Averill, 1981.

Schnabel, Artur. *My Life and Music*. St. Martin's Press, 1961.

Schonberg, Harold. *The Great Conductors*. Simon and Schuster, 1967.

———. *The Great Pianists*. Simon and Schuster, 1963.

Schwarz, Boris. *Masters of the Violin*. Simon and Schuster, 1983.

Seroff, Victor Ilyich. *Dmitri Shostakowich*. Knopf, 1943.

Sheppard, Leslie, and Dr. Herbert Axelrod. *Paganini*. Paganiniana Publications, 1979.

Slenczynska, Ruth. *Music at Your Fingertips*. Da Capo Press, 1976.

Smith, William Ander. *The Mystery of Leopold Stokowski*. Associated University Presses, 1990.

Sokol, Stanley. *The Polish Biographical Dictionary*. Bolchazy-Carducci Publishers, 1992.

Steinhardt, Arnold. *Violin Dreams*. Houghton Mifflin, 2006.

Stern, Isaac, with Chaim Potok. *My First 79 Years*. Knopf, 1999.

Steuermann, Edward. *The Not Quite Innocent Bystander.* University of Nebraska Press, 1989.

Stucky, Steven. *Lutosławski and His Music.* Cambridge University Press, 1981.

Temianka, Henri. *Facing the Music.* Alfred Publishing, 1980.

Viles, Elza. *Mary Louise Curtis Bok.* Bryn Mawr College: University Microfilms, 1983.

Szymanowski, Karol. *Szymanowski on Music.* Wightman, trans. Toccata Press, 1999.

Straeten, E. van der. *The History of the Violin, Vol. II.* Da Capo Press. 1968 (orig., 1933).

Vaughan, Roger. *Listen to the Music: The Life of Hilary Koprowski.* Springer-Verlag, 2000.

Viles, Elza. *Mary Louise Curtis Bok.* Bryn Mawr College: University Microfilms, 1983.

Villamil, Victoria. *From Johnson's Kids to Lemonade Opera.* Northeastern University Press, 2004.

Walsh, Stephen. *Stravinsky. A Creative Spring: Russia and France (1882–1934).* Knopf, 1999.

Weigley, Russell, ed. *Philadelphia, A 300-Year History.* W. W. Norton, 1982.

Welsh, Mary Sue. *One Woman in a Hundred.* University of Illinois Press, 2013.

Wieczerzak, Joseph W. *A Polish Chapter in the Civil War.* Twayne Publishers, 1967.

Wightman, Alistair. *Karol Szymanowski: His Life and Music.* Ashgate Publishing, 1999.

Wister, Frances Anne. *Twenty-Five Years of the Philadelphia Orchestra,* Edward Stein and Co., 1925.

Wormell, Sebastian, ed. *Poland.* Hong Kong: Pallas Guides, 1989.

Wytrwal, Joseph. *Behold! The Polish Americans.* Endurance Press, 1977.

Zavistovski, Leshek. *Children and Fish Don't Talk.* Sunstone Press, 2013.

# IS THERE MORE?

Rsearch often results in dead ends or incomplete histories when trying to discover and chronicle musical lives that are insufficiently documented, deserving of more recognition and remembrance. Sometimes even surviving family mmbers of an artist are unable to provide information due to the passage of time. No doubt there is more to be discovered about many of the artists in these pages and other artists who may have been unintentionally and regrettably overlooked. The reader is encouraged to unearth information about artists such as Zygmunt Dygat, Helena Morsztyn, Ada Sari (Jadwiga Szajer), Maria Fołtyn, Julian Pulikowski . . .and many others.

# INDEX

# ABOUT THE AUTHOR

Credit Jean Brubaker

Paul Krzywicki, a native of Philadelphia, was a member of the Philadelphia Orchestra for thirty-three years, performing in over four thousand concerts, more than 60 recordings and presenting master classes throughout the world. He is currently on the faculty of the Curtis Institute of Music. A full biography is in Part I.